D0918762

Japanese Religion and Society

Japanese Religion and Society

Paradigms of Structure and Change

WINSTON DAVIS

State University of New York Press

Published by
State University of New York Press, Albany

Printed in the United States of America

For information, address State University of New York
Press, State University Plaza, Albany, N.Y., 12246

Production by Diane Ganeles
Marketing by Dana E. Yanulavich

Library of Congress Cataloging-in-Publication Data

Davis, Winston Bradley.
Japanese religion and society: paradigms of structure and change
/ Winston Davis.
p. cm.
Includes bibliographical references and index.
ISBN 0-7914-0840-X (PB : acid-free).—ISBN 0-7914-0839-6 (CH :
acid-free)
1. Japan—Religion. 2. Religion and sociology—Japan. I. Title.
BL2203.D37 1992
306.6'0952—dc20 90-24745
CIP

10 9 8 7 6 5 4 3 2 1

For my parents,
Judith and Wesley Davis

Contents

Illustrations

Figures

Photos

Preface

It used to be said that, sooner or later, area specialists take on the characteristics of the countries they study. India experts become litigious, China specialists become bureaucratic, and old Japan hands isolate themselves in village cliques. Today this has all changed—at least in the Japan field. With journalists and students of other disciplines entering the field, scholarship on Japan is no longer an academic monopoly. The country itself is no longer the curio it once was. No longer is it merely a specimen in the orientalist's butterfly collection. Defying reduction to the conventional wisdom of the western academy, contemporary Japan poses an intellectual challenge rarely encountered in area studies. Neoclassical economists are nonplused by the country's economy, which seems to flourish the more it flouts the sacred laws of free trade. Political scientists are discomfited by Japanese democracy, a de facto one-party system dominated by the plutocratic Liberal Democrats and their unelected officials and bureaucrats. Western legal experts are dismayed at the Japanese legal system, a network of courts which routinely protects the powerful while convicting nearly all of those indicted by public prosecutors. And so on.[1] Happily, these conundrums have resulted in a new vitality in Japanese studies. Not only academics, but also journalists and other literate travelers are asking anew: What is there about Japan that makes it so different? Why is it so dynamic? What really makes it tick? In this book, I hope to throw some light on these questions by looking at an array of specific problems in Japan's religious history from the Tokugawa period to the present.

While this book is about Japanese religion, my goal is to frame the discussion in such a way that when readers put the book down, they will have a deeper knowledge of Japanese society and culture in general, and possibly even deeper insight into the nature of religion itself. The book deals with the relationship between Japanese religion, culture, and values on the one hand, and society, social change, and economic development on the other. I have written some chapters as a sociologist of religion, others as an historian. Most of the volume, however, falls under the mixed rubric of historical sociology. As an interloper in various fields, my work reflects what may be called the "poly-paradigmatic" nature of the contemporary social sciences and humanities. My theories, images, and methods are therefore unabashedly eclectic. Some chapters depend on the anthropologist's methods of observation and participation. Others rely on ex post facto interviews with people involved in the events of the recent past. Still other chapters are based on the historian's *Sitzfleisch* strategy, i.e., traditional library research. Many sections combine all of the above—plus random insights gained informally during various sojourns in Japan.

This is a book of paradigms and I invite the reader to approach it as such, and not merely as a collection of case studies—which it also is. While discovering the facts relevant to each study was no easy matter, in each case it was generating the appropriate theory, explanation, metaphor, or paradigm that proved to be the real challenge. It is this that I am most eager to share. Since the term *paradigm* is such a lively buzz word in the academic world today, I should say what I mean when I claim that this is a book of paradigms. But let me first say what I do *not* mean.

By the word *paradigms* I do not mean the transcendental archetypes of some historians of religion, i.e., patterns transcending cultural space and historical time. The paradigms I put forward are different from Mircea Eliade's universal "hierophanies" or "ontophanies" insofar as their ground is society and culture, not being itself.[2] Like Joachim Wach's "classical types" they are heuristic concepts; but they lack the normative, "light- and life-giving" dimension that Wach imputed to the classical. While Wach believed that his classical type was of greater worth than the examples which fell under it, I shall assume an axiological parity exists between my paradigms and their referents.[3] If my paradigms are not archetypes, neither are they structures in the sense of French structuralism. To reverse Jean Piaget's criticism of Foucault—that his work is an example of structuralism without structures—one could rightly say of the present volume that it is a study of structures without structuralism. As a practitioner of the *historical* sociology of religion, I would welcome a reaction of this sort not as criticism, but as praise. If anthropology really is "the process of trying to get a story out of a snapshot" (Jonathan Smith's description) I would have to agree with his conclusion: "It usually doesn't work."[4] Somehow, the synchrony and diachrony of the snapshot must be woven together, not just rhetorically, but as fundamental strategy for understanding and explaining what the snapshot is all about.

It would be gratifying to associate myself with the paradigm theories of Ludwig Fleck, Thomas Kuhn, and other historians, sociologists and philosophers of science. But again, differences seem to outweigh similarities. Unlike the natural sciences, the disciplines in which I move do not feel an obligation to adjudicate decisively between the claims of rival paradigms, or to move one dominant paradigm to another seriatim. In post-Parsonian social science for example—a field in which Weberians, neo-Marxists, structuralists, and a host of others ply their trades side by side—few try to falsify paradigms systematically, rally support for new, exclusive or encompassing paradigms, or move their disciplines towards theoretical or paradigmatic closure. Like other fashions, academic paradigms may be in today, out tomorrow. But it is difficult to say of the social sciences—and impossible to say of the humanities—what Kuhn says of the natural sciences, namely that "the choice between competing paradigms proves to be *a choice between incompatible modes of community life*."[5] From time to time, the social sciences and humanities undergo radical fluctuations in fashion, metaphor, and jargon, but for the most part they are free from the revolutionary paradigm shifts which Kuhn attributes to natural science. Their convolutions may be trendy, even playful, but revolutionary they are not. While tempers occasionally flare over the application of this or that paradigm or methodology, the contemporary academy has become nearly polymorphously perverse in its celebration of poly-paradigmatic approaches to religion, culture, and society.

The approach I take is neither complex nor unprecedented. In the *Politicus,* Plato outlines a paradigmatic method which in some ways is remarkably similar. In that dialogue, Plato has the Foreigner from Elea ask the young Socrates to imagine some children who are having difficulty with their phonics lesson. The children know some of their syllables, but become confused when the syllables they already know are combined in unfamiliar ways. How can one help these children? The Eleatic Foreigner proposes a simple remedy: "Take them to the syllables in which they have identified the letters correctly; then set them in front of the syllables they cannot decipher; then place known syllables and unknown syllables side by side and point out to them the similar nature of the letters occurring in both." A "parallel examination" of both hopefully will lead to a "single true judgment about each of them as forming one of a pair." Setting great store on his comparative use of paradigms (*paradeigmata,* in Greek) Plato introduces the technique into the method more widely associated with his name, the dialectic. Punning on the Greek work *stoicheia* (which means both the letters of the alphabet and the physical elements which compose the world) he suggests that the same method can be used to explain the "letters [*stoicheia*] with which the universe is spelled out." Paradigms will not only help the child read all of his letters; the young, enthusiastic Socrates boldly declares that paradigms will enable us "to solve *all problems!*"[6]

The paradigms I am working with are also intended to unlock the mystery of the unknown. If they do not solve "all problems," they at least help us to penetrate the allegedly inscrutable cultural patterns of Japanese society. Unlike Plato, who says that his own paradigm (weaving) is smaller in scale and inferior in value to his explicandum (statecraft), I feel under no obligation to evaluate my paradigms vis-à-vis what they explain or illuminate. This, again, is a matter of axiological parity. Parity of this sort entails still another obvious difference between my use of paradigms and Plato's: I have no hope that a mastery of paradigms will lead to a knowledge of fixed norms or absolute Ideas. For better or worse, lofty ideals of this sort are no longer the goal of the academic, nontheological study of religion. I use 'paradigm' simply to refer to patterns of thought, behavior, or values which can be used to explain and/or understand still other thoughts, behaviors, or values. Far from being universal or eternal, the religious paradigms I am concerned with are simply patterns that are strong enough to guide, defy, or confuse the history of the short run. Paradigms, in this sense, must be validated (or falsified) like any other empirical events—by observing not just the profound, ecstatic *mysteria tremenda* of prophets, sages, and shamans, but also by keeping a sympathetic but critical eye on the routines of institutional religion, the hocus-pocus of faith healers and quacks, and the desperate evening prayers of the common man. Used this way, the paradigm becomes an extended metaphor that illuminates one's subject matter in a comparative way.

The footloose paradigms that I work with sometimes border on theory itself. Historians, by profession inveterate nominalists, often pride themselves on their blissful ignorance of, or studied indifference to, theory. In contrast to social scientists who make their bread and butter by applying nomothetic paradigms (and jargon) to specific research projects, historians—*some* historians, I should say—are determined merely to "stick to the facts" and "tell it like it is." Many convince themselves that if they need theory at all—and some remain dubious about this to the very end—they will make up their own ("thank you very much!"). In this way, some historians claim that theirs is the idiographic discipline par excellence, and that they are the last rugged individualist left in the theory-ridden, copy cat world of academe.

Idiographic idiocy of this sort has culminated in the formation of various "orchid sciences," to borrow a term from the wit and wisdom of Professor Chalmers Johnson. The orchid sciences (as I understand them) are those undisciplined disciplines which gratuitously take upon themselves the random comparison of exotic cultural phenomena. The orchid scientists seem convinced that their only responsibility to scholarship is to describe their own rare specimens to others—"phenomenologically[?]"—and then step back to admire their "finds." In the "History of Religions" this is called, I believe, "appreciating" other religions. Since comparative work in the orchid sciences is guided neither by a serious purpose nor by substantive theories or hypotheses, they ultimately make no serious contribution to scholarship. In general, they seem content to describe whatever it is that catches their fancy. For those of us interested in Japan and the history of religions, orchid scientism is especially vexing simply because it is so wide-spread. It seems to me that the most effective remedy for this malady would be the cultivation of a deeper appreciation for the basic logic of sociological and historical explanation. Hermeneutics is not enough; it is just the beginning.

In some ways, the robust naiveté of chroniclers, archivists, and other orchid scientists is delightfully refreshing. But, naiveté is still naiveté. Against these flat-footed (and hopefully stereotypical) savants, I would argue that historical research, even in its idiographic mode, is theory-laden and paradigm-bound. This is especially obvious when we look at the study of foreign cultures. To select something from the confusing mélange of historical and cultural Otherness and domesticate it—say, by giving it a proper English tag (or in religious studies, a "Christian" name)—is, in effect, to compare the Other with the Familiar. *To compare, however, is to have a theory,* i.e., a conceptual bridge linking the one to the other. The real difference between the social scientist and the historian is that the nomothetic outlook of the former is based on a research language which is widely shared, honed, and criticized by a community of scholars, while that of the latter is more freely invented (and reinvented) in the writing of every new monograph. In the end, however, neither the historian nor the social scientist can do without theory or, at the very least, without a set of implicit paradigms embodying theory.

The paradigms I am working with in this book include Alfred Schutz's analysis of motives and obligations (chapter 1); Japanese religious notions called *hare, ke,* and *kegare* (chapter 2); conflicting political patterns of decision-making and tension-management (chapter 3);

Victor Turner's theory of structure and antistructure (chapters 2 and 6); my own analysis of the Pan-Asian motifs of Pure and Mundane Activity (chapters 3 and 6); a modified version of Robert Bellah's concept of civil religion (chapter 8); and theories of exchange, development, modernization, and secularization which run throughout the book. Some of these paradigms elucidate social and cultural structures that stabilize society by rewarding conservative behavior and gentling dissent (chapters 2 and 6); others deal with values that create a sense of restlessness with "the way things are" and generate open conflict in society (chapter 3). In general, the paradigms I employ vary from a phenomenological use of *emic* discourse (the language of the natives) to an analytical use of *etic* categories (the language social scientists use when they talk about the natives). The astute reader will notice that these paradigms are not only heterogeneous, but that they fly at very different epistemic altitudes. If readers object to this, I can only remind them that I am using "paradigm" in its classical sense, and not in the contemporary, Kuhnian way. They are intended to be simply "known syllables" held close to unknown ones, familiar snapshots laid side by side with unfamiliar ones. Thus, when I say that my paradigms are footloose, I mean that with them, I hope to move and operate freely in the vast, fallow land stretching between Kuhn's restrictive templates, on the one hand, and idiographic modes of research, on the other.

Theory and paradigms always find themselves in a curious dialectical tension with what natives have to say about themselves. Some of our best interpretive paradigms come from our informants themselves. Others prove to be quite useless or misleading. The question then is: Who is right—the scholar or the native? For years now, critics sympathetic to the plight of colonial and third world peoples have condemned the arrogance of western scholars who have presumed to explain, or even understand, the non-Western world. Much of this criticism of orientalism, as it is now called, was long overdue. And many, anthropologists in particular, have learned (or have learned to display) a new humility in their encounters with the Otherness of Asia and the rest of the non-Western world. Clifford Geertz sums up the New Humility nicely in his aphorism: "We are all natives now."[7] Today, however, there seems to be a New Arrogance abroad which might be called "the arrogance of the native." The New Arrogance can be summed up in the attitude "don't tell *me,* I *live* here!," or "I *am* one, so I *know!*" It is as though the native had transformed the time-worn speculation of psychological anthropology—described some time ago by Evans-Pritchard as the "If I *were* a horse" strategy—into the insolent posture "I *am* a horse, so let me tell *you* about horses."[8] In other words, "Let me (the native) write the book!" Now, this immodest, but admittedly interesting, proposal rests on the rather primitive epistemological theory that the native has *direct* access to the meanings of his or her own culture, whereas the scholar, as an outsider, can only infer or speculate about these meanings indirectly. The natives, however, presumably have not read Schutz or any other phenomenological sociologists and therefore do not realize that their own cultural insights are also interpretations, i.e., meanings they (or other members of the tribe) have created after "stopping and thinking." That is to say, at some point in time someone has removed himself, or herself, from the immediate flow of events and has creatively constructed or reconstructed these meanings and interpretations for the tribe. While one must always listen respectfully to what natives have to say—after all, it is their story that we are trying to tell—their interpretive structures are not necessarily the only, or the best explanations available.

I would like to draw the reader's attention to the tension that exists between some of the paradigms which I have used and the intuitive, romantic, and even nationalistic interpretations of some of the natives, i.e., Japanese professors, journalists and other opinion-leaders. The careful reader will notice a sustained criticism of many of these neonativist self-images—called "Japan theory" *(Nihon-ron)*—running, like a subtext, throughout the present work. This is no mere academic matter. In this case the choice of paradigms is crucial for our basic understanding (or misunderstanding) of Japanese society. For example, if we follow the Japan theorists and assume that Japanese society is by its very nature harmonious we will be tempted to ignore its signs of tension or stress. Yet there is ample evidence of conflict in contemporary Japanese society, including, for example, the recent uprising in Airin, a rundown section of Osaka, during which fifteen hundred rock-throwing rioters battled twenty-five hundred police officers for five nights in October 1990. In part 2, I therefore take the opposite tack from Japan theory and assume that conflict in Japan is as real as it is anywhere else. The problem, then, is to find the paradigms that best model this conflict. My criticism of Japan theory comes to a head in chapter 8, where I discuss it as a relatively secularized civil religion in the making.

I should also say a word about my use of the concepts *structure* and *dynamics*. The historian does well not to allow the "diachronic" framework of conventional historiography to dominate the tale he or she has to tell. The right of structure to interrupt that story must be recognized and respected, *absolutely.* While I have formally divided the book into one section on structure (Part 1), and three on dynamics (parts 2–4), it will be obvious that both themes pervade the whole volume. The interpenetration of the structure and dynamics of religion is not only a stylistic matter; it has to do with substance and theory. While 'dynamics' obviously implies some kind of social and/or historical change, one should not take it as connoting something uninterpreted or purely objective. On the contrary, both the structures and the dynamics of religion are products (and objects) of interpretation. The structuralist who disregards the dynamics of religion as mere "fraudulent outlines," to use Lévi-Strauss's expression, is as misguided as the historian of religion who shies away from them because he feels he can interpret religion "as religion" only if he confines himself exclusively to its deep structures or archetypes. Both, it seems to me, are tilting with windmills. As creatures of change, structures and dynamics differ only in that structures change more slowly and reveal themselves more obliquely in the hurly-burly of everyday life.

I have outstanding intellectual debts to many scholars, to sociologists and anthropologists in particular. Chapters 2 and 6 rely heavily on the concepts of 'structure', 'anti-structure', and 'liminality' developed by the late Victor Turner. The baseline of my research, however, is the view that religion—whatever else it may be—is a social construct. The philosophical underpinnings of this bold but simple idea have been worked out rather elegantly by Peter Berger and Thomas Luckmann in their general theory of "the social construction of reality."[9] While most scholars today put a linguistic spin on this theory, I still find Berger's *The Sacred Canopy* one of the most "user friendly" paradigms in the sociology of religion.[10]

This book would not be what it is (or what it is not!) if it were not for a long, admiring, but somewhat querulous relationship with the thought of Max Weber. Whether the position I take in chapters 4 through 7 should be called neo-Weberian or anti-Weberian, is a question I leave with the reader. I must say, however, that respect for Weber's lasting contributions to scholarship prevents me from assuming the kind of anti-Weberian posture which has become de rigueur among historians. Nevertheless, the reader will find in these chapters a genuine alternative and/or supplement to Weber's own theory concerning religion and the rise of capitalism. Since the research presented in these chapters has already elicited considerable interest, I should elaborate a bit more on what is at stake in this part of the book.[11]

The problems I have with Weber's "Protestant ethic" thesis have been felt by many, and for many years. Bernard Mandeville, for example, writing against the Weber thesis some two hundred years before it appeared, argued that "the Reformation has scarce been more Instrumental in rend'ring the Kingdoms and States that have embraced it, flourishing beyond other Nations, than the silly and capricious Invention of Hoop'd and Quilted Petticoats." From this he concludes: "Religion is one thing and Trade is another."[12]The reader will see from the concluding section of chapter 5 that I do not want to go quite this far. While not trying to discount completely the role of religion and values in the modernization of society, I have tried to relativize the Weber theory, much as Weber himself relativized Marx (without completely gainsaying Marx's own concept of development). My theory—or rather my plea—is simply that we give more attention to the way in which religion has passively allowed (or enabled) societies like Japan to industrialize, and spend less time discussing the "direct impact" of religious ideas on social and economic change. Alexis de Tocqueville saw the development of America in the nineteenth century in similar terms. American clergymen, he pointed out, are interested in "progress"—what we would call modernization or development—"and they applaud its results." They "really adopt the general opinions of their countrymen *and they allow themselves to be borne away without opposition in the current feeling and opinion by which everything around them is carried along*."[13] Tocqueville's clergymen clearly were not leading the charge; they were bringing up the rear. Some probably were simply trying to get out of the way of the advancing troops marching along toward "modernity."

Readers familiar with Weber's writings on this subject may wonder whether, by stressing the passive role of religion in modernization, I am able to explain the appearance of "this-worldly asceticism" and its alleged role in the process of industrialization. To those who would defend Weber along these lines, I might point out that Mandeville and Adam Smith (who relied heavily on *The Fable of the Bees*) were not troubled by this question at all. For them riches were not the fruit of asceticism, but the wherewithal of human vanity—a perspective that naturally deflects scholarly attention away from the role of asceticism in general. Tocqueville is less cynical than Mandeville, but has just as little use for the theory of this-worldly asceticism.[14] If Mandeville, Smith, and Tocqueville are right about the relationships among religion, asceticism, and the rise of capitalism, it is high time we took a fresh look at the role values really play in the development of modern institutions.

In part 3, I have tried to bring together a new paradigm of development based on the insights of people like Mandeville, Tocqueville, Karl Polanyi, R. H. Tawney, and Jacob Viner with my own reading of Japanese religion and society. I am acutely aware of how much remains to be done in this field, especially in Japanese studies. The altogether too brief sections on Confucianism and the folk tradition in chapter 4 are intended simply as a foil for those who are tempted to speak glibly about the "direct impact" of religion on social and economic change. What is ultimately at stake here is the paradigm itself.

The essays is this book owe much to many. I am endebted, first of all, to my wife, Linda, who has unstintingly supported my extravagant (and certainly time-consuming) habits of reading and writing, and who generously helped with the preparation of several manuscripts. She also took the photograph ("The Coke Vendor's Buddha") used on the cover of this book. Taken on a bustling commercial street in Kyoto, this photo seemed to be a perfect, if somewhat incongruous, expression of my own interest in religion and society. I am especially thankful for the long friendship of several colleagues in various universities and disciplines. Several years ago, Professor Harumi Befu of Stanford's Anthropology Department initiated me into the mysteries of exchange theory with, in a modified form, I have used in chapter 1. Andō Seiichi, Professor Emeritus at Wakayama University in Wakayama City, Japan, was instrumental in introducing me to the religious life of Western Japan, the part of the country where most of my subsequent research was done. Several missionaries, Japanese pastors, and seminary professors in the United Church of Christ in Japan provided useful information for chapter 3. Because they stand on both sides of an acrimonious controversy that continues to divide their church, I believe I can thank them best by keeping their names anonymous. Likewise, I remember with great fondness the members of the Ittōen community in Kyoto who helped me understand, in my own, limited way, the Ittōen way of life described in chapter 6.

I would like to express my thanks to the National Endowment for the Humanities and the Sam Taylor Fellowship Program for their financial support of my sabbatical research. Southwestern University's Cullen Faculty Development Program made several summer projects possible. I would like to acknowledge a special debt of gratitude to Evie Jo Wilson and her husband, the late Arthur Wilson, of Houston, Texas, for their generous endowment of the Wilson-Craven Chair in Religion which it has been my privilege to hold since joining the faculty of Southwestern University in 1983. A visiting professorship in the Department of Religion at Princeton University during the Spring semester of 1990 enabled me to put the finishing touches on the manuscript.

A number of individuals deserve special thanks for their invaluable help as research assistants during the four years I spent in the Faculty of Sociology at Kwansei Gakuin University in Nishinomiya, Japan, above all Kinoshita Hiromichi, Kumagai Yuka, Fujiwara Nobuko, and Matsuda Takeshi. Finally, it is a pleasure to thank once again those who have taken the time to read and comment of the various parts of this book, especially Robert Bellah, David Blumenfeld, Weldon Crowley, Steven Davidson, Jan Dawson, James Foard, Leonard Giesecke, T. Walter Herbert, Jr., Dan Hilliard, Chalmers Johnson, Edward Kain, Susan Matisoff, Timothy O'Neill, Gwen Neville, James Peacock, Mark Reames, David Reid, and Kenneth Roberts.

Although the chapters of this book are arranged in a logical sequence, readers will have no problem dipping into the text at whatever point they wish. While rewritten and updated, each chapter stands on its own. Chapter 1, which may prove to be more difficult reading than the following sections, does set forth some of my basic presuppositions concerning the social organization of Japanese religion, but it too can be skipped or read out of sequence.

I would like to acknowledge with gratitude the following publishers and journals for the use of previously published materials:

Chapter 1. "Japanese Religious Affiliations: Motives and Obligations," *Sociological Analysis* (Summer 1983), Vol. 44, No. 2, pp. 131–146; *Toward Modernity: A Developmental Typology of Popular Religious Affiliations in Japan*. Ithaca: Cornell University East Asia Papers Series No. 12, 1977.

Chapter 2. "Pilgrimage and World Renewal: A Study of Religion and Social Values in Tokugawa Japan," Part I: *History of Religions* (November 1983) Vol. 23, No. 2, pp. 97–115; Part II: (February 1984) Vol. 23, No. 3, pp. 197–221.

Chapter 3. "The Cross and the Cudgel: The Ordeals of a Japanese Church," *Religion* (1985) Vol. 15, pp. 339–371.

Chapter 4. "Religion and Development: Weber and the East Asian Experience," in *Understanding Political Development,* edited by Myron Weiner and Samuel P. Huntington. Boston and Toronto: Little, Brown and Co., 1987, pp. 221–280.

Chapter 5. "Buddhism and the Modernization of Japan," *History of Religions* (May 1989) Vol. 28, No 4, pp. 304–339.

Chapter 6. "Ittōen: The Myths and Rituals of Liminality," *History of Religions,* Parts I–III (May 1975) Vol. 14, No. 4, pp. 282–321; Parts IV–VI (August 1975) Vol. 15, No. 1, pp. 1–33.

Chapter 7. "The Secularization of Japanese Religion: Measuring the Myth and the Reality," in *Transitions and Transformations in the History of Religions: Essays in Honor of Joseph M. Kitagawa,* edited by

Frank E. Reynolds and Theodore M. Ludwig. Leiden: E. J. Brill, 1980, pp. 261–285.

Chapter 8. "The Hollow Onion: The Secularization of Japanese Civil Religion," in *The Challenge of Japan's Internationalization: Organization and Culture,* edited by Hiroshi Mannari and Harumi Befu. Tokyo: Kwansei Gakuin University and Kodansha, 1983, pp. 201–211.

PART I

The Structure of Religious Groups

CHAPTER I

Japanese Religious Affiliations: Motives and Obligations

The first convenience the sociology of religion should provide for students of foreign religions is a typological bridge that will enable them to move out of their own culture to exotic lands beyond. One wants to be able to look at groups in strange, new lands and say, "That's a religious sect," or "This looks like a church." Unfortunately, the direct application of the paradigms of the sociology of religion to the non-western world often results in monstrous distortions. In foreign religions we often encounter socioreligious configurations which do not match the social and/or theological presuppositions of the west. Should we then simply throw out the traditional categories of church, sect, denomination, cult, and mysticism and do our work in the language of our informants, i.e., the "emic discourse" of the foreign religion itself? I think not. In the first place, being stylistically awkward, this would invite confusion of a different, more fundamental sort. In the second place, completely giving up our traditional language would make it impossible to make the comparative judgments which ultimately make the study of foreign cultures interesting to us. In this chapter, I therefore would like to begin the construction of a typological bridge which we can use as we move from western culture to the sociology of Japanese religion and society. To do this, we must first lay foundations that will be secure enough to bear the weight of a bridge connecting (at least) two civilizations. In the end, however, we must avoid the temptation to use our bridge as a crutch. After all, a good bridge is one that helps us to move forward, beyond the familiar. Once it has been crossed, we may leave it behind and be on our way.

In this book, our bridge leads us to a land in which basic religious affiliations have traditionally been divided into Shinto parish (*ujiko*) and its guilds (*miyaza*), the Buddhist family temple (*bodaiji* or *danna-dera*), the Buddhist prayer temple (kitō-dera), the confraternity (*kō*), the New Religions (*shin-shūkyō*, or *shinkō shūkyō*), and various less formal, ad hoc relations with faith healers, shamans, and mediums. Each of these terms has a rich, in fact a confusing, history which I shall only touch on in this chapter.[1] Suffice it to say that each type has undergone significant change as Japan developed from a primitive confederation of clans to the modern industrial giant it now is. While I shall say a few things about the historical development of these groups, the religious affiliations I deal with in this chapter are primarily those of the modern period.

To establish our new paradigm we must temporarily put aside the familiar Christian categories of church, sect, and denomination and develop a set of more abstract notions. To do this, I would like to apply to these religious affiliations a modified version of what today is called "exchange theory." Although there is a sizable literature on social exchange both in sociology and in anthropology, dissatisfaction with much of this material puts stringent limits on its application to religious affiliations.[2] While some believe that exchange theory can explain *all* aspects of religion, including its basic values, symbols, and ideas, I shall restrict my use of the theory to religion's social expression.[3]

Because of the reductionism implicit in many sociological theories of exchange, I would like to begin our discussion by looking at exchange from a new perspective. Following the lead of mainline exchange theorists, we can develop our concept of social and religious exchange by looking first at the exchange of *economic* goods and services. In its simplest form, economic exchange "is a relation between two (or sometimes more) persons each of whom offers a benefit in order to induce a response."[4] For example, A may give X to B in order to induce B to give Y to him. But offering benefits is not all there is to exchange. Accepting A's inducement obliges B to respond to A by repaying him with Y. In other words, there are two moments involved in any simple act of exchange: 1. the moment when A acts in order to solicit a response from B, and 2. the moment when B, having benefited from A's initiative, is obligated to act in turn.

Even in economics, the concept of exchange takes us beyond the purely economic or materialistic sphere. The perceptive economist therefore recognizes that exchange is "not merely a method for reshuffling the possession of things." On the contrary, it "is a method of controlling behavior and of organizing cooperation among men." In the end, "exchange is possible only in a society in which a moral code and authority keep social peace."[5] In other words, our two moments of exchange always take place within a specific framework of culture, values, and norms.

The fact that even economic exchanges take place in the context of values means that if we are to apply the concept to social and religious relationships, we must give more attention than exchange theory usually does to *obligatory* experiences. To do this, and to move beyond the purely economic level of exchange, I turn now to the work of Alfred Schutz, specifically to his distinction between *in order to* motives and *because* motives.[6] By 'in order to' motives Schutz meant an actor's orientation and intentional movement towards a desirable future state. This imagined future state itself can be regarded as the terminus ad quem of the actor's conduct. Schutz's 'because' motives, on the other hand, are determined by "past lived experience," which he describes as the terminus a quo of action. We can relate this dichotomy to our two economic moments by associating A's interested, intentional action with Schutz's 'in order to' motives, on the one hand, and B's felt obligation to repay A with Schutz's 'because' motives, on the other. In a very elementary sense, much of the meaning we assign to economic and social intercourse can be described as a swinging back and forth between these two moments or motives. For Schutz, the sociological interpretation and understanding (*Verstehen*) of human action begins precisely at this point. "Human activities are only made understandable by showing their in-order-to or because motives."[7]

Applied to religious behavior, 'in order to' motives seem to have an almost childlike simplicity. The ancient Latin prayer *do ut des* and its Sanskrit equivalent *dadami se, dehi me* are examples that come first to mind. Both formulae imply a willingness to sacrifice or exchange something with the gods *in order to* achieve one's aims. There is an ancient Jewish custom which also illustrates this simple religio-economic exchange. A father would approach a priest in order to "redeem" his firstborn son (see *Numbers* 18: 15–16). The priest inquired, "Which do you prefer, your son or your money?" The father, declaring that he preferred his son, handed the priest five shekels. The priest would then intone the works "This [money] in place of that [the child]. *This in exchange for that.*"

Duty, devotion, loyalty, gratitude, and selflessness—virtues which one associates with 'because' motives—pose problems for exchange theorists, especially when their concept of exchange is too closely tied to economic exchange.[8] Because of the importance of such values in Japanese religion and society, we must carefully hold in check the cultural bias built into exchange theory, a theoretical persuasion which generally reflects the western market economy and its psychology of possessive individualism.

EXCHANGE WITH A GOD. On some stone lanterns at the Kitano Shrine in Kyoto, there are bas-relief carvings of Daikoku, one of Japan's Seven Gods of Luck. Visitors put pebbles in Daikoku's hollow eye sockets hoping that the god, in turn, will bring them good luck.

In Japan, obligation is regarded in terms of the "return of benefits or favors" (Japanese: *on, giri,* or *gimu*). Traditionally, the Japanese began life under the heaviest of obligations. As children, they were obliged to their parents for their food, clothing, shelter, and for life itself. As adults, they were obliged to village gods and to their family's sacred ancestors for their land, possessions, and occupations.[9] In the prewar family-state ideology, in the factory, and in various religious institutions, individuals found themselves bound by various obligations incurred by the real or imaginary benefits *they had already received.* It seems to me that Japanese ethical reflection, whether philosophical or popular, always begins at this point.

I once walked into a tea shop in Tokyo just before business had officially begun. As I sat waiting, the employees joined hands and chanted the following credo:

> We are grateful to the people of the world.[10]
> We will not forget that our shop has been set up for the sake of the customer.
> Sharing both happiness and sorrow, we will cooperate

and not forget to encourage each other.
  Setting aside the past and anxiety of the 'morrow
we will not forget to give our all
  to the work set before us today!

Hearing this, the westerner might want to ask *why* these young people felt so "grateful to the people of the world." For the young people performing this business ritual, however, such a question does not seem to arise. The conviction that one has already received blessings, benefits, and favors from one's superiors (e.g., customers, gods, ancestors, landlords, shoguns, and emperors) is the terminus a quo of moral feeling, the basic presupposition of ethical discourse and conduct. Gratitude is therefore a key value in nearly all of the country's religions. In this chapter such feelings and values will be treated in a nonreductionistic way as examples of the 'because' motives underlying obligatory conduct.

While positively inspired by previous acts of kindness, feelings of obligation and gratitude are also reinforced by negative sanctions, viz., by consideration of the consequences that would follow if the individuals did *not* express their "gratitude" or fulfill their obligations when expected to do so. In Japan these negative sanctions range from a temporary loss of face to long-term social ostracism. Since religious obligations are usually sugarcoated with fun and games, and since they offer individuals many opportunities to demonstrate their social or moral integrity, explicit negative sanctions seldom come into play. Their importance increases, however, as the obligation in question becomes more burdensome.

In the pages that follow, I shall use Schutz's ideal-typical contrast between 'in order to' and 'because' motives to classify and analyze popular religious affiliations in Japan. We shall look first at the Shinto par ish and its guilds, the Buddhist family temple, and the "civil religion" of the prewar period as examples of institutions based on obligatory conduct (or 'because' motives). After this, we shall examine Buddhist prayer temples, Sudden Death Temples, and New Religions as organizations which (ideal-typically) rest on motivated conduct (or 'in order to' motives). Then we shall discuss religious confraternities, groups which embody a mixture of obligated and motivated intentionalities. In this context, we can also take up the problem of syncretism, the basic framework of religio-political relations in Japan. Finally, we shall see that the paradigm we have developed for the study of religious affiliations may have wider implication for understanding the organization of industrial relations in Japan.

MIYAZA PREPARING OFFERINGS. In Ao, a small fishing village in Wakayama Prefecture, the preparation of food offerings for the kami is still the exclusive privilege of the male descendants of nine hereditary miyaza families.

Obligated Religious Affiliations

The local parish (*ujiko*) is the most common institutional expression of the Shinto religion. Since the beginning of the Tokugawa period (1603–1867), the parish has generally been regarded as an inclusive territorial unit composed of families having rights and obligations in the cult of the local tutelary deity (*ujigami* or *chinjugami*). Because Shinto is primarily a layman's religion, the kind of professional exchange between priest and lay worshipers that one finds in Buddhism is often less highly developed. Where it does exist, it is usually complemented by a strong lay leadership determined by heredity, rotation of offices, lot, or election. In Western Japan, many parishes were controlled by cliques (called *miyaza*) which consisted of the oldest, most prestigious families in the community. As time went on, these monopolistic parish guilds gave way to a more inclusive parish system.[11]

Although the festivals of the Shinto parish sometimes originate in, or reflect a collective 'in order to' purpose (such as warding off plagues or pests), relations with the parish and its guilds generally are obligatory. The parish and its guilds are part of a network of community obligations into which individuals are born. Since they are made members of the parish as infants—by a rite called *ujiko-iri*—their affiliation with the parish is anything but voluntary.[12] Throughout life they will feel a responsibility and loyalty to this particular ujigami and ujiko. Because the authority of the parish and its deity is quite effective, there usually is little need to enforce these obligations with sanctions. To put it in economic terms: the authority of the parish in cost-effective. Nevertheless, should individuals shirk their role in the village festivals or fail to make their stipulated contribution to the upkeep of the shrine, they might be shunned or isolated from the community, a form of ostracism called *mura-hachibu*.

At the beginning of the Meiji period, the government deliberately extracted Shinto from its age-old union with Buddhism and made it a symbolic vessel of the newly concocted imperial system. Since the ancestors of the imperial family were venerated as Shinto deities, Shinto parishes throughout the country were recruited to serve as outposts of the government's nationalistic and militaristic propaganda. Japanese morality had traditionally been measured by the degree of honor or shame the individual brought upon the ancestors of his family. By spreading the worship of the imperial ancestors as the ancestors of all Japanese, the obligations individuals owed to their families and the local Shinto gods were sublimated and transformed into loyalty to the state. Thus, by grafting its ideology into the traditional folk practices of Shinto and ancestor worship, the state manipulated the people's primitive, *volkisch* feelings of pride, guilt, and conscience, making these the emotional base for a new civil religion.[13]

An excellent example of the creation of civil-religious obligations is an episode in a novel by Murayama Tomoyoshi, a writer originally active in the antigovernment, proletarian art movement. Arrested in 1932, Murayama underwent *tenkō* (ideological conversion to the imperial ideology) and, for two years after his release from prison, devoted himself to writing "conversion novels." In his book *The White Night (Byakuya)*, he describes the psychology of tenkō. The following passage vividly illustrates the role of ancestors as symbols and agents of conscience.

> After his second summer there [in prison], absolutely shut away from fresh air, his mind was eroded by something undefined and invincible. He felt as though his flesh and blood, or rather something mysteriously a part of his own father and mother, and of their forebearers from time immemorial, whose faces, names and lives had long since perished was eating away his existence, which was after all an infinitesimally small particle of their posterity. However hard he tried to

> cry out at them, to push them aside, and to drive them out, it was of no avail. In his struggle with his invisible foes, day in and night out, he groaned, struck his head with his fists, and scratched the wall with his nails.[14]

In this way, the ultranationalistic civil religion promoted by the government transformed the will of ancestors, *kami,* and buddhas into the mandates of the government itself. Obligations to the emperor "knew no end." Under the American occupation, leaders at SCAP did their best to destroy the obligatory nature of the Shinto parish and make the religion a voluntaristic or democratic denomination in the American sense of the word. Some have argued that demographic change itself may have had an even greater eroding effect. Morioka Kiyomi, for example, found that new residents in suburban Tokyo have little sense of identity with the local ujigami.[15] Nevertheless, the same study shows that relations with the parish become stronger the longer the family lives in the area. The decline in obligatory ties therefore does not mean that the Shinto parish is on its way to becoming a voluntary association. Population dislocation seems to be only a temporary disruption of this essentially obligatory kind of affiliation. As a social custom, making contributions to the local shrine continues to be virtually obligatory in many parts of Japan, even for Christians and other non-Shintoists.[16]

In contrast to Shinto, the values and institutional affiliations associated with Buddhism might seem to be more universalistic and voluntaristic. After all, Japanese Buddhism has been successfully transplanted to Hawaii, California, New York, Brazil, and other places the kami themselves seem loath to visit. Actually, the voluntaristic aspect of Buddhism can be traced back to ancient India, where the religion developed as a "specifically religious" movement in contrast to the ambient "natural religion," Hinduism.[17] In Japan, before the Tokugawa period, only the Nichiren sect had insisted that all members of a family be members of the same temple. The government itself played a decisive role in destroying the voluntary nature of Buddhism. The new temple system (*tera-uke*) established by the Tokugawa shogunate transformed the motivated affiliations of previous centuries into the obligatory ties of the family temple common throughout Japan today. The growth of temple cemeteries during the Tokugawa period also hastened the development of particularistic, obligatory conduct in Buddhism. Graves contributed to this growth of particularism by virtue of the fact that they are even less mobile than the earthbound shrines of the Shinto gods. In the twentieth century, demographic change (i.e., urbanization and subur-

BUDDHIST FAMILY TEMPLE AND GRAVEYARD.

banization) has seriously weakened the ties between urban families and family temples, which often are located in the distant countryside, far from the family's present residence. When they move to the city, many families not only leave their family temples and memorial tablets behind; sometimes they even forget the name of their danna-dera. Unless there is a death in the family, a Japanese seldom would think of approaching the priest in his new neighborhood to ask to be made a "member" of his temple. In this context, 'in order to' motives would simply be out of place.

Motivated Religious Affiliations

Among Japan's motivated, 'in order to' religious affiliations are included Buddhist prayer temples, voluntary pilgrim bands (e.g., those discussed in chapter 2), utopian communities like Ittōen (see chapter 6), new Sudden Death Temples, and various New Religions which appeared during the course of the nineteenth and twentieth centuries. Motivated affiliations can be subdivided into the behaviors of clients and devotees. By 'clients' I mean those people who establish only transient, ad hoc relations with religious institutions (e.g., temples and shrines), or with holy men or women [e.g., fortune-tellers, mountain ascetics, faith healers, and the *oshi* priests (discussed in chapter 2)]. By 'devotees' I have in mind stalwart believers who maintain self-sacrificing, loyal, long-term relations with religious institutions. They are especially active in utopian communes and the New Religions.

The millions of Japanese who crowd into Tokyo's Meiji Shrine and other nationally known shrines at New Year's are probably the best examples of what I mean by religious 'clients.' As clients, these people do not have the enduring sense of loyalty to these institutions that members of the ujiko have to their ujigami. Typologically speaking, clients are simply erratic pilgrims. When they attend festivals or visit a shrine, they play the role of guests—in contrast to the active member of the Shinto parish or Buddhist family temple, who often is called upon to play the role of a host or sponsor of religious events. Since they are bound to shrines and temples neither by kinship nor by neighborhood, questions about ritual rights, duties, and privileges—issues which preoccupied members of the miyaza and some Shinto parishes—are naturally of little or no concern. The object of their devotion is often a deity with specific religio-magical boons to offer. A young female client, for example, may go to a medium to get advice about her marriage prospects. Or she might go to a shrine recommended by friends to buy amulets that (hopefully) will help her to find a husband. If the amulets work, her next pilgrimage might be to purchase still another one to ensure safe childbirth. Later, when the family buys a new Toyota, her husband might assume the client's role and drive the car to the Narita Fudōsan temple to buy an amulet for "traffic safety." When their son becomes a high school senior, he might become a temporary client of the god Tenjin (Sugawara Michizane) and pray for good luck on his college entrance examinations. As specific, goal-oriented, ad hoc activities in search of this-worldly benefits, none of these acts needs to be repeated. While pilgrimage and other client-type activities have a long history in Japan, the growth of fleeting clienteles is closely related to the atomization of Japan's urban population, and to the secularization of the traditional parish and temple in particular. The phenomenon is also a response to the expansion of professional priesthoods which has tended to encourage the commercialism of festivals and has made possible the sale of amulets and blessings in the shrine throughout the whole week.

In recent years, elderly clients have been attracted to Sudden Death Temples (*pokkuri-dera*), institutions which are surely among the most curious religious innovations—some might say the most macabre—in postwar Japan. Appearing around 1960, these temples ensure the client a quick and easy death, followed by a safe rebirth in Amida's Pure Land. The Sudden Death Temples are clearly a response to the problems of Japan's rapidly aging population. As the size of the average family decreases, the elderly have increasingly begun to live apart from their children. Presently, about twenty-five percent of them maintain separate residences, which is few compared with western countries but a great increase compared with prewar Japan. This is a population cohort which came to age when great stress was laid on the family and filial piety. From their perspective, the preference of the younger generation for small, nuclear families and separate homes naturally seems selfish. Spending their final years in a situation which Japanese critics call the "use and throw culture" (*tsukai sutete bunka*), the elderly feel that they too have been used and cast aside. Because postwar legislation encourages the equal distribution of inheritances, in many families no one child has the material resources to take care of the parents. Many of the elderly are therefore passed around from one child to the next (*tarai-mawashi* or *babakorogashi* as it is called), a routine which can be extremely unsettling for the aged. Suicides among the elderly have increased ominously.[18] Under these circumstances it is quite understandable that the some of the aged would turn to the Buddha and pray for a quick end to the sorrows of this life.

Tours to the Sudden Death Temples are organized by Buddhist Ladies Associations, senior citizens clubs, and travel agents. Only a few clients travel by themselves. The tour includes stops at two or three such temples and an overnight stay in a temple inn. At the Kichidenji temple in Nara, for example, a complete pilgrimage consists of three separate calls: the first to pray for a long life and good health; the second for protection against accidents; and the third for a quick and easy death and rebirth in the Pure Land (*anraku ōjō*). Because old people often fear the embarrassing "diseases of the lower parts," or *shimo no byō* as the Japanese put it, visitors to the temple are asked to bring a special set of underwear with them to be blessed. Those who forget to bring underwear with them may purchase it at the temple. These garments are blessed by the priest who sprinkles them with holy water and utters a spell over them in the name of a toilet deity called Uzumasa.[19] After this, the priest gives a fifteen-minute sermonette adroitly mixing light entertainment with the sober thoughts of traditional Japanese Buddhism. He assures his congregation that death is not something to be feared, but is merely like the falling of autumn leaves. With simple daily effort, one can be reborn in the Pure Land. One should therefore always wear a smile, use gentle words, and keep one's heart pure.

SUDDEN DEATH TEMPLE. The priest is blessing the underwear on the altar.

As a mode of religious affiliation, the Sudden Death Temple tour is obviously ad hoc and transient. No one gets to know the priest or his family well. Nor does the priest have time to talk personally with the thousands of elderly clients to whom he ministers every week. The relationship is, in fact, based on a simple exchange: admission is charged and underwear is blessed for a set fee. Looked at as a total event, only part of the "therapy" of the tour takes place in the temple itself. Back in their comfortable excursion buses, the old folks have a chance to talk with each other about their health, tension with their children, and the other problems of aging.[20]

We turn next to the 'in order to' affiliations of devotees, the most notable of which are the so-called New Religions (*shinkō-shūkyō*, or *shinshūkyō*), syncretistic sects with founders, scriptures, and mass followings.[21] Joseph M. Kitagawa describes these movements in the following words:

> Their teachings are eclectic and not well systematized, but their simple, direct, and practical beliefs and practices appeal to the masses who do not feel at home with the complex doctrines of established religions. . . . Most of them are highly centralized in their organizational structure, utilizing cell group systems as well as incentive plans. A few of them have semimilitaristic disciplines. All of them use mod-

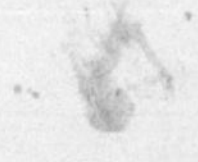

ern mass media of communication and have efficient methods of tithing or its equivalent.[22]

The clients of Buddhist prayer temples (*kitō-dera*) and Shinto shrines (*omiya, jinja, or jingū*) establish temporary relations with these institutions in order to recover their health, ward off accidents, ensure safe childbirth, or admission to the university of their dreams. The relationship of the devotee with his or her New Religion grows out of similar 'in order to' motives. But the relationship in this case is usually longer lasting. In response to the devotees' all-too-human needs, the New Religions display a universalistic, "whosoever-will-may-come" kind of attitude. Some, like Sōka Gakkai, have assumed a more aggressive posture, threatening that whosoever-does-*not*-come will be damned, or will at least get sick. While the actual beliefs of these groups may not appear to be *substantially* rational, the behavior of their adherents is based on a *functional* rationality and clear-cut 'in order to' motives.[23] This does not mean, however, that the individual who joins a New Religion is in all ways similar to the "religious joiner" in Western societies. Berger and Luckmann have described the latter a person strolling through the supermarket of suburban denominations, selectively (i.e., comparatively and rationally) making his or her ecclesiastical purchases.[24] In Japan, few individuals seem to select their religion on the basis of such cool, comparative analysis. While people are naturally interested in the cost-benefit factor (i.e., the ratio of miracles per yen and time invested), chances for one-to-one comparisons of prices, products, and services are limited. Believers generally stay with a sect as long as they are blessed with miracles or good fortune. When their luck sours, or when the cost of their involvement becomes greater than the satisfaction they derive from it, they simply drop out. If they join another New Religion later on—and movement between these groups is considerable—it usually will be in response to a coincidental meeting or conversation with a friend, relative, or neighbor. Proselytizing by strangers, while practiced by most of the New Religions, seems to be less effective.[25] Thus, the traditional obligatory influences of *Blut und Boden* continue to play a role even in religious groups based explicitly on motivated conduct.

Confraternities: A Mixture of Motivated and Obligatory Behavior

Thus far, we have seen that Shinto parishes and Buddhist family temples are based on the historical dominance of obligatory conduct, while Buddhist prayer temples, Sudden Death Temples, New Religions and communitarian movements take as their sociological point d'appui the functional rationality of 'in order to' motives. The confraternities (*kō* or *kōshū*) which we shall now examine run the gamut from those which are nearly identical with the particularism of the local community cults, on the one hand, to those based on universalistic faith-commitments, on the other. In some confraternities, 'because' motives seem predominant. In others, 'in order to' motives stand out. Most, however, are a mixed bag.

While the history of religious confraternities in Japan goes back to the time of Prince Shōtoku (573–621), it was the New Buddhism of the Kamakura period (1192–1338) which gave rise to the institution as we now know it. From the beginning, these groups benefited both from the individual motivations and the family obligations of their members. The Pure Land Ikkō sect, for example, held meeting to "pay back the blessings" (*hō-on-kō*) which members felt they had received from their founder, Shinran Shōnin (1173–1262). On the face of it, this sounds like obligatory conduct: piety here is a response to spiritual and material blessings *already received.* On the other hand, the express purpose of the Pure Land confraternities was to assemble *in order to* strengthen a common faith in Amida Buddha. Thus, religious voluntarism seems to develop in this sect much as it did in the Protestant movements of the west, viz., churches and sects which were also based on "faith alone" (*sola fide*). In both cases, the result was the emergence of a type of religious affiliation which had at least the potential for transcending the bonds of kinship and local community. Amida Buddha of the Pure Land sects therefore functioned as a specialized, adventitious deity within the local community. He was an alternative, or even a rival, to the inclusive, obligatory festival-faith of the Shinto parish.

To put this in European terms, the Pure Land confraternities were virtually Free Churches surrounded by the *Landeskirchen* of Shinto and Buddhism on the one hand, and by the private *Eigenkirchen* of the warrior class on the other. Varying in size from ten to one thousand members, these groups cut across the community's traditional pastoral and geographical borders. A confraternity often did not include all of the members of the same village, or even all of the followers of a given priest. On the other hand, a single chapel (*dōjō*) might house several kō. To use European terminology again, one might think of these groups as *ecclesiolae in ecclesia,* i.e., pietistical or devotional conventicles within the church. In some cases, the kō incorporated all of the believers of one village with those of neighboring communities. It was this *translocal* mode of affiliation that made the sect a political and

CONFRATERNITY. This nembutsu confraternity in Wakayama City also functions as a club for older women in the area.

economic power to be reckoned with in premodern Japan. While composed initially of peasants, these confraternities were not simple, egalitarian associations. On the contrary, they were merely links in a long ecclesiocratic chain leading up to the powerful Honganji patriarchs at the top. Other, less highly structured confraternities formed for the purpose of, say, venerating a local deity, did have a relatively horizontal or egalitarian organization.

Ikeda Yoshisuke has reduced this bewildering variety of confraternities to the following threefold typology:[26]

1. Those which *transcend* the local community
2. Those which are *coextensive with* the local community
3. Those which are *subsumed by* the local community

While Ikeda regards confraternities of the first type as the most likely to create social tensions in the community, it seems to me dubious that the translocal nature of these groups alone accounts for this fact.[27] For example, was it merely the translocal nature of the Pure Land confraternities that led to the fifteenth century *Ikkō Ikki* rebellions in the Kinki, Tōkai, and Hokuriku areas? I think not. While their translocal nature undoubtedly added great strength to the movement, groups of this sort tend to create social tension primarily because of their overall 'in order to' orientation. Such groups naturally lend themselves to organized, purposeful activity. Thus it seems to be religious groups which have both a translocal social organization and a capacity to express purposeful or instrumental intentionalities that are most likely to foment social change. By way of contrast, more conservative religious groups (such as the Shinto parish or Buddhist family temples) based on ascriptive obligations and duties are less wieldy and tend to become involved in social change only in a defensive way, e.g., in connection with local disputes over privilege and prestige.[28]

Japan's confraternities are based on a rich mixture of motivations and obligations, some of them religious, some secular, but most inseparably religious and secular at the same time. Whether their aim is to affirm a common religious faith, organize a pilgrimage, or hold a sweepstakes (*mujin-kō*), confraternities often demonstrate a high level of goal—or functional—rationality. Nevertheless, hierarchical and *Gemeinschaft*-like elements can also be found in their makeup. Because they were intimately tied to traditional patterns of social and economic interaction, many confraternities have now disappeared. While laymen blame priests for their demise, and priests chide laymen for their lack of zeal, the truth is that in Japan, as elsewhere for that matter, it is notoriously difficult to maintain groups *sola fide*. Hence the importance of the social and material exchanges (e.g., feasting, fun and games) which took place in the kō when the institution was in its heyday. The disappearance of these secular or parareligious exchanges is therefore not unrelated to the decline of the kō in postwar Japan.

Syncretism

We are now in a position to expand our basic paradigm and show how a combination of obligations and motivations led to the formation of religious syncretism, not pluralism in the western sense of the word. But first a word about the distinction between these terms. Syncretism and pluralism are both cultural systems resting on a multiplicity of alternatives. It is the structuring of these alternatives that makes the difference. Pluralism is a differentiated system of genuine religious and/or cultural alternatives. I say "genuine" because in this case society recognizes that adherence to one alternative may legitimately make commitment to other alternatives impossible. Since the alternatives in a pluralistic system seem to be moving apart from one another, I like to think of pluralism (ideal-typically) as a system of *centrifugal cultural differentiation*. Syncretism, on the other hand, I shall call a system of *centripetal cultural differentiation*. While there are cultural alternatives available (and practiced) in syncretistic systems, these alternatives coalesce, or dovetail, and, over the course of time, tend to become *layered, obligatory modes* of behavior and/or belief.

A brief historical digression is in order. In Japan's premodern period, alternatives from the outside world were transmitted to the closed society of manor and village primarily by wandering, unordained holy men. Together with itinerant entertainers, traders, and craftsmen, they gathered at large shrines and temples or in market places, i.e., places in which life was relatively unconstrained by magistrates and political authorities. The holy men carried with them a mixed bag of religious goods and services—Taoist magic, Shinto spells, and various Buddhist practices. Some were evangelists of one of the "single practice" sects. Relying on their own charisma rather than on official ordination, they organized their followers in small confraternities or other cultic orders.[29] Thought to possess special, esoteric knowledge about the spiritual world, these peripatetic holy men helped to spread the high culture of the capital throughout the provinces.

Since the deities and Buddhas of these holy men came from the outside world and provided an alternative to the indigenous cult, I shall refer to them as *adventitious* deities (*marōdō-gami*). The attraction of the adventitious deities was both thaumaturgical and soteriological. As functional deities, they were thought to have special miraculous virtues (*reigen*) such as the ability to ensure safe childbirth, a good harvest, or the cure of various maladies. Others guaranteed instant enlightenment—or at least assured the believer of immediate rebirth in the Pure Land after death.[30] In the eyes of the villager, the deity and his messenger were not always clearly distinguished. In fact, the missionary's residence sometimes evolved into the shrine of the marōdō-gami. In other cases, the local people themselves brought the adventitious deity home to the village, enshrining it in the precincts of their own ujigami. By giving their heretofore nameless clan god the name of a prestigious provincial or national god they sought to win for themselves the magical benefits of more powerful deities while simultaneously enhancing the good name of the village itself.

We can see two types of religious affiliation emerging from all of this: the one based on 'because of' obligations to the local deity, the other originally growing out of 'in order to' motivations focused on faith in a god or Buddha from the world outside the community. These alternatives can be summarized as follows:[31]

Locative and Adventitious Affiliations

The Locative Pattern (*Ujigami*)	The Adventitious Pattern (*Marōdō-gami*)
integrates community and kinship groups	establishes a community of believers apart from the local community and its kinship groups
exclusive, "particularistic" relations based on genealogy and/or geography	inclusive, missionary faith with relations between the sacred and the congregation based on faith and/or a demanding religious monopraxis
deity has undifferentiated functions	deity and missionary have specific functions and strong "personalities"
authority of deity reflected in political, economic, social, and cultural circumstances of the community	authority of deity reflected in the magico-religious power of its transmitter (missionary, shaman, hero), his techniques of ecstasy, and social position
(generally) routinized leadership based on rotating lay-priesthoods	(often) a charismatic leadership developing later into hereditary priesthoods

Figure 1

The process whereby the confraternities of an adventitious deity become established in villages gives us some idea of the ways in which external cults were indigenized in general.[32] Often the confraternity had a dual leadership made up of local stalwarts and missionaries from the outside world. The cult was propagated most successfully when the missionary was able to befriend the local priest and religious establishment. In recently founded villages, or in villages where the cooperative spirit of the community had weakened, the new faith made rapid headway. The adventitious god was often amalgamated with the indigenous deity. When this happened, the local deity assumed the name of the adventitious god, a set of specific functions, and a more definite "personality."This process of acculturation was hastened when the village was located close to the main shrine of the outside god. Near Kyoto, for example, many village deities were called Ise-sama (since Ise is relatively near Kyoto), whereas in distant Hokkaidō missionaries from Ise were able to establish only branch shrines of their cult. Often the temporary residence of the missionary served as an ersatz pilgrimage site for those unable to make the long journey to Ise. Aside from sheer distance, the process of assimilation could also be slowed down by the strangeness of the new god. The more the cult of the marōdō-gami resembled that of the ujigami, the more readily it was accepted by the community. Once accepted, the confraternity became integrated into the structure of the local religious system by patterning its festivals and concepts on those already familiar in the vicinity, and by gradually substituting for its own discipline the distribution of wonder-working amulets.

Such were to logistics of acculturation. But the question remains: why did the interaction of locative and adventitious patterns result in syncretism and not in pluralism as such? The ultimate reason, I believe, lay in the vulnerability and dependency of the local community. The traditional Japanese village was open to attack from outside, yet beholden to the same outside world for its defense. While it had its own internal political culture and leadership, ultimate power and authority came from political centers beyond its borders. The mythical charter of sacred kingship itself (the *tenson-kōrin* myth) was based on a shamanistic or marōdō-gami kind of scenario.[33] Thus, unlike the Abrahamic traditions in which social integration rested on belief in one God, one faith, and one religious practice, the political and social integration of Japan has traditionally been based on a *multiplicity* of gods and faiths. Significantly, the theological articulation of this syncretism (the *honji-suijaku* system) first appeared during the tenth through the twelfth centuries when the manorial system was becoming dominant. Shinto deities which had long been regarded as "sentient beings" in need of the Buddha's salvation themselves, or as guardians of Buddhist temples, were declared to be manifestations of the various Buddhas. After they lost imperial support in the middle of the Heian period, temples made use of this syncretistic theory in order to amalgamate Buddhism with the indigenous religious customs of the manors they controlled.

Whereas in the west it was heresy (or pluralism, as it is called today) which seemed to threaten the unity of Christendom, in Japan, it was monopraxis (emphasis on a single religious practice) that posed the greatest spiritual menace to the traditional integration of society. In the course of time, both the True Pure Land Buddhists and the Nichiren sects became deeply involved in rebellion. Under such circumstances, in order to avoid conflict with the religious establishment of the community, the new religious alternative (say, Amida Buddha) was generally treated as a supplement to the traditional devoirs of village and family. Grafted into these primary groups, participation in the confraternity of the adventitious deity gradually became obligatory, and finally hereditary. As the 'in order to' motivations of the first generation gave way to the 'because of' obligations of posterity, the adventitious deity ceased to be much of an alternative at all. The result therefore was not pluralism, but syncretism.

Refining and Restricting the Paradigm

Field researchers familiar with the messy motives of daily life will quickly sense that Schutz's motivational dichotomy cannot be directly translated into an interview schedule. And they are right. One problem is that there is a *verbal* overlap between the expressions 'in order to' and 'because of' (see note 7). This however, is not as much of a problem as the *systemic* or *historical* overlap commonly witnessed in the motives which typify institutions. Since motives are likely to change over the lifetime of the individual member—and, more obviously, over the course of his family's interaction with the group—this ambiguity *in re* may be more significant than the ambiguity *in theoria*. For example, a family which originally joined a Buddhist confraternity in order to worship Amida Buddha, in later generations may participate in the same rites simply as a family devoir. Similarly, while most Japanese join a New Religion in order to find a cure for illness or bad luck, subsequent experience may have a transforming effect on their original motivation. Miraculous experiences or significant personal relationships often generate new obligations to sects and deities. In this way, groups which originally depended on the intentionalities of magic and voluntarism develop new outlooks based on more rational, devotional obligations. Simultaneously, as these groups become more stable or mature (e.g., as they move into their second generation), they naturally tend to become more inclusive and quietistic. No longer is it mandatory for a person to authenticate his membership by wrapping himself in the mantles of magic and charisma. Gradually, the group may put on the whole armor of an obligatory institution. Hence the well-known metamorphosis of sects into denominations, a transformation which, abstractly at least, can be spelled out in terms of a history of motivations and obligations. While people will continue to convert out of specific 'in order to' motives, younger family members often join merely out of filial piety. Thus, within the same family, motives for joining and continuing to participate in a group will vary widely.

Religious affiliations based on obligatory conduct often undergo a similar change, but in the opposite direction, i.e., by generating new 'in order to' motives. For example, during the ultranationalist period, Japanese politicians advanced the cause of their own factions by cloaking their political ('in order to') ambitions in the obligatory rhetoric of civil-religious slogans. This use of political slogans differed hardly at all from the purchase and use of religious amulets, both being instances of goal-oriented (*zweckrational*) behavior.[34] Or, to take a more general example: an individual born in a Shinto parish might get the urge to run for public office. His obligatory connection with the shrine may turn out to be a golden opportunity to influence the votes of other parishioners. Religious obligations thus become a front for the political will-to-power.[35]

Because of the fluidity of our motives and obligations, those who would operationalize Schutz's schema for use in the field are advised to do so with caution. The primary value of his distinction is its usefulness in sorting out fundamental or ideal-typical modes of religious and social affiliation *over the long run*. The intentionalities expressed by the words 'in order to' and 'because of' should therefore be thought of as hegemonic motives, i.e., dominant motives which repeatedly (or historically) seem to initiate or sustain social or religious affiliations. They are the motives that seem to come to the surface primarily "when push comes to shove." In nearly all cases, they are reinforced by their ideal-typical opposites: 'because' motives by 'in order to' motives, and vice versa.[36] As such, hegemonic motives may or may not be congruent with a respondent's conscious motives. For these reasons, the position elaborated in this chapter may appeal more to historians of religion able to survey in a leisurely way decades or even centuries of continuity and change than to sociologists or anthropologists working in the field on a six-month grant.

Comparative Use of the Paradigm

Since the theology and history implicit in the typology of western churches, sects, and denominations are virtually without parallel in East Asia, it is highly misleading to apply these terms directly to religious affiliations in Japan, China, or Korea. Although the English language may force us to speak of Buddhist "churches" and Shinto "sects," enough has already been said about the social structures of Japanese religion to make us painfully aware of the inaccuracies of this borrowed vocabulary. Although our new paradigm cannot be easily or directly applied to fieldwork at this point, it does offer us a way of comparing religious affiliations east and west in a relatively controlled way. What follows is an attempt to do so in terms of the underlying hegemonic motives and obligations of religious groups in Japan and in the west.

The 'because' motives which characterize Shinto parishes and Buddhist family temples in Japan also seem to have dominated the traditional churches of Europe. Membership in these groups was generally determined by birth, or rather by infant baptism, while popular support was closely related to national and/or family identity. The 'in order to' motives which underlie the ad hoc ties the Japanese client establishes with prayer temples, faith healers, fortune-tellers, or functional deities—as well as the longer-lasting ones devotees strike up with the New Religions—have their parallel in the purposefulness and psychological drive of first-generation sects, cults, and evangelistic campaigns in the west. Between these extremes fall our North American "mainline denominations," institutions which typologically are parallel to some of Japan's older New Religions. These organizations help to perpetuate cultural or familial identities while, simultaneously, providing a milieu in which individuals can pursue their own spiritual goals. These comparative relationships are summarized in figure 2.

Looked at from this rather ambitious, global perspective, we can now hazard some broad generalizations about the relationship between hegemonic motives and the socioreligious profiles of the institutions they influence. Both in Japan and in the west, religious affiliations with a 'because' base tend to have more inclusive, stable memberships. However, they are susceptible to attrition due to shifts in population, losses which are seldom made up simply by devoting more time and energy to evangelism. On the other hand, more highly motivated 'in order to'

Obligations, Motives, and Religious Institutions

Motivated Conduct ('in order to' motives)	Mixed Motives	Obligatory Conduct ('because' motives)
	Japan	
Ad hoc affiliations with holy men, fortune tellers, and functional deities		Shinto parish (*ujiko*); Shinto parish guild (*miyaza*)
Buddhist prayer temples (*Kitō-dera*)	Confraternities (*kō*)	Buddhist family temple (*danna-dera* or *bodaiji*)
New Religions	Older New Religions	Civil Religion
Sudden Death Temples (*pokkuri-dera*)		
	The West	
Sects; cults; evangelistic campaigns and moral crusades	"Mainline" North American denominations	Traditional European churches and/or parishes

Figure 2

groups are prone to high dropout rates due to the instability of charismatic leadership and the disappointment of magical or apocalyptic expectations. They can however recoup these losses through evangelism and thereby achieve much higher growth rates than more conservative groups. In contrast to 'because' groups, which generate socially inclusive congregations, 'in order to' sects, cults, and New Religions generally appeal to definable groups or to special interests, e.g., to the sick, disabled minorities, or to groups based on gender, culture, or age.

While it is difficult to generalize about their political orientations, the inclusive social composition of 'because' groups generally makes it difficult or impossible for them to espouse specific positions or causes. Religious ethicists, pontiffs, prelates, and other ecclesiocrats claiming to speak for their churches do, of course, issue manifestoes from time to time on this or that social problem. Pronouncements of this sort, however, tend to be few in number and politically innocuous. When they are not, they run the risk of religiously polarizing congregations that are already divided socially and economically. As we shall see in chapter 5, the most significant political role of religions based on obligatory conduct is their silent acquiescence in "the way things are" and their open cooperation with the powers-that-be. When radicalism does break out in institutions of this sort (e.g., in Latin American Catholicism or in Japan's Jōdo Shinshū), it is often a reflection of class struggles too strong to be contained any longer by the "transcendental" ("above-it-all") political style of the leadership. Aside from this, however, there seems to be no "elective affinity" at all between 'because' groups and the political left. Sometimes, more homogeneous 'in order to' groups are able to take more specific political stands, in so far as other-worldly interests and apocalyptic expectations do not completely turn them away from the problems of this world. An example of social action of this sort is the active role of Afro-American churches in the American civil rights movement of the 1960s and 70s. In general, however, as sects become "denominationalized," they tend to abandon the critical postures assumed by their founders and become "all things to all men," i.e., political nonentities. The Japanese New Religions, Tenrikyō and Ōmotokyō, are excellent examples of this process of religious and political *embourgeoisement*.

The rank-and-file members of religious groups based on 'because' motives tend to display a low level of religious knowledge and a high level of theological ambiguity. Among the members of 'in order to' groups, however, knowledge of sacred lore and mastery of magical techniques is more widely diffused and highly developed, even among the rank and file. Examples of this would include the memorization of scriptures, prayers, and incantations in some sects, and the development of healing arts or theosophical speculation in others. The magic of 'because' groups is generally diffuse and traditional, while that of the 'in order to' sects is dispensed in more efficient and profitable ways. In both cases, the distribution of charms, spells, or healing prayers may help to support the institution financially. Usually, only the leaders of sects, cults, and New Religions—or individual fortune-tellers, healers, and shamans—are able to earn their keep solely or primarily through the purveyance of magic.

'Because' and 'in order to' groups also differ in the ways they celebrate their faith. In groups founded on obligatory affiliations, sport (Japanese: *asobi*) is incorporated into a cyclical or liturgical renewal of the community. Be it the uproar of ritual combat in a Shinto festival or the tomfoolery of the Mardi Gras in Latin America, play is part of an "eternal return." While such goings-on are often frowned upon by ascetic sects, many 'in order to' groups incorporate sport as part of their "youth work." As such, play, or asobi, instead of spontaneously renewing the whole community, is used as an evangelistic technique to expand or perpetuate the sect itself.

Japanese Groups: A Broader Look

From the beginning of their recorded history, the Japanese have been telling themselves and the rest of the world that they are a "group-oriented" people. The so-called Seventeen Article Constitution attributed to Prince Shōtoku in the early seventh century emphasizes the importance of values highly regarded even today: harmony, consensus, obedience, and decorum. In contemporary Japan a spate of books and articles known rather grandly as "Japan theory" (*Nihon-ron*) seeks to create a sense of national identity primarily by expounding on these values.[37] Among western Japanologists, the outlook expressed by this literature is sometimes referred to as the "group model". This theory or model seeks to explain nearly all aspects of Japanese life in terms of 1. the *value system* just described, 2. the *homogeneity* of the Japanese people, 3. the *uniqueness* of their culture, 4. the existence of a *modal personality* based on ego-repression and dependent collectivism, and above all 5. *the tendency to do nearly everything in groups*.

Some scholars have tried to debunk the model completely, claiming that the Japanese are actually more heterogeneous than they seem, that their society is not unique, that their fabled politeness and loyalty are merely the strategies of self-interest, and that the individual is ultimately as important as the group. In industrial sociology there is a new hard-nosed trend that rejects *any* discussion of the impact of traditional Japanese culture and values on the country's astonishing economic growth. While I, too, regard the group model and Japan theory in general as idealized, ideological self-portraits, the approach I have outlined in this chapter may help us to avoid both the gullibility of the Japan theorists and the reductionism of the western realists.

It is indeed true that the Japanese tend to realize their personal goals within the protective framework of groups dominated by paternalistic ideals. Because of the relatively limited horizontal mobility among Japanese firms, the workplace itself displays some of the characteristics of the obligatory religious affiliations I have discussed above, especially their particularism and ascriptive sense of identity. Accepting a position with some firms is similar to being adopted into a family. It follows that the claims these groups make on their employees, as well as the obligations management imposes on itself, go far beyond the "labor-management relations" of most companies in Europe or North America. These claims are legitimated largely in terms of an "ideology of obligation" based, in turn, upon Schutz's 'because' motives. Accordingly, many, perhaps most, Japanese have a rather idealistic way of talking about their work. An official of the Matsushita company put it this way:

> Service, not profit, is the objective. Profit is not what we can earn—it is given to Matsushita in appreciation of its services. If the company fails to make its profit, it has committed a social blunder or sin, according to our philosophy. The society to which Matsushita belongs entrusts it with capital and manpower for Matsushita to get results. Profit is the appreciation of society, the reward to Matsushita for what it has done.[38]

This way of talking tends to transform the most mundane, self-seeking kinds of activity into idealized, or even spiritualized, efforts to "return the benefits" (*hō-on*) one has already received. A company president can move his employees to tears when he reminds them how the founder of their firm suffered and sacrificed on their behalf. The "suffering of the founder," a common theme in both religious and secular groups, creates an a priori obligation which makes members (be they religious devotees or employees of a firm) feel that they must devote themselves wholeheartedly to the group. To promote a spirit of devotion and hard work, many companies sponsor "spiritual education" (*seishin kyōiku*) programs for their employees. These programs (which are often obligatory) include retreats at famous shrines and temples, lessons in flower arrangement, and even paramilitary drills on a self-defense force base. During these sessions, employees are reminded of the many benefits they have received from their company, and of their duty to work hard and faithfully in return.[39]

The paradigm I have outlined in this chapter offers us an alternative both to the group model and to some of the extreme attacks made on it. Explaining loyalty and obligation in terms of benefits and exchange gives us a deeper appreciation of Japan's group values. On the other hand, by putting equal weight on 'in order to' motives and self-interest, it causes us to appraise more realistically the utilitarianism and individualism also at work in this seemingly consensual and collectivistic society. Many social scientists have rightly stressed the fact that we cannot account for Japan's economic miracle in terms of her culture or values alone. Specific institutions and rewards (such as a decent sharing of profits, respect for workers' opinions, and job security) have also contributed to Japan's sustained economic growth. Some, however, reacting negatively to the overemphasis on culture in James C. Abegglen's early work, have gone to the opposite extreme, maintaining that industrial and bureaucratic organization, strategy, technology, and self-interest are the necessary and *sufficient* causes of the country's success.[40] From my point of view, to argue that the Japanese sense of loyalty is an illusion—because only institutional arrangements "count"—is as misguided as to say that in the west because "honesty pays"—that is, because it has its own material rewards—there is no such thing as honesty. This radical dichotomizing of culture and institutions, morality and rewards, is a methodological bias that is apt to blind us to the real dynamics and sensibilities at work in Japanese society. In this chapter I have tried to go beyond the group model, not by reducing its idealism to more selfish drives but by recognizing the importance of both motivations (including self-interest) *and* obligations (including a lively sense of gratitude, loyalty, responsibility, and dedication to the task at hand) in our paradigm of exchange relations. Detailed studies have shown that the exact mixture of motivation and obligation in any given group will depend in large measure on members' sex, education, age, and potential for mobility, as well as on the group's own size and other specifics.[41]

The alleged uniqueness of Japanese society which proponents of the group model insist on can be reduced to two things which, while seldom encountered in the west, are hardly unusual in the history of traditional civilization. In the first place, there is a pronounced tendency in Japan for institutions to absorb the 'in order to' motives of individuals, binding them to the 'because' principles of what could legitimately be called "moral communities." Within these communities, the aspirations of individuals—just as real in Japan as in the west—are harnessed to the needs of groups. This discourages the growth of an *explicit* western-style psychology of possessive individualism. Instead, individual claims and rights are subtly blended with collective obligations and duties. 'In order to' motives are sublimated (i.e., transformed, but not destroyed) and raised to the nobler level of ideals. In the second place, there is in Japan a historical tendency for the hegemonic motives of institutions to evolve from an instrumental, 'in order to' orientation to an obligatory, moral one. Over time, the instrumental motives of the groups listed in the first column in figure 2 tend to shift to the right, becoming virtually indistinguishable from the obligatory conduct of the groups represented in the second two columns. It is therefore not unusual to find both Japanese companies and New Religions (groups one ordinarily associates with clear-cut instrumental, 'in order to' orientations) stressing the importance of loyalty and the "return of benefits" (values associated with obligatory modes of conduct).

PART II

The Dynamics of Social Conflict

CHAPTER 2

Pilgrimage and World Renewal

Having discussed the basic structures of Japanese religious life in chapter 1, I turn now to consider some of its dynamics. I would like to look first at what may seem to be the very opposite of structure, namely conflict. While mainline sociology (following Durkheim) has focused primarily on the structures and functions of society and culture, some sociologists (often, but not always, inspired by Marx) have become interested in society's tensions and contradictions which, they believe, provide the ultimate explanation of its structures. In other words, conflict has more explanatory power than structure. My own position, which could be called a variation of "conflict structuralism," falls somewhere between the two extremes.[1] Like Coser, Dahrendorf, and other conflict structuralists, I regard both consensus and conflict as "partial" theories. They tell the truth, but not the whole truth. Nevertheless, in contemporary Japanese studies, the moderation of conflict structuralism is difficult to maintain. On the Japanese side (i.e., in the "emic discourse" of the "natives"), one is constantly reminded that Japan is a "harmonious society." As I indicated earlier, this is an ideal the Japanese have cherished at least since the Seventeen Article Constitution. Supposedly written by Shōtoku Taishi in 604 C.E., this document begins:

> Harmony is to be valued, and an avoidance of wanton opposition to be honored. . . . When those above are harmonious and those below are friendly, and there is concord in the discussion of business, right views of things spontaneously gain acceptance. Then what is there which cannot be accomplished?[2]

In the final chapter of this book, we shall see that the view of Japan as a consensual, harmonious society continues to be part of the country's formal and informal ideology. If anything, the image is even more powerful today than it was in the seventh century. Most contemporary

Japan theorists (professional producers of the emic discourse) are persuaded that Japan is not only a consensual and harmonious society; they also believe (as Prince Shōtoku did not) that Japan is virtually a classless state.[3] Outside of Japan, this idealized image has been picked up by western Japanologists, some of them distinguished Japan hands. Under their influence, a nonconflictual group model of Japanese society became an article of faith in Japanese studies for many years.

Happily, this is no longer the case. Scholarly (or etic) discourse on Japan today is divided between those who accede to the group model and those who stress institutional, or more nitty-gritty, conflictual factors.[4] Even in Japan, there are scholars who reject the ideological preoccupation with consensus. For example, some of the historians whom I otherwise rely on in this chapter tend to see in nearly any manifestation of symbolic resentment the seeds of "revolution." One of my aims in writing this study of pilgrimage has been to correct and modify this approach. While the carnival atmosphere of pilgrimage did indeed give vent to suppressed feelings of resentment and frustration, I argue that it often is more important to see how religious structures help to contain conflict and prevent it from degenerating into pure chaos. I shall therefore try to show how "synchronic" religious structures (combined with plain self-interest) put restrictions on the resentment expressed in the "diachrony" of events.

In chapter 1, we saw that would-be realists have tried to explain Japan's economic success without reference to consensus, gratitude, loyalty, and other emic ideals. I suggested there that a via media could be found between the methodological extremes of the gullible idealism of the proponents of the group model, on the one hand, and the hard-nosed realism of some institutionalists, on the other. I would like to make a similar claim here. While structure and dynamics, synchrony and diachrony, are not absolute opposites, we are not justified in reducing the one to an epiphenomenon of the other. On the contrary, it seems to me that the task of the history and sociology of religion is to see how they come together to constitute "the religious event." This, at least, is my aim in this chapter.

Karl Marx was not entirely wrong when he declared religion to be the opium of the masses. But he did err in his choice of the words *opium* and *the masses,* a blunder which caused him to overlook the multiplicity of roles religion plays at all levels of society. 'Opium' here suggests a soporific function which, as R. J. Zwi Werblowsky has shown, is more typical of the religions of the bourgeoisie (with its cushioned pews and pastel vestments) than of the proletariat itself.[5] If religion does not, then, merely narcotize the masses, what social function does it have?

In general, we can say that, at the lower levels of society, religion plays two rather contradictory roles. In the first place, it has (pace Marx) *energized* the masses for both toil and revolt. It has kept workers on the job, off the streets, off the bottle, and away from opium. It has idealized monotonous, dangerous, and low-paying jobs as the worker's "calling." As Weber and others have shown, this energizing function has enabled religion to play an important role in social change. With the right kind of apocalyptic inspiration, religion has energized the faithful for crusades, holy wars, and rebellion—and, I might add, the subsequent slaughter of pagans, apostates, oppressors, and civilians who happen to get in the way. On the other hand, by accenting miraculous, ecstatic, or otherworldly experience, the churches of the disinherited tend to take social—and a fortiori economic—issues off the agenda of pious concern. This second function of religion is clearly what Marx had in mind in his famous dictum.

This chapter will decipher the social attitudes and political values of participants in large-scale pilgrimages to the Grand Shrines at Ise during Japan's Tokugawa period (1603–1868). That popular movements of this scope often degenerate into bedlam and anomie is, of course, common knowledge. Revolutions turn into mayhem, crusades degenerate into massacres, and limited wars escalate into total ones. Although one does not usually expect such outcomes from pilgrimage, we shall see that in this period of Japanese history rebellion and popular religion were no strangers. Both were, to use Victor Turner's helpful expressions, "antistructural" or "liminal" movements that tended to turn the world upside down. By examining why the world did not *stay* upside down, I hope to throw light on the conservative, unrevolutionary nature of the resentment that appears during such periods of liminality. I also hope to show how, by limiting its own liminality and establishing among pilgrims a sense of "normative communitas"—another Turnerism—these pilgrimages achieved their sacred purpose.[6]

To grasp the political significance of popular religious movements perhaps we need to replace Marx's "opium" with a fresh paradigm. Later in this study, I shall borrow and (experimentally) apply a phrase coined by Bryan Wilson who described the function of Methodism in English life as "a massive gentling of the people."[7] As sacrilegious as it sounds, this expression—which I presume he takes from animal husbandry—is quite apt since the gentled (or gelded) unlike the narcotized or lobotomized, continue to function quite well in most areas of life.

They seek no change in their condition, change being beyond the pale of their imagination. The gentled passively accept economic exploitation and political authoritarianism; they shy away from liberation movements calling for a change in the status quo or the destruction of masters.

This leads me to point out an important difference between 'opium' and 'gentling' as paradigms. In the case of opium, although there are "pushers" who make it available, one can argue that taking the drug is ultimately the individual's own responsibility. While some, like Origen, have made themselves eunuchs for the kingdom of heaven, usually gentling is carried out by someone else, by "gentlers." In the present study, this role was played (mutatis mutandis) by priests, daimyō and merchants, individuals and classes determined to maintain the status quo. By assuming this role, these individuals simply enabled religion to perform the gentling function it had played in Japanese society since prehistoric times.[8]

In the following pages, I shall describe the nature and scope of these pilgrimages and the uproar they caused. Then I will comment briefly on the general relationship between peasant rebellions and the religion of the common folk in the Tokugawa period. After this, we shall see how government policy, the charity of the upper classes, the moral guidance of the Ise priesthood, and, finally, the ritual structure of pilgrimage itself all helped to curtail social chaos and anomie. Finally, to complete the historical picture, I shall discuss how pilgrimage and rebellions "to renew the world" were finally repressed, and how their themes were revalorized and used by various New Religions—and by the Meiji regime itself—to continue the "massive gentling" of the Japanese people.

Okage-mairi: What It Was

Okage-mairi was a pilgrimage (*mairi*) to the Grand Shrines of Ise. The word *okage* probably originated in the fact that these pilgrimages were made possible "thanks to" (*okage*) the largess of almsgivers who supported indigent pilgrims along the way. Or, it may simply refer to the pilgrims' desire to thank the gods for their "blessings" (*okage*).[9] Although the pilgrimage was supposed to take place every sixty-first year, only the large-scale okage-mairi of 1705, 1771, and 1830 approximated this ideal.[10] Smaller pilgrimages took place randomly, in 1638–39, 1650, 1661, 1701, 1718, 1723, 1730, 1748, 1755, 1803, and 1855. Other still smaller pilgrimages failed to reach the nationwide level. The *ee-ja-nai-ka* ("Ain't it hunky-dory") movement of 1867 was sometimes called okage-mairi (especially from Nagoya to the east where it took a more orderly form). But since this movement consisted largely of ecstatic dancing in situ and seldom included any actual pilgrimages to Ise, it is best to think of the ee-ja-nai-ka as a separate movement.[11]

To get an idea of the size and scope of these movements, let us look at the three largest pilgrimages of the Tokugawa period. The first nationwide okage-mairi took place in the spring of 1705 when children aged seven through fifteen left their homes in Osaka, Sakai, and Kyoto to go to Ise. As many as 3,620,000 individuals ultimately joined in, coming from as far away as Edo and Hiroshima. Although a group of women and children from Tango set out for Ise in March of 1771, the pilgrimage of that year actually began the following month when about twenty or thirty women and children from the tea farms around Uji in Yamashiro abruptly left kith and kin to visit the Grand Shrine. The movement soon spread to Osaka and Kyoto, and by July took in all but the extreme northeast and southwest of the country. While estimates of the pilgrim population of that year vary from one to two million or more, some scholars believe it may actually have been larger than the okage-mairi of 1705. Priests at the Outer Shrine distributed between thirty thousand and forty thousand amulets every day. The pilgrimage of 1830 (which, because of its size and the richness of its documentation, will be the primary focus of this paper) began in the intercalary third month in Shikoku when word spread that amulets from the Ise shrines were falling from the sky (a phenomenon called *ofuda-furi*). Although this pilgrimage had little impact on Kantō, Tōhoku, or Kyūshū, as many as five million pilgrims made their way to Ise that year. Thus, if the estimates which put the number of pilgrims traveling to Ise in ordinary years at about three hundred thousand to four hundred thousand are correct, okage-mairi caused their number to increase by a factor of ten or more. Whenever enthusiasm grew dim, rumors that amulets were falling would reignite the imagination of whole villages and set the pilgrimage in motion once again. In October, when the pilgrimage itself seemed to be waning, ecstatic dances (*Ise-odori* or *okage-odori*) broke out in Settsu, Kawachi, Yamato, and Ise.[12] The dancing reached its climax in December but continued through April of the following year, disrupting normal life and work schedules for weeks on end. Dancers carrying open umbrellas were accompanied by gongs, bells, shamisens, and drums. Enormous amounts of money were spent on fanciful costumes, elaborate ornaments, and banners made out of velvet, damask, and other expensive materials. One source tells us that the Ise-odori resembled the dances of the *gannin-bōzu,* lower-class mendicant priests who went about reciting ballads, riddles, or nonsense sutras for a small handout.[13] Geisha from the cities were sometimes hired by community leaders to teach the dances to the country folk. On the Tōkaidō roads, most of the dancers were underlings and servants attached to the post stations. The dancing that broke out in Yamato was largely confined to young men and women in their late teens. Many of these dances—ecstatic as they might have been—were methodically organized by community leaders. When this was the case, participation often became mandatory. Usually, rich farmers and merchants were expected to pick up the tab. In Itami, dances were carefully rehearsed and then performed before local shrines. After that, the dancers went throughout the entire region performing in a total of thirty-eight other communities. Dance contests (*odori-sumō*) were also held between villages.

Contemporary sources give us a vivid picture of the transformation of the spirit of the pilgrimage during the Tokugawa period. In earlier okage-mairi (through 1650), participants usually dressed in white and had the pious manner of medieval pilgrims. As time went on, these pilgrimages, like Shinto festivals in general, fell under the spell of the gaudy and lavish culture of Japan's few but burgeoning cities. In the okage-mairi of 1771 various sorts of "secular" entertainment were provided for the pilgrims.

Throughout the Tokugawa period, cities played a dominant role in recruiting pilgrims. The okage-mairi of 1650 began among the merchants of Edo. In 1705, Kyoto and Osaka were the starting points of the movement. While the okage-mairi of 1771 began in rural Yamashiro, Osaka quickly became its mainstay. Likewise, the 1830 okage-mairi, while beginning in Shikoku, spread to urban centers which then became the major catchment areas. From the cities the excitement spilled over into the backwaters of rural Japan. It would therefore not be an exaggeration to think of okage-mairi as largely an urban phenomenon.

While most of the pilgrim recruits came from the lower urban and rural classes, okage-mairi was a social hodgepodge. By 1553 it was said that high and low had joined the pilgrim bands.[14] Scattered among the thousands of day laborers, apprentices, and farmhands who walked to Ise and back on foot, we catch glimpses of well-to-do pilgrims being carried aloft in palanquins the whole way. Servants trudged along behind their master's litter carrying the baggage or making merry with drums, flutes, and shamisens. The author of the *Ukiyo no arisama*, whose eye never missed an incongruous situation, describes a procession to the Grand Shrine led by the aged but apparently successful master of a brothel in Shizuoka. The old man's carpeted palanquin was spread with silk *futon,* lined with crêpe de chine and decorated with artificial cherry blossoms. At either side marched an entourage of about twenty prostitutes all in the same costume. Following them came more than thirty porters and coolies, also in livery, with the bags. Over their heads fluttered an enormous banner with the words, "Our Second Pilgrimage."[15]

People's attitudes toward pilgrims were greatly influenced by class differentials. Rich pilgrims could expect good treatment in the inns but might not be given many handouts along the way. Most of the well-to-do pilgrims carried ladles as ornaments and not as tools for begging. Lower-class pilgrims often fell into disrepute, those from Osaka and Wakayama excelling others in opprobrium.

The pilgrimage of the runaways, or the "French-leave pilgrimage" (*nuke-mairi*) was another important feature of okage-mairi.[16] In 1650 and 1771, the French-leave pilgrims seem to have organized themselves, to some degree, by neighborhood and occupation. In other cases, however, women, children, servants, farmhands, or apprentices spontaneously and surreptitiously left for Ise without the permission of their husbands, parents, masters, or lords. While other pilgrims often made the trip in special garb, the French-leave pilgrims generally ran off in their work clothes. Since many of the "children" mentioned in our documents were actually servants, the French-leave pilgrimage seems to have been a way for the underlings of society to enjoy a temporary respite from their toil. While other pilgrimages usually took place when agricultural workers, servants, and apprentices were least busy (between New Year's and March or after the middle of June), nuke-mairi often took place during the busiest seasons of the year, thus contribution to the economic turmoil caused by the pilgrimage.

Along the highways, pilgrims were met by jesters, bards (often priests with earthy vocations), musicians, geishas or other fair ladies waiting to entertain them with a joke, a tale, a song, or a bed. More important were the almsgivers, individuals, and groups whose generosity made the pilgrimage possible for the lower classes. Almsgivers, outnumbering the pilgrims in some places by as many as seven to one, stood by the roadside to drop gifts into the pilgrims' outstretched ladles. Wayfarers were given tobacco, dried seaweed, fish, tea, beans, rice, bamboo or reed hats, noodles, lanterns, miso soup, and even bags to carry the gifts away in. Gift giving (*segyō*) also included a wide variety of services: haircuts, hot baths, rides on horseback, in boats, or palanquins and lodging for the night. In their zeal to help, people were even seen chasing after pilgrims, stuffing presents up their sleeves. Coolies, "as though they had gone completely mad," forced people to ride in their palanquins.[17] In Tsu, a town in the Ise area, samurai retainers with their customary two swords turned out in large numbers to give rides to the pilgrims.[18] Large-scale, individual segyō of this sort began in the okage-mairi of 1705. In the pilgrimage of 1771, segyō became both more generous and more highly organized. Group segyō became common. For example, in Kyoto the Confraternity of the Sacred Dance, an organization of wealthy families from the center of the city, donated umbrellas, raincoats, sandals, money, paper, fans, and various kinds of food to passersby. In other places "welcome wagon groups" (*settai renchū*) were set up. Donations often were compulsory. In Osaka, for example, ward elders went around to householders with subscription lists to see that all contributed.[19] In 1830, the custom of mandatory contributions spread from the cities to the countryside. Rich farmers pooled their donations so that even the poorest sort could go to Ise. This kind of corporate segyō directed toward individuals within the community supplemented direct handouts made to strangers on the highways. All told, this outpouring of good will helps to account for the massive proportions the pilgrimage assumed that year.

The motivation behind this potlatch of generosity was no simple altruism. Giving to pilgrims was believed to result not only in happier rebirths, but also in good health, good luck, and wealth in this world. A rice merchant by the name of Kashimaya Tōshichi, writing under the interesting pen name "The Old Fisherman Who Seeks Profits by Casting His Nets in the Markets of Dōjima," gives us a clear insight into the spirit of segyō. Kashimaya praises okage-mairi as a time when "the sincerity of the Japanese spirit is made manifest *and markets automatically prosper*" (my emphasis). "Thanks to the great blessings of our emperor we can joyfully form groups to help people, and go about day and night walking with our feet in the sky. Rice merchants who are sincere in their dealings will be the reflection of flowers blooming in the distant mountains. Ah, the *flowers of gold* that will bloom here in Osaka. They will be our pride and joy!".[20]

Pilgrims had many reasons to go to Ise. The French-leave pilgrims generally went in order to get away from the duties of farm, shop, and home. Many joined the pilgrimage simply because no one else was staying home. Others went to fulfill vows (in return for some kind of magical boon), to apologize for moral or ritual misdeeds, to seek relief from disease, or heaven's assistance against future ills. While pilgrimages before the Tokugawa period may have been an expression of more pious ambitions, the *Shiojiri*, a miscellany published in 1782, tells us that the pilgrims of that day sought for pleasure, prosperity, and long life in this world, or simply escape from disaster. Others hoped to be reborn rich and carefree, perhaps as kings or men of distinction. Still others vainly followed along in order to go "sightseeing among the shrines in the high mountains."[21] Swept away on such short notice, many pilgrims did not bother to learn the proper songs or prayers. Some did not even know who the god of Ise was.[22]

Trials and Tribulations

Since much of our information about the not-so-pretty side of okage-mairi comes from the *Ukiyo no arisama,* I would like to preface my remarks about the trials and tribulations of the pilgrim with a few words about this anonymous document and its author. Born in Katsuyama (Mimasaka), the author later moved to Osaka to practice medicine. In 1806, he began to record the events of his day, producing an invaluable chronicle of Japanese history through the late 1840s.[23] The book was written for the private edification of the author's descendants and consequently was never published in his own lifetime. His critical attitude toward the okage-mairi of 1830 caused him to accent the dangers and moral outrages of the pilgrimage. It therefore stands in striking contrast to other documents which dilate on the miraculous cures and wonders that are said to have occurred. True grace (*okage*), he held, is not to be found in pilgrimage (*mairi*); but rather:

> Born alike 'midst quiet sea
> True grace can ne'er but just this be.[24]

Grace or thanksgiving is best expressed not by "floating away" to Ise (as he was wont to say) but in the settled piety of everyday Japanese life. He thought that people should make their "pilgrimage to the Plain of High Heaven" by tending to their family's business and calling (*tenmei*), by honestly and compassionately obeying lords and respecting parents, and by maintaining close ties with other relatives.[25] Not an unbeliever himself, the author grudgingly conceded that the pilgrimage was probably inevitable in this "mixed up world" (*midaretaru yo*).[26] At times his condescension turns contemptuous, as, for example, when he discusses the pilgrims' begging.[27] The plagues and illnesses which spread along the highways leading to Ise he attributed to heaven's indignation at the pilgrims' own turpitude. Nowhere in his chronicle do we read about the fun or fellowship that pilgrims must also have enjoyed as they marched along together. Instead, in story after story, we encounter thieves, kidnappers, deceitful moneychangers, counterfeiters, slavers, adulterers, incestuous lovers, sexual maniacs, greedy innkeepers, and bogus pilgrims interested only in a handout. While he also related the divine punishment which resulted from their misdeeds, the author's emphasis always falls on the sin itself and not on heaven's intervention or the spiritual restoration of the fallen. He shared the common, upper-class view that pilgrimage was an omen of impending natural disaster. He believed, rightly I suspect, that okage-mairi was especially dangerous for the "better sort," and that under such conditions well-to-do people (*mi o moteru hito*) should not mingle with the crowds.[28] It goes without saying that in these pages healing miracles are few and far between, or are actually discounted. In short, the author's negative attitude toward okage-mairi was typical of the urban upper classes in general.

Keeping the outlook and biases of the author of our primary document in mind, we can now return to our pilgrims and the story of their hardships. The very magnitude of the 1830 okage-mairi made it inevitable that the 'liminality' of the movement would be threatened by antinomianism and lust, and that its 'communitas' spirit would be periodically soiled by crime. The *Ukiyo no arisama* and other documents give us a wealth of information about the chaotic conditions which developed. So many pilgrims were on the road that many, unable to find lodging at the end of the day, were forced to sleep in the fields. Others trudged along through the dark only to fall into the clutches of thieves. Those lucky enough to find a place in an inn were forced to share their mat with three or four others. During the night people getting up to relieve themselves stepped on sleeping children, creating such an uproar that no one could sleep. Innmasters brought breakfast to their weary guests in the middle of the night and urged them to be on their way so that they could welcome a second shift of guests from those still marching by. Crowded inns became breeding grounds for the plague. Some pilgrims (especially those who had taken French leave) starved to death after the almsgivers lost their initial enthusiasm. Other travellers became ill and died on the way. Pregnant women sometimes gave birth in tea shops or inns along the way. Some had miscarriages or died in childbirth. One woman, accompanied by a six- or seven-year-old child and an infant, became ill and died on the way. Later on, passersby found the older child weeping at his mother's side, while the infant vainly sucked her cold breasts. Another woman was bewitched by a fox and threw herself into a pond and drowned. Some went mad when they lost their children in the crowds. With roads so crowded, mothers who could not find a place to change their children's diapers were forced to walk on and on while the infants on their backs stank and squalled.

Some children were kidnapped. As many as thirty slavers were arrested for kidnapping teenage boys. (Even Lord Itō of Hyūga in Kyūshū was involved in this nefarious traffic.)

Various other crimes also helped to turn the world upside down. Counterfeiters passed along their homemade wares and tried to circulate money that was no longer legal tender. Petty thieves of all sorts preyed upon unwary pilgrims. Coolies offered free rides to ailing pilgrims, only to take them down dark alleys to rob or rape them. Some, pretending to be samurai, befriended the wayfarers and later picked their pockets. On their return, exhausted pilgrims often refused to eat. Some acted like madmen, walking around in the middle of the night, going out into storms, and subsequently falling ill.

Mysterious pranks also contributed to the excitement of that annus mirabilis. In one place, gravestones which normally could be moved only by four or more men were silently removed during the night and buried several feet below the ground. Worse yet, the posthumous names of the dead painted in black had been repainted in red, and vice versa.[29] The lord of the domain stationed watchmen in the graveyard with strict orders to arrest all suspicious-looking individuals. But, try as they would to stay awake, the guards mysteriously became drowsy and fell asleep. When they awoke, they found new signs of mischief. One night they tried to seize a strange woman who appeared in the graveyard. The woman, however, disappeared and an invisible foe attacked the watchmen, cutting off their hair and mutilating their ears and noses. Later on, similar damage was reported in Edo itself. Rumor had it that these sacrilegious pranks were the work either of Hidden Christians or *tengu*.[30]

The breakdown of normal sexual restraints was another aspect of the moral anomie that marred the pilgrimage. Some pilgrims made three-dimensional representations of the genitalia and carried them through the streets shouting obscenities and clapping their hands. The brothels of Furuichi were a special attraction for the pilgrims. One pilgrimage song even sings the praises of the "vaginas [a lustier word is used in the text] of the prostitutes of Furuichi" which "out of gratitude" had become "octopuses" (to entangle male pilgrims?).[31] Since prostitution had always been a liminal supplement to marriage in Japan, the existence of brothels near the Grand Shrines is not, in itself, clear evidence of a breakdown in public morality. Nudity and transvestism, while seen more often in the later ee-ja-nai-ka, were also noticed in the okage-mairi of 1830. In many places men and women exchanged clothes and went about offering free rides to pilgrims. In one town a young woman stood on the street shouting, "They're giving stuff away to the pilgrims, but I don't have anything to give. So I'll give you this," and then exposed herself.[32] The mingling of the sexes in dark, crowded inns and deserted fields or woods also contributed to the ill repute of the pilgrimage among the "proper" sort of people. Husbands naturally doubted, apparently with good reason, the intentions of wives who slipped away as French-leave pilgrims. Nuke-mairi offered many a woman the once-in-a-lifetime chance to be rid of husband and children. The author of *Ukiyo no arisama* overheard one woman pilgrim say as she passed his door, "When I go on a pilgrimage it's annoying to look at my hubby's face. And the boy! I'd like to get rid of him!"[33]

Beautiful girls captured on their way to Ise were sold to brothels or made the playthings of the pilgrim routes. A couple from Temma in Osaka set out on pilgrimage with their eighteen-year-old daughter. Along the way, the daughter injured her foot and was offered a ride in a litter that happened to be passing by. The parents joyfully accepted the offer and continued their journey walking along beside the litter. Before long, however, they got caught in a large crowd and the mother and father lost sight of the girl. The coolies, seeing their chance, quickly turned down an alley where they raped the girl several times over. After that, they tried to sell her as a prostitute. Finally, yielding to her protests, they had her tattooed from head to foot instead. Then they took the girl to the Namba Bridge. "Temma's not far from here so you can go on by yourself," they said, shaking the girl out of the litter into the street.[34]

Inflation, the natural result of five million people suddenly converging on a single place, was another source of confusion. Within weeks, or even a few days, the price of rice, straw sandals, lodging, and other necessities began to skyrocket. Most of this inflation can be traced to the unprecedented demand placed on scarce resources. Indulging pilgrims whose usual diet was yams and barley with an expensive rice diet was, itself, highly inflationary. Outright profiteering accounted for other price hikes. As soon as word of a new pilgrimage began to spread, innkeepers, ferrymen, merchants, and laborers became excited about the windfalls they hoped would come their way.[35] In Mie, local officials had to issue orders controlling the fares being charged for horses and litters. In Nara, where profiteering was rife, some pilgrims had to turn back because of the high prices. Conditions there finally became so bad that officials were sent from Osaka to upbraid and arrest profiteers and to warn pilgrims not to expect gifts or lodging along the road. In the end, inn fees and the price of shoes and other items had to be officially controlled.

If inflation was hard on the common pilgrim, the chaotic, carnival atmosphere was also a nuisance to the sober merchant. For example, a paper merchant by the name of Yamatoya Rihei went to Kameyama to collect some debts. There he found that the pilgrimage had thrown everything into pandemonium. He finally was able to find a place to stay in the home of a sixty-four-year-old tobacconist who, with his son, was busy giving free rides to pilgrims. "At a time like this, how can we refuse!" the old man said. "Why don't you pitch in too?" Rihei, seeing no way out, was obliged to drop his own business and carry pilgrims as far as the edge of the town. Finally, realizing that no one was interested in settling his accounts, the disconcerted Rihei returned home without making a single penny.[36]

Another merchant, a wholesaler dealing in fertilizers, went from Osaka to Yamato to collect some debts. When he came to the shop of one of his customers he learned that the man's brother had recently died and that the family was in mourning. Not wanting to bring up business matters abruptly, the merchant politely extended his condolences to the family and then asked whether it was true that the Ise dance had become popular in Yamato. "It certainly has," said the bereaved brother, "we'll show you." With this, he jumped to his feet and started to dance, accompanied by his wife and child on the shamisen and drums. Soon the neighbors heard the music and joined in, and before long there were thirty people dancing. The merchant, unable to say anything about his bills, went back to Osaka with nothing to show for his trip.[37]

The Spirit of World Renewal

The crime, disease, and inflation which took place during okagemairi were obvious burdens to the common pilgrim. More vexing to the upper classes—to landlords, merchants, and the warriors who lived off taxes—was the way in which pilgrimage disrupted business and agricultural routines. The gravest threat to the social order, however, was the occasional act of insubordination by indigent pilgrims toward individuals of wealth and authority. Because the episodes which I shall relate later seem to reflect the spirit of contemporary peasant rebellions "to renew the world" (*yonaoshi ikki*), I must digress briefly to describe the general relationship between Tokugawa peasant rebellions and the folk religion of the day. Only then will we understand why the upper classes viewed popular religious movements with such alarm and distaste.

The religious aspect of many uprisings was patent. Angry peasants hatched their plots in the woods surrounding Shinto shrines, during religious vigils, or while attending meetings of confraternities. They sent representatives to Ise to present their grievances to the goddess Amaterasu. In some places, rebellious peasants presented their manifestoes to the local gods or Buddhas and then exchanged holy water in their presence. In 1772, some disgruntled peasants purified themselves, fasted for seven days and nights before the Buddha, and prayed to Akiba Gongen before presenting their petition to the authorities. In Iyo (Shikoku), several thousand people took part in an uprising in 1750 to demand an end to excessive profits being made by monopolistic merchants (*tokken shōnin*) and called for the dismissal of the headmen of six villages. After deciding to take action, they prayed to their tutelary deity, Tenjin, for the success of their venture. "If you grant our request, we'll build you a new shrine; but if you don't grant it, we won't." In case Tenjin failed to get the hint, they dramatized their demand by wrapping a long rope around the shrine threatening to pull it down.[38]

In 1837, Ōshio Heihachirō publicly announced the beginning of his insurrection in Osaka by distributing copies of a manifesto wrapped "in saffron-colored silk bags with a Shinto litany from the Great Ise Shrine." The inscription on the front read: "Given down from heaven." While Ivan Morris, tongue in cheek, regarded these words as a "modest inscription,"[39] Osaka residents, who in the okage-mairi of 1830 had witnessed amulets falling "from heaven" upon their own rooftops, may have taken these words more literally! Ōshio's followers took to the streets, hoisting banners with the words "The Great Shrine of the Goddess Amaterasu." Rebels in other insurrections went into battle carrying large banners bearing the names of famous shrines such as Kasuga, Hachiman, or Ise, ensigns which were, in effect, amulets writ large.

The legends of rebel heroes (called *gimin,* that is "saints" or "righteous men") who had sacrificed themselves and their families for the community were nothing short of hagiography. The mere recitation of such tales as the story of Sakura Sōgorō was enough to incite peasants to rebellion.[40] Because the authorities would not allow rebels a proper burial or grave, peasants venerated their fallen leaders under the guise of the Shinto god Inari, as Jizō the Scary (Nirami-Jizō) or some other deity.[41] Many heroes, such as Sano Masakoto, assassin of the hated Tanuma Okitomo (d. 1784), were worshiped as "gods of world-renewal" (*yonaoshi daimyōjin*). The spirits of deceased rebel heroes were also thought to cure diseases of various sorts. For example, a leader of an uprising in Mimasaka was venerated as the god of headaches. After recovering from a headache, people in the area used to express their thanks by offering a small model sword before the shrine of their rebel god.[42]

Some rebels were directly influenced by such religious thinkers as the unorthodox Shinto priest Umetsuji Norikiyo (1798–1861) or by scholars from the action-oriented Wang Yang-ming school of Confucianism. Like the founders of the New Religions of the late Tokugawa period, the leaders of insurrections founded confraternities or academies to spread their ideals. Leaders also had religious experiences. Ōshio Heihachirō experienced a "personality transformation vision" of Wang Yang-ming while crossing Lake Biwa in a violent storm. Shortly after the arrival of Commodore Perry in 1853, Kanno Hachirō, leader of a yonaoshi uprising in Iwashiro, had a vision of an old man with white hair who presented him with plans for the defense of the country and the establishment of "the prosperity and happiness of all people." Kanno was also told that his own family lineage could be traced back to the seventh-generation descendants of the gods Izanami and Izanagi (divine parents of the sun goddess Amaterasu). Among the common folk, rebel heroes were ranked together with emperors, shoguns, wizards, and other religious charismatics as *ikigami,* living deities. It is not impossible that some were regarded as adventitious deities (*hito-gami* or *marōdo-gami*) or as gods who suddenly appear, prosper, and then disappear (*hayari-gami*).

Rebellion itself was sometimes regarded as the advent of the gods of world renewal, that is, as the manifestation of gods who had come to avenge the sufferings of the oppressed. Rebels in the Kamo rebellion in Aichi in 1836 taunted their oppressors, saying: "Hear this! How can you rich folks escape the punishment now falling upon you for cornering the rice market, turning your rice into sake, and selling it at high prices? You neglect the suffering of the poor and commit robbery. *The gods of World Renewal are arriving to punish you here and now. So be ready!*"[43] With this, the rebellious "deities" set about destroying both homes and storehouses.

In times of peace, social discontent tended to show itself indirectly, for example, in ballads (*jōruri*) celebrating the leaders of past insurrections, in folksongs and folktales, in the songs of mendicant priests (*chobokure* or *chongare*), or in the nonsense sutras (*ahadarakyō*) which they recited, or, finally, in antiestablishment lampoons and satirical verse (*rakushu*).[44] When rebellions broke out, however, peasants dared to attack their social betters more openly as "fools," "thieves," "evil wolves," "leeches," "dogs," "foxes," and "apes."[45] Nevertheless, Japan was a culture without a strong sense of ultimate or absolute evil. Unlike the medieval European rebel, in whose apocalyptic imagination the enemy might be identified with the Whore of Babylon or the Antichrist, Japan's peasant rebel was restrained by a culture in which a "logic of relative contrasts" displaced the absolute dichotomies of good and evil, oppressor and oppressed. Japanese scholars have often pointed out that, perhaps for this very reason, peasant rebellions in Japan never saw the carnage or terrorism of the Peasant Wars, the Taborite uprising, and other European conflicts.[46] In Japan, as elsewhere, rebellion was a tradition based on implicit moral understandings. This tradition both legitimated the rebel and set limits to his wrath and indignation. Thus, in some peasant uprisings, rebels imposed ascetic rules of restraint upon themselves—not to steal, not to kill, not to take pawned goods ("they belong to people"), to be careful with fires, and so on—all on the grounds that "this movement is not based on selfish desire; it is for all the people."[47] Those who stole so much as the blade of a hoe were turned over to the authorities. The violence that did take place was aimed at the destruction of material wealth (overturning barrels of sake or shōyu, scattering rice, barley, and money in the streets, burning promissory notes, and so on), not at the appropriation of the "means of production." As long as they were dominated by relatively small, integrated leadership groups motivated by a deep sense of injustice, peasant rebels displayed a remarkable level of self-control. Discipline was apt to break down only when the starving rural *Lumpenproletariat* joined the ranks. Even then, we are still talking about rebellions and not about revolution. More than anything else, it was the *traditional* nature of rebellion which allowed it to absorb elements of the folk religion.

Okage-mairi, Ee-ja-nai-ka, and Rebellion

During okage-mairi—times which could hardly be called ordinary—resentment took both direct and indirect forms. The homes of village headmen, Buddhist priests, and other authorities who tried to stop the pilgrimage were often put to the torch. As early as 1673, farmers in Mimasaka who had gone on pilgrimage pressed the authorities for a reduction in their taxes.[48] In the okage-mairi of 1705 this song was heard:

O marvelous age!
'Tis the Year of the Bird,
And everyone's old debts
Will be wiped away![49]

In the okage-mairi of 1723 the urban upper classes in Kyoto who had dressed up as the forty-seven rōnin and as Minamoto no Yoritomo were criticized for acting "rudely." In some villages youths dressed in elaborate costumes and staged impromptu farces, pretending to be, for example, imperial messengers presiding over rituals at Ise.[50] Costume parades of this sort were prohibited by the government not only because of their expense but also because of their symbolic disregard for authority.[51]

Since the okage-mairi of 1830 took place during the Tempō era (1830–44) when peasant rebellions reached their apogee, it is little wonder that the pilgrimage itself often gave vent to feelings of discontent. The momentum generated by such a massive mobilization of common people inclined even the humblest to acts of audacity. Minowa Zairoku describes a large group of pilgrims which passed by the retinue of a daimyō without so much as a bow. The daimyō is said to have forgiven the lack of manners of these individuals because they were pilgrims. More realistically, the incident illustrates the relative weakness of the power structure in the face of such enormous dislocations of the population.[52]

Most of the social friction that erupted during the okage-mairi of 1830 grew out of the ecstatic dancing which began in October. The use of dance and ritual processions as a means of expressing discontent has a long history in Japan. During Shinto festivals, rowdy *omikoshi* (god cart) processions often degenerated into still more violent attacks on the homes of unpopular or greedy families. The Sand-Hauling Festivals (*suna-mochi*) popular in the Osaka area around 1800 often resulted in a refusal to settle year-end accounts. During a harvest dance called the Butterfly (*chōchō odori*) held in Kyoto in 1839, rich and poor alike dressed up in lavish costumes and frolicked about. Forming groups of as many as two hundred people, dancers broke into the homes of strangers and brazenly pranced around on the tatami mats with their shoes still on. Such dances, called *odori-komi* or "dance-ins," became common in later okage-mairi and were raised to the level of an art in the ee-ja-nai-ka of 1867.

The area which stretches from Takarazuka to Itami used to be the home of many rich merchants.[53] When the dancing spread to this region in April of 1831, the merchants haughtily refused to have anything to do with it. Incensed, the common people shouted that there was "no longer any difference between the towns and the countryside" and that the merchants should therefore send their daughters out to them. The merchants, of course, would hear of no such thing. "Instead of sending out our girls," they said, "we'll give you one hundred pieces of silver for each one of them. Be satisfied with that." "It's not a matter of money," the people cried. "Since we are all one (*ittō no koto nareba*) everyone must dance!" After some haggling, the merchants were made to pay an even larger amount, each contributing according to his means. The money was put to good use—paying for festival floats, costumes, and other things needed for the dance.[54]

Dancing disrupted agricultural work, as well as loan and tax payments. In Amagasaki and other places, peasants danced throughout the barley harvest, the rice transplanting season, and the time of weeding. In extreme cases harvests were lost. In the hurly-burly of the dance, some peasants tried to evade their taxes and other financial obligations, while others tried to get their payments reduced or postponed. In a post town between Osaka and Kyoto, people danced for so long (about thirty days) that they neglected their work and were forced to demand a cut in their taxes. While a tax break was finally granted, it amounted to only one-third of what they initially asked for. Because they had spent so much money, they were forced to borrow to pay even their reduced taxes. Later on, villagers who were unable to repay their loans threatened those who were about to pay theirs back, saying that "if there's anybody who's going to pay his debts, he should pay for the whole village!" Much to the dismay of the merchants who had put up the money, no one made any payments at all.[55]

How Chaos Was Avoided

The confusion of okage-mairi was curtailed by 1. government policies of repression and/or compromise, 2. the sagacious charity of the upper classes, 3. the guidance provided by the priests from Ise, and, ultimately, 4. the unrevolutionary, ritual nature of pilgrimage itself.

Government Policy

The Tokugawa shogunate was fully aware of the danger posed by okage-mairi and other large-scale religious movements. In earlier centuries, the Jōdo Shinshū and Hokke sects had proved to be serious sources of disorder. Military confrontations between Oda Nobunaga and the Tendai and Shinshū sects were still fresh in mind. The shogunate still had to contend with periodic acts of defiance from various recusant underground religions (e.g., Hidden Christians and Buddhists from the Fuju-Fuse and Kakure-Nembutsu sects). As for Shinto, the regime feared not only its loyalist elements but also its potential for initiating new popular movements which might slip out of control. Above all, Edo authorities wanted to avoid the fatal conjunction of a popular uprising and an educated leadership, such as occurred in the rebellion of Ōshio Heihachirō.

It was not only Confucian asceticism and the martial code (*bushidō*) that inclined the warrior against the opulent nonsense of festivals and pilgrimages. Warriors whose economic strength was declining deeply resented the way peasants and urban riffraff wildly threw their money away on costumes, ornaments, food, and drink. Those who deliberately tried to stir up religious enthusiasm by devious means were quickly apprehended. In 1830, authorities in Osaka arrested two or three rogues, charging them with amulet fraud. This was their crime: they had apparently taken pieces of string and tied fried bean curd and fish guts to one end and amulets from the Grand Shrine to the other. They placed these sacrilegious contrivances on rooftops where crows would find them and fly off, dropping the amulets among the gullible crowds below.[56] The same authorities also declared that people who heard about falling amulets should immediately report their stories to the office of the *bugyō*.[57] Government documents condemned those who left old people and children behind and berated single people who, with no thought for their landlords, abandoned their rented quarters to rush off to Ise. Although the government could find no reason to apprehend those who made the pilgrimage in good faith, it directed all pilgrims to get permission before leaving. In other words, only nuke-mairi was condemned.[58] In Awa (Shikoku), notices were posted warning women and children against leaving the domain without written permission and ordering those caught at the border without such papers to be returned to their homes.[59] Government announcements also expressed concern about the threat posed by the pilgrimage to the economy. The lord of Himeji announced that "the people of this domain can go on pilgrimage as they see fit, providing it does not interfere with the rice transplanting."[60]

Had it dared, the shogunate would probably have outlawed the pilgrimage the way it had other religious movements. But in the face of such massive throngs, it assumed a more discreet posture. The most that it could do was to restrict what it regarded as the excesses of the movement. One has the impression that, as a result of its growing financial embarrassment, the government was forced to take a weaker stand on the pilgrimage of 1830 than it had in earlier years. In Awa, for instance, the local daimyō had banned the earlier okage-mairi. But in 1830, he donated three thousand *koku* of rice to pilgrims in Osaka and provided one hundred and fifty palanquins for their use. In places like Yagyū in Yamato, officials ate humble pie, reversed their long-standing restrictions on the Ise dances, and ordered that "if there is an *okage-odori* the people should dance a lot and not just one person from each family."[61] In short, the attitude of the government toward the pilgrimage was supportive only when a more forceful policy of "gentling" seemed unwise. In all cases, the authorities did whatever they could to curtail the breakdown of law and order, on the one hand, and to assure the stability of the economy and the steady flow of tax payments, on the other.

The Support of the Upper Classes

When we discussed the *Ukiyo no arisama* we saw that the urban upper classes had little sympathy for mass movements like okage-mairi. Even Shinto scholars of the School of National Learning (*Kokugaku*) held mass pilgrimages to Ise in contempt. This is not surprising since many of the Kokugaku scholars were from the merchant class.[62] These scholarly, rich merchants and farmers developed close ties with lower-ranking samurai, including the antiregime (*tōbaku*) faction that would ultimately overthrow the Tokugawa establishment. From their point of view, movements like okage-mairi were "crazy," "absurd," and "worse than vile."[63] Tanigawa Kotosuga (1709–76), an early Kokugaku scholar from Ise, regarded okage-mairi as a bad omen, an opinion which was shared by the upper urban classes and authorities alike. Kotosuga pointed out that, in the past, okage-mairi had portended the death of a shōgun, the rebellion of Yui Shōsetsu, and various terrifying storms. The okage-mairi of 1705 prepared the way for earthquakes and a fire at Ise. The pilgrimage of 1771 preceded an enormous tidal wave in Nagasaki, a typhoon in Kyoto, a devastating fire in Edo, floods, and so on.[64] The great Kokugaku scholar, Motoori Norinaga, also a resident of Ise, carefully recorded the number of pilgrims converging on the Grand Shrine in his *Tamakatsuma* but says nothing more about the event, probably because he held it in such low regard. He discounted rumors of falling amulets and other miracles as the work of foxes, dryads (*kodama*), or other evil *kami*.[65] Thus, nothing could have been further from the spirit of popular pilgrimage than Kokugaku, even though, like okage-mairi itself, it was a Shinto movement which held the gods of Ise in high esteem.

Disdain the pilgrimage as they might, daimyō, merchants, and other "worthies" (*utokujin*) were in the front ranks of those giving segyō to the pilgrims. In 1830, the fabulously wealthy Kashimaya Sakujūrō alone was said to have distributed a total of 10,000 *ryō* to pilgrims, while the Konoike family gave away between 765 and 3,000 *ryō*. Other prominent donors included such well-known merchant families as Mitsui, Kobashi, Iwaki, and Masuya. Some merchants sincerely believed that their beneficence had nothing to do with their long-term profits and that their gifts brought pleasure to giver and receiver alike.[66] The author of the *Ukiyo no arisama*, however, paints a different picture. He points out that, while merchants in the Dōjima area of Osaka were proud of their good works, their charity was entirely aimed at enhancing their own good name and prosperity. Not a penny, says he, was given out of true benevolence.[67] In Saitōmachi, where the author himself lived, people living in better homes were assessed one hundred *mon* as a mandatory contribution. He and two others were made to contribute three hundred *mon*, something they understandably resented. He did not think this kind of allotted, community segyō was true philanthropy. He also criticized those who gave presents to pretty female pilgrims, hoping for unseemly favors in return. True segyō, he said, was that practiced by great merchants like Kōnoike Zen'emon, Ten'ōjiya Gohei, and Hiranoya Gohei who had their servants impartially stuff a few pennies in the hands of all who passed by. While the author of *Ukiyo no arisama* held these wealthy merchants up as paradigms of disinterested benevolence, Minowa Zairoku, representing a more popular view, points out that, in fact, the Osaka merchants actually gave more to pilgrims coming from areas where they had commercial interests at stake than they did to others.[68] Like the daimyō, rich merchants probably gave more out of fear than out of the goodness of their hearts. After all, they were not deaf to the rumors about the revenge that heaven, and resentful pilgrims, had taken on pinchpennies in other parts of the country.[69]

Ise Priests and Their Legends

There was a rich folkloric tradition associated with okage-mairi which may also have contributed to the preservation of the movement and to the gentling of its excesses. Pilgrim tales circulated by priests from Ise were designed to castigate those who would hinder the pilgrimage or exploit is sacred liminality. The function of these stories was to preserve the antistructural tendencies of the pilgrimage by situating them within the structured norms, values, and taboos of everyday Japanese life.

According to legend, the gods themselves played a role in maintaining public order in the turbulent days of okage-mairi. Hundreds of tales have been preserved of divine retribution directed against those who, in various ways, tried to obstruct the pilgrimage or give it a bad name. Greedy merchants, foiled by divine justice, failed to make their usual profits. Robbers who preyed on pilgrims were mysteriously lured back to the scene of their crimes and captured. Others fell ill. A landlord in Osaka who tried to prevent his renters from showing hospitality to pilgrims was suddenly struck dumb.[70] People's arms were paralyzed when they tried to strike pilgrims or flog family members who insisted on going to Ise. A Buddhist priest of the Jōdo Shinshū sect who tried to prevent his parishioners from worshiping the Shinto gods at Ise unexpectedly died in his sleep. It was rumored that when members of this sect did go on pilgrimage the gods had their revenge by causing them to lose their children along they way. Those who refused to join the okage-odori became ill. The cynical and ungrateful risked similar reprisals. When a skeptical blind man in Awa declared it was impossible for amulets to fall from the sky, his clothes suddenly ignited as though by spontaneous combustion. Convinced of his error, he set out for Ise.[71] Along the Harai River, some farmers who had no horse gave rides to pilgrims on their cow. A band of pilgrims was suddenly struck dumb when they complained that they would rather walk than ride on such a beast.[72]

One motif running through these tales of divine retribution can be called the "theme of sticking revenge." In Harima, a thief who was trying to rob the home of a family which had left home on pilgrimage found, to his dismay, that he could not get his hand out of the money chest he was working on. In Mitaka, a burglar was caught when he could not move from the door of a house.[73] Another thief stole some rice from pilgrims and later could not free himself from the rice bag itself.[74] A samurai who had made fun of some pilgrims was unable to dismount from his horse and became a prisoner in his own saddle for four or five days.[75] The *Ukiyo no arisama* gives us some interesting variations on this theme. A sixty-year-old man and his daughter-in-law once joined a pilgrim band going to Ise from Harima. One night the old man raped his daughter-in-law but, by an act of divine revenge, was not able to withdraw from her body. Both subsequently had to be carried home together on a pallet. A Buddhist priest who insisted on visiting the Ise shrines suffered a similar fate when he committed incest with his mother. When they were discovered, the son was unable to withdraw.[76] Stories of this sort seem to have been directed against those who, by disregarding everyday morality and taboos, impugned the integrity of the pilgrimage.

One potential threat to the pilgrimage was the resistance offered to Shinto worship of all kinds by the more exclusive ("single-practice") sects. To understand this a word must be said about the religious affiliations of the Japanese people which, over the centuries, have manifested two contradictory tendencies. One—symbolized by the tutelary deities of the local community—is based on the closed, particularistic world of the traditional village and its social hierarchy. The other—which we see in the extension of enlightenment to both sexes and all classes in Kamakura Buddhism, in the decline of exclusive shrine guilds in Shinto, in the development of popular pilgrimage, and even in the development of "civil religion" in prewar Japan—is a movement to extend religious privileges to those previously unenfranchised. Whether it was the result of a gracious proclamation of universal salvation or the outcome of class struggles, the trend toward enfranchisement made possible a wider participation in religious events. As we saw in chapter 1, voluntary relations with religious institutions tend, over time, to become inherited obligations. While the first converts, say to Jōdo Shinshū, might join a confraternity as earnest believers, their descendants, whether firm believers or not, are expected to continue to participate by virtue of their family's responsibility to the community. The same was true of pilgrimage to Ise. Originally only members of the imperial family were allowed to worship at the Grand Shrine. Later, the nobility in general, the warrior class, and finally the common people were enfranchised in the Ise cult.[77] Gradually, social conformity and religious syncretism conspired to transform this right into an obligation. Once a pilgrimage began, extraordinary pressure was put on individuals to go to Ise, to support the dancing, or to give alms to pilgrims.[78]

Christianity was not the only exclusive religion whose claim to ultimacy caused it to run afoul of the all-embracing syncretism of Japanese religion. The Jōdo Shinshū and Hokke sects of Buddhism likewise tended to demand the unequivocal devotion of their followers. This often caused a serious dilemma for the faithful who, as members of the community, were expected to participate in the rites of the local Shinto shrine. Pilgrimage to Ise with its Shinto shrines also brought this tension between community and sect into the open. In the okage-mairi of 1771 and 1830, very few pilgrims came from Noto or Hida, strongholds of the True Pure Land faith, or from Kazusa, Awa (Chiba), or Kai where the Nichiren sect was strong. Needless to say, the attitude of these sects and their adherents was deeply resented by other Japanese.

When the priest of Shinshū temple in Nada (Kobe) prevented his congregation from giving gifts to pilgrims, those passing through the town were heard muttering to themselves, "With all these big houses and no one giving handouts, why, they must have leprosy!"[79] Actually, not all believers in this area followed their priests' instructions willingly. When the Buddhist priests forbade them to go to Ise, some parishioners complained so bitterly that the local temple had to send to Higashi Honganji, the sect headquarters, for priestly reinforcements to help put down the apostasy. The young people of the temple were incensed at the arrival of these special emissaries. "In this land of the kami, the Grand Shrine at Ise is the most renowned of all for its miracles. *Everyone* has faith in it," they protested. Convinced that a fire which had recently destroyed their temple was an act of divine retribution, the young men of the temple threatened to kill the priests, and finally did chase them out of town.[80] In some places, Shinshū priests themselves broke rank and joined the pilgrimage.[81]

As in the later ee-ja-nai-ka, sheer trickery may have induced some strict Buddhists to join the pilgrimage. The following story, which may well be fictitious, bears retelling. Hiraga Gennai (1729–79), a popular writer, experimenter, and herbalist, went to Echigo and discovered an entire village that had refused to go on pilgrimage because of its steadfast devotion to Amida Buddha. Feeling somewhat irritated by this, Gennai collected some amulets and attached them to a kite. Then he climbed a nearby mountain and flew the kite over the village, letting the wind scatter the amulets over the houses below. The village immediately began to boil with excitement. People offered rice cakes and sake to the Shinto gods and set off for Ise en masse.[82]

Stories of divine punishment also helped to reinforce traditional prejudice and taboos, thereby binding the antistructural elements of okage-mairi to the structures of everyday life. Religious taboos, such as the avoidance of "red and black pollutions" (*aka fujō* and *kuro fujō* associated, respectively, with blood and death) were strongly reinforced by these tales. In one story, a man set up a tea shop for the refreshment of the pilgrims in Yamada. One morning he was unable to get a fire started for the tea. Thinking this strange, he did some investigating and learned that his maid was having her menstrual period. After this he was able to start the fire. But he still could not get it hot enough to boil water. Continuing his investigation, he discovered that the boy who was fetching his water was in mourning. When he heard this, the man built a new, "clean" fire and the water quickly came to a boil.[83] Other stories make the same point. Minowa Zairoku tells the story of a woman who was on her way to Mount Koya to bury the ashes of her husband who had died less than a month before. Overcome by the hullabaloo of the pilgrimage, the woman forgot her original errand and headed for Ise, her husband's ashes still in hand. When she stopped at an inn run by an oshi priest, the woman suddenly went berserk. Only after she confessed to the priest what she had done and turned away from the Grand Shrine did the woman regain her senses.[84] Similarly, the great fire that broke out at Ise in 1830 was attributed to the breaking of various taboos. Some thought that it was punishment for the participation by outcastes (*Eta*) in the pilgrimage. Others pointed their fingers at the merchants of Yamada who were too busy making money to observe the tradition of "a separate fire" and at women who did not live apart when having their periods. Still other people blamed the fire on the unprecedented mixing of strangers at Ise or their defecation in front of the shrines.[85]

Tales of revenge gave vent to the xenophobia which, after the middle of the nineteenth century, raged throughout the land. In 1853 the court requested Ise and other Shinto shrines to recite prayers for the "expulsion of the barbarians" or, as we would say today, for national defense. Dread of foreigners was as widespread among the folk (e.g., the *yonaoshi* activists) as it was among nativist thinkers and other members of the elite. During the ee-ja-nai-ka a stone weighing seventy or eighty pounds fell from the sky on the home of a foreign admiral living in Yokohama. In the harbor, a mysterious sandbar rose up "like a mountain" to prevent foreign ships from passing by. As a result of these mysterious goings-on, the foreigners allegedly learned to fear the "divine country" and returned home.[86] A contemporary song told how "okage-mairi" (i.e., ee-ja-nai-ka) restored order in the country after the gods, offended by the opening of trade with foreigners, afflicted the people with unheard of diseases, battles, and natural disasters.[87]

Divine retribution (*shinbatsu*) also preserved the religious decorum of the pilgrimage. While the roads leading to Ise were often a bedlam of noise and confusion, once the pilgrims reached the precincts of the Grand Shrine, silence reigned. In 1830, however, a group of pilgrims from Ōmi created a scene in front of the shrines, singing in loud voices and hurling insults at one another. When they refused to heed the warnings of the officials at the shrine, their leader suffered a mysterious seizure and fell to the ground. When the others saw this, they turned pale and ran off. Thus traditional respect for the shrines was maintained in the midst of what otherwise might have become an unholy uproar.[88]

Heaven also intervened in a positive way to promote the pilgrimages. The most important of these acts of divine intervention are recounted in tales of miraculous guidance, healing, and resurrection. Mysterious "uncles" and "aunties" appeared to restore lost children to their parents or to provide the children with food, lodging, and money. Equally mysterious white horses materialized to carry young pilgrims to Ise and back. Their good deeds accomplished, these equine angels would disappear, leaving behind, as their calling cards, as Ise amulet and a small pile of horse dung. Generally, the implication was that the horse, in some sense, *was* an amulet which had undertaken the responsibility of guiding the children to the Grand Shrine. The parents of one eight-year-old boy in Awa refused to let their son go to Ise and finally had to tie him to a post. The next morning the boy was gone and an amulet was found dangling from the rope. Four days later the boy returned home, much to his parents' relief. Asked how he could make the trip to Ise and back in such a short time, the lad replied that he had met an old man leading a "white paper horse." When the old man told him to get on the horse, he was whisked away for a tour of both shrines, all in record time.[89]

Children were also the heroes of resurrection narratives. A certain family once entertained pilgrims in their home even though they were holding a memorial service for their son who had died recently. Helping the pilgrims, they thought, would be an act of merit for the repose of the boy's soul. Their piety paid off abundantly, for the next day the son they thought was dead appeared at the door with a friend. When he told his parents that he had been to Ise, the family opened the grave and discovered that an amulet from the Grand Shrine had taken the place of the boy's ashes.[90]

In a similar tale, a nurse in the employ of a samurai retainer insisted on going to Ise in spite of her master's demand that she stay home and take care of his little boy. She had not been gone long before the boy she left behind became ill and died. Knowing nothing of the child's death, the nurse continued on her way until she came to Osaka. There she met a strange Buddhist priest walking hand in hand with the child. The priest turned the boy over to his nurse and vanished. When the two finally returned home, the grieving father at first refused to see the woman. But when a servant told him that the boy was alive and with his nurse, the samurai opened the child's grave and, to his amazement, found only an amulet from Ise.[91]

Aside from their inspirational or entertainment value, resurrection tales of this sort seem to say various things. The first story seems to imply that charity shown to pilgrims may be rewarded by the most glorious of miracles, resurrection from the dead. In the second story, the miracle of resurrection overcomes the resistance of a samurai to the pilgrimage, justifies what seemed to be the reckless faith of his son's nurse, and finally, shows that not even death itself can stop the pilgrim's progress.

Amulets themselves were part of the triumphant spirit of the pilgrimage. While falling amulets are usually seen as symptoms of social hysteria, *ofuda-furi* also contributed to maintaining a harmonious, community spirit. During the okage-mairi of 1705, an amulet from the Grand Shrine suddenly fell from the sky and came to rest between some people in Osaka who were about to come to blows in an argument. When the people in the area saw how the amulet had restored peace, they became more "circumspect"—or gentled—in their behavior.[92]

In 1830, an amulet fell on a rented house in the castle town of Himeji. When the landlord saw how fervently his renters worshiped the amulet, he demanded it for himself. The renters, however, refused to give it up. The quarrel was finally brought before the lord of the domain who decided the case in favor of the landlord, ruling that whenever amulets fall on rented houses they belong, by right, to the owner of the property. Just as the renter was about to turn the amulet over to the landlord, it miraculously split in half.[93] Another amulet fell between two houses in the same town. While the two families were arguing over who should have it, the amulet, of its own accord, rose up in the sky, divided in half, and descended once again on each of the two houses, effectively putting an end to the argument.[94]

Amulets were also affective in negotiating with government officials who tried to block the pilgrimage. During the okage-mairi of 1830, authorities in Tango forbade the people to go on pilgrimage. But when amulets started to fall on the lord's own castle the ruling was reversed.[95] Other amulets fell on the roof beams of pious or generous villagers as a reward for the roles they played in okage-mairi. Still others fell from the sky to encourage the fainthearted to join the pilgrimage.

The tales that we have examined reinforced the normative parameters of the pilgrim's world. As religious and moral "action guides" they supported a moral vision of a world that *should be*.[96] Since okage-mairi was a movement of the common folk, its norms must be sought for in the basic value orientation of the common people which provided the backbone of their morality, indignation, prejudice, and taboos. Although this orientation often manifests itself in folktales, folksongs, and other artifacts, it is not necessarily the immediate expression of the common man himself. All expressions of justice, popular or otherwise, reflect the outlook and interests of the specific individuals or groups which articulate them. To discover the real face of the value orientation of the folk, one must therefore try to peer behind the various masks that religious leaders, village headmen, parish intellectuals, scholars, and rebels from more substantial social backgrounds have created in their various attempts to dramatize, sublimate, or conceal the plight of the common people.

Although okage-mairi and other popular movements of the Tokugawa period have been criticized by Japanese scholars for being leaderless and therefore "unrevolutionary," the pilgrimages actually did not want for proper guidance. The sense of justice that underlies the tales of okage-mairi comes not from the pilgrims themselves, but indirectly, through priests from Ise called *oshi* or *onshi*.[97] These priests were especially active in the Kinai but plied their sacred arts throughout the country, save in those parts dominated by the Honganji sect. Their primary work was to organize congregations and confraternities which would serve as an infrastructure for the pilgrimage, to distribute amulets to the faithful, and to put up pilgrims in the inns which they owned or managed. Toward the end of the Tokugawa period, their role as innkeepers became increasingly important.

Like professional clergy everywhere, the interests and outlook of these priests were both similar to, yet different from, those of their supporters. While close enough to the common people to be their indirect ideological spokesmen, their bread was buttered on the other side. Unlike the oshi from Kumano who employed middlemen (*sendatsu*) to manage their congregations, the Ise priests usually enjoyed direct, personal relationships with their followers. When an oshi visited a village, he brought with him small gifts of tea, sashes, cosmetics, or fans. The congregation reciprocated by taking care of his road tolls, lodging, and other expenses and by giving him offerings of rice or cash. In the communities in the Kinki region where the faithful were in the majority, the oshi was supported by public funds or by mandatory contributions collected by the village headman. They regarded their congregations as personal fiefs to be traded, transferred, or sold at will to other oshi. Those who were able to acquire a large number of congregations amassed sizable fortunes which could be put out at interest. Indubitably, such usurious practices created a distance between the oshi and his followers. Some priests are said to have sold their congregations in order to buy prostitutes. Nevertheless, like the servants of other adventitious deities—for example, *sendatsu, yamabushi, hijiri, shugenja,* and the missionaries of the later New Religions—the oshi was regarded as a holy man by the people. Disregarding the *Shintō Gobusho's* proscription of shamanistic practices, the oshi appealed directly to the earthly needs of the miracle-thirsty masses. Even the water from the oshi's bath was saved and drunk as an elixir in times of illness.[98]

While the oshi's religious services brought him close to the people, his quest for material well-being gave him a vested interest in maintaining social order and stability during the ballyhoo of the pilgrimage. As a "gentler" of the pilgrims, the oshi took his stand with the authorities and merchants against any and all rabble-rousers. His material interests inclined him to be less concerned about the class enemies of the people than about the enemies of the pilgrimage, be they daimyō, merchants, jealous husbands, or plebian toughs. To express his concerns, the oshi created the folklore of miracles and divine judgment which I have already described.[99] Like the leaders of some of Japan's New Religions today, one of the main functions of the oshi was to collect, encourage, fabricate, edit, and publish miraculous tales. These tales were designed to discourage suspicious husbands, stingy masters, and tax-hungry lords from impeding the pilgrimage. Other yarns were meant to prod the hesitant to join the movement. While the folktales they spun reflected the folk justice of the common people, they also helped to tame and contain it. So successful were they that even a skeptical chronicler like the author of the *Ukiyo no arisama* made use of them and was influenced by them, *malgré lui.* One could speculate that the more violent upheavals which took place during the ee-ja-nai-ka were due not only to the influence of the yonaoshi rebellions but also to the loss of symbolic and moral control of the movement by the Ise priesthood.

Here one might ask, Did the tales of heavenly retribution transmitted by the oshi priests really make a difference? Were their stories effective in promoting interest in the pilgrimage? Did they help to curb the chaos that appeared at the margins and interstices of the movement? Unfortunately, to answer these questions we have only the witness of the tales themselves to go on. And the answer there, of course, is invariably yes. Miracle tales often end with the triumphant refrain: "And seeing this, the whole village set out for Ise," or "after this, everyone contributed more zealously to the pilgrims." Stories of divine retribution also seemed to "work." People sometimes went on pilgrimage just to avoid the misfortune others suffered after refusing to go. The same was true of the dances. In one village a rumor spread that if someone refused to join the dance his family would catch the plague or his house would burn down. The lesson was clear to all: "So dance! (*saraba odore*)." Everyone chipped in some money to cover expenses, and at four in the morning the drums in the local shrine awakened the village for breakfast. Soon the drums were beaten a second time calling all to line up. At the third roll of the drums—still before sunrise—the dancing began and continued for some thirty days![100]

We have already seen the positive effect that falling amulets had on authorities in Tango. A more colorful story with the same intent comes to us from the ee-ja-nai-ka. In Shiga, amulets from Ise fell on an inn where a troupe of samurai happened to be staying. When the people began to dance around chanting "Ain't it great, aint' it great!" one of the samurai took offense, brandished his sword over the heads of the dancers, and ordered them to stop. Suddenly the menacing, uplifted arm of the samurai became paralyzed. When the other warriors saw what had happened, they cried out in alarm, "Isn't there a priest or a wizard (*onmyōji*) around here? We need a prayer!" "You don't need a prayer," the dancers replied. "When there's a pilgrimage going on, dancing's as good as a prayer. So dance, samurai, dance!" Thinking he would never get his arm down unless he did, the samurai joined the dance for about an hour. Finally his arm returned to normal. Out of gratitude and humiliation, the samurai made offerings to the gods and departed the next morning without giving the people any more trouble.[101]

Eternal Return and Counterrevolution

The word *revolution* has many meanings. If by 'revolution' we mean "the organization of zealous men for sustained political activity"—Michael Walzer's minimalist, neo-Weberian definition—pilgrimage obviously is entirely *un*revolutionary.[102] Although tagged a "liberation movement" by a number of Japanese scholars, okage-mairi tended to take place in years of plenty when rebellion itself would have been unexpected. While temporary relief from toil must have been an important incentive for women and servants who took French leave to go to Ise, the lure of the sacred and the promise of miracles were equally significant factors behind their pilgrimage. To conclude that okage-mairi was an "escape from the town or village community made possible by divine authority,"[103] or a "yearning for reform,"[104] or a "liberation movement,"[105] "mass hysteria," or "mock revolt,"[106] is therefore to name the pilgrimage after what lower-class pilgrims were getting away from, not what they were going to.

Not since the destruction of the armies of the Honganji sect at Ishiyama in 1580 and the Christian forces at Shimabara in 1638 had any group in Japan successfully challenged the bakufu in the name of a religious ideology. The Kakure-Kirishitan (Hidden Christians), Kakure-

Nembutsu, Kakure-Daimoku, or Fuju-Fuse (recusant Buddhists of the Tokugawa period) were all unrevolutionary groups (in Walzer's sense) motivated by specifically religious imperatives. *Kakure-mairi* (as nuke-mairi was sometimes called) differed from these Underground Religions by being tacitly accepted by society. While it did give women and servants a chance to participate in the pilgrimage which the Ise-kō (confraternities more solidly grafted into the male-dominated power structure of the village) did not provide, nuke-mairi was hardly revolutionary. Sakurai Tokutarō suggests that it originated in the initiation rituals of village youth which often featured a secret pilgrimage to Ise.[107] Masters who were afraid of losing their servants when they "ran away" to Ise organized parties for them on their return. The French-leave pilgrims, for their part, brought back presents or even money (as "interest") for masters and relatives who had stayed at home. This exchange of gifts signified the resumption of the social interaction of everyday life and helped to reintegrate the pilgrim into his quotidian routine.[108] Seldom were French-leave pilgrims seriously punished or abused.

If revolution is distinguished from rebellion by its decisive, once-and-for-all nature, it is obvious that okage-mairi, which occurred sporadically throughout the Tokugawa period, was closer to the rhythmic pattern of rebellion. Miyata Noboru has analyzed okage-mairi, okage-odori, and ee-ja-nai-ka in terms of the cult of the Gods in Fashion (*hayari-gami*). These gods are thought to have miraculous powers to cure such ills as toothache, hemorrhoids, smallpox, measles, and the plague.[109] Some hayari-gami could even put an end to a spouse's extramarital affairs. The defining characteristic of the hayari-gami is the inconstancy of their worshipers' attention: they enjoyed no routine veneration. On the contrary, as soon as the worshiper's troubles were over, he forgot all about his hayari-gami. In some cases, such as plague, a straw effigy of the hayari-gami—for example, a disease god (*eki-jin*) or an evil deity (*aku-jin*)—was made and then burned or thrown into a river. In some areas, villagers danced en bloc with these symbols to a neighboring village. This village, in turn, would transmit them to the next village, and so on, until the plague was run out of the area. This custom, called *kake-odori*, was closely related to familiar rites for expelling harmful insects (*mushi-okuri*).[110]

Miyata has clearly demonstrated the structural relationship between such mass movements as okage-mairi, ee-ja-nai-ka, and other religious "fashions" or "fads." The shortcoming of this thesis is that it tends to underestimate the importance of the ideal recurrence of okage-mairi every sixty-one years. Based on the traditional Sino-Japanese calendar, this cyclical repetition is perhaps the strongest piece of evidence we have linking these pilgrimages with what Mircea Eliade calls the "eternal return."[111] It also speaks strongly against interpretations of pilgrimage as "liberation movements." One can grasp this readily by comparing pilgrimage with the Japanese custom of celebrating an individual's sixty-first birthday (*kanreki*), another practice growing out of the sexagenary calendar. At his kanreki, the person being feted is dressed ceremonially in a bright scarlet cap and jacket which Japanese children used to wear. This symbolizes the successful completion of the full sixty years of the calendar. On reaching the age of sixty-one, the individual is said to have returned to infancy. He then must begin a new cycle. It used to be said that the person who reached this age was "reborn." From then on he was expected to obey his children who, having reached maturity themselves, were ready to take over the family's affairs. The custom therefore symbolized the orderly relinquishing and transmission of domestic authority and a cyclical understanding of the course of human life.

The gentling, religious nature of okage-mairi is best understood when we situate it among the fundamental categories of Japanese religion: *hare, ke*, and *kegare*.[112] The basic element in this triangulation is *ke*, the magicoreligious power of everyday life and of agricultural production in particular. As this power declines (say, with age, sickness, cold weather, a woman's menstrual period, or child-birth), it becomes *kegare*. While *kegare* is usually translated "pollution," Sakurai Tokutarō maintains that its essential meaning is the "withering (*kareru*) of *ke*." Although the word *kegare* can mean "pollution," it is not simply the opposite of "purity." It implies a powerless or rundown state of affairs. Finally, *hare* is the ritual means for reproducing or stimulating *ke*. The best example of the interaction of these spiritual states is the Shinto festival itself. During the course of a festival, prayer, orgies and ritual combat (*hare* activities) remove the "withered" or rundown condition (*kegare*) of the community and its land, thereby restoring the power (*ke*) needed for a vigorous, productive society.

If we think of okage-mairi as a kind of *hare* movement, both the "secular" and the "conservative" aspects of the pilgrimage become clear. As an agent of renewal, *hare* contains within itself both structural and antistructural elements, that is, both formal ritual activity and orgiastic eruptions of energy. One might even say that *hare* includes elements which other cultures would regard as sacred *and* profane. (Foreign visitors often remark that Japanese festivals and pilgrimages have become very secular. Actually, judged from their basic structure, they have always been secular events.) Although festivals and pilgrimages became increasingly commercialized and spectacular during the Tokugawa period, sport and entertainment were part of their reinvigorating dynamism (*hare*) from earliest times. This role of play, and dance, is echoed in the following ditty from the Ise-odori:

> Even in Kantō and Tōhoku far away,
> Young and old, men and women together. . . .
> How wonder-ful the pilgrimage!
> Dancing, dancing
> The Ise dance;
> *If people have fun* [nagusami]
> *The country will prosper forever. . . .*
> How wonder-ful! [My emphasis].[113]

Far from aiming at insurrection, the okage-mairi and nuke-mairi—like the Shinto festival—had as their purpose the magicoreligious restoration of productive energy. Like Japanese folk religion in general, these events were dominated by an earthy pragmatism. The truly popular shrine at Ise was not the Inner Shrine where Amaterasu was worshiped but the Outer Shrine promoted by Watarai Shintō. This was the fane of Toyouke, a deity of fertility. Returning pilgrims often posted amulets from the Grand Shrine in their rice paddies in order to secure abundant crops. The veneration of the God of the Hoe (Okuwa-sama) was an important feature of both the okage-mairi and the okage-odori. Symbolic of the farmer's unending prayers for rich harvests, Okuwa-sama probably helped to popularize the Ise faith among the rural masses. Inscriptions of prayers on stone lanterns commemorating the okage-mairi in the Osaka and Nara areas still bear witness to the driving force behind the pilgrimages. On these lanterns are engraved such words as "thanksgiving for a good harvest," "the safety of the whole village," "peace on earth and flourishing crops," and even "good luck to the army."[114] The *Kasshi Yawa Zokuhen* tells us that in 1830, anticipating rich harvests, people began to talk about "okage-mairi."[115]

The Ise dances often had the function of warding off plagues and natural disasters. The words to a dance held in Nabari (Mie prefecture) warned that "people who have stopped dancing have to go to the doctor and take medicine."[116] A song from Itami connects the dance with both fertility and world renewal:

> The Thanksgiving Dance exorcizes evil spirits [*akuma*];
> Pray to the gods for a rich harvest.
> The heavenly gods of Ise bid us dance.
> If we dance the world will be renewed.[117]

Little wonder, then, that in places where amulets did not fall from the sky people started to dance just to make sure they were not cursed!

Other closely related symbols which surfaced during the social ferment of the nineteenth century—for example, World Renewal and Maitreya's World (or Boat)[118]—also had their roots in agrarian magic. The world (*yo*) that was renewed in yo-naoshi was originally the fields, not society. Similarly, Maitreya's world originally referred to a year of great abundance said to occur once every twelve years. If we look at the use of the terms *yonaoshi* and *Maitreya's World* in the contemporary Fujidō sect, it seems that both ultimately referred to the union of the sexes (or yin-yang) and the fertility of the earth. Thus all of these terms—okage-mairi, nuke-mairi, yonaoshi, Miroku-no-yo, as well as the more inclusive concepts of *hare, ke,* and *kegare*—arose in a religious world in which renewal was part of a cycle of ritual activities aiming at the periodic revival of the powers of the earth. Because the rejuvenation of the community itself was always a part of the Shinto festival, it is not surprising that in the nineteenth century this religious vocabulary was creatively extended to include the transformation of society per se. Yonaoshi came to mean the renewal of the entire nation; the expression "a festival of World Renewal" (*yonaoshi no matsuri*) could be used to refer to rebellion itself.[119] In some cases, it assumed a more explicitly political (or "rational") form and turned into a truly revolutionary movement.[120]

The Repression or "Gentling" of the Folk Tradition

Albert Camus once pointed out that the modern rebel is one who seeks to replace "the reign of grace by the reign of justice."[121] Dissidents in traditional societies like Tokugawa Japan were more flexible and perhaps even a bit more humane and sensible. They sought for justice, not only in open rebellion, but also in various forms of indirect, symbolic protest. They even looked for it in grace, miracles, divine retribution, not to mention an eternal round of rituals whereby their communities were renewed and made whole. The social and political values which came to the surface during the okage-mairi were of this sort. They were the result of a mixture of prejudice, superstition, class interest, and poetic justice (in which the greedy and overbearing always get their comeuppance). Perhaps their sense of justice helped the pilgrims and their priestly guides integrate the extraordinary, antistructural experiences of the pilgrimage with the fairness, resentment, conformities, and taboos of everyday life. In this chapter we have seen how this basic value orientation, together with sagacious government policies and the calculated charity of the upper classes, sustained and gentled the pilgrim and kept the pilgrimage itself within its traditional bounds. Without this elementary sense of order, the chaos generated by pilgrimage and rebellion might easily have slipped into sheer anomie.

Although a small-scale okage-mairi occurred in 1890, after the reorganization and institutionalization of the new Meiji authoritarianism in 1871, no mass pilgrimages to Ise took place.[122] After that, the religious and social aspirations formerly expressed in pilgrimage, ee-ja-nai-ka, and peasant rebellions to "renew the world" were stamped out or forced to assume new, sublimated forms. Under the new State Shinto system, ward headmen (*kuchō*) replaced the oshi as distributors of amulets from Ise. The Shinto ideology enabled the Meiji oligarchs to assign new valences to various elements of the repressed folk tradition and thereby exploit the people within the context of a newly concocted national eschatology. Ise itself, which after centuries of exclusive patronage by aristocratic and warrior families had become the heritage of the common folk, was once again transformed and became the national palladium, the Holy of Holies of the imperial system itself. Even ee-ja-nai-ka, which one associates with the sublimated protest and ecstatic tomfoolery of 1867, was absorbed by the spirit of Meiji nationalism. E. H. Norman relates the following anecdote: "An American friend of mine who spent his boyhood in the city of Shimonoseki told me that he well remembers that following the announcement of the defeat of Russia in the war of 1904–5, spontaneous processions were held in the city and outskirts which took on gradually a hysterical character. The refrain *eija nai ka* [*sic*] occurred in the singing and shouting of the crowds."[123]

The word *yonaoshi,* if not its spirit, was incorporated into the messianic dreams of several of Japan's New Religions. Likewise, faith in Maitreya Buddha, associated throughout East Asia with popular rebellion, was taken over by the new sects and made part of their syncretistic smorgasbords. Under these new political circumstances, religious concepts like yonaoshi and Maitreya had to be used ambiguously if they were to be used at all.[124] As symbols of otherworldly hope and salvation they could be counted on to attract the exploited masses. And finally, as expressions of the cosmic pretensions of the new Japanese messiahs, the same symbols could be used to advance the interests of the sects themselves.

Symbols of renewal are generally most disruptive while in the ingenuous bloom of youth. At this stage, their challenge to the established order is marked by ecstatic dreams of a new world, anarchistic heroism, and the martyr's blood. Once organized, these symbols, and the movements they inspire, tend to lose their vitality. Ideologists and ecclesiocrats—the movers and gentlers of the new age—vie with each other to assign new meanings to old symbols, turning the articles of faith against the interests of the very people, or classes, who first believed. This, in effect, is what happened to yonaoshi, okage-mairi, and faith in the Future Buddha—movements which once, to varying degrees, had been deeply implicated in the hopes and values of the common folk. Born in the soil of agrarian magic, these folk movements had developed, willy-nilly, into expressions of social unrest during the *bakumatsu* period. All were part of a very traditional moral economy and ritual cycle that called for the periodic renewal of the earth. After the Meiji Restoration these visions were either nationalized by the state and made to apply to the renewal of Japan herself, or they were spiritualized by New Religions and extended to the transformation, and healing, of the human condition itself. Ironically, this final metamorphosis of the symbols of renewal helped to promote the exploitation of the lower classes by landlords, industrialists, and officials and served to continue the "massive gentling" of the Japanese people.

CHAPTER 3

The Cross and the Cudgel

In the last chapter we saw how religious structures can be used to curtail social and political conflict. Although I prefer to talk about the "gentling" rather than about the narcotizing of the masses, up to this point my discussion of religion and social conflict has been quite in keeping with "conflict sociology." Unfortunately, the paradigm of gentling deals with only one aspect of our problem, for under the right circumstances, religious and political structures also *generate* conflict. This adds additional support to my contention that religious "events" can best be understood by seeing how "synchronic" structures—latent and manifest—disclose themselves in the "diachrony" of history.

Ever since it was introduced in Japan in the sixteenth century, Christianity has repeatedly found itself at the center of controversy. There are several reasons for this, not the least of which are the religion's foreign origins. While nativists used the same argument against Buddhism, Buddhism, at least, had many centuries during which it could become more or less indigenized. Christianity's western connections, however, were too recent and obvious to be convincingly denied. In many cases, the foreign missionary was literally just around the corner. Many fledgling churches were still beholden to foreign mission boards for financial support. Another source of tension was Christianity's exclusive, monotheistic claims. Translated into Japanese idiom, Christianity itself was a "single practice" sect. In chapter 1, I pointed out the tension that often arises between the syncretistic claims of the local community, on the one hand, and the ritual monopraxis of sects like the Nichirenites or the followers of True Pure Land Buddhism, on the other. Tension of this sort could become extremely dangerous since political power itself rested on a syncretistic imperative. To insist on "one Lord, one faith, one baptism"—or, in the Buddhist case, one way to nirvana—was to invite head-on confrontations with the powers that be, and the enmity of other sects vying for the support and protection of the same powers.

Tensions of this sort—caused by the foreignness of Christianity and its exclusiveness—help to fill in the background of the story I am about to tell. But, in this case, the real source of conflict lay not in the relationship between the religion and society, but within the religious group itself, or rather, within its own contradictory value-structures.

The Kyōdan Struggle

In the autumn of 1969 a violent struggle broke out in the United Church of Christ in Japan (*Nihon Kirisutokyōdan;* hereafter: Kyodan). Radical seminarians and university students put on riot helmets, covered their faces with towels,[1] and, brandishing long cudgels,[2] invaded various meetings of the church. Once inside, they seized microphones, intimidated the participants, and completely dominated the proceedings. For hours they harangued delegates with their "problems,"[3] hurling abusive language and catcalls at the church's most venerable theologians and laypersons. The few delegates who dared to speak out were booed, pushed back into their seats, or roughed up. In some cases, meetings went on like this throughout the night. After one such encounter in the Tokyo district, the chairman of the meeting was taken to the hospital and treated for exhaustion.

At about the same time, leaders of church-related universities were going through similar ordeals. Radical students pelted the chancellor of Meiji Gakuin with eggs, poured milk over his head, and broke one of his limbs. At Aoyama Gakuin, they beat up the chaplain in the university chapel itself. Radicals in the seminaries disrupted ministerial examinations and tore up exam papers. Seminary buildings were taken over and barricaded by student protesters. For about three years, ordinations throughout the country were forcibly postponed. To restore law, order and property rights, theological faculties felt compelled to call in the riot control police. Several seminarians and radical students were arrested; some were later indicted and given jail sentences. In Tokyo, two radicals committed suicide.

In major metropolitan areas the turmoil spread to local congregations. Deeply divided over the issues, churches split and attendance and offerings seriously declined. In Nishinomiya, a minister who dared to compare the painful experiences of his radical son to the suffering of Christ on the cross was dismissed for preaching "unchristian sermons." In Kyoto, students interrupted a pastor's sermon with various "problems", and then, advancing to the pulpit, tore off his robe and demanded his resignation. After the incident, the minister was hospitalized with a heart condition. Throughout the church, word spread of worship services that had been similarly disrupted, of collection and Communion plates that had been dashed to the floor and desecrated. In some churches, radical pastors suspended Communion services, and banned the use of the Lord's Prayer and the pastoral benediction. Throughout the 1970s, charges and counter-charges of heresy and violence filled the pages of church publications and even made their way into the secular press. For years, district assemblies and national boards were unable to meet for fear of unpleasant encounters.

Statistics tell an equally dismal story. Of all the church's vital statistics, only membership, contributions and pastors's salaries showed an improvement during the period from 1948 to the beginning of the struggle. During this period, attendance at Sunday morning worship services remained steady, but all other indicators were in decline: church school enrollments and attendance, baptisms, and the percent of the membership regarded as "active resident communicants." These figures suggest that even before the Kyodan struggle broke out, the church was far from a healthy, dynamic institution. During the years of the controversy, contributions and salaries continued to improve. But telltale U-curves were noted in the figures for 1. church school enrollments and attendance, 2. baptism, 3. attendance at Sunday worship services, 4. average membership, and 5. active resident communicants.[4] Statistics indicating a rise in contributions to the church during this period are probably an indication both of inflation and a rapidly rising GNP. More significant is the fact that by 1980 the Kyodan had accumulated debts amounting to some $700,000. Both personnel and programs sponsored by the national headquarters in Tokyo had to be cut back severely.

Before we can make sense of this struggle we need to know more about its historical development and the world view of its participants.

The History of the Dispute

The Kyodan was formed by a merger of thirty-four Protestant denominations in June, 1941. While the Japanese churches had discussed an ecumenical merger for many years, it took pressure from the fascist, wartime regime to bring the new church into existence. For this reason, while conservatives to this day continue to regard the union as an "act of divine Providence," radicals insist that the church is a creature of the state. Soon after the end of the war, the Anglican Episcopal Church of Japan, the Japan Lutheran Church, and various Baptist groups withdrew from the union. Nevertheless, the Kyodan continued to be by far the largest Protestant Church in the country.

The roots of the controversy go back to disputes between the Social Gospel faction *(shakai-ha)* and the more evangelistic elements *(fukuin-ha* or *kyōkai-ha)* active in the various denominations that joined the Kyodan. A more recent factor was the publication of two highly controversial documents by the church. In 1954, a new Confession of Faith was adopted by the Kyodan. Many liberals feared that this creed, while it contained nothing novel, would be used to restrict theological freedom, especially should it be used as the basis of ordination examinations. Conservatives, on the other hand, worried that without a creed-based examination system, the doors of the ministry would be flung open to the unorthodox. The second document was a declaration dealing with the church's role during World War II. Although the Kyodan had made a brief statement in 1946 admitting its part in the war, by the middle 1960s some felt that this was not enough. Therefore, on Easter Sunday, 1967, a "Confession of War Responsibility" was issued in the name of Suzuki Masahisa, moderator of the church. The Confession stirred up a heated debate. While not many were willing to admit they were opposed to its contents, a large number of conservatives felt that the document had been foisted upon them in an autocratic way. Even liberals felt that the church should have had more time to discuss and digest the new Confession. These documents had the effect of polarizing the leadership of the Kyodan into a liberal wing that felt the Gospel should be expressed in political and social action, and a conservative branch that believed the church's true mission was evangelism and the salvation of individual souls.

The fuel already spread over the church by the disputes of the 1950s and 1960s was suddenly ignited by the question whether or not to participate in the building of a "Christian Pavilion" at the International Exposition to be held in Osaka in 1970 (commonly called "Expo 70"). In 1968, the National Christian Council endorsed the idea of the pavilion. Costs were to be shared in about equal thirds by Japanese Catholics and Protestants, and by overseas Christians. In October 1968, the 15th General Assembly of the Kyodan voted to participate in the construction of the pavilion. This decision immediately raised howls of protest, especially from leftists and liberals in the Osaka and Tokyo districts who suspected that the government was using the exposition to distract public attention from the most controversial issue of the day: the renewal of the US-Japan Security Treaty (Japanese abbreviation: Ampo). They reasoned that the government had concocted this "festival of Baal" in order to avoid the mass demonstrations that had taken place when the treaty was renewed ten years earlier. Conservatives, however, supported the idea of the pavilion, saying that it would offer an excellent chance to "witness for Christ." On 14 July 1969, just as the debate was reaching its boiling point, Moderator Suzuki, a strong and dynamic figure, died from cancer. He was succeeded by Vice-Moderator Ii Kiyoshi, whom both sides came to regard as a weak and vacillating leader. The stage was now set for the chaotic performances of the next decade and a half.

On 1 September 1969, over 150 helmeted student radicals took over a meeting of the church's executive committee. The students disrupted the agenda, violently insulting the more conservative members and interrogating them concerning their stand on the pavilion. Some students took up positions by the doors where they prevented members from leaving, or going to the restrooms. About thirty or forty radicals surrounded and badgered Professor Kitamori Kazoh, a faculty member of the Tokyo Union Theological Seminary (TUTS) and one of Japan's foremost theologians.[5] Some, armed with slingshots, hurled hard paper pellets at him and broke his glasses. At one point, when Kitamori suddenly tore up a confession he had just been forced to sign, a student struck the professor in the face. Finally, after continuing on like this throughout the night, the radicals extracted a promise from the committee that it would call a special assembly of the church to discuss the problem of the pavilion. The meeting was finally adjourned at 7:30 A. M. on 2 September. On 11 September, radicals forced the Executive Committee to hold another open meeting which, again, turned into an all-night affair. A special assembly of the church was finally convened, but it too was paralyzed by the violent tactics of the radicals so that no vote could be taken on the question of the pavilion. It is said that the meeting concluded with the singing of "The Internationale" rather than with the usual hymn.

Hamstrung in this way, the church was legally bound to abide by its previous decision and the Christian Pavilion was finally built, paid for in part by funds from the Kyodan. Throughout the country, district assemblies were forced to allow radical participant-observers without voting rights *(baisekisha)* to attend meetings. Repeatedly, the baisekisha disrupted the proceedings with their "revolutionary" tactics. Violence, and rumors of violence, prevented the major urban districts (Tokyo, Kanagawa, Osaka, Hyogo, and Kyoto) from selecting delegates for national church assemblies. Finally, the question whether or not to admit baisekisha to meetings became as heated an issue as the pavilion itself.

As a result of the "Kitamori Affair", a serious rift developed between the TUTS faculty, on the one hand, and the Tokyo clergy and the executive committee, on the other. The seminary claimed that participants in the 1–2 September meeting should have protected Professor Kitamori from harm. The executive committee and the Tokyo clergy countered by attacking the seminary's transcendental, above-it-all attitude. In October 1969, students at TUTS, protesting the stand their teachers had taken, went on strike and demanded "mass negotiations" *(taishū dankō)* with the faculty. In November, they occupied and barricaded the seminary buildings. Later, student radicals broke into a professor's home and were indicted for illegal trespass. Finally, on 11 March 1970, the TUTS faculty called in a 150-man police squad to drive the students out. When the police arrived on the scene at seven in the morning, only a handful of students were on the premises so that only four were arrested. Three students were later indicted. On 17 March, when registration was held, about 20 percent of the student body decided to leave the seminary. Three years later, the general assembly of the Kyodan passed a resolution demanding that TUTS drop its legal charges against the students. The seminary, however, refused and the students were sentenced to suspended prison terms.

Throughout the struggle, the radicals sustained and coordinated their operations through various struggle-committees on their home campuses. There were various, small New Left groups organized on an *ad hoc,* single-issue basis. These groups often had no elected leaders and, apparently, little or no formal, or hierarchical, structure. They deliberately sought to avoid the top-heavy regimentation of youth groups sponsored by the Socialists and the Japanese Communist Party. Among these rather short-lived groups was an anti-Expo organization called Hanbanpaku Kyōtōkaigi which had grown out of Beheiren (Citizens' Alliance for Peace in Vietnam). There was also a Caucus of Independent Christians (Jikiren) formed by student radicals and a Caucus of Independent Pastors (Jibokuren) for radical Kyodan ministers.

Although a number of conservative caucuses had existed in the Kyodan even before this, in 1977 a new group called the Federation of Evangelical Churches (Japanese abbreviation: Rengō) was formed by conservatives in order to prevent (what they perceived as) the complete takeover of the church by radicals. Their express purpose was, as they would put it, to keep the church, as "the Body of the Lord Jesus Christ, *clean*." Instead of having their time and energy consumed by endless debate and so-called "dialogue," they wanted to invest their energy in evangelism and "the mission of God." Thus they condemned the seventeenth, eighteenth and nineteenth general assemblies of the church, meetings of the executive committee, and other boards and commisions which had "compromised with heresy" by denying "the canonicity of the Bible, the Confession of Christ as Lord and Savior, and the Faith of Redemption." Conservatives were also upset about a decision by the Kyodan in 1975 that "no positions will be excluded" in answers to ministerial examinations concerning the meaning of the creed. While the decision to exclude no positions had enabled the church to resume ordinations, conservatives feared that it had opened the ministry to pagans and heretics. By 1978, Rengo had grown to 61 congregations and had 292 individual members. By 1980, it had a budget of $148,000.

In 1979, in defiance of Kyodan rules, Rengo held its own ministerial examinations and proceeded to ordain five candidates. Although Rengo's purpose was simply to assure a steady supply of orthodox clergy, the Kyodan refused to recognize the validity of these examinations and ordinations. Even though the conservative group was originally intended as a "purifying" force within the Kyodan, and not as a new sect or denomination, a few Rengo congregations voted to withdraw from the church.

Today the controversy has subsided considerably. All districts save Tokyo (made up of some 350 congregations) have been able to reconvene their annual assemblies. Nevertheless, unpleasant incidents continue to occur. As recently as 1982, a seventy-three-year-old conservative leader in Osaka was knocked to the floor by chairs and teacups hurled by radicals. Now and then one pastor, known as "the hit man of the radicals," disrupts meetings, usually by knocking books and papers out of the hands of delegates with whom he happens to disagree, or by pulling chairs out from under them.

Two Worldviews

Although I will later explain the Kyodan struggle in sociological terms, the debate that went on cannot be reduced to social (let alone "material") factors. Unpleasant as it was, the controversy had its own epistemic (i. e. theological) integrity and, in fact, touched on fundamental questions about the role of the church in modern society.

The "theology" of the controversy appeared in a flood of position papers, speeches, sermons, and published articles. In the heat of the battle, words, events, and things *all* became symbols. These symbols, in turn, became signs of still other symbols, producing in the end a theological grotesquerie difficult for outsiders to comprehend. Both sides dilated endlessly on a host of "problems"—e.g., the Christian Pavilion, the declaration of war responsibility, ministerial examinations, reunion with the Okinawan church, relations with the Korean churches, the Yasukuni Shrine Bill, the Security Treaty, rearmament, and Japan's economic "reinvasion" of Asia—with all the subtlety, passion, and venom of medieval schoolmen. To this cacophany, theological adepts added descant voices two octaves higher relating these "problems" to the loftier symbols of the faith itself—e. g., faith, good works, redemption, resurrection, evangelism, and the creed of the church—and to the still more arcane concerns of twentieth century theology: eschatology, salvation-history, praxis, and so on. In the end, the "dialogue" between the two sides sounded like a double chorus simultaneously reciting a litany of frenzied, mutual curses.

While the theological pedigree of the radicals ultimately can be traced back to Anglo-American Neo-Calvanism and the social gospel, its roots also go deep into the subsoil of Japanese Protestantism. In the postwar period, the teachings of various Western theologians were introduced in Japan calling for a "servant church" ready to dismantle or dissolve itself in social action to save the world. Japanese thinkers also played a role. Takizawa Katsumi, student of the famous philosopher Nishida Kitarō and the Swiss theologian Karl Barth, developed a philosophical position said to be congruent with the teachings of Marx, Buddha, and Jesus, but from which one can criticize all of the ideologies and institutions later developed in their names. The works of Tagawa Kenzō played an important role in the radicals' understanding of the Bible and of the historical Jesus in particular. At TUTS and other seminaries a dispute called the "Jesus or Paul?" controversy broke out in tandem with the other quarrels of the day. Under Tagawa's influence, some radicals came to regard Saint Paul as a reactionary—apparently because be instructed Christian slaves to be content with their lot, and because he seemed to enjoin Christians to obey the state blindly. This led some to question the validity of the Pauline-Lutheran doctrine of "justification by faith alone," the very heart of Protesant theology. Paul's theological formalism was contrasted with the "humanism" of Jesus.

The conservatives in the church include a wide spectrum of believers, from pastors with a holiness or fundamentalist background to erudite theologians who, perhaps for the first time in their lives, found themselves labeled conservative simply because they opposed the violent tactics of the radicals. While their diversity makes a summary of their positions difficult, a survey of their writings reveals the influence of the evangelistic pietism of their American missionary teachers, an almost Augustinian sense of political realism and church order, a virtually Confucian respect for their *sempai* (elders or predecessors, including the wartime leadership of the Kyodan), and a serious committment to a free, pluralistic society (a belief growing out of Japan's postwar liberal democracy and, to some degree, out of their own Protestant heritage). In their eyes, the thought of the radicals stems not from theology, but from the "Marxism, Maoism, and paganism" brought into the church by recent converts. Some believe the problems of the Kyodan originated in the failure of the Japanese churches to preach "redemption through the Cross." At times, a sectarian stridency can be heard in their voices. "We are small, but *we* are the real church," says one Rengo leader. "*We* have preserved the creed, the theology, church order, and a high level of morality. After the so-called church destroys itself, it will realize *we* were right!"

What symbolized the heart of the controversy for the conservatives were the radicals' *gebabō*, staves which in conservative eyes were the truncheons of the Goths, the clubs of the Red Guard, and the cudgels of the Circumcillians rolled into one. For conservatives, the radicals' violence was the real cause of the whole rumpus. Among the radicals, age-old Puritan and sectarian sensibilities awoke once again. Church buildings, sacraments, ministerial garb and titles (e. g, *sensei* or Reverend), not to mention the politeness that permeates the Japanese language, were all rejected as the whited sepulchers of the Ampo Establishment. Since the church had joined forces with the state by participating in Expo, the students felt that by struggling with conservatives in the church's "solemn assemblies," they were confronting the state itself. For this reason they refused to take off their helmets in church meetings. As they put it, helmets were a "sign of the struggle."

Throughout the controversy, attention on both sides was focused on the Christian Pavilion. Conservatives regarded it both as a real opportunity for evangelistic outreach and as an example of voluntary action in a democratic church. Radicals, however, saw in it the menace of a "new Japanese fascism," a "reenactment of wartime apostasy," and a "festival of Baal (or capitalism)" celebrating the triumphs of materialism, rearmament, and the exploitation of workers, peasants and colonial peoples everywhere.[6] For them, the Christian Pavilion was no different from the Yasukuni Shrine. Both were sticky filaments in an ideologician web spun by the insidious spiders of militarism and monopoly capitalism.[7]

Another pivotal symbol was the Confession of War Responsibility.[8] Although inspired by the Stuttgart Confession of the German church, the Japanese confession was really quite different. In Japan, there had been no *bekennende Kirche*. The confession was drawn up by pastors who had come to maturity during the war (the so-called *senchū-ha*). These men, being younger, were better able to adjust to the democratic ideals of the postwar period than were their sempai, the wartime leaders. Many in the older generation felt that, far from confessing their guilt, they were being criticized by the confession and by a younger generation which knew nothing of the hardships they had endured. From their point of view, the compromises the church had made between 1931 and 1945 were made under conditions of extreme presssure and actually had had the effect of saving the Kyodan from more serious persecutions. On the left, the person who had most to say on this subject was Doshisha's radical church historian, Professor Dohi Akio. What follows is a paraphase of the radicals' perception of the Church's "war guilt" based largely on Dohi's research:

> After Uchimura Kanzō's so-called *lèse-majesté* affair the Japanese churches tried to defend themselves more vigorously by proving their patriotism and "Japaneseness" whenever they could. Although the Protestant churches had opposed government efforts to control religious groups in the 1920s, resistance became soft during the increasingly tense decade of the 1930s. In 1933, officials from the Ministry of Education addressed the delegates of the Japanese Christian Federation, calling on them to recognize the *Basic Principles of the National Essence (Kokutai no hongi)* and urging them to "Japanize" Christianity itself. The federation officially replied to this challenge by proclaiming:
>
> > We are fully aware of the trend of the national movement. We grasp the true meaning of the Japanese spirit and will protect all that is good and beautiful therein. . . . We believe that Christian thought and faith are the best that we can offer for the clarification of the foundation of the national movement and the precious glory of our Imperial Family.
>
> In 1939, the Religious Corporation law was finally passed by the Diet. Under this legislation, the Ministry of Education was given control of the establishment (and disestablishment) of all religious groups, as well as the certification, appointment, and general oversight of religious leaders. Christians finally acquiesced in this law, hoping that by securing state recognition they would finally escape adverse public opinion. Under these conditions, the Kyodan was established in 1941 by a majority vote of denominational delegates. This made the Kyodan the illicit offspring of Protestant churches which had willingly offered themselves to the militarist regime.
>
> Even before this, Japanese Christians had actively been participating in their country's military adventures with gusto and naiveté. Some church publications urged believers to participate in the rites of State Shinto as a matter of etiquette and "plain common sense." Still, the worship of the Shinto gods and the emperor was a vexing question.

> While articles urging resistance did appear, the churches fell completely silent on the issue as Japan got more deeply involved in the war. A song called "The Greater East Asia Co-Prosperity Sphere" was added to hymnals. Church leaders declared that worshipers should bow in the direction of the imperial palace before services began. Pastors were encouraged to make pilgrimages to Ise and other Shinto shrines. Church officials visiting the Japanese colony of Korea encouraged native Christians to participate in Shinto rituals—a suggestion the Koreans fiercely rejected. In Manchuria, churches were built with the support of Mantetsu, the national railroad, in the hope that they would create a "better atmosphere" in the colony. Japanese Christians regarded such contributions as acts of Providence designed to promote patriotism, industry, and evangelism alike. The church responded to the Manchurian Incident with renewed calls for national unity, prayers for peace, and plans for conducting "special, emergency evangelism" in northern China and in Japan itself. With slogans like *dendō hōkoku* (serving the country through evangelism), the church expressed its naive faith that, somehow, the ritual of Protestant evangelism would make a significant contribution to the war effort. Money was collected by the church to purchase aircraft for the armed forces and, as in the Christian west, prayers were offered up for the victory and safety of the men serving their country. The few Holiness and Nazarene ministers who dared to oppose the emperor system were instructed by the Kyodan to repent and resign from their churches. The Kyodan also tried to dissolve their churches and expropriate their property. One Nazarene minister who had refused to worship the emperor was stripped of his ordination by the church.

Such were the events which, from the radical perspective, had prompted the church, in its Confession of War Responsibility, to "seek the mercy of our Lord and the forgiveness of our fellow men."[9] What is important for us is the *symbolic use* of this material in the controversy that erupted in 1969. It seems highly unlikely to me that repressed feelings of "war guilt" were, in any sense, a "cause" of the Kyodan's controversy. Although I cannot prove it, I strongly suspect that the "war guilt" of Japanese Christians was not the festering of a superego troubled by the sins of the past, but the brooding of an ego over the possibility of losing face in the present or future. If I am right in my assessment of the psychology behind the confession, the social function of the radicals' muckraking was not simply to bring the church to its knees in repentance, but to embarrass its conservative opposition. In other words, the purpose of this painful excavation of the past (which took place primarily after the Expo fracas broke out) was to prepare a moral indictment against the ecclesiastical establishment. Dohi and other radicals have used history to demonstrate the illegitimate birth of the Kyodan, its infantile nastiness during the war, its adolescent dependence on missionaries and foreign funds in the postwar period, and its adult corruption as seen in its collaboration with the Ampo Establishment at Expo 70. History, therefore, was made to bear witness to the total depravity of the church and its conservative leadership.

Behind it All

Since Japan is widely touted these days as a harmonious, consensual society, many will wonder how such a violent feud could ever have taken place, especially in a Christian church. Those more familiar with Japan and Christianity will realize, of course, that conflict is a stranger to neither one. But even they may want to ask why this squabble took place. This question has been asked by two very different groups. It is asked, first of all, by the interested parties themselves, usually out of anger, or out of a need to point the finger of blame at the other side. Such is not my purpose. The question is also asked by social scientists and historians in their search for the cause of events. Since legitimate doubt has been raised concerning the explanatory power of "cause" in historiography—doubts which should also arise in the sociology of religion—we must approach this problem with due caution and self-restraint. The Kyodan controversy is extremly complex. Its events, differently perceived by each faction, if not by each individual, are widely distributed in time and space. Behind each encounter and episode lie concealed, subtle, and long-standing networks of personal friendships, loyalties, and animosities which do not lend themselves well to research or scholarly publication. In the rest of this chapter, I shall therefore avoid any discussion of the "real causes" of the dispute and restrict myself to an analysis of its *enablements,* i. e., various factors which, brought into play in the same "time frame" facilitated the eruption and continuation of the struggle.[10] After disposing of (what I regard as) the minor enablements, I shall devote the remainder of this chapter to what I regard as the major ones: the historical impact of the university struggles of the late 1960s and 1970s and the structural influence of various incompatible political systems at work in the organization of the Kyodan.

First, let us look at some explanatory theories which do not seem to work. Many church members explain the church struggle in terms of an age or generation gap. This is not very convincing. After all, not every new generation tries to overthrow its church and university.

While most radicals were students aged eighteen to twenty two, older radicals and sympathizers could also be found. Furthermore, the radicals were not even a majority of their own generation. The vital factor was not age itself, but the specific historical experiences which this particular age cohort had had—a subject to which I shall soon return. Social class, too, was not a significant factor. The Kyodan is, in general, a middle-class church. No one on either side seemed to regard the struggle as one between haves and have-nots. Likewise, while each side claims a profounder theology, neither can objectively demonstrate that it has a monopoly on erudition. Each side has its professorial supporters; each has its intellectuals. And, it must be said, each has its aggresive and tactless hot-heads. While more churches with a fundamentalist or Holiness background may be affiliated with Rengo, the split in the church did not run along the lines of the denominations that originally joined the Kyodan merger. Nearly all of the "mainline" denominations had had their liberals and conservatives, their social action factions, and evangelical caucuses before the merger. By the time the Kyodan struggle began, a whole generation had been raised without any significant exposure to the old denominational identities. Some conservatives contend that most of the radicals are recent converts and that the nonradicals tend to come from Christian homes. But this charge seems to be a slur rather than objective insight. Simply being a first generation Christian does not dispose individuals to ecclesiastical radicalism.

While class is not a major factor, economic considerations have not been without their influence. Although evangelists working for a pittance in rural areas were deeply upset about the money spent on the pavilion, their churches, being smaller and more dependent, tended to stay out of the quarrel. The smaller churches simply could not afford to take sides. Thus, in many cases, economic considerations tended to *prevent* polarization. Many pastors were said to be afraid to affiliate with Rengo because they feared the radicals would gain control of the church and cut off their pensions. Young ordinands may have espoused a more conservative line in order to avoid charges of "Jesus-ism," something that could cost them their future livings. Economic prudence also encouraged young academic assistants in seminaries to keep a low profile during the controversy. On the other hand, the economic factor sometimes kept the pot of confrontation boiling. Because churches did not want to lose the financial support of liberals and radicals, no moves were made to excommunicate them. At TUTS, contributions from conservative or neutral congregations now more than make up for the funds the church withdrew from the seminary budget. This newly achieved economic independence enabled TUTS to resist the denomination's proposal that the seminary criticize itself for having called in the riot police. This, too, has prolonged the affair.

The University Struggle

Early in 1968 violent student riots broke out at Nihon and Tokyo Universities and spread quickly throughout the country. Whether private or national, religious or secular, Christian or Buddhist, Japanese universities were soon paralyzed by kangaroo-courts, mass confrontations between students and administrators, and outright criminal activity—including arson, murder, gang rapes (in classrooms), and the kidnapping of faculty members and their children. In response to the New Left uprisings on campuses in the west, a new, amorphous, nonsectarian student movement called Zenkyōtō (the Joint Struggle Committee) made its appearance in Japan. As a "postmodern" movement, Zenkyōtō attacked what it saw as "the restrictive structures of modern society: technological rationality, utility, uniformity, and goal-directedness. Complete emancipation from all restrictive ideologies and oraganizations was the final objective."[11] Opposed to all rational debate and hierarchical organization, the movement was deeply suspicious of all formal democratic procedures. On the more positive side, it advocated direct or participatory democracy and the cultivation of a sense of personal authenticity, independence, or selfhood (variously called *dokuritsu-shugi, jiritsu-shugi,* or *shutaisei).* It also called for spontaneous revolutionary activity and the criticism of internalized social evils (e. g., "the university within," or "Narita within").[12] It stressed that by profiteering in the Korean and Vietnam wars, Japan had once again become the victimizer *(kagaisha)* of Asia. This "victimizer-consciousness" *(kagaisha-ishiki)* was widely used to indict existing patterns of authority. At the same time, students saw their generation as the "victim" *(higaisha)* of the monopoly capitalism and fake democracy of the older, hypocritical generation.

In 1969, the National Diet passed the University Control Bill giving the Minister of Education authority to close any university that could not maintain law and order on its own campus. The law took effect on 19 August, and by November the number of campuses under siege had decreased by about three-fourths.[13] The student movement was not only attacked form the outside; it also tended to self-destruct. Violent fights (called *uchigeba*), often resulting in death and injury, erupted among the various revolutionary sects.[14] The utopian idealism of the student movement finally soured and turned into mock heroics, a studied fascination with death and destruction, and sheer anomie.[15]

All parties involved in the Kyodan struggle admit that the turmoil in the universities had a powerful impact on the church. While the squabble might well have taken place even without it, it is unlikely it would have taken the shape it did had not the universities already passed through similar ordeals. In other words, the university struggle provided the Kyodan radicals with a pattern or model of confrontation which enabled the struggle in the church to take place the way it did.

A brief review of the spatial and temporal relations of the two struggles makes their connection quite obvious. Church districts with the most serious problems were located in those parts of Japan where the major student rebellions had taken place—Tokyo, Osaka, Kyoto, and Hyogo prefecture. Many radical ministers had churches near the universities.[16] The timing of the church struggle is also significant: it reached its peak of violence (from the fall of 1969 through the spring of 1971) soon after the University Control Law had swept the radicals off the campuses. One pastor sympathetic to the radicals pointed out that many of the students who became leaders in the Kyodan struggle had been relatively passive in the university uprisings. Since the church was their own "turf"—and since by this time they had become experts in handling "hypocrites and reactionaries"—the Christian students felt that the controversy in the Kyodan was an opportunity to show their mettle and become leaders in their own right. Whether this pastor's "deprivation theory" is valid or not is hard to say. What is clear is that by this time these young people had suffered a series of deep moral frustrations. They had seen Japanese democracy renew the hated Security Treaty and offer their country's territory and services to the United States for use in its "unjust war" with North Vietnam. They had seen the same kind of "formal" or "fake" democracy at work in their own church which, only two years after confessing its complicity in the Pacific War, agreed once again to offer the state its services by participating in Expo 70. On all sides then—in politics, on the campuses, and in the church—they felt themselves surrounded by compromise and corruption. Like their non-Christian comrades in the university struggle, they longed for a life free from the evils of politics, money, war, repression, and rationality. They looked for, and in revolutionary praxis may momentarily have found, a life of Pure Activity. I will argue that Pure Activity—the religious experience of flowing, free, unfettered, spontaneous, innocent, or absolute action taught and practiced by Taoism, Zen and other Asian traditions—has deeply colored the Japanese understanding of revolution, praxis, and authenticity.[17]

Against this background, it is little wonder that the ideas, rhetoric, and slogans of the Kyodan radicals were nearly carbon copies of what they had heard on the campuses a few months earlier. "Destroy the university" *(daigaku kaitai)* became "destroy the church" *(kyōkai kaitai)*. Demands for "free" or "independent classes" *(jishu kōza)* turned into calls for "independent worship services" *(jishu reihai)*. Demands for "open meetings" *(kōkai kaigi)* and "mass negotiations" *(shūdan kōshō* or *taishū dankō)* were heard both on the campuses and in the pews. Both institutions were plagued by the problems of unelected representation *(baisekisha* or *daihyōsei)* and other basic questions about parliamentary order *(kaigisei)*. Student radicals taunted university officials saying that if they called in the police they would be proving once and for all the faculty's collusion with the state. The same gauntlet was thrown down before officials of the church and its seminaries. Calling in the police would be an open confession that the Kyodan was the product of the state and could be sustained only by its power.

Radicals in both struggles spoke the language of Chairman Mao. Radical ministers were called "opposition pastors" *(zōhan bokushi)* from the Maoist expression *zōhan yūri,* meaning "there is reason in opposition", or "oppositon has its own logic". The idea that "no positions should be excluded" in ministerial examinations was a reflection of the ideological openness of Zenkyōtō itself.[18] University and church officials alike were forced by students to prepare *sōkatsu,* position-papers (literally "syntheses" or "summaries"), usually of a self-incriminating sort. The revolutionary practice of self-criticism *(jiko-hihan* or *jiko-hitei)* seemed to have an "elective affinity" with the Christian teaching of repentance—at least the connection was made by the zōhan bokushi. Likewise, the students' emphasis on political autonomy (the *dokuritsu-shugi* of the Democratic Youth League) and the "standing-on-one's-on-feet-ism" (the *jiritsu-shugi* celebrated by the poet Yoshimoto Ryūmei and preached by Zenkyōtō) seemed to resonate, albeit at weird frequencies, with the Protestant stress on individual responsibility and selfhood.[19]

The problem of *shutaisei,* a philosophical term meaning "subjectness," autonomy, authenticity or independence, beset church and academe alike.[20] The term was claimed, and used, by both sides in the church struggle. Radicals like Professor Dohi claimed that because the church had been created by the state it had no shutaisei until it issued the Confession of War Responsibility. Church and university authorities who called in the police were merely shoring up the inauthentic, heteronomous foundations of their respective organizations. In the eyes of the radicals, the sanctification of parliamentary procedures by the conservatives also ran against the spirit of authenticity. "When the church which looks in faith to God and Christ gets bogged down by its own organization and rules, it loses its independence and raison d'être."[21] Radical students who invaded the executive committee's meeting on 1 September 1969, allegedly had as their aim making members of the committee "wrestle with this problem *in an authentic way (shutaiteki ni kono mondai ni torikumu)*."[22] The term *shutaisei* also crops up in the discussion about the reunion with the Okinawan church (February 1969), radicals and liberals worrying that the Okinawans, overwhelmed by union with the larger church, would lose their shutaisei.

Although shutaisei was used in Japanese intellectual circles with universalistic overtones, it was also used "to imply an opposite totalization of a *Japanese* ethos, in the form of something akin to national character."[23] Like Yoshimoto's "standing-on-your-own-feet"— described by the poet himself as the "nationalism of the common man"— shutaisei became a battle cry in the church against acquiescent or "heteronomous" relations with foreigners.[24] While the church, as a "foreign religion," could not push the idea of national autonomy too far, shutaisei did emerge as a key concept in discussions about the indigenization or de-westernization of the faith. Conservatives and radicals alike felt that using foreign funds for the support of Japanese church personnel was humiliating. But while conservatives were willing to accept such contributions for "pioneer projects," the radicals called for still greater self-reliance—in the name of shutaisei.[25] As early as 1961 similar concerns had prompted some church leaders to oppose the World Vision evangelistic campaign as a "foreign mission" to Japan that compromised the independence and integrity of *Japanese* evangelism. Although the Kyodan had failed to take a decisive stand against the renewal of the Security Treaty in 1960, opposition to this campaign may have been, in part, a reflection of the anti-Americanism still in the air. In the controversy over the Christian Pavilion, the concept of shutaisei was, again, used by both sides. While radicals held that the pavilion was a surrender of the Kyodan's shutaisei to the state, conservatives like Kitamori Kazoh complained that the radicals' secular humanism was a de facto denial of God's own shutaisei![26]

Political Paradigms

Had a controversy of this magnitude taken place in America, the church probably would have quickly split, and the heretics (i. e., the losing side) would have been banished to the backwoods of Rhode Island or the salt flats of Utah. But it took place in Japan and therefore reflects the social and political structures of that country. Unlike scandals in other contemporary Japanese religions, the problem in the Kyodan happily did not involve the misuse of money, real estate, or women. When paper pellets, teacups, and chairs were not flying through the air, the Kyodan fight was carried on at a rather high theological altitude. This too sets it apart from other "typically Japanese" squabbles. What then was Japanese about it?

The Kyodan controversy may have been touched off by such issues as the Christian Pavilion, but ultimately it was not a struggle about those issues. Had it been a disagreement over issues, it could have been settled without such turmoil. Basically, it was a political problem—not merely in the sense of who should make decisions, but *how* they should be made. Each side, in effect, had absolutized and sanctified its own mode of decision-making. Each therefore felt the other had trampled on its absolutes and desecrated what it believed was holy. If my analysis of the situation is correct, the religious issues can be seen virtually as catalysts which "enabled" long simmering tensions between *contradictory political systems* within the Kyodan to come to the surface and erupt.

To put these political systems in comparative perspective, I would like to step back and take a look at a similar problem in a Japanese village. Robert J. Smith describes a nasty affair that took place over the construction of a chicken-processing plant in Kurusu, an agricultural community. While the problems of Kurusu and the Kyodan may seem unrelated at first sight—church members may accuse me of levity in comparing them at all—we shall see that the extraordinary events touched off by the proposed chicken plant and the Christian Pavilion actually have much in common, and, I venture to add, much to teach us about Japanese "politics."

In 1973, the "Clover company" (a fictitious name invented by Smith), a subsidiary of a larger corporation, made an offer to set up a broiler-processing plant in Kurusu. At a meeting of the hamlet asssociation, the company's bid was discussed and four representatives were appointed to pursue the matter in greater detail. Before long, an agreement was struck and papers were signed for the construction of the new plant. Unexpectedly, a group of families became quite upset at this and demanded the contract be nullified at once. They claimed that since the village representatives were only supposed to investigate the offer, they had overstepped their charge by going ahead and concluding an agreement with the company. The representatives, however, stoutly maintained that they had done nothing but carry out the mandate given to them by the village government. This led to a long, bitter controversy which was even covered by mass-media newspapers and TV stations.

"Charge and countercharge were hurled; some people had stopped speaking to others; playmates had been separated and forbidden to associate even at school; houses had been stoned and windows broken; denunciatory placards had been posted, and there was even a public demonstration against the project."[27] Unlike the Christian Pavilion, however, the furor in Kurusu resulted in the cancellation of the contract with Clover and the chicken-processing plant was never built.

Smith hesitates—wisely I think—to say what really "caused" the to-do in Kurusu. The opposition stressed the environmental hazards of the proposed plant. Chickens, and later their feathers and entrails, would have been trucked right through the middle of the village. The effluent from the plant (including the chickens' blood) would have been poured into the river, and would finally have entered the community's irrigation system. Although the company was talking about a plant which would slaughter one thousand birds a day, some villagers feared the company would build a much larger plant, perhaps like the one built on the coast by the same company, processing forty thousand chickens a day.

Like the struggle in the Kyodan, the Kurusu controversy can be seen as a tug-of-war between traditional and modern politics. Perhaps it even included a bit of the "postmodern" politics discussed below. By traditional politics, I mean the politics of paternalism, consensus, and implicit understandings so typical of "old Japan." By modern politics, I mean the politics of formal rules and democratic procedures associated with the "new Japan." Unlike traditional politics, decision-making in modern political systems must be explicit. One senses that the trouble in Kurusu may have been set off by the failure of the protagonists to distinguish between these implicit and explicit procedures and entitlements. The determination of the matter at hand seemed to be rushed through the political system before everyone could have a say. Some people who had initially objected to the project complained that they had not been heard out. In fact, they failed to make their objections explicit. Consequently, no one went home from the original gathering of the hamlet association with a clear "sense of the meeting."

The young people in Kurusu added still another dimension to the problem: their opinions seemed *too* explicit. In effect, they were playing politics according to new rules. As one Kurusu resident put it, "I really don't know how the sides formed, but it seems to me that in the end the more vocal young people won because they are so clever with words—a lot more so than we were when we were young—and they say exactly what they think."[28] The problem with speaking one's mind is twofold: it causes some to lose face and, in consensual societies, it just is not the "done thing." In effect, the young people had abandoned the traditional politics of scripts—explained below—for a modern politics of explicit stands. This caused their elders (those who had concluded the agreement with Clover) to lose face—a problem that grew even worse when the story was broadcast by the mass media. As one villager put it, "Places like Kurusu are a bit like a stage where most of the action goes on with the curtain down."[29] This, at least, was the way things were supposed to happen in the past. When the curtain suddenly was raised, the actors were caught unawares. Their traditional scripts were ruined. After that the problem became, literally, *how* to act. What rules should be followed? How could the mess be resolved? The controversy actually came to an end without anyone confessing that he had been wrong or had gone too far. As Smith puts it, "Not one of these proud people had ever offered an apology to another for any action taken or word spoken in anger."[30] From that time, public meetings have been poorly attended "because everyone is wary of some unpleasant development."[31]

In short, the controversy in Kurusu seems to have erupted when the time-consuming consensus-building procedures of traditional politics were violated by the swift ("efficient"?) conclusion of a contract. People then began to say "what they really thought," causing deep embarrassment to those who (probably) had been acting according to the old implicit rules. After this, placards, broken windows, and insults began to disrupt the daily routine of the village. As in "old Japan," symbolic violence was the court of last resort for those who felt they had not been heard.

The controversy in Kurusu is a valuable example of the difficulty of combining the delicate etiquette of traditional politics with the formal rules, explicit stands, and delegation of authority one associates with modern (i.e. western-style) politics. But before analyzing the politics at work in the Kyodan's struggle, we must lay out, in a more general way, the basic political structures already touched on in the Kurusu case.

Broadly speaking, the Japanese have known four different political (i.e., decision-making and tension-managing) systems in their history.

Throughout their history, the Japanese have had considerable exposure to authoritarian and totalitarian rule. Kamishima Jirō calls this "hard rule."[32] During the war, the military government brought this style of politics to perfection. In the postwar period, the internal organization of the Japan Communist Party has shown a similar tendency. Although this politics has had a long history in Japan, it is hardly popular. Even during the war, Tōjō Hideki came in for heavy criticism when he began to mimic the histrionics of the European dictators. Although the question of political violence crops up repeatedly in the Kyodan controversy, totalitarianism fortunately has not been the real issue. We may therefore safely set it aside.

Secondly, the Japanese have known and practiced what I shall call "folk democracy." Closely allied to the sense of "folk justice" which developed in the traditional Japanese village, folk democracy is both particularistic and provincial. Like the traditional government of the village, it depends on voices, not votes. It aims at consensus, not majority rule. The public meeting itself, reduced to a recitation of prefabricated scripts, leaves little or no room for individual stands.[33] Since it evolved out of a society politically based on households and not individuals, responsibility for political decisions in a folk democracy is collective and diffuse. Consensus, in this system, is achieved not through rational, public debate—a practice that invites the loss of face—but through the informal persuasion that takes place primarily before formal meetings begin.[34] Since each major participant must be given a chance to speak, folk democracy is notoriously time consuming. Often a meeting, or even a series of meetings, will be called, not to solve a problem, but to mull it over and calm everyone's misapprehensions. Although folk democracy can be called "soft rule" it is generally dominated informally by the power structure of the community. Its consensual processes therefore work in tandem with the invisible authoritarianism of age, wealth, and rank. Succesful leaders, however, generally give the impression of reigning, not ruling.[35]

In a consensual political system of this sort, strong or persistent minority views pose a serious problem. As we have seen in Kurusu, a minority which feels itself unfairly treated may resort to some form of real or symbolic violence. Although the abstract notion of rights gained no recognition in traditional Japan, peasant rebellions and other violent disruptions of the community often helped to protect the powerless and restore the consensus-building process itself. Protestors in a folk democracy often have no alternative, constructive program of their own to offer. Their violence is justified, and *publicly condoned,* not because it clears the way for a better or more rational plan of action, but because it springs from a "pure heart." This widely shared understanding of symbolic violence in Japanese folk democracy suggests there may be a deep, unconscious relationship between the country's long history of peasant rebellions and political anarchy, on the one hand, and its religious tradition of Pure Activity, on the other.

The third political system found in Japan can be called formal democracy. A western import, formal democracy contrasts vividly with its *völkisch* predecessor. If folk democracy is a kind of government-byantechamber, formal democracy is government-by-chamber. Formal democracy depends on votes, and not merely on voices; on stands, and not on scripts. While folk democracy cultivates implicit understandings, formal democracy requires explicit positions. Responsibility in such a system is specific rather than diffuse. Majorities and minorities coexist on the basis of three fundamental principles: majority rule, the loyalty of the opposition, and a sense of fair play determined by abstract rules. If elected by a sizable majority, the leadership is empowered to assume an authoritarianism of office until its term expires. Modern or formal democracies restrain the political power of majorities by positing various a priori civil rights—an idea unknown to folk democracies. Finally, formal democracy rejuvenates (and /or perpetuates) itself not through violence but by periodic elections.

The system of formal democracy which I have just described is, of course, an ideal. Its actual practice, whether in village government, the church, the university, or the Diet itself, is quite a different story. At most crucial points, the Japanese practice of formal democracy is made possible by strategic compromises with the age-old customs of folk democracy. Votes are often heavily influenced by factions and gray officials. The stands an individual takes in public are carefully rehearsed in private with his patron or supporting clique. Sensitive issues will be talked over at dinner parties *(kondankai)* and other informal gatherings before they are taken up in public. Commonly, more time will be devoted to the presentation of reports (the modern equivalent of scripts) than to the discussion of individual stands. All of this takes time. Like the skillful village headman, the modern government, religious, or academic leader is careful to give the impression that he is merely presiding over meetings or mediating between conflicting parties. Thus the leadership style of Japanese democracy is basically "transcendental." In western eyes, Japanese leaders, even prime ministers, therefore seem to be weak, chronically ambiguous, or even devious. Leaders who do take a strong or clear-cut stand are routinely cut down for their "egocentric views" or "high-handed ways." The system itself therefore tends to generate a style of leadership that seems *structurally* weak. Truly strong and resourceful leaders can, of course, manipulate the system to their own advantage. Those determined to be *someone* can do so by cultivating a congenial humility before the masses, who are forced by tradition to give the appearance of wanting to be *no one*. The system will even tolerate a few charismatics, as long as they are hearty, humane chaps wise enough to refrain from "making waves." Like the leaders of the traditional village, the modern formal democrat must cooperate with the powers-that-be. The system breaks down only when a truly weak leader appears, i.e., a person who is unable to translate the ritual weakness of leadership into de facto power and action.

In spite of its election system, formal democracy generally allows powerful cliques to continue in office for decades. Little wonder, then, that student radicals in the late 1960s rejected the whole system as "fake democracy." The student movement itself introjected still another element—our fourth system—into this already complex array of political possibilities—one based on the notions of "participatory democracy" and "revolutionary autonomy" *(kakumei shutaisei)*. What they meant, or tried to mean, by participatory democracy was basically the same as the call for direct political action by the New Left in the west. In Japan, as in the west, the idea of participatory democracy entailed a deep distrust of formally constituted assemblies and duly elected officials. Democractic formalism was therefore regarded as just one more of the Establishment's tricks.

The idea of "revolutionary autonomy" is more interesting. At best, it challenged the formal democrats to take a serious look at the real meaning, and burdens, of political responsibility. At worst, it simply destroyed politics by reducing it to the chaos of the kangaroo-court, or the narcissism of revolutionary self-grooming. In the end, it made demands on the Japanese personality and social system that were as difficult to meet as the challenge of formal, western democracy had been in the early Meiji period. With their long tradition of "dependent collectivism,"[36] shutaisei was as mysterious to the Japanese as Protestant individualism itself.[37] It was therefore no accident that many students who cultivated a "postmodern" taste for revolutionary autonomy were later "recollectivized" by radical groups and sent out to destroy each other in the sectarian Armageddon of uchigeba.[38]

It was in this cauldron of political contradictions that the Kyodan struggle came to full boil. To members of the church, it seemed that the Kyodan had been polarized, and paralyzed, by two irreconcilable western political systems: the modified formal democracy of the Kyodan's government, on the one hand, and the participatory democracy of the radicals, on the other. At least the *theological* debate between the two sides suggests that this was their understanding of the situation. But this is not all there was to it. (As Peter Berger once remarked, "The first wisdom of sociology is this—things are not what they seem.")[39] What was universally overlooked was the similarity of the radicals and the conservatives due, in part, to the impact of folk democracy *on both sides*.

Neither side in the Kyodan struggle can claim a monopoly on good works or progressive policies. None of the conservative leaders I interviewed had ever voted for the ruling conservative party, the Liberal Democrats. Most seem to support the Socialists or the Social Democrats. Some radicals, on the other hand, are inclined to a cynical quietism and never bother to vote.[40] Some conservative congregations sponsor impressive social action and educational programs, while some radical pastors have nothing to show for their activism but a church-organized preschool run for their own financial gain. Among the conservatives are people who both supported the Confession of War Responsibility and opposed the Christian Pavilion. Both sides, influenced by the idealism of national autonomy (shutaisei), would like to see the Kyodan become less dependent on foreign aid.[41] As a result of this emphasis on autonomy, each side criticizes the compromises (and the subsequent loss of shutaisei) of the other. Both entertain vague ideas about de-westernizing the church. Both drained religious symbols of their mystery and deeper meaning, turning them into thin, unnourishing analogies for political action or ecclesiatical maneuvering. Both sides—and not just the radicals—could therefore be charged with "secularizing" the Gospel. Both have consciously assumed a "prophetic" stance vis à vis the other. The radical minister from Kansai whom I mentioned earlier says that he identifies himself with "the angry Christ" who drove the money changers from the temple. But conservatives also talk about "cleansing the temple," i.e., by getting rid of the radicals once and for all. One conservative leader in Osaka complains that, at every critical juncture, Kyodan leaders have blindly followed the line laid down by the New Left and the liberal (or quasi-Marxist) academic establishment. "I alone said no!" he boasts. Neither side believes that Christ's words about turning the other cheek were meant to be taken literally. If it is true, as conservatives sometimes allege, that non-Christian radicals were brought in to help disrupt church meetings, it would seem that *both* sides have been ready to avail themselves of forces outside the church.

When one adds up these similarities, one comes to the surprising conclusion that the protagonists have mistakenly been labeled radicals and conservatives. (In this chapter, I have employed these terms up to this point faute de mieux). In remarks that mix insight with bitterness, one so-called conservative observes that "at root the Kyodan problem is not a struggle between a "church faction" and a "society faction," or even between "conservatives" and "progressives." It is a vigorous conflict among progressives who are divided over whether or not physical force will be allowed to overturn democratic procedures.[42]

In many respects, the ecclesiology of the Kyodan conservatives was a sanctification of formal democracy. As members of Rengo like to put it, "the chairman of the church assembly, and the One who calls the meeting to order, is Jesus Christ himself." From this they conclude that any disturbance of the church's *kaigisei* is an act of disobedience against Christ. But the order that really developed in the church seemed to be one controlled by the "same old faces" year after year in an unholy succession going back to the unpurged wartime leadership. Radicals therefore tended to look upon the Kyodan's kaigisei with the same suspicion country rebels directed toward the ruling households and cliques in the villages. Are the leaders of the church truly responsible, informed, and concerned? Or are they merely those who have been "formally elected by the majority?" Had it not been by majority vote that the churches created the Kyodan in the first place, offering the denomination to the state as an ideological puppet? Were not the "democratic" procedures of the church the same ones the Diet use to ram through the renewal of the Security Treaty? Convinced that the rules of formal democracy were stacked against them, the radicals believed that symbolic deeds made more sense than rational debates. Christ cleansing the temple would henceforth be their model of political action. Like the dramatic acts of the biblical prophets, their revolutionary praxis would stop the majority in its tracks.[43]

Or so they thought. As it turned out, political traditionalism had a dampening effect on the ambitions of both sides. In Japan, where people prefer to "cover up things that stink" *(kusai mono ni futa o suru)*, as the saying goes, a truly free, public discussion of problems generally does not come about easily.[44] Both sides in the Kyodan's struggle showed great hesitation to enter into open conversations with the opposite party. Radical students feared that by participating in a rational dialogue they would be forced to compromise their life of Pure Activity and lose their shutaisei. Conservatives were equally reluctant to talk with the radicals. Dialogue seemed only to reward their violence. Many conservatives therefore came to regard the "way of dialogue" *(taiwa rosen)* as the spineless leadership's "way of making deals" *(torihiki rosen)* with radicals behind everyone else's back. We have seen that because Japanese folk democracy is uneasy about open debate, discussions have to be carefully scripted, rehearsed, and staged. Since this takes time, any discussion that is "over and done with" quickly is suspect, almost by definition. From Kurusu's Clover affair, we have learned how costly a speedy decision can be. In the church, all sides complained that major decisions—especially the church union of 1941, the proclamation of war responsibility in 1967, and the decision to reunite with the Okinawan church in 1969—had been made with undue haste. As one minister put it, "since democracy takes time, we should not be in a hurry."

Except when it falls into strong hands, like Suzuki Masahisa's, the moderatorship of the Kyodan is prone to all of the structural weaknesses of folk democracy.[45] Moderator Ii, who presided over some of the stormiest meetings of the church, initially averred that he had no "perpective" of his own and therefore refused to say in what direction he intended to lead the church. Had he maintained this low profile—so common in folk democracies—he might have survived unscathed. Unfortunately, he seeemed to drift into a more "radical" definition of his role, claiming that the moderator should be "the leading pitcher of the team, not an umpire." In the end, he seemed fit for neither role. Although he seemed to favour the radicals, the radicals themselves found him an indecisive people-pleaser *(happō bijin)*. Conservatives considered his "way of dialogue" an appeasement policy and claimed that he was merely acting as the "robot of the radicals." What both sides failed to see was the unlikelihood that leadership *structured in this way* would ever be able, on its own, to restore a working consensus in the church.

How, then, did the struggle come to an end, when and where it did?

It would be naive, of course, to expect that the controversy would be resolved the way the New Testament says enmity should be overcome, i.e., through confession, repentance, and reconciliation. The dénouement of the Kyodan controversy can be understood only in terms of a social psychology based on lower expectations. As in Kurusu, no one apologized. The *odium theologicum* was finally overcome not in large, head-on debates, but in small, informal groups. People who seemed to get along quite well in small groups became hostile when the group became large enough to become formal. In Osaka, when the district assembly was finally reconvened after an interruption of ten years, the floor was opened for a discussion of the whole affair. *No one rose to speak*. In some districts, "deliberations" *(kyōgikai)* replaced formal meetings *(sōkai)*. This provided a more leisurely forum for smoothing out ruffled feathers. To give the radicals a hearing, new committees were established to work on the problems of "the church and social action." In some areas, district assemblies and subcommittees labored month after month on *sōkatsu* that would serve as a symbol of the restoration of Christian fellowship.

The effect of these compromises has been the imposition of a dual or two-tiered structure on the church—at both the national and district levels—a pattern that actually was already beginning to develop under Moderator Suzuki.[46] This consists of an upper stratum of ecclesiocrats and activists who control official church proclamations and policies, on the one hand, and a lower stratum made up of basically conservative or politically indifferent pastors and local congregations preoccupied with evangelism, the cure of souls, and the repair of the church roof, on the other. This was the dual structure that Ōki Hideo is pointing to when he criticizes the "lack of real linkage between the Kyodan's superstructure and the local churches."[47]

Time itself helped to heal the wounds of the church. Radical students graduated from the universities, got married, and started to raise families—events known to have a lethal effect on revolutionary zeal. Some radicals left the church. Many conservatives began to devote more of their time and energy to Rengo than to the Kyodan. Some older members died and put the worldly battles of the *ecclesia militans* behind them once and for all. But most church members simple remained indifferent—to the problems of the Kyodan and to the larger issues of faith and society. The moralism the Kyodan had inherited from both Confucianism and Protestantism discouraged most members from seriously considering problems that could not be solved by, or reduced to, personal piety.

Finally . . .

The Kyodan controversy is interesting, first of all, for the things it was not. It was not a struggle between rival denominations. By the time the controversy began, denominational identities had largely been forgotten. It was not a battle between fundamentalists and liberals. Both sides had been exposed to large doses of theological sophistication. It was not a confrontation between a church and a sect. Churchly and sectarian tendencies were at work on both sides. I have also argued that, in the end, it was not even a matter of issues or a contest between the rival demands of social action and evagelism.

Our study of the major historical and structural influences on the uprising in the Kyodan does not enable us to explain *why* it took placc. But it does help us understand what *enabled* it to take place the way it did. It also throws light on the question why it lasted so long. In the first place, as a voluntary association, the Kyodan holds a rather special place in Japanese society.

> The internal disagreements and struggles within the Kyodan during the era of reappraisals from 1968 mirrored the growing polarization within the larger society. The church as one of the few genuinely voluntary groups in Japanese society was therefore one of the few places where such conflicts could freely come out into the open. The bitter-

> ness of the disagreements could not be so freely expressed and acted upon in legislative forums, political parties, schools, trade unions, social welfare organizations, or businesses, for all of these organizations were responsible in one form or another to act under public authority. In a word, when members of these other groups became unruly, the leaders of these organizations had the right and the duty to call in the police to restore order. . . . This was why a denomination like the Kyodan could become polarized in both ideology and activity and stay that way long after universities, trade unions. and political parties had gone through the same period of chaos and return to something resembling business as usual.[48]

The church, of course, had no equivalent to the University Control Law which it could invoke against radicals. Unlike university students, no one "graduates" from the church. Since members can take their leave only by dying or by voluntarily dropping out, all were locked into the problem as long as they wanted to remain in the denomination. Both sides, for practical and theological reasons, abhored the idea of becoming still another Protestant sect and therefore refused to give ground to the opposition. The only way to win was to convert the whole Kyodan to one's own side.

Another reason for the continuation of the struggle was the tendency of the Japanese to avoid unpleasant, "sticky" situations. Here again church members resemble the villagers of Kurusu. Although schooled by folk democracy to accept symbolic violence passively, many refused to attend meetings where they might be confronted by extremists, challenged to take a public stand, or put in some other embarrassing position. It was only in the fall of 1990, that the Tokyo District Assembly was able to reconvene. The nineteen years of deadlock in the Tokyo area churches hamstrung the meetings of the national church, forcing it to postpone indefinately such major issues as the nature of ordination examinations.

In the final analysis, however, the reason the struggle lasted as long as it did was because it was not merely a disagreement over issues. As we have seen, it was a struggle between parliamentary and radical progressives—both deeply influenced by the etiquette and procedures of a premodern political tradition—over the right way to make decisions and manage disagreements. But ultimately, the Kyodan struggle was even more than this. It is an example of the fundamental sociological contradictions that arise whenever a church takes a stand on public or moral issues in a class-based, pluralist society. The problem here lies neither in the prophetic self-image of church leaders, nor in the democratic polyarchy of secular society, but in their combination. At the

Eleventh General Assembly of the Kyodan held in 1960, two basic questions were raised which still await decisive answers. The first was: when the church takes a stand on a political issue does it violate the civil rights of members who happen to disagree with that stand? In other words, does it preempt its members' own political autonomy? The second: does the executive committee have the authority to take such stands in the name of the church? In other words, "who speaks for the church?" These questions are an expression of the basic problem all churches face as inclusive, but heterogeneous, institutions in a pluralistic society run according to the game-rules of formal democracy.[49] After 1969, radical demands for a "participatory democracy" (which, in turn, threatened to drag the church into the quagmire of revolutionary *amonie*) transformed this political dilemma into a constitutional crisis. I have tried to show that what made this crisis a "typically Japanese" one was the pervasive influence of folk democracy on both sides. In the end, both "radicals" and "conservatives" were forced to decide what elements of the indigenous political tradition of Japan—the practice of time-comsuming consensus-building, symbolic violence (or "Pure Activity"), the implicit "rights" of the powerless, collective responsibility, and the invisible authoritarianism of status—should be incorporated into the government of the church.

PART III

The Dynamics of Social and Economic Change

CHAPTER 4

The Weber Thesis and the Economic Development of Japan

Visitors to Japan often return home deeply impressed by the sedulous discipline and drive of the Japanese people. So well does the psychology of the Japanese meet the demands of industrial society that one wonders whether some benevolent, Invisible Hand has not at last made the perfect match between economics and the human psyche. (Perhaps this was the same Hand that made the Japanese short, their homes cramped, and their cities crowded.) Industry is clearly omnipresent in Japan—perhaps even omnipotent. Whether the individual Japanese is arranging a wedding or a funeral, renting an apartment, or planning a vacation, the *kaisha* (firm) is always there. The Japanese seem to live not only in a "kaisha-economy" and a "kaisha-society," but also in a "kaisha-culture." The industry that engulfs their lives seems to be a "total institution," the likes of which westerners encounter only in prisons or mental institutions.

If our travelers had time to bone up on Japanese history before they took off, they would also be impressed by the congruence between the country's religious faiths and the kaisha-culture of the present. Zen Buddhism seems to sanctify the secular activities of everyday life, including industry. Shinto lends to that activity a feeling of national identity, optimism, and plain good luck. Confucianism encourages the kind of close social bonds one encounters on all sides. Had our travelers gone back as far as the seventh century in their research, they might have come upon the Seventeen Article Constitution, an archaic template of Japanese morality which we have already discussed. The document—which is actually a sermon to the bureaucracy and not a constitution at all—seems to foreshadow many of the practices and values of today's kaisha-culture: its stress on harmony, hierarchy, authority, and decorous or ritualistic behavior. It calls for social concensus: "Decisions on important matters should not be made by one person alone. They should be discussed with many." And it sanctifies social conformism: "Let us follow the multitude and act like them."[1]

Unfortunately, the professional student of Asian society cannot return home with the same confidence in his first impressions. Like more casual visitors, he sees many parallels between the modal personality of the Japanese, their values, and daily activities. He also senses that probably all of these things are, somehow or other, congruent with Japan's religious traditions. But do such parallels or patterns unlock the "mystery" of this Asian society? Do they really explain its awesome economic success? Or is the sociocultural *Gestalt* we perceive just one more thing we need to explain? Unlike the tourist, the academic is duty-bound to go home and turn his hunches and intuitions into *defensible hypotheses and/or paradigms.*

In this chapter, I would like to reconsider one of the most intractable problems in the sociology and history of religions: the role of religion, values, and culture in economic development. In the following pages, I describe two alternative (but not necessarily contradictory) ways of looking at religion and development: Max Weber's (which I characterize as a theory of "hurdles and motivations") and my own version of Karl Polanyi's theory of embedded and disembedded markets

MEN PUSHING A FESTIVAL PALANQUIN. Both in religious festivals and in business relations, the Japanese tradition encourages close, cooperative, hard work.

(explored here in terms of the extended metaphors of "barricades" and "assaults"). I discuss the difficulties entailed by the Weberian approach by examining the claim that Confucianism prevented the rise of capitalism in China but caused it to flourish in Japan. Then I turn to the Japanese folk tradition to see whether or not it gave birth to a genuine work ethic. Finally, I point out some of the social costs entailed by Japan's work ethic (or work ideology). In some concluding afterthoughts, I try to persuade myself (and the reader) that there is some merit in my approach and drop some hints as to how others might continue this research. After surveying the Weber thesis in general terms in this chapter, I shall continue my discussion of the problem in chapters 5 and 6 by focusing more specifically on Buddhism and a Buddhist commune.

Weber's Paradigm: Hurdles and Motivations

In his research on non-Western societies, Max Weber was interested primarily in demonstrating the uniqueness of the *Entwicklungsformen* of "the specific and peculiar rationalism of Western culture."[2] While he himself did not apply this term to whole societies, his work quite naturally raised a much broader set of issues that subsequent researchers and theorists would treat as "development" or "modernization."[3] Therefore, what I am about to call Weberian may, sensu stricto, better be labeled Weberesque.

Weber treated development—or what *we* call development—as though it were an extended obstacle course stretching between traditional and modern societies. He saw this course as one laid out between the authentic human nature of simple societies (the starting line) and the deformed human nature of modern, capitalist society (the finish). In this race, runners (i.e., developing nations) who succeed in surmounting all of the hurdles of the course are rewarded with the trophies of modern civilization—but are also cursed with its "rationality." Because he thought the asceticism of early capitalist society was unnatural and (from a human point of view) irrational, Weber was convinced that these hurdles could be overcome only if the runners were initially motivated by something equally irrational, i.e., by something that would stimulate them to give up, subdue, or deform their own human nature. Only an inhumane, irrational drive would suffice as the motivation for achieving this inhumane, irrational goal. One could therefore say that Weber's investigation into the origins of capitalism was a kind of *sociology of pain*. What interested him was the question, Why would *any* society want to cultivate a spirit of asceticism, i.e., the voluntary suffering that is "the exact opposite of the joy of living."[4] Not convinced that the material rewards at the end of the race were sufficient to get the race started, he looked for some other motivating power—for a "mighty enthusiasm,"[5] or some secret, horrible anxiety like the Puritan's concern for his soul's salvation—that would send society racing pell-mell up the *via dolorosa* of rational development. While this metaphor may be a bit melodramatic, one comes away from a careful reading of Weber wondering, with his heavy-handed critic, Herbert Marcuse, "Does he by any chance mean to say: And this you call 'reason'?"[6]

Weber viewed the process of development in terms of three sets of hurdles. The first set consists of the basic characteristics of the capitalist system itself: its rationality, asceticism (at least in early capitalism), continuity (in production and markets), and (formally) free labor markets. The second set of hurdles relates not to the economic system itself, but to its social environment. Developing nations must establish institutions that will enable their economies to function under (formally) peaceful conditions. They must replace patrimonialism and the kinship base of the economy with rational administrative organizations and legal institutions. They must separate places of business and residence, corporate and private property. Finally, Weber put before the developing nations a third set of hurdles, those of motivation or *Geist*. Developers must also achieve the spiritual ethos Weber associated with the origins of western capitalism: the duty to work in one's "calling" (the so-called work ethic), the rejection of magic, and the cultivation of an existential tension between the world as it is and the ethical demands of a transcendent deity.

In regard to the last set of hurdles, the comparativist will naturally wonder whether it is reasonable to put before non-western nations spiritual hurdles that come from a different race track, i.e., "the specific and peculiar" ethos of an entirely different civilization. In the author's introduction to *The Protestant Ethic and the Spirit of Capitalism,* Weber repeatedly states that what he is interested in is the fact that only in the West does one find cultural and economic phenomena "having *universal* significance and value."[7] He makes clear that he is not saying that Protestantism is the only religion that can produce a rational economy—a disclaimer he seems repeatedly to forget in his comparative studies.[8]

The rise of capitalism in various parts of the non-Protestant world after Weber's death—especially in East Asia—suggests that history has removed the third set of hurdles from the path of the developing nations. Or has it? Some have tried to salvage Weber's scheme by searching for, and allegedly finding, equivalents or analogues to the Protestant ethic in Japan, Korea, Singapore, Nigeria, and other rapidly developing parts of the world. They have argued, or assumed, that if non-Western nations are not going to surmount the west's own spiritual hurdles, they must at least clear spiritual ones similar to those already cleared by the west. Presumably, other religions and gods can provide motivations similar to the Puritans' *Angst* over election. Those who have taken this line—I shall call them "the Weberians," though this is merely my own "ideal-type"—continue to look at development more or less from Weber's own point of view. While most do not share Weber's own approach-avoidance complex toward the spirit and achievements of capitalism, they continue to look at development as a quasi-evolutionary process of hurdles and motivations. Like their great culture hero (and most of the intellectuals of the eighteenth and nineteenth centuries), many Weberians continue to believe that the rationalization of society necessarily entails the secularization of religion and the decline of magic. Again like Weber, they are concerned primarily about the *Geist* produced by society's elite "culture-bearers" and religious virtuosi. And finally, they seem to believe that because this *Geist* takes root in "the central value system" of society, it applies univocally, or at least mutatis mutandis, to investors, entrepreneurs, inventors, merchants, consumers, and workers alike.

What then was the "impact" of religion on economic development? This question, perhaps like all questions of ultimate historical causation, seems to defy ordinary proof in terms of verifiability or falsifiability. My own reaction to the Weber thesis can be summed up briefly in the following "six principles of moderate skepticism":

1. It is impossible to determine the truth-value of the claims that:
a. religion has had *no* impact on development.
b. religion has had an impact of *a certain given magnitude*.

2. Given what we know about the overall strength of the social and economic variables involved, it is *unlikely* that religion has always been *a necessary or crucial factor* in development.

3. The difficulty of separating ex post facto legimitations of economic success from the actual motives lying behind rational economic behavior often makes the historical study of religion's putative ex ante role in economic life a thankless task. (In their memoirs, successful tycoons like to attribute their wealth to their own virtue and piety. But is this really how or why they became rich?)

4. Since religion sometimes provides clues for understanding the contours (if not always the causes) of development, the study of the role of religion in development *may* be of considerable importance.

5. Those who would investigate this problem should look at three questions:

a. How has religion motivated economic change?
b. How has religion failed to obstruct change?
c. How has religion promoted a quiescent acceptance of the social costs imposed by development?

In my later discussion, I shall refer to 5a. as the question of religion's "positive enablement" of development. This is the question that interests Weber and the Weberians most. Unfortunately, this is not all there is to the problem of religion and modernization. A complete accounting would also include issues raised by questions 5b. and 5c., questions that deal with religion's "passive enablement" of economic change.

6. It is possible that religions that inculcate a this-worldly asceticism have had *some* impact on development. Perhaps this "Weberian minimalism" can be put more realistically by translating it into negative terms: insofar as strict morality and zealousness in one's "calling" would be boons to any economy, it is unlikely that this-worldly ascetic religions—assuming they neither encourage hoarding nor discourage investing—do development any harm.

It seems to me that Weberian studies are least convincing when they focus their attention exclusively on question 5a., and when they assume a priori that religion is the source of some "central value system," which, in turn, directly influences all segments of society with an equal force, or in the same way. Exclusive emphasis on "value systems" is, of course, un-Weberian. In his comparative studies, Weber was deeply interested in the material factors of production, if only so that he could argue, counterfactually, that had the right *Geist* been present, such-and-such a country could have developed a "rational economy." Nevertheless, his stress on *Geist* often led him to underestimate the contradictions in "the central value system" and the *multiplicity of motivations* called for by market societies. Rather than one *Geist,* I see the possible emergence of several different "spirits" in the rise of capitalism. First, buyers and vendors must cultivate the spirit of "creditworthiness" in order to reduce the "cost of information" concerning their own reliability.[9] Second, entrepreneurs stand in need of a *Geist* that will promote risk taking. Third, investors need a spirit that will inspire delayed gratification. Fourth, management needs a disciplinary

Geist to impose on workers, i.e., a work ideology. Finally, while workers require no special *Geist* to inspire their involuntary suffering, by adhering to the *Geist* of management they are sometimes able to work their way up in the world. In some cases they may even develop a work-ethic separate from the work-ideology of management.

Another general problem with Weber's approach is his treatment of secularization. If modern society is composed of different "spirits," we need not assume that each one will be secularized in the same way. In fact, some "spirits" may not be secularized at all. Now and then, some may even undergo "resanctification"—e.g., the Moral Majority's recent legitimation of the spirit of the American booboisie (if I may use Mencken's apt expression). Secularization entails two very different concepts: *Entgötterung* (the decline of religion) and *die Entzauberung der Welt* (the removal of magic from the world). Weber's general scheme of secularization can be logically reduced to a minimal pattern consisting of three historical (or quasi-evolutionary) moments:

1. Society turns its attention from other-worldly religious pursuits to activities in this world and invests this world with new positive significance. It then begins to explore the world with magic, reason, and common sense.

2. Society frees itself from the archaic "garden of magic" and desanctifies the world so that it can manipulate it in a matter-of-fact way. This transformation is most radical, its results most dramatic, when it takes place as a response to a transcendental ethical imperative (e.g., in response to the "ethical prophecy" of the Bible or its revival in ascetic Protestantism).

3. Finally, as a result of the growing wealth and hedonism of successful development, religion itself begins to decline. The work ethic loses its religious foundation; this-worldly motivations, rewards, and constraints take the place of the "mighty enthusiasm" that formerly drove people to work in their callings.

Here, the first moment roughly corresponds to Weber's concept of this-worldliness; the second, to intellectualization, rationalization, and the decline of magic and magical religions; the third step is equivalent to the "routinization" of the work ethic and the decline of religious zeal in general. Once we reach the third moment of secularization, we encounter one of the primary "cultural contradictions of capitalism." At this point society seems to encounter one of the "perennial gales of creative destruction" that Schumpeter attributed to capitalism itself.[10] The new economy creates, in effect, "a critical frame of mind which, after having destroyed the moral authority of so many other institutions, in the end turns against its own."[11]

The problem with this view of secularization is twofold. First, although "Weber clearly stated that disenchantment is only a growing *possibility* in modern society, he also regarded it as part of the *fate* of Western civilization."[12] Curiously enough, he never seems to have seen the contradiction between this dogmatic view of secularization as fate and his condescending recognition that "the masses in need are *always* out for emergency aid through magic and saviors . . . "[13] Perhaps it was the logical architecture of his own thought that led him to the conclusion that secularization is the fate of modern society. That is, since rationalization has power *(Macht)* and domination *(Herrschaft)* at its disposal—rather than vice versa, as in Marx—its power to remove the hurdles of magic and traditional religion is a foregone conclusion. Ultimately, a rational society *must* cast out its gods, ghosts, priests, and shamans.

Weber seems to stress the fateful character of secularization for still another reason. He not only believed that the secularization of the world was a necessary precondition for, and by-product of, the rationalization of society. He also believed that there was an irreconcilable contradiction between the traditional teachings of religion and the competitive spirit of the market:

> The market community as such is the most impersonal relationship of practical life into which humans can enter with one another. . . . Where the market is allowed to follow its own autonomous tendencies, its participants do not look toward the persons of each other but only toward the commodity; there are no obligations of brotherliness or reverence, and none of those spontaneous human relations that are sustained by personal unions. . . . The "free" market . . . is an abomination to every system of fraternal ethics.[14]

Clearly, then, society must disabuse itself of its traditional religious morality before it can develop a rational economy. Again, the conclusion seems to follow: once development begins, the decline of religion and magic is inevitable.

Against this view, I would argue that the introjection of the romantic notion of fate into social science is a dangerous business.[15] I have also argued, on empirical grounds, that the "secularization process" does not always take place the way Weber says it should. Japan, at least, does not seem to fit the Weberian model of secularization.[16] Keith Thomas has demonstrated in magnificent detail that in the seventeenth century the English did rid themselves of magic, even before scientific cures for their ills and anxieties were available.[17] From this he concludes, with Weber, that "it was the abandonment of magic which made possible the upsurge of technology, not the other way round."[18] But should we treat this finding as a necessary condition for modernization everywhere? Since we shall deal with this question at greater length in chapter 7, we can put it aside for the time being. Suffice it to say that in the long run, more important than the "decline" of religion and magic are their internal transformation and pragmatic accommodation with the "spirits" of capitalism, science, and technology.

Hurdles or Barricades?

The obstacles in the way of development can simply be knocked over and dragged off the race course. This is the way the Kemalists took care of Islamic law *(shari'ah)* in Turkey and the way the Puritans disposed of Catholic magic. This is also the way Stalinists and Maoists have dealt with religion in general. This model of secularization looks at religion primarily from the point of view of aggressive modernizers and developers. But this is not the only way to look at the situation. One can also approach it from the standpoint of traditional societies seeking to protect themselves from the disruptive advance of economic values that are "an abomination to every system of fraternal ethics." What these societies fear is not progress but the social turbulence and moral turpitude caused by unrestrained trade and commerce. Because of their nearly static economies, many traditional societies look upon growth (or rather, *profit*) as though it were a zero-sum game. St. Jerome put it nicely: "It is not without reason that the Gospel calls the riches of this earth 'unjust riches,' for they have no other source than the injustice of men, *and no one can possess them except by the loss and the ruin of others*."[19]

As an alternative to Weber's hurdles cum motivations (which looks at modernization from the developers' point of view), let us look at the relationships between the economy, religion, and society from the point of view of "traditionalism." One could describe the situation from this vantage point by drawing three concentric rings: an inner ring representing the economy and its values (e.g., achievement and universalism); an outer ring—for society, its existing values, status, and power relations; finally, between these two, a middle ring standing for the "immunological barrier" that traditional societies erect against the economy, or rather against the pestilence they intuitively sense would be released by an unrestricted market (see figure 3). Within this barrier we must place taboos, magic, traditional religion, morality, law, philosophy, and folk values in general.[20]

Our new model, or paradigm, can incorporate Weber's notion of traditionalism by treating its various elements (e.g., kinship, patrimonialism, substantive justice, religion, and magic) as *defensive* institutions protecting society (A) from the market (C). Polanyi describes the defensive role of religion, and the "embeddedness" of economies in traditional society, in this way:

> Obscure as the beginnings of local markets are, this much can be asserted: that from the start this institution was surrounded by a number of safeguards designed to protect the prevailing economic organization of society from interference on the part of market practices. The peace of the market was secured at the price of rituals and ceremonies which restricted its scope while ensuring its ability to function within the given narrow limits.[21]

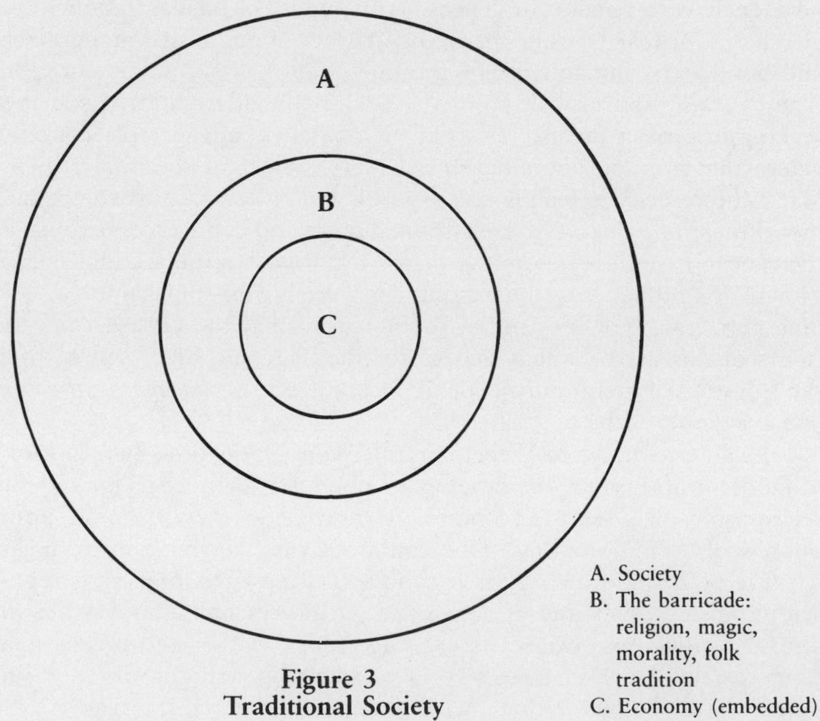

Figure 3
Traditional Society

A. Society
B. The barricade: religion, magic, morality, folk tradition
C. Economy (embedded)

From the point of view of our barricades paradigm, economic development takes place not just when an "enemy" (i.e., a modernizer or developer) scales the ramparts and invades the citadel of society, but when the barriers themselves grow old and weak, and finally begin to crumble, or when their defenders lose heart and surrender. Figure 4 represents the relationship between development and secularization from this point of view. Here, the porousness of the religious barricades (represented by a dotted line) has allowed the economy and its values to expand and penetrate the domain of society itself. It could be said, I think, that European society was already reaching this stage when, in 1651, a philosopher as eminent as Thomas Hobbes could say that the value or worth of a man is his *price*.

Without denying that secularization sometimes may proceed along the lines suggested by Weber and the Weberians (though not compelled to do so by "fate"), our new paradigm seems to encourage us to look at secularization from a different perspective—from *behind* the ramparts,

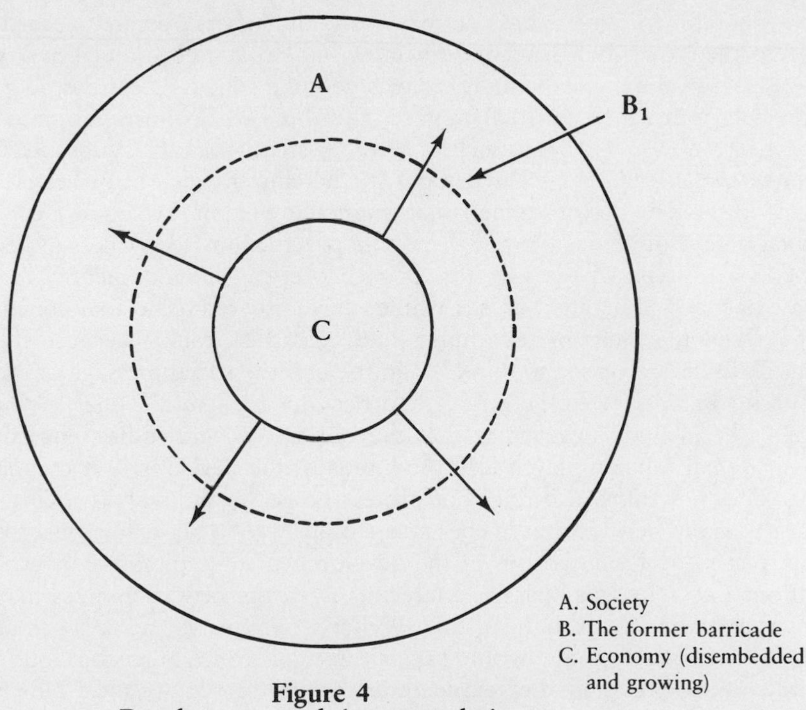

Figure 4
Development and Accommodation

i.e., from the point of view of traditional religion and society. It bids us pay greater heed to the ways in which the old defenses against the forces of Mammon grow weak, allowing society itself to be filled with that *amor sceleratus habendi* against which the preachers of old so ardently inveighed. Secularization of this sort—i.e., an internal secularization involving the complete "transvaluation of all values"—has been brilliantly discussed by Karl Marx, R. H. Tawney, Georg Simmel, and many others.

This viewpoint also helps to correct what would otherwise be a very one-sided interpretation of the role of religion in the development of European society. A rational economy came into being not only because "hot Protestants" filled the market with the "zeal of the Lord," but because lukewarm Christians offered so little resistance to exploitation. In England, as nearly everywhere, development spelled misery for those unfortunate enough to be caught in the "iron cages" of the developers and exploited by enclosures, engrossing, rack rents, poorhouses, or sweatshops. In the face of these moral outrages, the church had virtually nothing to say. "The old medieval doctrines were quietly dropped and Churchmen came to assume that economic affairs operated according to their own independent principles, and that riches and poverty were part of the divine plan. There was genuine solicitude for the poor, particularly for their spiritual welfare, and there was condemnation for some of the more extreme cruelties of the system—*but the system itself was unchallenged*."[22] As Tawney put it, the church was out of her element in the new age of "impersonal finance, worldmarkets, and a capitalist organization of industry. . . . " The practical ineffectiveness of her doctrines "prepared the way for their theoretical abandonment. They were abandoned because, on the whole, they deserved to be abandoned. The social teachings of the church had ceased to count, because the church itself had ceased to think."[23] In the end the social message of the church "was neglected, because it had become negligible."[24] The point not to be missed, however, is that the obtuseness and indifference of institutional religion played into the hands of the developers. A church that does not think also does not protest or get in the way. If it turns out (as many believe) that Weber was simply wrong about the positive role played by Protestantism in the development of capitalism, investigations into religion's "passive enablement" of the new economies may prove to be of greater moment than Weber's fixation on the activism of his Puritan saints. This, I would say, is the significance of Liston Pope's study of religion and the textile industry in Gaston County, North Carolina.[25] Later, I shall argue that religion played a similar collaborative role in the development of modern Japan.

Confucianism and Development

We turn now to the development of East Asia. Two books—one by Roy Hofheinz, Jr. and Kent E. Calder, the other by the Japanese economist, Morishima Michio—have recently appeared arguing that Confucianism played a major role in the development of this area. Hofheinz and Calder, in *The Eastasia Edge,* have pointed out the remarkable difference in real per capita growth between the "post-Confucian" states of East Asia and the Hindu, Buddhist, and Islamic states of South and Southeast Asia. In addition to statist and corporatist factors, the authors discern behind the region's success the impact of Confucian values and discipline. "Loyalty lies at the heart of what we call the 'Eastasia Edge'."[26] Throughout "Eastasia" one encounters nationalism, an emphasis on education (even in premodern times), single-party rule (de facto in Japan since 1955), mutual aid rather than public welfare (even in the People's Republic of China), respect for government and bureaucracy, and a "tradition of agriculturally-based family and lineage organization within centralized state systems."[27] Behind all of this stands the nonlegal moralism of Confucianism itself.[28] "Confucian benevolence" accounts for the weak labor unions and even the high rate of personal savings in the whole region: "Confucian philosophy, with its stress on proper behavior and respect for one's position in life, hailed prudence and frugality, demanded sacrifice for future enjoyment, and condemned parents who failed to provide for their offspring."[29] Although the authors credit Confucianism with so much of the success of East Asia, they make no attempt to account for the different rates of development *within* the "post-Confucian" region in terms of religion (see Figure 5).

Michio Morishima, however, rushes in where Hofheinz and Calder fear to tread. The difference between Japan's success and China's slow development can be attributed to the different kind of Confucianism that developed in Japan; a Confucianism that replaced the benevolence, humanism, individualism, and literary interests of the Chinese bureaucracy with the loyalty, nationalism, social collectivism, and technological interests of the Japanese samurai. Furthermore, because of the influence of the samurai on Confucianism, the Japanese rejected the west's liberalism, internationalism, and individualism when they imported its science, industry, and technology. Morishima concludes that "*Because of its ideology* [i.e., Confucianism] Japan's economy is very different from the free enterprise system of the West."[30]

Confucianism also explains the dual structure of Japan's modern economy, i.e., the split between its large industries with their systems of

Figure 5

How Eastasia Outpaces Its Neighbors
Real per Capita Growth in Asia, 1960–78

Eastasia	*Real Per Capita Growth Rate (%)*
Republic of Korea	9.9
Hong Kong	9.0
Republic of China	6.2
Singapore	6.0
Japan	6.0
Democratic People's Republic of Korea	5.4
China	4.9
Other Asia	
Pakistan	4.8
Thailand	4.1
Malaysia	3.4
Sri Lanka	3.4
Indonesia	3.1
Philippines	2.9
India	1.5
Vietnam	0.6
Nepal	0.5
Laos	0.4
Burma	–0.1
Kampuchea	–0.8

Hofheinz and Calder 1982, p. 6, citing Donald Wise, ed., *Asia Yearbook 1980* (Hong Kong: Far Eastern Economic Review, 1980) p. 10.

permanent employment and seniority advancement, on the one hand, and the small to middle-size companies in which employment depends on a free market in labor, on the other. Morishima maintains that the ex-samurai who founded and originally managed the larger firms imparted to industry their own Confucian sense of loyalty. For this reason, large-scale industry in Japan today depends on "loyalty markets" for its recruitment (i.e., on employees who "loyally" surrender mobility for the security of a permanent position). But the spirit of the smaller firms, founded and manned (or womaned) by people originating among the three lower classes of Tokugawa society (peasants, artisans, and merchants), is based not only on loyalty but on pure profit maximization (or "materialism," as Morishima puts it). Recruitment in these firms takes place in what he calls "mercenary" labor markets, i.e., free labor markets that guarantee no one employment and in which no one makes long-term commitments to his company.

Morishima concludes his book with a self-conscious attempt to update Weber by explaining the basic differences in the development of Europe, China, and Japan in religious terms. He first divides religion into three social or political types. Type 1 legitimates the status quo and is therefore the religion of the ruling classes. Type 2 is a religion for the ruled, i.e., for the individual subjects (or citizens) of a country. As a religion "for individuals," such a faith, in its more rational forms, is sometimes highly critical of the status quo. It may even legitimate a new political order in which those who are now ruled become rulers. Type 3 religions are also religions "for the individual." Compared with the second type, however, religions of this sort are less rational and more mystical, inclining the believer to a life of reclusion and passivity. Morishima associates the first type with Confucianism and Imperial Shinto, the second with Puritanism, and the third with Taoism or Shinto. These types are summarized in figure 6.

Morishima seems to be arguing (more strongly than Weber) that it is primarily a country's ideology, culture, or religion that determines its social, political, and economic organization. For him, ethos is not merely a necessary condition of development; it is its primum mobile. Such, at least, is the explanation he gives for the differences between 1. Japan and China, 2. Japan and the West, and 3. larger and smaller industry in Japan.

Figure 6

Summary of Morishima's Position

Type	*Function*	*Class Involved*	*Historical Example*
1	Legitimation of status quo	The ruling elite	Confucianism and Imperial Shinto
2	"For the Individual" and critical of status quo	The ruled	Puritanism
3	"For the individual" but passive and apolitical	The ruled	Taoism and Folk Shinto

Morishima goes on to make other bold comparisons. In the west, religion itself gave rise to the Puritans' rational spirit (as well as to internationalism, liberalism, and individualism). Lacking any rational religious tradition (i.e., Type 2 religion), the Chinese had to import their "rationality" artificially from the west, i.e., in Marxism.[31] Like China, Japan had virtually no Type 2 religions. Type 1 religion, the Confucianism of the samurai (and the Shinto of the imperial household), supported the status quo. Type 3, the Shinto of the common folk, inclined the Japanese masses to an ethos of passive obedience. In the end, the masses were saved from a life of passivity by their own biological (?) or ethnic (?) atheism: "The Japanese, though ethical, is non-religious *by nature*." Since "most contemporary Japanese are atheistic and irreligious," they are basically "materialistic."[32] This materialism of the masses, combined with the nationalism of the ruling class, makes for a potent, and potentially suicidal, cultural mix.

Morishima's book is difficult to evaluate since it is written in the genre of Japan theory. A sublimated form of nationalism, Japan theory tends to exaggerate the role of culture in order to account for Japan's essence—and success. Nevertheless, of all of Japan's religious traditions, one would think that Confucianism would be the most likely to inspire this-worldly, rational, economic activity. Even the Sino-Japanese word "economics" *(keizai)* comes from a Confucian expression—*keikoku saimin,* i.e., "rule the country and help the people." Joseph J. Spengler maintains that "Confucianism introduced and sustained a spirit of laissez faire in Chinese social thought."[33] To prove his point, he quotes the Confucian historian Ch'ien Ssu-ma (145–c. 90 B.C.E.).

> Each man has only to be left to utilize his own abilities and exert his strength to obtain what he wishes. Thus, when a commodity is very cheap, it invites a rise in price; when it is very expensive, it invites a reduction. When each person works away at his own occupation and delights in his own business then, like water flowing downward, goods will naturally flow forth ceaselessly day and night without having been summoned, and the people will produce commodities without having been asked. Does this not tally with reason? Is it not a natural result?[34]

Whether this was laissez-faire economics in the modern sense, however, is dubious. Considering its historical provenance, it might better be thought of as a recipe for a primitive or feudalistic kind of physiocracy. Confucius himself seems to have been opposed to competition for profit. The "economics" of *The Great Learning* aims not at growth but simply at having enough to live on: "There is a great principle for the production of wealth. If there are many producers and few consumers, and if people who produce wealth do so quickly and those who spend it do so slowly, then wealth will always be sufficient."[35] To have turned this truism into an economics of development would have taxed even Japanese ingenuity.

There are many points that could be raised against Morishima's thesis. Like other Japan theories, it fails to deal with horizontal social relations, the role of individual self-interest, competition, disloyalty, and conflict. On the basis of Morishima's loyalty theory, how would one account for the rejection of "administrative guidance" by some Japanese industries, or the difficulty Japanese groups have in arriving at a "consensus" on so many issues? If ethos counts for so much, how much weight should we put on the contributions of the banking system, tariffs, government and industry planning, wages and bonuses—factors that other authorities believe have been so important in the development of Japan? As I implied in the second of my "six principles of moderate skepticism," I find utterly incredible explanations of development that stress (as Morishima does) culture or ethos at the expense of such concrete factors.

Morishima's main argument about the Confucian influence on Japan assumes that the Japanese revalorized the Confucian virtue of loyalty. In China, loyalty had meant faithfulness to one's own conscience. In Japan it came to mean an unswerving devotion to one's lord, boss, or company. It seems to me, however, that even the samurai could not survive on a diet of absolute idealism. On the contrary, they lived in a world in which duties and obligations rested upon reciprocal exchange relationships. Thus, even in the Tokugawa period, pure (i.e., unstimulated and unrewarded) loyalty must have been a rare virtue indeed. Loyalty was always situated in a network of incentives, rewards, and constraints. The values of the samurai, like those of the lower classes, were based on an ethos of "hierarchical complementarity"[36] in which service was exchanged for patronage. This was an important aspect of Confucianism from the very beginning. As one of Confucius's disciples put it: "Our Master's teaching is simply this: loyalty *and reciprocity*."[37] Here, Morishima's culture-based theory of Japan's success gets him into trouble. If the loyalty of large-scale kaisha workers today is rewarded with high wages (and it is), is it not possible to argue that loyalty can be created, or even bought in the same way? Morishima is being far too idealistic (and condescending) when he explains Japan's dual economy in terms of the impact of Confucian loyalty on the upper strata of industry and the influence of "materialism" on the lower ones. When we look at loyalty as an exchange relationship, his distinction between "loyalty" labor markets and "mercenary" ones—at least as an absolute, cultural distinction—seems to break down. Furthermore, if loyalty and permanent employment were simply parts of industry's cultural inheritance, why were they not present when Japanese industries were first created? And finally, if loyalty was a Japanese absolute, how does one explain the change of masters that occurred so dramatically in 1868 and 1945—and, indeed, throughout Japanese history?

From the standpoint of the history of scholarship, the most surprising thing about Morishima's thesis is its obvious clash with Max Weber's own opinions—not that Weber is the final authority on the development of East Asia! Weber, after all, had dogmatically proclaimed that "a people among whom a stratum of the character of the samurai played the decisive role could not attain a rational economic ethic of their own . . . "[38]—words that, in retrospect, look both pompous and silly.

As for China, Weber was convinced that "from a purely economic point of view, a genuine bourgeois, industrial capitalism *might have* developed. . . . "[39] What ultimately prevented development was the failure of the Chinese to create the right kind of *Geist.* Although the Chinese were legendary for their capacity for labor, work discipline in the impersonal, capitalist sense was beyond them.[40] Individuals were protected from exploitation and economic disaster by their families, i.e., by groups whose primary identity was established by the rites of ancestor worship. Because it was thought that the kinship group (Weber: sib) had received its land from sacred ancestors, land could not easily be sold—a fact that put severe restrictions on the development of commercial agriculture (which presupposes the ready alienation or "commodification" of land). Weber therefore seems to be arguing that the failure of the Chinese to develop free markets in labor and land was directly or indirectly the result of the worship of ancestral spirits by the sib. Furthermore, because the rural sib was regarded as the individual's true home, a genuine urban spirit did not develop in the cities. Since Chinese cities were merely outposts of the central government, they afforded no free space in which social experiments or economic innovation could take place. Like the countryside, the city was forever under the watchful and suspicious eye of a patrimonial state that was always ready to interfere in the economy—either for its own gain or in the name of "substantive justice" (i.e., distributive justice in the classical sense). For this reason, the social and economic organizations that did develop (e.g., guilds, communal workshops, and clubs) were organized defensively—as "barricades," I would say—to protect the "individual against the danger of proletarization and capitalist subjection."[41] Because of the moralistic, antilegal influence of Confucianism, the state failed to produce the kind of rational administration and law necessary for a capitalist system. "Patrimonialism, being ethically oriented, always sought substantive justice rather than formal law."[42] Like the moralism of Confucianism itself, Chinese law (which Weber calls " 'Solomonic' Cadi-*[qadi]* justice") was aimed at contests between persons, not at the impersonal litigation between abstract organizations (e.g., corporations) or situations.[43] Because of the weak sense of transcendence in Chinese religion, there was naturally little or no tension between sacred (or "natural") law and positive law. Since, for Weber, there is no social change without such tension, religion again seems to have been the ultimate impediment to China's development of a rational economy. Ultimately, it proved to be the insuperable hurdle.

Although Confucianism developed along rational, utilitarian lines, it failed to generate the "mighty enthusiasm" that alone can initiate the transition to modernity. The life-style of the Confucian bureaucrat was, itself, antithetical to the spirit of capitalism. Scholarship imbued his position with a magical, traditional authority. His education (like the humanism of Catholic Europe described elsewhere by Weber) was innocent of mathematics, natural science, and geography.[44] His philosophy was an undialectical, or categorical, species of thought. His rationalism was a "rationalism of order" incapable of initiating profound social or economic change. Study consisted of the "assimilation of existing ideas" and texts.[45] Academic specialization was discouraged because the superior man *(chün-tzu)* regarded himself a generalist. In contrast to the Puritan, who regarded himself a "tool" to do God's work on earth, the Confucian literatus thought of himself as a "personality" to be cultivated, as an end in himself.

Here we get to the crux of Weber's analysis. Unlike the Puritan, who tried to transform and master the world, the Confucian sought merely to accommodate himself to it:

> The Confucian desired "salvation" only from the barbaric lack of education. As the reward of virtue he expected only long life, health, and wealth in this world and beyond death the retention of his good name . . . all tension between the imperatives of a supra-mundane God and a creatural world, all orientation toward a goal in the beyond, and all conception of radical evil were absent.[46]

In spite of his disclaimer, cited previously,[47] Weber believed that this tension was possible *only* in a society where the religious ideal was established by "an absolutely super-creatural, supra-mundane, personal creator and ruler of the world."[48] From this, it seemed to follow logically, and not just as a matter of fact, that China had not "developed" because the Chinese had developed no "ethical prophecy" strong enough to challenge traditional ways of life. Because of its lack of ethical transcendence, Confucianism failed to overcome the magical manipulation of the world—a failure that the ethical prophet took as an affront to divine majesty. Because Confucianism regarded mankind as essentially good, it was untroubled by the sinfulness of a "fallen humanity." Nothing more radical than a solid, classical education was needed to make the world as good as it ever was, or could be. No mediating priesthood was necessary, no "cure of souls," no "church discipline."[49]

From his comparative point of view, Weber believed that the Chinese had failed to develop a capitalist economy because they had failed to harken to the God of Deutero-Isaiah and the Puritans. Only He can generate the kind of motivation, tension, and anxiety needed to "goose" society over the hurdles on the road leading to a rational economy. Put more formally, the problem with Confucianism *as a religion* was that its deity was too rational, too immanental, and too impersonal to make the kind of ethical demands people need to hear if they are to break out of their traditional bonds. It failed to generate the irrational, "mighty enthusiasm" required to "rationalize" the world. Its problem *as ethics* was that it was too personalistic, or particularistic, to break the hold of kinship on the individual. In short, Confucianism gave the Chinese no reason to espouse the unnatural, voluntary suffering (i.e., *innerweltliche Askese*) that early capitalism allegedly depended upon. "Alien to the Confucian was the peculiar confinement and repression of natural impulse which was brought about by strictly volitional and ethical rationalization and ingrained in the Puritan."[50]

While some scholars have perceived the ethnocentrism of Weber's comparative studies, the subsequent development of capitalism in the non-Christian world should make it obvious to all. Weber, of course, would retort that, while capitalism was bound to spread throughout the world, it could make its *initial* appearance only in Protestant Europe. But this seems to be a very peculiar argument. It seems to me that no historian can show why something had to appear anywhere *first*. Whether Weber was right about Chinese Confucianism, I cannot say. But, then, who can? Did capitalism fail to develop in China because, as Weber puts it, the Confucian gentleman sought only to "adjust" to the world, while the Puritan saint tried to "master" it? The question itself assumes a symmetry between man's spiritual and economic lives which is not always forthcoming in the historical record. Did the Confucian bureaucrat fail to become a modernizer because he was a Confucian, or because he was a bureaucrat (i.e., because of the way his offices and opportunities were structured)? Again, it is enormously difficult to separate these critical variables—assuming they *are* critical.

If Weber was right about China and Chinese Confucianism, one can understand why Morishima has to stress the *exceptional* nature of Japanese Confucianism if he is to show how the latter gave rise to a "rational economy." When Weber died (in 1920) there were few who could have predicted the breathtaking economic development of Japan in future decades. Even though Japan had already won a war against a European nation, Westerners could argue that her opponent, Russia, was neither modern nor really European. Japan could therefore still be excluded from the western concept of "modernity." Had Weber foreseen some of the salient features of subsequent Japanese capitalism, he would have had even less reason to predict its future triumphs. Japanese development relied to a large extent on bureaucratic *dirigisme*. Weber, however, failed to see the dynamic role a "developmental bureaucracy" could play. For him, bureaucracy aimed primarily at the regulation, not at the stimulation of the economy. The Japanese have also relied on a meritocratic examination system to supply industry and government with reliable "human capital." Weber, on the other hand, thought that, by discouraging entrepreneurial charisma, systems of this sort encouraged stagnation. The Japanese economy—or rather its "upper tier"—has also developed a system of "lifetime employment." Weber would have regarded this as inviting an unacceptably high level of risk-aversion and, again, stagnation. And so on. In other words, Weber failed to see that a non-Christian *Volk* could, and would, be the *first* people in the world to come up with a *new kind of capitalism,* one that may even be more dynamic (or powerful) than the Euro-American variants which thus far have dominated the world's economy.

Does this mean that Morishima Michio provides us with the kind of paradigm that we need to account for the development of East Asia in the post-Weberian world? One could argue in Morishima's defense that the concern the samurai of the Meiji period (1868–1911) had for the safety of their country was a motivation equivalent to the anxiety of the Puritans over their election, and that it was the "mighty enthusiasm" or the irrational goad to rational activity that Weber was looking for. Undoubtedly, this concern was an important factor behind the decision by the Meiji government to establish industries with state funds. But, again, we must ask the question we asked about the Chinese literati: did the samurai play a role in the development of industry because they were Confucians or because they were (cultural) warriors? Did lower-ranking samurai take positions in these new companies because of their ethic or because, after the disestablishment of their caste, they found themselves out of work? Questions of this sort make moderate skepticism seem a generous attitude.

Truth may not always reveal herself as the golden mean, but it seems to me that Weber and Morishima have gone astray by espousing extreme positions. Weber clearly erred when he failed to see the moral "tension" implicit in the Confucian concepts of the Tao, T'ien, and "the golden age." As Confucius himself put it, "If the Way *(Tao)* prevailed in the world, I should not be trying to alter things."[51] Throughout its long history, Confucianism repeatedly lent itself to critical social analysis and political action. Its emphasis on "the investigation of things" inspired a spirit of curiosity and inquiry. But to regard this attitude as "science and technology" (as Morishima does) is, again, to exaggerate. While Confucianism gave rise to "practical studies" *(jitsugaku)* in Japan, jitsugaku itself satisfied only the protoscientific curiosity of the amateur collector. It fused, and confused, ethical and natural knowledge. Only in the Meiji period, under the impact of Western science, did Japanese thinkers learn to differentiate clearly between the principles (Japanese: *ri;* Chinese: *li*) of nature and those of morality.[52]

It is possible that Confucianism (in its diffuse form) has had something to do with the diligence, sincerity, and frugality of "post-Confucian" East Asia—or, at least, with the articulation of these virtues. It is possible that the Confucian examination system paved the way for the development of the meritocracies and "diploma societies" of the present. It is not impossible that the moral tutelage of the Confucians prepared the Far East for the "preceptoral systems" that later would guide its economies—from the "massive unilateral persuasion" of the People's Republic of China to the "administrative guidance" of capitalist Japan.[53] It is also possible that the kind of consensual system of decision making and responsibility sharing one finds in Japan today had its origin (at least in part) in the kind of "discussions" commended by the Confucianism of the Seventeen Article Constitution. I think that the spirit of cooperative, ethical reciprocity one finds in Japanese industrial paternalism probably does go back to the moralism of Confucius. (I also think that this "spirit" is largely an ex post facto beautification of industrial relations. While resonating in a positive way with popular tradition, I do not think it was "the cause" of the industrialization of Japan and East Asia). In all of these cases, all that one can say is that these propositions are possible, probable, or likely. In most cases, I find no way to evaluate Morishima's claims at all. For example, how can we know whether it was Confucianism that caused Japanese workers to accept the limited horizontal mobility of their tier-one labor markets, or exploitation by "capitalists and the labor aristocracy"?[54] How can one know whether it was Confucianism—and not Shinto or the indigenous social system—that accounted for the tendency for the Japanese kaisha to evolve into a "complete society in itself"?[55] How can one say with any certainty that Confucianism, and not Buddhism, caused the (alleged) lack of competition between individuals in Japanese industry[56] or the rare phenomenon of groups competing only to show their loyalty to the firm? In short, how can one identify and control the relevant historical variables?

Japan's Vernacular Religions and Economic Development

Whether we are looking at Confucianism, Buddhism, or a mixture of the two, there are obvious pitfalls in beginning our search for an Asian work ethic in the obiter dicta of pious entrepreneurs or the sacred texts of the founders of the great traditions. Unfortunately, this is where Weber and most of his followers have begun. This ultimately encourages a purely textual and elitist ("top-down") approach to the problem. In the following sections, I turn from the venerable spokesmen for religion and industry and look at some of the leaders of the folk tradition. Because the Japanese government has always exhorted peasants and other workers to be diligent and frugal, we cannot say that the work ethic springing from the vernacular tradition is absolutely free and spontaneous. But, because these virtues benefited households and government alike, such values cannot be lightly dismissed as mere "false consciousness" planted in the popular mind from above.

Perhaps it will help us understand the development of the popular work ethic if we temporarily replace Weber's hurdles, runners, and motivations with the imagery suggested earlier of barricades and an advancing army of developers. Unlike hurdles, barricades and ramparts must be peopled. This means that we must rewrite our development scenario and people it with *two* sets of actors. In addition to our advancing army (the former runners), we must now write parts for the defenders of the ancient bastions of faith, magic, tradition, and good works. We must be careful to attribute to our new actors the same capabilities we ascribed to the advancing troups. They must be able to think for themselves and maneuver in their own defense and self-interest. We must endow them with the ability to dodge, huddle, feint, fall back, regroup, conspire, collaborate, betray, compromise, and even surrender to the foe. As we saw in chapter 2, the strategy of religious groups caught in the fray is often determined by the material interests of their spiritual leaders—interests that usually differ considerably from those of the laity. Religions of the oppressed led by clergy intellectually or materially beholden to new wealth may be among the first to give in to the demands of development.

We must add two final scenes to our skit. In the first, we must tell the story of the failure of the defenders of the faith to obstruct social and economic development. We must relate how they retreated, compromised, and grew silent or indifferent to the breakdown of traditional communities and social values. We can even add a dash of pathos by relating how they turned their backs to the social inequities appearing in their own midst. In our final scene, we shall see how our erstwhile defenders became passive or even active collaborators with the foe, how they grew as proud of development as the developers themselves, and how their rhetoric and strategies were coopted by the victors and made part of the master plan of modernization.

The Next-to-the-Last Scene: Passive Enablements

First, we must tell the rather paradoxical story of religion's passive contribution to the growth of the modern economy. For lack of space, I shall merely summarize the plot as it unfolded in Japan.

Although the Tokugawa period (1603–1868) was formerly thought to be a time of economic stagnation, research has shown that the country was actually undergoing remarkable structural change during this time. Nevertheless, when the period began, no one could have predicted what lay ahead. In nearly every way, the cards of fate seemed to be stacked against the small island country. It had few natural resources. Government policies did nothing to foster growth and much to hinder it. The regime had cut off external trade out of fear that rival domains might profit too much from it. Domestic trade was in the hands of a hereditary merchant caste that stood at the low end of the Confucian social scale. Officially, commerce was divorced from prestige and honor. There was even a common saying that "the offspring of a toad is a toad; the offspring of a merchant is a merchant."[57] Tolls and poor land transportation limited trade, while sea transport was thought to be too hazardous for most purposes. As in China, peasants were reluctant to sell land they had received from their sacred ancestors. The economy of most villages was embedded in the fictive kinship of extended households. Many crafts and markets were cornered by monopolistic guilds *(za)*. In western Japan, households that monopolized economic and political affairs sought to dignify their secular authority by controlling religious guilds *(miya-za)* as well.

In the nineteenth century, when Japan finally opened her ports to the world, she already had many advantages that third-world countries today would envy. Literacy was widespread. In western Japan, the prolonged practice of double cropping had created an economic surplus that, in turn, gave rise to a widespread money economy. The hereditary servants and kinship base of agriculture of the early Tokugawa period gradually had given way to the labor of a rural proletariat. Increasingly, a family's welfare was determined as much by distant markets as by its own shrewdness and hard work. The social and moral bonds that previously tied patrons and workers together were shattered and replaced by impersonal relations between landlords and tenant farmers. Employment became a matter of "relations entered into for the convenience of the moment, so that instead of being the guide lines of a way of life, they were episodes that passed and were quickly forgotten."[58] Thus, even before Meiji, the economy was becoming "disembedded." To put the same thing in the language of development studies, the commercialization of agriculture and the development of urban trade during the latter half of the Tokugawa period constituted a gestation period that enabled the economy to take off during the reign of the Meiji emperor.

As development (or disembedding) proceeded, up-and-coming families began to demand their just share of power and prestige. In Western Japan, hereditary village offices were opened to election. Guilds were disbanded, reestablished, and then destroyed through de facto competition. For many families, the costs of the disembedding of the economy were high. Under the reactionary slogan "revere grain, despise money" *(kikoku senken)*, some demanded the new money economy be curtailed or abolished. As we saw in chapter 2 conservative limits were built into social protest during most of the Tokugawa period. Peasant uprisings were common enough, but they were rebellions, not revolutions. The vast majority aimed at temporary relief and not at permanent structural change. When rising families protested the control of the Shinto parish by the old families in their villages, they sought only to be included in the cult, not to abolish the religious status system itself.[59] In the most rapidly developing parts of the country, these protests resulted in the religious enfranchisement of more and more families. These expanding enclosures of the population around the shrine amounted to the development of an active "participant citizenry" in the religious microcosm of village Japan.[60]

Since the beginning of recorded history, Japanese religions have largely been under the control of national and local authorities. In

Shinto, secular and religious leadership was often identical. Buddhism was muzzled as soon as it was brought from Korea to Japan and was made the monopoly of an elite that hoped to reserve the religion's magical powers for itself. Even after Buddhism became a popular religion, sect leaders continued to vie for official patronage—which inevitably brought about state control. During the Tokugawa period, Buddhism was used directly by the government to control the masses. We shall see in the next chapter that the religion proved to be as pliant in the hands of the autocratic Meiji developers as it had been under the Tokugawa regime. More concerned about the suffering and illusions of the individual than about the misery and injustice of society, Buddhism was not a faith that "made waves." Unlike Islam, it sought to impose no sacred law upon society that could possibly obstruct change. While Theravada Buddhism in Southeast Asia may have helped to prevent the social fragmentation of rural areas, Buddhism has done nothing to prevent the rapid overdevelopment of the Japanese countryside.[61]

Shinto was just as obliging. Because it had no universal prelates to enforce its claims. Shinto readily gave in to the demands of the developers. In chapter 7, we shall see that if a festival interfered with new work schedules, it was postponed, curtailed, or simply dropped from the calendar. Ancient taboos limiting social intercourse with outsiders were prudently overlooked or forgotten. The emperor himself, the high priest of Shinto, was equally compliant. Accustomed for centuries to reign without ruling, he presided over meetings of the Japanese cabinet like the *deus otiosus* of primitive religion. One of the leaders of the Meiji period even complained that, unlike the west, Japan had no "spiritual axis." The imperial system was therefore the very opposite of Weber's "sultanism," i.e., the extreme form of patrimonialism which so often stood in the way of development. It could even be argued that the emperor's greatest, unsung virtue was his *failure* to obstruct "progress."

To understand the real influence of religion on the development of Japan we must look at it as it actually functions in daily life, i.e., as a comprehensive, tolerant, syncretistic system composed of various elements. Although Weber maintained that toleration had nothing to do with the origins of capitalism, earlier observers, such as Sir Josiah Child in the seventeenth century, noted that "toleration in different Opinions in matters of religion" did contribute to prosperity. Charles Leslie even complained that "toleration is a sacrificing of God to Mammon."[62] In Japan, political order was predicated on mutual toleration and a recognition of the practical value of multiple religious affiliations. We have already seen that, in general, the only religions to cause any problems were those that insisted exclusively on their own "single practice"—

e.g., the True Pure Land, Hokke, and Fuju-Fuse sects of Buddhism; Christianity; and some of the New Religions such as Soka Gakkai.[63] Over the course of time, some of these religions learned to compromise and even developed "mixed practices" of their own. Sectarian rivalries were generally held in check by practical (and political) calls for mutual respect. One could argue that this kind of toleration was another way in which religion failed to get in the way of development. (One has only to compare the declining GNPs of countries torn apart by religious or sectarian strife to see my point.) Toleration (the religious face of pragmatism) and flexibility (the secular side of toleration) have undoubtedly enhanced the stability of Japan's rapidly developing society. They have also enabled the Japanese to borrow (at minimal psychological cost) from the science, technology, and cultures of the rest of the industrial world.[64]

From the beginning of the Meiji period, Japan's development imposed a devastating burden on the common people—a fact Japanologists, social scientists, and "Atari Democrats" in this country, bewitched by the Japan-as-Number-One-ism of the 1980s, tended to forget. Many of the oppressed turned to the New Religions for miracles and magic. Founders of these movements condemned grasping merchants, selfish landlords, and the authorities themselves. They warned vaguely about a "renewal of the world" and the coming of a "Future Buddha" who would set everything aright. In 1838, in the midst of the turbulence of the Tempō period, Nakayama Miki founded a sect called Tenri-kyō, a movement that later became one of Japan's largest New Religions. Like other founders, Miki had her own vision of "world renewal." She bluntly criticized the leaders of the Meiji regime ("the High Mountains"):

> Till now they've said "it's a High Mountain"
> But down in the valleys everything is withering.
> The authorities in this world do as they will.
> Don't they know the sorrow of God?
> Know this: henceforth the power of God will
> Rival that of the authorities!
> Up to now the authorities have done as they would,
> Boasting, "we are High Mountains."
> Trees which grow on the High Mountains
> And those at the bottom of the valley are the same.
> Harken unto me! Whether on top of the High Mountain
> Or in the valley below—all are God's children.
> Every day God's heart is impatient to show us our freedom *[jūyo-jizai]*.

For these and other impolitic remarks, Miki was repeatedly arrested and harrassed by the "High Mountains."

Another prophetess to suffer a similar fate was the colorful and irrepressible Kitamura Sayo (1900–67), who founded the "Dancing Religion" (properly, Tenshō-Kōtai-Jingū-Kyō) in the last years of the Pacific War. On 6 August 1945, a pious follower rushed to the Kitamuras' house to tell the foundress that an atomic bomb had been dropped on Hiroshima. There she found Sayo eating a bowl of rice gruel. The foundress's response to the news was typical of the self-possession of the traditional charismatic. "Calm down and keep quiet," Sayo growled. "The atomic bomb is now eating rice gruel right here."

A few days later Sayo had a revelation that she had become "the only Daughter of the Absolute God of the Universe." Her message consisted largely of an unending stream of vitriolic attacks on people she called "maggot beggars" (social climbers, or "developers"), "beggar officials" (petty functionaries who lived off bribes), and "traitor beggars" (militarists responsible for Japan's defeat).[65] Even the emperor was not spared a tongue lashing. All of these "maggots," Sayo said, are still enslaved in a "meaningless, useless, profane civilization."[66]

After the war, Mrs. Divine (Ogamisama), as she was called by her followers, was arrested for refusing to pay her rice taxes. According to the district attorney's own statement:

> The defendant claims that the world of today consists of nothing but egoistic "traitor beggars." She believes the farmers should not till their fields to feed such beggars, and therefore, she issued instructions for them not to submit to the government even one ounce of rice until the people realize their heavenly calling and are ready to render their services for the establishment of God's Kingdom on earth.[67]

At the trial, Mrs. Divine stood up "and sang out the following sermon in Her loudest voice":

> Do not worry about position, honor, and fortune
> But discard them, together with your egoism.
> God has already descended and has taken over
> The maggot's world into His hands and rules it,
> At this time of the human-world's downfall.
> You beggars of the defeated world, open your eyes—
> Wake up before it is too late.[68]

After her death, Mrs. Divine's followers summarized her attitude toward Japan's new economy and values in the following words:

> With all the technology and scientific advancements, many jobs have been eliminated. People tend only to think of themselves. Competition is keen and unsavory practices have developed. People scheme to deceive, cheat, rob, and steal; and humans are pawns for industrial, religious, and political intrigues. In the world of competition, people live in uneasiness and labor suffers, because they are merely used for production. They live for the material things of life but do not improve themselves spiritually. The more they acquire the more they want, so they are never satisfied or happy.[69]

The Dancing Religion's own solution to these problems was, first of all, that, with "Ogamisama as the central figure of life,"[70] people should devote themselves selflessly and thankfully to the work karma has bestowed upon them. They must curb their appetites and not resent the good fortune of others:

> Ogamisama says that in the degenerated beggar's world, if you do not get rid of your selfishness you will never be saved. Since we are human beings, we possess the instincts of self-preservation. We must have certain things in order to exist but we must not want in excess of our needs. Be thankful and satisfied with what you have and live a clean life. If you have what you need, do not be extravagant and if you do not have all you need, do not complain.[71]

These examples of social protest from the underground world of popular religion should not mislead us into thinking that the New Religions were a covert form of social or political activism. They were not. Mrs. Divine probably spoke for most of the New Religions when, in an interview, she exclaimed: "Political parties are entirely useless . . . I will dissolve the Diets one after another and will confiscate all the belongings of the maggot beggars."[72] Her final solution to the problem of society and industry was a religious one.

Miki and Sayo were extreme cases—charismatic women whose disgust for "High Mountains" and "maggots" could not be repressed. In general, the social protest of the New Religions took safer, more symbolic, or even cryptic forms. Preachers said just enough about the evils of Japan's "meaningless, useless, profane civilization" to establish rapport with those forced to look upon development from the bottom up. Kawate Bunjirō (1814–83), founder of the Konkō sect, condemned the "progress and development" of his day when he said, "They talk about the world 'opening up'; I say it's falling apart!" Again, Itō Rokurobei (1829–94) of the Fuji sect openly lamented. "Enlightenment [i.e., the Meiji word for overall "development"] is the downfall of mankind."

Usually, the messiahs of the New Religions touched on social problems only as examples of a more fundamental religious plight: the impending end of the world, possession by evil spirits, rampant egoism, manifestations of bad karma, and so on. By "touching on" social issues in this way, the preacher could keep silent about the "negative externalities" of development while seeming to make a great deal of racket about them. By reducing social problems to instances of otherworldly or demonic predicaments, the founders of the New Religions were able to keep a safe, grumpy silence on problems of the greatest social importance. Whatever his diagnosis might be, the preacher's remedy was always a religious or magical nostrum: an amulet, a spell, or a ritual that would take care of everything. Whether in peace or in war, New Religions of this sort—for all their fuss—seldom got in the way of development.[73] On the contrary, like Japan's older religions, they passively enabled economic development to go forward.

I have argued elsewhere that, contrary to Weber's notion that development rests upon the "disenchantment of the world," magic and miracles are entirely compatible with the "rationality" of industrial society.[74] Although magic was "sober and rational" when it first appeared, Weber was convinced that the "highly anti-rational world of universal magic" among the religions of Asia could never give rise to "rational, inner-worldly life conduct."[75] This conclusion seemed to follow from the dubious distinction Weber drew between the *miraculous* religions of the west and the *magical* ones of the east—the former being more "rational" than the latter. Where there was magic, *all* of life was affected, Weber seems to believe. Thus the logic of his argument precluded the possibility that workers could be faithful to their industrial "callings" by tending their "gardens of magic" on weekends or on their days off. Because of his preoccupation with the *origin* of capitalism, he gave no attention to the question of whether magic could adapt itself to the rational temper of a modern economy *once that economy was in place*. It seems to me that as long as magic is situational (i.e., as long as it can retreat under inappropriate circumstances) and functional (i.e., subordinate to the controlling rationality of the "better sort of people"), it poses no serious threat to modern institutions. In fact, one might argue that modern economics (and politics) have become quite dependent on the magician's legerdemain. If so, I would argue against Weber that magic, magical religions, and development are not antithetical at all. On the contrary, wherever we look, the magician and the general, the shaman and the developer, the preacher and the industrialist all seem to be following the same drummer, marching to the same beat.

The Final Scene: Positive Enablements

The idea that preachers, shamans, and magicians indirectly contribute to development by keeping their mouths shut (or vacuously open) rests on an argument *ex silentio* more easily sensed than proven. This does not mean that religion's passive acceptance of development is unimportant. On the contrary, it is as vital to development as the positive enablements I am about to discuss. To put the relationship between the two in the terms of theology: the passive is to the positive enablement what a *nihil obstat* is to an *imprimatur*. One facilitates the process by not objecting; the other, by giving the "go-ahead" and blessing.

Throughout the premodern world, religion and magic were used to enhance the productivity of contained or embedded economies. "What the common man looks for in religion is not metaphysics, but a kind of spiritual, or thaumaturgical, pragmatism. He wants his cow to calve, his wife to bear, the drought to end, the plague to pass him by . . . "[76] In all of the countries of East Asia, religion provided ritual techniques to promote the fertility of fields (and wives) and to bring merchants and artisans good luck. Each occupation had a festival day for its own guardian deity. Even other worldly faiths like Buddhism developed their own this-worldly magic and work ethics.

The religious work ethic one finds in Asian countries just before the modern period is, typically, a mixture of magic and common sense, a striving for achievement, and a genuine concern for the well-being of kith and kin. None of the Japanese figures usually mentioned in this context—e.g., Ishida Baigan, Hakuin Zenji, Suzuki Shōsan, or Ninomiya Sontoku—could conceive of a "work ethic" that would encourage a moral disembedding of the economy. Quite to the contrary, all of them sought to motivate people to work and achieve as much as they could in the context of the feudal society in which they lived. All presupposed, and sought to reinforce, the social and kinship restraints of traditional Confucian society.

A good example of the work ethic of the folk (and the mixture of traditional and modern elements in it) is found in the Fuji sect. Originating in the ascetic and shamanistic practices associated with Mount Fuji, this sect was popular among the merchants and artisans of Edo (Tokyo) and among the peasants of the surrounding Kantō plain. The sect developed its own social ethic, which is said to have influenced Ninomiya Sontoku himself. Among the virtues it extolled were benevolence, self-restraint, frugality, and diligence. Preachers of the sect stressed the importance of developing strong farming and fishing villages, hygiene, and agricultural technology. They urged members to be active in community projects such as the building of roads and bridges. One should labor, they said, not merely to enrich oneself, but in order to support one's family and indigent neighbors. The Fuji sect attacked various magical practices, even those traditionally practiced by the sect itself. Its attitude toward women was also relatively "modern." Itō Jikigyōmiroku (1671–1733), the sect's messiah, declared that women are not polluted by their menstrual period (regarded by Shinto as a source of "red pollution"). On the contrary, if a woman "did not harm, poison, or bewitch her husband"—and as long as she did her housework and followed the traditional Rule of the Three Obediences[77]—she was a man's equal. "Both male and female are human beings."

In addition to these relatively progressive doctrines, the Fuji sect also believed in a fuzzy kind of eschatology called "world renewal" *(yonaori)*, "the shake up" *(furikawari)* or "the renovation" *(on-aratame)* of the world. The eschaton was believed to have started when the "male and female ropes" of the god Sengen Daibosatsu were joined together on 15 June 1688 at Shakamuni's Crevice in Maitreya's Fushita Heaven (equal to Mount Fuji itself). This esoteric event ushered in the age of Maitreya's rule *(Miroku no yo)*. One of the early leaders of the movement, Gatsugyō Sōjū, called upon the emperor himself to inaugurate the world of Maitreya![78]

If the Fuji sect was at all typical of the kind of religion that had the greatest appeal to the common folk—and I think it was—it is evident that the religious "work ethic" of early modern Japan was steeped in otherworldly expectations *and* in the values of familyism, community, and political authoritarianism.[79] The individual was expected to follow the line of work of his own ancestors. In short, *it was an ethic for a society with an embedded economy.* Since it justified diligence without generating any unnatural or "mighty enthusiasm" for it, I would hesitate to call the Fuji sect's work ethic the analogue of the Puritan's (alleged) work ethic. Nor do I find any evidence in the writings of other Japanese moralists for any purely religious, irrational goad to rational labor that would disregard the claims of kith and kin.

The same must be said of the social teachings of the New Religions of the twentieth century. Many, perhaps most, continue to preach a feudalistic morality in the context of a modern competitive economy. When not blatantly feudalistic, the morality taught by the postwar New Religions is usually rich in the ascetic, nationalistic, and authoritarian values of Japan's wartime "civil religion." Mrs. Divine, for example, taught that "occupation and religion are both wheels of the same cart."[80] While in jail, she wrote a letter to her son with the following practical advice:

> The beans in the fields should be picked while they are green because this will save lots of labor and besides, if you don't pick them while green, the stems cannot be used for fertilizer. Next, do not waste but be as frugal as possible and appreciate what you have. This is one of the most important fundamentals of religious practice.[81]

Like other Japanese moralists, she taught that the way out of economic strife is to accept the karmic determination of one's economic and social position. "Each person should remind himself of his responsibilities to God and his employer and make certain he renders his best efforts to both."[82] Employers, on the other hand, must treat their workers as human beings. While outsiders may treat these words as pious platitudes, the faithful believe that "by this, Ogamisama taught us how to rise above the economic system."[83]

Throughout the modern period, the traditional morality of hard work, achievement, and social concern has been modified and reworked countless times, both in secular and in sacred ways. In its most effective form, it has been co-opted and woven into the civil religion and civil theology that took shape and dominated Japanese life between 1868 and 1945.[84] Confucianism itself encouraged ambition to hide behind the folding oriental fans of benevolence and patriotism. During the Tokugawa period, Confucian schools aimed at producing men who would be useful to their fiefs. Later on, the same ambition was legitimated in the name of Japanese nationalism. The nouveaux riches in Japan justified their wealth in the name of family and nation, much as early English entrepreneurs dedicated the fruits of their labor to the "glory of God and the improvement of man's estate."

During the Meiji period, businessmen sought to justify their activities in terms of Confucianism, nationalism, and the Way of the Warrior (*bushidō*). In the end, however, the business elite failed to "formulate a persuasive rationale for capitalism."[85] Throughout the 1920s and 1930s, the traditional Confucian "barricades" held, and businessmen were excoriated for their selfishness and profit mongering. This ideological failure helped to polarize social criticism at the extremes: between conservative ultranationalists, on the one side, and radical Marxists, on the other. Each group had its own organic vision of society. The western ideals of economic individualism, liberalism, and parliamentary democracy were finally squeezed out and replaced by militarism and fascism pure and simple. The mixture of civil religion and business ideology proved to be far less successful in the end than the mixture of civil religion and the work ethic itself. If it is true that religion often influences the economy through the medium of politics,[86]

Japan's civil religion *may* have had more to do with implementing the popular work ethic than any other symbolic factor. In spite of its failures in the prewar period, the "business ideology" and other "superordinate goals"[88] continue to be used by Japanese industry to legitimate itself and to motivate its work force. These values are transmitted or instilled in workers (from the "top down") through various initiation rites, training sessions, and "spiritual education" *(seishin kyōiku)* weekends.[89]

Today, work in Japan is made part of an inclusive reticulation of such values as harmony, unity, consensus, loyalty, sincerity, and altruistic service to the individual's family, company, and nation. As such, the work ethic has been imposed on workers both from below (by popular religious leaders, moral entrepreneurs, and even by the workers themselves) and from above (by government, industry, and the official ideology). Here again, it is helpful to distinguish between a work *ethic* (the former) and a work *ideology* (the latter). In part, these values are what the Japanese call *tatemae;* principles averred in public. They are part of the rituals of the office, shop, and factory. The worker subscribes to them the way he or she participates in morning calisthenics—sometimes with gusto, sometimes with lethargy—but always by going through the motions. Allegiance to the rhetoric and values of a firm may be thought of as the expressive side of the socioeconomic exchange of service for patronage that lies beneath the individual's overall relationship with his or her company. According to a Japanese proverb, everyone should "wrap himself in something long." Usually this means everyone should find a strong and reliable patron. But by extension, it could just as well refer to the company uniform and the long, invisible cloak of values and etiquette that goes with it. Many find the moral bonds with their company deeply satisfying. Many Japanese are convinced that wrapping themselves in these virtues is the sure way to success. For these reasons, the ideals of loyalty and service have become inextricably intertwined with material rewards, the quest for higher status, and the affirmation of family and national identity.

Denouement: Embedding Society

Today, not much remains of the barricades that once defended traditional Asian society against development. Victorious developers have built their own castles where the ramparts once stood. Above the former citadels now rise the towering spires of Tokyo, Osaka, Seoul, Singapore, and the other dazzling emporia of East Asia. Were we to update figures 3 and 4 and make them correspond to the situation today, we would have to transpose A and C to show that society itself is now virtually sequestered or "embedded" in the economy. Today, it is industry that asks to be made safe from society and *its* claims, i.e., the social welfare and justice that, like quasi-religious superstitions, continue to remind us of our tribal past. The new barricades protecting the economy are manned by secular preachers of the gospel of wealth, Reaganomics, and Japan theory. Standing beside them, however, are the evangelists, shamans, magicians, and high priests of both traditional and New Religions who now bless the very institutions they once cursed.

The relationship between society, religion, morality, and the economies emerging in some of the countries of East Asia today can be represented by figure 7. Notice that the barrier protecting the economy in figure 7 (B_2)—now a solid line—is being rebuilt and restored to its pristine condition. Here, the organic model of *society* (e.g., the ethic of "hierarchical complementarity") that once fended off the disequilibrating forces of the economy has been turned into an organic model of

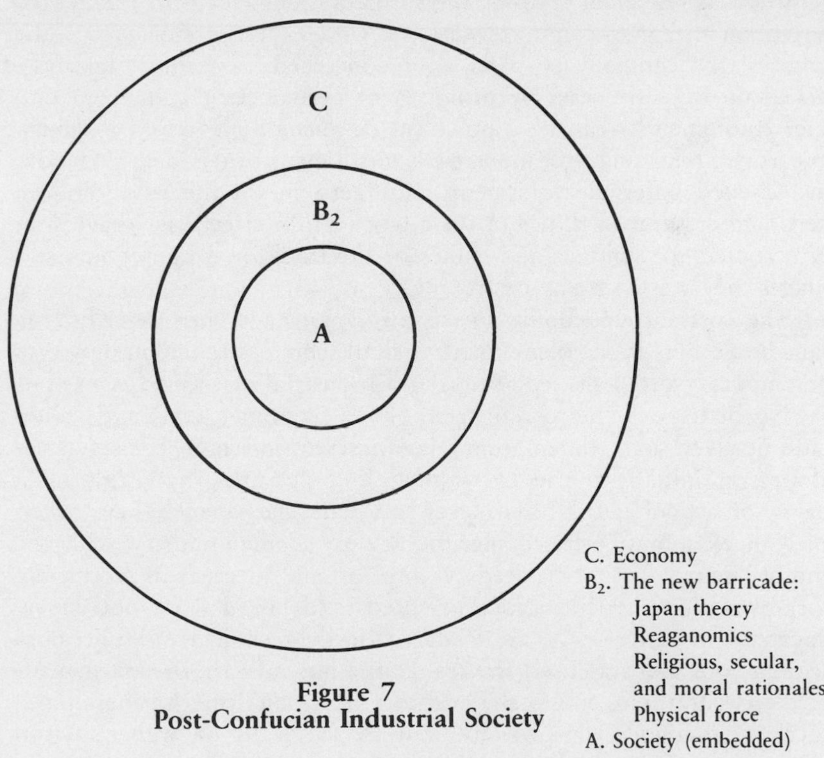

Figure 7
Post-Confucian Industrial Society

industry. Figure 7 represents only an exaggerated ideal type of a society still in the process of "development." Some will regard it as a figment of the imagination, or perhaps a nightmare. Others will defend it as one of the most successful experiments in postmodernity. Perhaps its closest approximation is modern Japan. In other parts of East Asia, military dictatorships dominate society (A) and industry (C) alike. In Japan, however, a struggle continues between the forces of society and the all-but-dominant economy. The willingness of so many Japanese to put up with the claims of industry (at the expense of their own "entitlements") has a great deal to do with their own improved financial condition. The economy has paid off handsomely.

Part of this payoff has been ideological and moral. It is deeply gratifying to belong to a large, powerful, and successful organization that seems to "care." The "universal and mutual distrust" that Weber saw in the traditional economies of Asia ironically reappears with a vengeance once the "rational depersonalizing of business" has been pushed to its logical conclusion: quick layoffs for quick profits, the flight of capital, and so on.[90] But once business reaches the point where stability is as important as immediate profits, the ruthless ("universalistic") disregard for workers becomes counterproductive. Under these circumstances, the image of the company or bank as a concerned, benevolent family—backed up in some cases by promises of permanent employment and other emoluments—can be a powerful *de-alienating* force in the business world. Realizing this, industrialists in Japan, Korea, and Singapore have created paternalistic systems that zero in on the psychological needs and cultural identities of their workers. In effect, they have simply co-opted the symbols and values of the traditional households and villages they were actually destroying.

The costs of embedding society in Japan have been described by Hane and others in moving detail.[91] I shall therefore touch on only two contemporary problems, education and industrial discipline.

No better example of the triumph of economic goals and values could be given than contemporary Japanese education. The costs of development, initially borne by women and peasants, now rest most heavily on school-age children. Over the years, the Japanese have developed an examination-based meritocracy to supply industry with the kind of "human capital" it needs. It aims at, and succeeds in producing, workers who are docile, group-oriented, and broadly but not deeply educated—or better—who are *socialized* in the technical and functional rationality of industry itself. To realize the bureaucrats' dream of making the twenty-first century the "century of Japan," the Japanese have, in effect, chained their own children to the walls of Weber's "iron cage." Some children spend as much time at their desks at school and in *juku* (after-school tutoring or "cram" schools) as English children did at their workbenches in the early nineteenth century. This system of "education" is probably the main cause of one of the country's ugliest social problems, violence in the home and at school.[92] On college campuses, educators and psychologists worry about students who have become "moratorium men" unable to commit themselves to *any* social or industrial institutions.[93]

Another problem for the rapidly developing societies of East Asia is coercion. The ideological and religious defenders of the new industrial order are backed up by physical force. This time the defenders literally "mean business." Industries, armed with their own patrols and spies, brook no opposition. Shortly after the Pacific War, Japanese industry deliberately set out to destroy the militant labor unions. Today, workers who are dissatisfied with the company union are harrassed and sometimes even beaten. Those who take sick leave are sometimes "visited" by company police to see how sick they really are. At Toyota, rebellious union members circulate an underground newspaper similar to the *samizdat* publications of the USSR before *glasnost*. Union elections are supervised by the labor aristocracy (generally a clone of management itself); voting is sometimes conducted in public view.[94] Restrictions on horizontal mobility, a system of seniority pay, and other practices severely limit the freedom of the working force. In other parts of East Asia the working population is kept in line by the general mobilization of society against foreign enemies. Since the same troops are used against internal dissenters as well, their *real* purpose is open to question. I bring up these unsavory facts to make the simple point that industrial discipline in Japan and the rest of East Asia depends on more than a "work ethic."

Our examination of the religious and cultural barricades between society and the economy finally brings us back to our starting point, Max Weber's own *sociology of pain*. Looking at Japanese young people today, one wonders how they can endure such massive repression. To be sure, the primordial togetherness of after-hours drinking and cavorting provides workers with some relief from the demands of the office or factory—far more than singing the company song! But in the end, the Japanese will probably contain dissent and make the next century their own by falling back on some kind of nationalism. Today, Japan seems to be hankering for a new civil religion that will legitimate the country's postwar success and provide a theodicy for the suffering it has caused. Both Japan theory and the New Religions seem to be groping in this direction.[95]

Afterthoughts

Because of the theoretical nature of this chapter, I would like to conclude with a *caveat lector.* Figures 3, 4, and 7 are not intended as a simple, unilinear paradigm of development per se. Rather, they symbolize *one* way in which the religious rationales sanctifying society and the economy have changed. While not denying the possibility that religion may sometimes have a positive, stimulating effect on social change and economic development, I have emphasized the importance of its functional or legitimating role, and the ways in which that role itself has changed in order to accommodate development. While there is evidence of a work ethic among the working classes, this ethic achieved national significance only after it was rationalized and propagated as a part of civil theology, business ideology, and the new national image-making of Japan theory. Whether or not there is such a thing as a "central value system," there clearly is a *resonance* here between the work ethic of the common people and the work ideology of the cultured and industrial elites. That resonance is not natural or accidental; it was planned.

Weber and the Weberians have generally approached the problem of religion and development by analyzing the religion and values established before the onset of industrialization, and by postulating a correlation (or "elective affinity") between them and subsequent historical events. I would suggest that more attention be paid to the religious attitudes which appear *while development is taking place.* For example, one can learn far more about the religious background of American capitalism by reading the sermons of Bishop William Lawrence of Massachusetts, Henry Ward Beecher, or Russell H. Conwell than by pouring over Richard Baxter's *Christian Directory.* Perhaps a good example to follow would be research on a parallel problem: the role of religion in colonialism. While missionary zeal paved the way for colonial adventures in some parts of the world, most missionaries simply *followed* the imperialist into the field and collaborated with him.

Weberians have often treated religion as a crucial but unchanging variable in the maelstrom of social and economic change. Here I think we should return to Weber's own interest in the (internal) transformation of the religions that are (externally) affecting development. We must also be aware of similar changes in values in general, e.g., how they are turned into rhetoric, and how rhetoric, in turn, gives rise to new values. Also, we should periodically remind ourselves that values do not generally act on their own, but rather as part of a "team" of factors including physical rewards, constraints, etc.

Before any meaningful work can be done on the problem of religion and development, we must subject the concept of secularization to a thoroughgoing review. We need to recognize the importance of the "disenchantment" of certain strategic elements of society and the economy; but we must be very suspicious of, and finally reject, a priori theories that postulate the *Entzauberung* of the whole damn *Welt*. For the same reason, the decline of religion itself can no longer be taken for granted as a necessary concomitant of some "universal process of modernization." In no case should we allow theory to blind us to the subtle ways in which very "primitive" kinds of religion and magic continue to coexist and collaborate with modern economic and political institutions. The recrudescence and revalorization of religious emotions, ideas, and symbols take place in *all* periods of history. We must therefore pay more attention to the *aggiornamento* of magic and religion, and not focus our efforts exclusively on the tension between them and development. On this point, Weber and other theorists bewitched by the Enlightenment's idle myths of "science and progress" have badly misled both the sociology of religion and the study of social and economic change.

CHAPTER 5

Buddhism and Modernization

Like the nouveaux riches in countries around the world, wealthy Japanese businessmen like to pause now and then to reflect on the secrets of their own success. Most attribute their wealth to old-fashioned hard work. Others, looking deeper, try to explain their wealth and work habits in terms of their country's unique culture, values, or religion. In the Meiji period, entrepreneurs like Kanbara Meizen claimed that their entire lives had been spent in the single-minded pursuit of Buddhist truth.[1] More recently, the president of TDK (Tōkyō Denki Kagakukōgyō Company) boasted that the inspiration behind his company, one of the most successful in Japan, is Buddhism.

> Making a profit is important, of course, but it is not the ultimate goal. Character building is much more important. At TDK we attach great importance to discovering the meaning of work. As far as valuing relationships goes, it seems to me, Japan is second to none. And at the bottom of this lies Buddhism.[2]

Specific Buddhist sects have also claimed to be the ultimate reason for Japan's success. Zen Buddhists like to attribute the decisiveness of the Japanese businessman to the creative nihilism of the Rinzai and Sōtō sects. Shingon (Esoteric) Buddhists claim that belief in *its* doctrines "may well be one of the underlying reasons for the Japanese devotion to work."[3] Still others explain the ethos of Japanese business in terms of the Way of the Warrior (*bushidō*), a mixture of Buddhist, Confucian, and Shinto ideals.

It is one thing for wealthy tycoons and pious bishops to attribute their country's success to their own religion and virtue. It is quite another for scholars to do so. Ironically, the self-images of contemporary Japanese seem to dovetail at just this point with the Weber thesis, again bringing into question the ability of the latter to penetrate or transcend what, to outsiders, seem to be largely ideological claims. Without rehearsing all of the points made in the previous chapter, let me say that, in my opinion, Weberian studies of this sort have often been hamstrung by two critical weaknesses. First, they typically begin with an analysis of value-systems existing in the period *before* rapid economic development begins. Some Weberians even leap to the conclusion that economic development takes place *because of* previously existing values, thereby falling into the trap awaiting all lazy historians: the logical fallacy *post hoc, ergo propter hoc.* The second weakness is this: Weberians often assume that the relation between religion and development is exhausted by an examination of positive and negative causes. They feel they have fulfilled all professional duties once they have shown, comparatively, how religions and values promote and/or hinder the rise of capitalism.

In this chapter I reexamine the relations between Buddhism and the modernization of Japan, avoiding, I hope, the pitfalls of conventional Weberian analysis. To avoid the "post hoc" trap, I shall concentrate on Japanese values at the time industrialization actually began, the Meiji period (1868–1912). By so doing, I hope to make my study congruent with contemporary research on the origins of British capitalism.[4] To avoid the trap of speculation, I shall look not only at abstract ideas, schools of thought, and individual thinkers but also at the role played by specific religious institutions in the development of the country. Finally, in order to avoid the grand simplicities of positive and negative causation, I shall focus on the "passive enablements" of history introduced in chapter 4. History often is most deeply affected by things that fail to happen, by leaders who do not lead, by groups that acquiesce in the flow of events, by prophets who do not protest, and by churches and sects that, for reasons of fear, greed, or sloth, compromise with the world and "make no waves." In the history of economic development, passive enablements of this sort are an untold story but possibly one of greater moment than the twice-told tales about the putative "impact" of values. To tell the story, we must pay special attention to the ways in which institutional religions accommodated themselves to political institutions and economic change. We must give heed to their strategies for dealing with change, being especially attentive to the strategies of compromise, ambiguity, and silence.[5] In a word, we must concentrate on the *cooptation* of religion by political and economic developers. By following these prescriptions, or home remedies, I hope to do what I can to nurse Weberian scholarship away from its unhealthy fixation on "necessary causes"—the conditions necessary for the rise of capitalism—and try to generate a healthier interest in the *rhetoric of development.*

The Legacy of Buddhist Social Teachings

Weberians are not necessarily wrong when they point out the influence premodern values have had on the modern world. A value system, after all, is a legacy of priorities. Traditionally, Buddhist values helped to reinforce the moral barricades that protected Japanese society from unfettered competition and "embedded" the country's markets in the mazeways of the community itself.[6] For example, in the *Nihon Ryōiki*, a book of miraculous tales collected around 800 C.E., we read about a rich woman who

> lacked faith and was so greedy that she would never give away anything. She used to make a great profit by selling rice wine diluted with water. On the day when she made a loan, she used a small measuring cup, while on the day she collected, she used a big measuring cup. Or, when she lent rice, she used a lightweight scale, but, when she collected it, she used a heavyweight scale. She did not show any mercy in forcibly collecting interest, sometimes ten times and sometimes a hundred times as much as the original loan. She was strict in collecting debts, never being generous. Because of this, many people worried a great deal and abandoned their homes to escape from her, wandering in other provinces. There has never been anybody so greedy.

After the woman died, her family did not cremate her body, but

> called thirty-two monks and lay brothers to pray to Buddha for her for nine days. On the evening of the seventh day she was restored to life and opened the lid of the coffin. When they came to look in it, the stench was indescribable. Her body above the waist had already turned into an ox with four inch horns on the forehead; her two hands had become ox hooves, with the nails cracked like the insteps of an ox hoof. The lower body below the waist was human in form. She did not like rice but grass, and after eating, ruminated. She did not wear any clothes, lying in her filth.

Kyōkai concludes the tale with a Buddhist moral.

> She did not know the law of karmic retribution, being unreasonable and unrighteous. . . . If you make a loan, don't use excessive force to collect the debt, for, if you are unreasonable, you will be reborn as a horse or an ox and made to work by your debtor.[7]

This story is hardly unique. Japanese folktales are filled with miraculous tales which warn the greedy and deceitful of their ultimate comeuppance. Buddhism simply adds its own twist to the tale: the idea of *karmic* retribution. One should not think, however, that the Buddhist attitude towards the economy was entirely negative. On the contrary, since the *sangha* (the cloistered monastics) depended on the laity for material support, the Buddhist lay ethic naturally encouraged economic activity, or what I would call *the asceticism of embedded economies*. For example, in the *Admonition to Singāla* found in the *Dīgha Nikāya* (3.180ff.) we read that

> The wise and moral man
> Shines like a fire on a hilltop,
> Making money like the bee,
> Who does not hurt the flower.
> Such a man makes his pile
> As an anthill, gradually.
> The man grown wealthy thus
> Can help his family
> And firmly bind his friends
> To himself. He should divide
> His money in four parts;
> On one part he should live,
> With two expand his trade,
> And the fourth he should save
> Against a rainy day.[8]

The compiler of this text actually seems to get carried away by his own work ethic. The "deferred gratification" he calls for is, by today's standards at least, truly extraordinary: the layman is to live on a mere 25 percent of his income. Fifty percent of his profits should be reinvested in his business, and another 25 percent should be put in the bank, as we would say. If any Buddhist families actually followed this advice, they must have been remarkably well-to-do, or, at the very least, terribly frugal. The compiler also forgets something few preachers would ever omit: the layman's material obligation to the monks. Other scriptures, however, make good this omission by treating religious donation as one of the layman's primary means of merit-making—merit-making, in turn, being the means to better rebirths in the future.

While the Buddhist economic ethic in ancient India encouraged the asceticism of an embedded economy, its norms lacked moral, and certainly legal specificity. It was the rare monk who said anything explicitly critical about the financial dealings of his own patrons (*danapati*). (Explicit criticism of this sort was more easily given indirectly, as, for example, in the recital of folktales or in the informal transmission of rumors about supernormal, or karmic retribution). Ultimately, the nebulousness of the Buddhist ethic was enlisted in the movement to unfetter or "disembed" the market.[9] But before we discuss the Buddhist contribution to Japan's disembedded economy, we must take a closer look at the moral resources available to the Buddhists of Meiji Japan when they first turned their attention to the problems of industrialization.

The social teachings of Meiji Buddhism rested largely on the unpacking of traditional "numbered teachings" (e.g., the *Four* Noble Truths, the *Eightfold* Path, the *Twelvefold* Chain of Co-Dependent Originations, and the *Ten* Virtues) and various other religious slogans, that is, holophrastic clusters of one to four Chinese ideographs functioning as mnemonic or catechetical devices for transmitting the Dharma. Some slogans stressed Buddhism's ancient ideals of social harmony (*kōkyō wagō*) and harmonious unity (*chōwa yūgō*). Others reflected core Japanese values. Among these, the most important were the concepts of *on* and *hō-on*.[10] As we saw in chapter 1, Japanese morality begins with the a priori premise that the individual has already been "benefited" when he first comes into the world. By virtue of his birth, he has received *on* (benefits) from the kami, the Buddha, his parents, ancestors, the country, and the emperor. As life goes on, he will receive other *on* from his village, patrons, bosses, and neighbors. Moral obligation is therefore understood as *hō-on* (the return of benefits), morality itself as an exchange of scarce material and emotional resources within a hierarchy of benefactors and the benefited. Benefits of life, nourishment, protection, and guidance flow from above; responses of gratitude, love, and loyalty rise from below. Traditionally Buddhists had Four Duties based on the Four Benefits (*shi-on*) received from 1. parents, 2. the sovereign, 3. the Three Treasures (Buddha, Dharma, and Sangha), and 4. all other sentient beings.[11] Responding to imperial benefits was one's first and foremost duty.[12] Because labor itself was thought to be a response to favors already received, the morality of *on* stood, indeed stands today, at the heart of the Japanese work ethic.

Under the influence of Confucianism, the Buddhist morality of *on* assumed an essentially hierarchical coloration. The doctrine of Original Awakening might seem to suggest that all human beings were equal, but Japanese Buddhists seldom pushed the idea to the extreme. Instead, they were content with a "soft equality." According to the teachings of Mahayana, making ontological distinctions (*sha-betsu*) within the totality of the Buddha-mind was equivalent to wandering in pain and illusion. For this reason all dualities and differences had to be overcome. What then could one make of the actual differences in wealth, power, and ability pandemic in human affairs? Japanese Buddhists sanctioned these differences with the slogan "discrimination (or difference) is equality; equality is discrimination" (*shabetsu-soku-byōdō; byōdō-soku-shabetsu*). In Meiji Japan, the ideal of a discriminating egalitarianism could, and easily did, accommodate a considerable degree of inequality.

Another slogan that played a decisive role in Buddhist teachings in the Meiji period was *shinzoku-nitai,* the Pure Land doctrine that religious truth can be divided into absolute and relative teachings. In Japan, where the Jōdo Shinshū sect identified the absolute with the Dharma, the relative with civil law, *shinzoku nitai* was understood as a call for an undivided obedience to established religious and political institutions. The slogan therefore had the effect of absolutizing the will of the authorities, while nullifying moralities that were independent of state power. It also lent an aura of Buddhist respectability to the government's campaigns to "increase industrial productivity" (*shokusan kōgyō*) and create a "rich country and strong army" (*fukoku kyōhei*). Related slogans—for example, "revere the emperor and serve the Buddha" (*sonnō hōbutsu*), "love the country and protect the Dharma" (*aikoku gohō*), "protect the country by promoting Zen" (*kōzen gokoku*), "pacify and preserve the country (through Buddhism)" (*chingo kokka*)—express a similar conflation of religious and political obedience and underscore the importance of Robert Bellah's discovery that "Japan is characterized by a primacy of political values."[13]

While individual thinkers like Ishida Baigan, Suzuki Shōsan, Takuan Sōhō, Bankei Yōtaku, and Hakuin Ekaku preached a traditional (e.g., socially "embedded") work ethic, the Buddhist tradition was far from justifying the relentless quest for profit or the gratification of self-interest one associates with modern capitalism.[14] A good example of the Buddhist attitude toward work can be seen in the *Lives of Pious Folk (Myōkōnin-den)*, biographical sketches of pious farmers, merchants, samurai, outcastes, beggars, and prostitutes published by the Honganji sect from the eighteenth century through the 1920s.[15] Many of the stories have an otherworldly orientation. The saints are generally more interested in departing this world for the Pure Land (*ōjo*) than they are in returning to it and doing good as bodhisattvas (*gensō*). While waiting for his departure, the saint should devote himself wholeheartedly to the hereditary occupation of his family (*kagyō*) and be benevolent and charitable. Reflecting the asceticism of the samurai ethic, the Buddhist saint strives to be diligent about his work, yet indifferent to wealth. In no instance do the saints countenance "money grubbing" or the spirit of "acquisitive individualism." Work, as Hōnen taught, supports one's birth in the Pure Land. Humble souls who do not insist on their own rights are singled out for praise.

A Weberian would probably see evidence in other stories of a "this worldly mysticism." Take the tale of Asahara Saichi (1851–1933), a humble, semiliterate cobbler from Shimane Prefecture. Rising early every morning, Saichi went to a nearby temple to hear a sermon. Then he returned home and spent the rest of the day diligently working at his bench. Although he sometimes gambled with the young men of the village, work alone brought him pleasure. At night Saichi scribbled simple hymns of praise on chips of wood from the floor of his shop and offered them before his Buddhist altar. Later he made clean copies of them in a schoolboy's notebook. The following is a sample of his work:

> Oh it's wonderful! This world and this, my work, have turned into the sublime Pure Land itself. How strange, how passing strange!
>
> How does Saichi make his living? Saichi makes his living by chanting "Namu Amida Butsu."
>
> *Namu Amida Butsu! Namu Amida Butsu!*
> "Namu Amida Butsu" comes to my heart;
> My work (kagyō) *is* "Namu Amida Butsu."[16]

Saints like Saichi are as indifferent to wealth as they are to their own poverty.

> I may be poor, but still I'm very happy
> taking pleasure right here in the Pure Land.
> *Namu Amida Butsu!*[17]

Ideal saints like Saichi knew how to be content with their lot, but never failed to make their contributions to the local temple. Money given to temples would bring good luck to one's children, or would turn into other kinds of wealth later on. Even fathers who sold their daughters to brothel-keepers in order to have money to give to priests were praised as "men of great faith."[18]

There was, however, a subtle shift in emphasis in the Myōkōnin collections of the Meiji period. New emphasis on respect for the emperor brought the life of Meiji saints into line with the Imperial Rescript on Education and the Pure Land ideal of *shinzoku nitai.* The "debt of gratitude" they owed to the emperor was scarcely different from that which they owed to Amida Buddha. Editors singled out for praise the filial child, the faithful wife, the obedient servant, and those who helped the poor, succored the sick, and gave aid to victims of natural disasters. Thus the Meiji saint was on his way to becoming a collaborator of social change and development.[19]

Criticism and Persecution of Buddhism

Weberians often go wrong by assuming that the values expressed by religious slogans have a life of their own or directly influence the course of history. Would that things were so simple! One could argue that the most decisive influence on the (partial) implementation of Buddhist social teachings in this period was their initial *rejection.* In the Tokugawa period, Buddhism was attacked on ethical, political, and economic grounds by thinkers as diverse as Yamagata Bantō, Hayashi Razan, Ogyū Sorai, Kumazawa Banzan, and Nakai Chikuzan. Buddhism was seen as a useless, otherworldly religion, a cloaca of superstition, sloth, and turpitude. Priests were attacked as parasites living off the poor and gullible, a charge that became especially serious during the lean years of the late Tokugawa period. If people were to spend all their time meditating or chanting the *nembutsu,* who would till the soil, write books, pay taxes, or do good deeds? In the Meiji period Ukita Kazutani, Tokutomi Sōhō, Inoue Tetsujirō, and others attacked the religion's spirit of resignation and passivity. Confucian thinkers criticized the seemingly asocial nature of Buddhist ethics. Protestants questioned the appropriateness of the ideal of non-ego in a world that (in their minds) increasingly demanded individual autonomy and a sense of personal responsibility. They also made light of traditional Buddhist attitudes toward women and the failure of the religion to enforce its own teetotalism. Shinto priests attacked Buddhism as a "foreign" religion. Ultranationalists criticized its pacifism. Political progressives of all stripes asked how, if there *is* no self, an individual could assert his civil rights and liberties. If there are no ontological boundaries between the self and others, can there be such a thing as justice? Without *real* actors, can public or political discourse take place at all? If anger and resentment endangered one's own enlightenment, how could exploited workers express their natural sense of indignation against their capitalist masters?

The criticism of Buddhism culminated in open persecution. In the Tokugawa period, domains like Okayama, Aizu, Mito, Tsuwano, Satsuma, and Chōshū drastically reduced the number of their temples, priests, and nuns. In the Meiji period, the government initiated a series of politico-religious experiments. Since Buddhism had been closely associated with the bakufu, the government decided to separate Buddhism from Shinto, making the latter the religion of the state. While the government aimed only at purging Shinto of its Buddhist accretions, the purification campaign got out of hand and turned into outright persecution. From 1871 to 1876, the number of temples throughout the country was reduced from an estimated 465,049 to 71,962. The number of priests declined from 75,925 in 1872 to 19,490 in 1876.[20] In 1872 the government announced that priests were henceforth free to marry and follow nonvegetarian diets, a move that struck a deep blow to the dignity of the priesthood and its sense of discipline. All in all, the attack on Buddhism during the first eight years of Meiji was so severe that one leading priest, Fukuda Gyōkai, predicted an Imperial Rescript would soon be announced prohibiting the practice of the religion once and for all.

Whatever the truth of the charges brought against Buddhism—that it had become a religion of stagnation, resignation, and so on—persecution miraculously transformed the religion into a supporter of the political and military policies of the Meiji state and made it a collaborator in the development of Japanese capitalism. To analyze this transformation, we must look at the institutions and movements that served as the mediators between traditional values and the exigencies of the day. To do this, we must examine the "*four Buddhisms*" that made up "the Buddhism" of the Meiji period, namely, the outlooks of 1. the praxis masters, 1. the thinkers of the Buddhist Enlightenment, 3. the "progressive" Buddhist movements, and 4. the temples, or institutional Buddhism itself.

The Four "Buddhisms" of the Meiji Period

The Praxis Masters

We begin with the praxis (or *kairitsu*) masters—Jiun Sonja Onkō (1718–1804), Fukuda Gyōkai (1809–88), and Shaku Unshō (1827–1909)—because they were primarily responsible for transmitting the "strategy of accommodation" of the past to the Meiji period. To protect the Dharma, these priests elaborated a conservative strategy based on a firm reaffirmation of the religion's loyalty to the throne. Various slogans proclaimed that the Dharma was virtually coextensive with the law of the land. Buddhist leaders argued that Buddhism was "useful" (*buppō kokueki*) because it could magically and morally "protect" the nation (*gohō gokoku*). From this they reasoned that the state, in turn, should protect Buddhism by reestablishing it as an official religion (*goyō shyūkyō*). Shaku Unshō even looked to the state for the purification of the Sangha. Buddhism belonged not to the people, he argued, but to the emperor. The government should therefore regulate the Sangha and oversee its transmission of the precepts. In fact, what Shaku was advocating was a restoration of the ancient Sōniryō system of the Nara period, or Ritsu-ryō Buddhism, as it is called.

The Buddhist strategy rested on two subordinate tactics. The first was a widespread campaign to reform the Dharma by putting into actual practice the moral and religious disciplines spelled out in the ancient Buddhist precepts, monastic rules, and doctrines like the Ten Virtues (*jūzen*) and the Three Teachings (*sangaku*).[21] The renewed emphasis on moral praxis was not just a movement to rejuvenate Buddhism. It also provided "plausibility structures," to use Peter Berger's term, enabling Buddhists to deal with persecution philosophically.[22] The failure of Buddhists, especially in the Tokugawa period, to follow their own discipline was used to explain the suffering that Buddhism now had to endure. Praxis therefore came to function virtually as a theodicy for persecution. On the other hand, the rediscovery of praxis promised to transform the Buddhist masses into disciplined, loyal citizens. Praxis could therefore be used not only to rehabilitate but also to "legitimate" the Dharma. It could be used as part of the ubiquitous argument that Buddhism should be officially recognized once again because—by mass-producing good behavior—it was "useful" to the state.

The second set of defensive tactics had to do with relations with other sects. Putting aside their sectarian differences, Buddhist leaders began to draw on, and mix, the teachings of their several traditions more freely. They called for the restoration of the syncretistic ties they traditionally had enjoyed with Shinto and Confucianism. The Buddhist attitude towards Christians was a different story. Under the slogan "reject evil and establish truth" (*haja kenshō*) they launched a campaign against the legal rights of Christians.[23]

In many ways, the moral reformation launched by the praxis masters was conservative to the point of being reactionary. In 1872 Fukuda fired off several petitions to the government resolutely protesting the relaxation of the monk's traditional vows. In the same year, Shaku tried to prevent the opening of Mount Kōya and other sacred mountains to female pilgrims. Both deeply distrusted "the World of the Five Impurities." Both opposed the spread of Christianity. Neither was a friend of the materialism and acquisitiveness unleased by the government's program of Civilization and Enlightenment. After the movement to "modernize" Buddhism had come into its own (ca. 1890), the praxis advocated by Shaku Unshō lost most of its appeal. "Enlightened" thinkers attacked it as pessimistic, unsystematic, and overly defensive. By trying to free Buddhism from its dependence on ancient thought, on the one hand, and the corrupt values of modern society, on the other, the conservative campaign to "reject evil and establish truth" unintentionally found itself in a position that simply ignored history.

In spite of their shortcomings, the kairitsu teachers of early Meiji made a powerful impression on the religious life of their day. Above all else, they sought to provide ordinary people with spiritual and moral guidance. By insisting that Buddhist discipline be extended to all of the faithful, men like Fukuda and Shaku gave their support to the religious enfranchisement of the entire nation. Their message was the gospel of a "broad church" that, by ignoring narrow sectarian claims, was able to translate Buddhist discipline into simple universal norms. In this way, the praxis masters of Tokugawa and early Meiji added their support to the "value generalization" of Japanese Buddhist life—value generalization being a process that often accompanies the emergence of "modern" societies.[24]

Enlightenment Thinkers

Although the Buddhist Enlightenment is conventionally treated as a phenomenon of the 1870s and 1880s, it is difficult to specify its time frame with any precision. It begins with thinkers like Inoue Enryō, Shimaji Mokurai, Ishikawa Shuntai, Akamatsu Renjō, Hara Tanzan, Katō Kurō, and Ōsu Tetsunen but, in effect, continues on into the Taishō period (1912–24) with figures like the learned Watanabe Kaigyoku (1872–1933). Philosophically, the men of the Buddhist Enlightenment were preoccupied with a new hermeneutic that would spell out the Dharma in western philosophical terms. The journals for which they wrote were filled with articles on Socrates, Epictetus, Jesus, Martin Luther, Goethe, Mohammad, Kant, Schopenhauer, Schleiermacher, Emerson, and Bergson, as well as Confucius, Mencius, and other eastern sages. Like the spokesmen of the secular Enlightenment, Buddhist thinkers denounced the corruption of the clergy, feudalistic customs, like disembowelment (*seppuku*), and habits like public nudity and mixed bathing which were offensive to western eyes. Like their traditional confreres, the praxis masters, they cast a suspicious eye on Christian rivals. But unlike the traditionalists, they used the concept of haja kenshō to analyze religion and society in general and to critique the historical development of Buddhism.

Like its secular inspiration, the Civilization and Enlightenment Movement, the Buddhist Enlightenment was progressive in form, but conservative in substance. While leaders sometimes used the language of "natural rights," "freedom," and "progress," they remained firmly attached to the absolutism of the Meiji state. Their social ideals rested on the traditional notions of karma, filial piety, "discriminating equality," and the "benevolence of the sovereign." Many continued to argue along the lines developed by the praxis masters that the persecution of Buddhism had been brought about by the religion's own moral failure and that the situation could be remedied only by binding Buddhism to the state in a pact of mutual "benefits" and protection. This did not mean that the Enlightenment thinkers were committed to the state's religious program. But even those who opposed interference by the state in religious affairs were deeply influenced by the traditional doctrine of the inseparability of civil and religious duties (*ōbō buppō* or *shinzoku nitai*).

As modernizers of the Dharma, the Buddhists of the Enlightenment fully deserve the high reputation they have achieved in Japanese scholarship. Above all, they deserve respect for their attempts, however feeble, to make sense of their own religious tradition in light of the western philosophical and scientific thought inundating Japan at the time. Like the praxis master, they were quick to draw attention to the weakness of Buddhism and to call for necessary reforms. They helped to eradicate clerical evils and promote a more appropriate ethic for the family and for Japanese society in general. Unlike the French and Scottish Enlightenments, the Civilization and Enlightenment Movement in Japan was largely a government-sponsored program.[25] Enlightenment thinkers therefore tended to be critical of society but not of political absolutism. Like the Restoration itself, the secular Enlightenment of Fukuzawa Yukichi et alii ultimately was anything but liberal or democratic. The Buddhist Enlightenment followed suit. Its leaders continued the conservative strategy of the praxis masters, albeit in a more sophisticated, academic way. After the late 1870s the Enlightenment's emphasis on rights, which had always been equivocal, gave way to an intense nationalism that accented the rights of the state itself. Natural rights were not conceived as individual entitlements limiting the power of the state but as morality in keeping with nature. In short, Buddhism's primary defensive strategy did not encourage the faithful to stress their own civil rights but to dilate on their "usefulness" to the state. While nation and society were not clearly distinguished by most thinkers in the Meiji period, it was (literally) to the nation, and not to society, that benefits (*koku-on*) were to be "returned."

Conservative and Otherworldly Buddhist Movements

The social and political orientation of Buddhist movements in the Meiji period varied widely. When they could be pinned down to anything specific, groups like Nishida Tenkō's Ittōen or Kiyozawa Manshi's Spirituality (*Seishinshugi*) turned out to be conservative, or even feudalistic. Others, such as the members of the New Buddhist Movement, stood at the more progressive end of the spectrum.

Spirituality was very much the outcome of the personal pilgrimage of its founder, Kiyozawa Manshi (1863–1903).[26] Kiyozawa managed to combine in his own life and thought the discipline of the praxis masters and the absolute fideism of the Pure Land School.[27] Like Martin Luther, Kiyozawa approached the problem of morality after drinking deeply from the heady wine of faith. This raised a unique problem. If salvation is by faith alone—in Kiyozawa's case, faith in Amida Buddha—why be moral or bother about this world at all? Kiyozawa was no more an antinomian than Luther was. *After* a man has trusted in the Power Beyond Self, Kiyozawa writes, "he may live a moral life. He may seek academic knowledge. He may engage in politics or business. He may go fishing or hunting. When his country is endangered, he may march to war with a rifle on his shoulder."[28]

Before trusting in the Other Power of Amida, morality rests on the Self Power of the finite creature. To be moral in this sense is to be fettered to constraining responsibilities. The more one enters into the Power Beyond Self, the more disciplined one becomes. By allowing Amida Buddha to do good through oneself, the blindness of Self Power is gradually dispelled. Human goodness is therefore the work of the infinite or absolute (*mugen*), a power that transcends the finite ethical world of the "deluded spirit of Self Power" (*jiriki meijō*). Since the finite develops out of internal, karmic factors it cannot reach the absolute. The infinite, however, acts *ab extra* upon the finite self and, by taking the initiative, draws the finite to itself. In this process, the religious experience reverses the dynamics of morality. Freed from Self Power, morality becomes, so to speak, an effluent flowing out of the reservoir of faith. Morality is no longer a religious problem; it is a religious phenomenon. Kiyozawa therefore defined Spirituality as a "pragmatic way (*jikkōshugi*) for dealing with the world." He believed that although spiritual obedience was a form of "subjectivism," it was simultaneously "activistic" to the point of denying existing reality.[29] True morality is therefore part of the effortless Pure Activity that springs from faith.[30] It is the "work of the Buddha," not something we decide and then do.

Thanks to Shaku Unshō's influence, Kiyozawa, even after his conversion to the Power Beyond Self, continued to insist on the need for Buddhist praxis. He taught that the believer should seek to promote social welfare in a spirit of cooperation and harmony. He firmly rejected the self-interested idea of "Buddhism to protect the country." For him, "rich country, strong army" could never be a religious ideal. He was also critical of imperialism, even though he failed to see that, after its intervention in the Boxer Rebellion (1900), Japan itself had, de facto, entered the ranks of the imperial powers.

Kiyozawa did not seem interested in detailed critiques of Japanese capitalism. When he speaks of "freedom," he has in mind a purely religious experience. Freedom is whatever brings about enlightenment, i.e., "freedom from the self, not freedom from external conditions or circumstances."[31] Since the self cannot liberate itself, Kiyozawa's notion of freedom has no direct relationship to self-initiated action or political (let alone economic) freedom. On the contrary, freedom is virtually the same as religious humility. Thus he argued that "perfect freedom and perfect submission are not antagonistic."[32] In short, Kiyozawa's "freedom" seems to be an example of the absence of "autonomy" (*shutaisei*) in Japanese society that critical Japanese intellectuals constantly lament.[33]

In spite of the tension between the otherworldly or pietistical *Innerlichkeit* (Japanese, *naikanshugi*) of his thought, Japanese historians of religion often refer to Kiyozawa's conversion to the Power Beyond Self as a harbinger of "modern" Buddhism. But, aside from his openness to modern scholarship, it is difficult to see what is so "modern" about his general position. As for social action, the combination of fideism and rigoristic praxis led Kiyozawa, as it did many European pietists, to confine his reform effort to ecclesial politics. But even as a reformer of his own sect and its schools, Kiyozawa turned out to be a failure. Like Fukuda Gyōkai and Shaku Unshō, he finally tried to achieve his goals by establishing a group that he could control, the Spirituality Movement. The offspring of failed reforms, Spirituality developed into an alienated, pietistical *ecclesiola in ecclesia*. Thus Kiyozawa, the church reformer, had little influence on worldly reforms or social change. As a graduate of Buddhist schools set up in early Meiji to further the goals of "rich country, strong army," Kiyozawa was actually a product of institutional Buddhism's strategy of accommodation.[34] As a social thinker, he ranks no higher than the servile Myōkōnin saints of the Shinshū tradition. Through his piety, Myōkōnin hagiography was grafted into the Buddhist understanding of the emperor system itself. Consequently, Spirituality turned out to be, in Fukushima Hirokata's words, an "unconditional affirmation of existing reality."[35]

Relatively Progressive Movements

Viewed from the political left, groups like Spirituality would have seemed reactionary indeed. The more distance lay movements put between themselves and the temples, the more progressive they seemed to become. Although they welcomed priests as members, and even as leaders, paraecclesial organizations of this sort laid special emphasis on the layman's calling as a householder-bodhisattva. Groups of laymen like the Kyōkai Myōdō, founded by Torio Tokuan (1847–1905), sought to put into practice the Four Obligations and Ten Virtues and thereby implement the conservative strategy of "protecting the country by protecting Buddhism." In 1886, Daidō Chōan left the Sōtō priesthood to found the Kuzekyō, a layman's group devoted to the worship of the bodhisattva Kannon. Daidō, who was highly critical of institutional Buddhism, hoped to overcome the charge that Buddhism was a pessimistic religion by putting the precepts into actual practice. The Warp and Woof Society (Keiikai) founded in 1894 by Furukawa Rōsen, attacked the Buddhist establishment and, like Kuzekyō tried to rebut charges of otherworldliness. Members like Sakaino Kōyō agreed that Buddhism in the past had indeed been a "pessimistic religion." What was needed was a new Buddhism not based on prayer or magic (*kitō Bukkyō*), but one that would deal responsibly with this world and not just wait for the next. The Warp and Woof Society disbanded in 1899, but its work and spirit were inherited by the Spirituality and New Buddhist movements. In some cases, laypersons were "monasticized" in lay Buddhist communes (without taking vows of chastity).[36]

As time went on, Buddhist movements became more nationalistic. For example, the National Pillar Society (Kokuchūkai) begun in 1914 by the ex-Nichirenite priest, Tanaka Chiugaku (1861–1939), tried to combine aggressive evangelism (*shakubuku*) and emperor-worship. Tanaka condemned the patron-family (*danka*) base of institutional Buddhism and called for the reorganization of the religion as a "church" (*kyōkai*). For all his fanaticism, Tanaka was a highly respected Buddhist who had a decisive impact on Takayama Chogyū, Anesaki Masaharu, and even the Christian preacher, Uchimura Kanzō.

The New Buddhist Movement

The Most progressive of the Buddhist movements of middle and late Meiji was the New Buddhist Movement, an organization that grew out of a meeting held in 1894 by Furukawa Rōsen, Sugimura Jūō, and others.[37] Most members were middle-class, unaffiliated Buddhists in their twenties. The New Buddhists picked up and developed the radical ideas of the Warp and Woof Society. They rejected the traditional rituals and priesthood of the "Old Buddhism," blaming it for overlooking the individual and for obstructing "progress" in ethics, education, and religious research. Like Inoue Enryō, they denounced magic and superstition. In their *Statement of General Purposes,* the group vowed to work out a "sound religious faith" and to exert itself "for the fundamental betterment of society." They called for free scholarly research on Buddhist history and doctrine. Rejecting all schemes to "protect Buddhism," they boldly denounced state support of, and interference with, religion.[38] Sakaino Kōyō decried the way Tokugawa Buddhism had transformed believers into mere temple patrons. In an article published in the movement's journal, *The New Buddhism*, Sakaino declared that the "sound faith" the group was seeking was a "this-worldly," "activist," "ethical," and "optimistic" religion—adjectives carefully chosen to accentuate the differences between the new and old Buddhisms.[39]

The New Buddhists were among the few Buddhist organizations actually to engage in social protest. In 1902, they protested the Ministry of Education's heavy-handed treatment of the Tetsugakkan Affair.[40] They criticized the moral rearmament philosophy of the Hōtoku Movement, the Confucian revival, bushidō, the Boshin Rescript, and the National Morality Movement as "old-fashioned."[41] While they could not publicly oppose the Russo-Japanese War, some members, like Hayashi Takejirō, assumed a public stance of "war weariness." In 1909, New Buddhists protested publication of the Ministry of Education's infamous Order Number One prohibiting "dangerous thoughts." They were opposed to militarism and lavish displays of patriotism. Some became involved in protesting the Ashio copper mine affair. As middle-class reformers, the group never adopted socialism as part of its platform. While some tried to move toward the workers, like other "bourgeois intellectuals," their sympathies usually stopped short of direct political action.

The Economic Perspective of the Buddhist Movements

Some Buddhist intellectuals showed considerable interest in socialism. In 1882, long before the abortive Social Democratic Party was conceived, Tarui Tōkichi founded the Eastern Socialist Party on the idealistic notion that the "children of Buddha" should "look at the people with compassionate eyes." Some, like Tanaka Sōgorō, believed socialism was essentially a mixture of Buddhism, Confucianism, and western thought. Some thought socialism was the same as the Mahayana ideal of "cooperative assistance" (*kyōdō fujo*).[42] Katayama Sen (1859–1933), an early member of Abe Isoo's socialist circle, initially advocated a "spiritual socialism" based on the Buddhist ideals of non-ego and altruism. Some of the New Buddhists—Mōri Shian, for instance–enjoyed close relations with socialists and members of the Heiminsha. Kiyozawa vaguely proposed the establishment of "Buddha's Country" (*Nyōrai no kokka*) as an alternative to capitalism and political authoritarianism. Itō Shōshin's Selfless Love Movement was a pacifistic movement bordering on, but never quite becoming, socialist.

As the capitalist system spread, some Buddhists became aware of a new kind of poverty. Moved by the economic panic of 1890, Murakami Taion began to publish detailed articles on poverty and hunger. Honorable poverty (*seihin*) was superior to ill-gotten wealth, he said. The rich who provide no assistance to the poor can make no claims against them. If the government takes no steps to help the poor, Buddhists should do so out of considerations of "egalitarianism." Buddhists should try to evangelize the "lazy poor" and awaken them from their sloth.

Goodwill notwithstanding, the "socialism" of the Buddhist movements generally fell short of political action. Most members could only be called socialist "sympathizers." In contrast to later movements in Southeast Asia, "Buddhist socialism" or "spiritual socialism" in Japan therefore turned out to be a tepid affair. It called for "equality with order" or "discriminating equality," a nebulous position that actually made room for inequality on a grand scale. It was the fuzzy kind of social idealism that paternalistic, ultranationalistic National Essence Socialism (Kokutai Shakaishugi) could, and later on did, coopt. Nevertheless, there were many socialists—Kinoshita Naoe, Sakai Toshihiko, Kōtoku Shūsui, Morichia Unpei, and Ishikawa Sanshirō among them—who were on good terms with the members of the more progressive Buddhist movements.

The most radical Buddhists were those implicated in the Lèse Majesté Affair.[43] In 1911, life sentences were handed down to Takagi Kemmyō (a priest in the Ōtani sect), Sasaki Dōgen (Shinshū), and Mineo Setsudō (Rinzai). Takagi earlier had worked for the liberation of outcastes (the *Eta* or *Burakumin*) and for the abolition of prostitution. In 1904 he wrote a book called *My Socialism* in which he declared the Buddha to be a "socialist in the spirit world" and Shinran "the ally of the common man." He declared that the "corrupt world" described in the scriptures was the world of class struggles.[44] The Ōtani sect finally excommunicated him for breaking its religio-political ideals, *shinzoku nitai* and *ōbō ihon*.

The most interesting figure involved in the Lèse Majesté Affair was Uchiyama Gudō (1874–1911), a member of the Sōtō sect. Uchiyama's social thought was essentially a mixture of Zen, socialism and anarchism. Anarchism, Uchiyama believed, was the natural expression of the Buddhist spirit of self-sacrifice. Egalitarianism he equated with Buddhist Enlightenment. He attacked the divinity of the emperor as a base superstition, challenged tenant farmers not to pay their taxes, and urged conscripts to desert the army.[45] He called for "freedom"—obviously not the freedom advocated by Kiyozawa Manshi—for the respect of the individual, the dignity of workers, and the public ownership of land and the means of production. With radical credentials like these, Uchiyama's execution by the state in 1911 was hardly surprising.

The most progressive of the Buddhist groups we have been discussing was probably the New Buddhist Movement. On several occasions the government prohibited the sale of its magazine, *The New Buddhism*. In contrast to the old Buddhism, the New Buddhists emphasized not the "return of *on*" due to the emperor or the nation but that owed to the Three Treasures and to "all sentient beings," that is, to society itself. What the subject owed the sovereign was a debt of gratitude for giving and observing the constitution and preserving "political righteousness" (*kengi*). In this way, they sought to weave the ancient morality of *on* into the new constitutionalism of the day. In contrast to Spirituality, they focused their attention on the "deterioration of humanity" sweeping through Japanese society. Since movements of this sort were often shaped by (and "played to") secular political or literary groups, conservatives raised questions about their "religiousness." Articles in *The New Buddhism* itself asked whether the movement was truly Buddhist. Ōuchi Seiran criticized them on the grounds that they had failed to produce a "new faith" and had degenerated into a purely social movement. "The old house has been destroyed. The new one is not ready. One is therefore made to camp out of doors."[46] Because the Movement *was* a movement and not a settled corpus of ideas, the New Buddhists had no ready answers to criticism of this sort. In fact, they were in the midst of a transvaluation of all Buddhist values—philosophical and social. Nevertheless, the New Buddhists would not have recognized a purely secular salvation as enlightenment, or an enlightenment experience without the spirit of emptiness, self-control, and non-ego as salvation.

The Conservatism of Temple-Based Buddhism

Up to this point we have discussed the transsectarian responses to modernity of the Buddhist movements in the Meiji period. While novelty always captures the historian's attention—and in some ways these movements were unprecedented—it is important to bear in mind their limited "statistical significance." They were primarily elite phenomena, movements "staged" by educated leaders for middle-class students and a sympathetic press. To grasp the real nature of the Buddhist response to modernity we must look at the Buddhism that was numerically, socially, and politically dominant. To do so, we must turn from relatively ephemeral movements to temples and to the thinking of the priests who served them. As we reexamine the social teachings of temple-based Buddhism, the relatively progressive nature of movement-Buddhism will stand out in clear relief.

In chapter 1, we traced the conservatism of the Buddhist family temple (*bodaiji*, or *danna-dera*) back to the hegemonic "because" motivations of its supporting members. We must now expand our analysis by taking a closer look at the institutional networks surrounding the temple. Institutional Buddhism was an integral part of the social and political *Gemeinschaft* structure of rural Japan. At the community level, its leading families included village headmen and landlords or the so-called gentry. Attached to the temples was a wide variety of confraternities (*kō* or *kōsha*), which likewise reflected the micropolitical order of the village. Vertically, the local temple was at the low end of a "parent-child" hierarchy of temples extending up to the head temple of the sect. At the prefectural and national levels, the ecclesiocrats of the head temples were well connected with secular and political elites. The patriarchs of the Honganji sect, for example, were related by marriage to the imperial family itself. Sandwiched between, and silenced by, the elites were the common masses, often living in abject poverty. Conspicuously missing was a middle class.

We have already seen that the persecution that took place in early Meiji was the primary cause of the reactionary campaign to "protect Buddhism." While peasants sought to protect their family temples by force, in uprisings called *gohō-ikki*, more effective strategies of self-defense were drawn up by the temples. Institutional Buddhism responded to persecution by frantically proclaiming its loyalty and devotion to the regime. Among the temples one could see the same kind of competition-in-loyalty one sees today among rival industries in Japan vis-à-vis some government agencies. Each sect vied to demonstrate its fidelity not only to the nation and the emperor but also to the basic policies of the state: economic development, nationalism, and even war.

In keeping with its social base, the reaction of institutional Buddhism to modernity was conservative and often reactionary. Its overwhelming concern was the recovery of its own privileges, comfort, and security. The link between these institutional imperatives and the strategy of accommodation was patent in the Buddhist campaign to achieve official recognition by the state. In May 1889, thirty-six sectarian Buddhist leaders petitioned the home minister asking for official recognition. The next month, the same group, meeting in the Tsukiji Honganji temple in Tokyo, resolved that Buddhists must work for "social harmony," give aid to the poor, help spread education, and give encouragement to industrial production. One suspects that the intentions of these two meetings and their respective resolutions were not unrelated. They are a perfect example of the attempt to trade mutual "benefits" for "protection" in a strategy of accommodation. To prove its "usefulness" to the state, Buddhism posed as a cornucopia of good works. Hundreds of patriotic Buddhist youth groups, charitable foundations, and devotional organizations sprang up around the country. Buddhist sects began to train and dispatch home missionaries to conduct evangelistic work in prisons, schools, and factories. Foreign missionaries were sent out to "pacify" the new colonies. Buddhist chaplains began to accompany the army in its sallies abroad.

A Strategy of Accommodation

A strategy of accommodation can be seen behind many of the specific programs devised by the Buddhist sects of the Meiji period. Here I shall examine Buddhist responses only to the Imperial Edicts, the Ashio copper mine affair, and Japan's growing militarism.

Buddhist Commentaries on the Imperial Rescripts

After the Imperial Rescript on Education appeared in 1890, several commentators tried to give the document a religious twist. Buddhist writers argued that the doctrine of the Four Benefits (*Shi-on*) was, without modification, identical with the teachings of the rescript. Buddhism supports the rescript, they said, because it is the basis of filial piety in general. They enthusiastically endorsed the government's union of religion and government (*saisei itchi*)—implying, of course, that it should include Buddhism. They extolled the nobility of dying for one's country. On Kigensetsu (the festival of the founding of the Japanese Empire), 1911, the Imperial Rescript on Rescuing the People (*Kyūmin Chokugo*) was published announcing the dispersal of one and a half million yen from the emperor's own treasury for free medical assistance. Buddhists used the occasion to point out that Buddhist charity was in accord with the emperor's own magnanimity and that they shared his fear of left-wing radicals.

On 13 October 1908, the Meiji government responded to the economic recession following the Russo-Japanese War by issuing the Boshin Rescript. In it, the emperor urged the people to be frugal, obedient, sincere, to "toil arduously" and not succumb to the growing temptations of individualism, hedonism, and socialism. Buddhists again responded by publishing numerous tomes of their own on related topics. In 1909, the Hōzōkan publishing house brought out a compendium of stories about frugal people, replete with quotations from the scriptures on the virtue of diligence for use by Buddhist preachers. Some regarded support for state programs as Buddhism's raison d'être. Pure Land zealots declared that spreading the Boshin Rescript was the principal calling of the Honganji sect and instructed believers that hard work was identical to believing in the Sacred Vow of Amida. The faithful were also urged to treat working hours and material things produced with frugality as though they were the Buddha himself. Priests devoted themselves to preaching the Boshin gospel to landlords and tenant farmers. Implicit in their message were the (tendentious) ideas that the vicissitudes of a nation depend on the morality of its people and that prosperity is a karmic reward.[47]

The Ashio Copper Mine Incident

In some cases, Buddhism was compelled to accommodate itself to the state's negative mandates. The Ashio pollution affair is a case in point. In the 1870s a copper mine run by Furukawa Ichibee began to dump pollutants into the Watarase River, poisoning the rice paddies in about 1,366 villages in Tochigi, Gumma, Saitama, and Chiba prefectures. The health and livelihood of some three hundred thousand people were put at risk. Before long, Ashio became of a widely discussed problem, even in Buddhist circles. Buddhist priests pointed out that the Ashio tragedy was not just the result of "bad karma." It was a case of avoidable human misconduct. Temples in the area set up offices to coordinate an antipollution campaign. In 1902, however, the Religion Bureau of the Ministry of Home Affairs warned all religious bodies in Japan to avoid political discussions of the affair. Discussions of this sort, the government noted, served only to stir people up and had a particularly bad influence on students. A Shingon temple in Gumma Prefecture was told it could no longer allow antipollution activists to use its premises for their meetings and that it would have to close its "pollution office." In obedience to the government order, Buddhists began to discuss the Ashio problem as a humanitarian, social issue rather than as a problem of the massive political clout of unfettered capitalism. Ōuchi Seiran warned fellow Buddhists not to hate Furukawa or resent the government's foot-dragging policies. In the end, Ashio ceased to be a political problem for institutional Buddhism. It became a matter of "charity" instead.

Militarism

While economists tend to isolate the "development" of Japan from the country's military adventures, the truth is that development was not limited to the "rise of capitalism." Militarism, nationalism, imperialism, and capitalism might be *separable* developments, but they are *inseparable* in their real, internal relations. Our story would therefore be incomplete without a passing reference to Buddhism and war.

It is sad and ironic that Buddhism, like Christianity, has done so little to curb the modern world's thirst for imperialism and war. During the Meiji persecution of Buddhism, priests sometimes participated in uprisings to protect their temples (*gohō-ikki*), while strongly condemning similar uprising by peasants protesting high taxes and rents (*nōmin-ikki*). During the Seinan War, Honganji sent large sums of money to the government troups in order to "benefit the nation." By the early 1890s, Buddhists (like other Japanese) had been swept away by the tide of anti-Western feelings and patriotic emotion. Enlightenment Buddhists like Ōuchi Seiran strongly supported the Sino-Japanese War. A federation of Zen sects urged all temples to be frugal in order to be able to contribute patriotically to the war effort and to the relief of soldiers. In the same way, Shinshū encouraged its members to buy war bonds and donate money and valuables to the armed forces. Two years after the war, the Shinshū patriarch, Ōtani Kōzui, was given an imperial citation for his many contributions to the war effort. It goes without saying that the assistance of the temples enabled the government to devote more of its resources to the military effort itself. To put the matter more bluntly, religious charity was coopted by militarism and an imperialistic foreign policy.

Most Buddhist sects legitimated the Russo-Japanese War on the grounds that Japan was only seeking to establish law and order (the Dharma) in East Asia. Some, like Inoue Enryō, justified the war as a crusade against Christianity. In 1904, Buddhists joined Shintō, Confucian, and Christian leaders to proclaim that the war with Russia was aimed at the "eternal peace" of Japan and East Asia, and that it was being waged "for the sake of civilization, righteousness and humanity."[48] From the Buddhist perspective, the struggle with Russia had become a holy war, even a manifestation of Buddhist "compassion"! The Buddha had given Japan his guidance and blessing for a complete victory over the traitorous, *klesha*-ridden (sinful) Russians. Killing the enemy was therefore not an infringement of the Buddhist precept of noninjury but a sign of devotion to the Buddha himself.

The only Buddhist opposition to the war came from those beyond the pale of institutional Buddhism or from those willing to risk its wrath. Uchiyama Gudō wrote an antiwar tome called *Motto for the Imperial Soldier (Teikoku gunjin zayū no mei).* In Wakayama, the "Eta priest," Takagi Kenmyō, incensed the Buddhist establishment by attacking priests who prayed for victory and set up memorials for the war dead. Some members of the New Buddhist Movement also held pacifist views. Sakaino Kōyō condemned the war from the beginning, predicting that it would enrich the capitalists by exploiting the poor. In the face of war, Kiyozawa Manshi talked evasively about the "ironies of karma" and the "need for faith." Others, like Itō Shōshin, waited until the war was over to express their antiwar feelings.

The Official Buddhist Response to Issues of the Meiji Period

We have seen that the "progressive" Buddhists had no unified viewpoint on social ethics and economic justice. The same was true of institutional (or temple-based) Buddhism, although here the range of opinion moves decidedly to the right. At first, the temples were largely silent about political and economic changes. When they did speak out, their message was highly ambiguous. As time went on, however, the Buddhist response to capitalism and other issues of the day did become clear.

The Economic Perspective of the Buddhist Temples

Where did institutional Buddhism stand in regard to the massive economic growth of the Meiji period? What did it have to say about the suffering it created? Institutional Buddhism responded to the Lèse Majesté Affair with horror and disgust. Priests inveighed against socialism as an unpatriotic cult based on a doctrine of "bad equality" (*akubyōdōsei*). They resented the way socialists scoffed at "karmic relations" and attributed to their ignorance of karma their failure to recognize the "obvious differences" between social classes. After 1911, when the government began to clamp down on dissent in earnest, Buddhist preachers increasingly laid emphasis on the "return of benefits," "thankfulness," the "consequences of karma," the "mutual reliance of the rich and the poor," and "orderly (i.e., unequal) equality." During the Enlightenment period, thinkers like Shimaji Mokurai condemned socialism as an egalitarian theory running counter to the Buddhist teaching of "discriminating equality." In 1872, the Ōtani Shinshū sect proclaimed that "in the end, to evade taxes and neglect business is to bring poverty, misery and hunger upon the people."[49]

Buddhism was constitutionally opposed to the "struggle for existence" and the "survival of the fittest"—the interpretation given to western capitalism in the nineteenth century by the Social Darwinists. But it did not reject capitalism per se. On the contrary, it trotted out its ancient slogans of "social harmony" in support of the competitive economy and the government's "rich country, strong army" policy. In 1909, on the eve of the Lèse Majesté Affair, Shaku Sōen was arguing that the Zen ideal of seeking for enlightenment in this samsaric world was the real energy behind the economy.

After the Affair, the government turned to Buddhism to help stem the flow of socialism, anarchism, the labor union movement, and other "dangerous ideas." Since the Buddhists were always ready to prove their "usefulness," they readily accommodated the Dharma to fit the new situation. As tensions between capital and labor mounted, the temples tried to take a transcendental stand above the fray. In fact, they were safely in the pockets of the state and the "developers." The problems of labor were to be solved, they said, not by strikes but by returning to the ancient morality of *on* and *hō-on*. Those who helped to increase industrial productivity were often ranked with workers in reformatories and other charitable institutions as exemplary models of the "heart of compassion" (*jihi*).[50] Buddhist economic wisdom came down to this: managers should be paternal; workers should "return the benefits" received from their bosses and work out of "gratitude." A worker's rights must give way to his duties.

Attitudes Toward Workers and Poverty

The Buddhist attitude toward workers was not entirely negative. After the financial panic of 1890, Buddhist publications began to publish detailed reports on the lot of the poor. The capitalists' vicious response to the strikes of 1907 was condemned as a misuse of power that created still more violence. Buddhist authors challenged their fellow believers to address the various social problems created by the maldistribution of wealth. Other publications drew attention to the ancient precept that the starving cannot understand the Dharma and urged the faithful to come to the rescue of the poor, especially if the rich and the powerful failed to do so. They drew attention to the plight of the female work force and called for meetings to discuss cruelty in the factories. Some sought to "protect" factory operatives, postal workers, bank employees, and even the police. In 1910, the Honganji sect organized a group called the Buddhist Friends of the Railway to work with the national railroad. It later extended its mission to the spinning mills.

Sympathy aside, the Buddhist response to labor unrest was extremely cautious. Its basic social philosophy rested on a policy of "mutual assistance between the rich and the poor." The poor need the work and protection only the rich can provide; the rich need the hard work of the poor. Buddhists saw this as an application of the Mahayana teaching of the "unity of self and other" to the new factory system. In fact, it was a new use for the medieval, indeed ancient, ethic of "hierarchical complementarity." Some interpreted the doctrine of the "Middle Way" as a neutral stand between labor and capital. On this reading, the Middle Way meant that the rich should show mercy to the poor and that the poor should be diligent in serving the rich. At the prompting of Itagaki Taisuke, the home minister, the Higashi Honganji patriarch wrote to all priests urging them to exhort wealthy temple patrons to perform acts of charity and to warn trade unionists not to go on strikes or "recklessly" stir up other workers. Buddhist factory evangelists preached up the government's ideals of "rich country, strong army," corporate familialism, and the need for cooperation between management and labor. Most priests, however, had no understanding of the new factories and instinctively took the side of capital in most disputes. They lost no time in denouncing the "socialist agitators" who "stirred up" strikes and protest movements. By becoming the "friends" and "allies" of the workers, factory evangelists tried to present an alternative to radicalism. To make the workers aware of the "Light of Amida Buddha," they sought to provide them with "temples in the caverns of poverty."[51] Even though tuberculosis was the greatest danger to female mill workers, Buddhists priests fretted more about the preservation of their chastity. However benign their intentions may have been, the evangelists eventually came to be deeply resented, especially when they took the side of management. In some cases, such as the Ōmi Silk Thread Strike of 1931, the workers protested the evangelists' "religious coercion" and demanded the "complete abolition of factory evangelism."[52]

Like the Dissenters and Nonconformists in Britain, the Buddhists of the Meiji period generally regarded poverty as the natural result of sin, or "bad karma," as they would say. Shimaji Mokurai put the blame for poverty on the shiftlessness of the poor themselves. "They just don't work!" he complained. What the poor needed was "morality," "education," "thrift," "good manners," and, of course, "spiritual culture."[53] Private sins seemed more obvious and important than the most heinous institutional crimes. Buddhist priests, like Protestant clergy in the west, lamented drinking, sexual debauchery, gambling, and other "working-class vices." Economic recessions and depressions (e.g., the period

1881–85) were also explained in terms of moral failure: the people had not been "frugal" enough.

Charity

Buddhists initially found it difficult to adjust to the new ideal of charity. Their social thought was based on a limited repertoire of ideas, values, and slogans, for example, "friendship and solidarity" (*dōmei*), "altruism" (*rita*), "repaying one's obligations to all sentient beings" (*shuyō-on*), "returning to the world as a bodhisattva" (*gensō ekō*), and so on. Charity (*fukuden*) given to monks, to the poor and the sick, or to aged parents was an opportunity to "return benefits" and thereby improve one's own karma. Usually, people gave to those whom they knew personally. Charity, in other words, was proudly particularistic. Since the suffering of others was thought to be the result of their own evil deeds (either in this life or in previous ones), the doctrine of karma limited the scope and effectiveness of charity. While karma notoriously followed families from generation to generation, there seemed to be no such thing as "social karma." (This was not strange since the abstract idea of "society" itself hardly existed.) Western Protestants and Japanese Buddhists drew virtually the same conclusion from all of this: poverty is the fault of the poor. To most Buddhists, the Confucian nostrum "reward good, punish evil" (*kanzen chōaku*) therefore seemed a perfectly natural response to the social question. Only a few realized that it was impossible to apply the idea in a complex society. If international markets and business cycles sometimes punished the diligent and rewarded the indolent or crafty, who could say who was "good" and who was "evil"? Relations between morality and capitalism were not that simple. Nevertheless, the simplistic moralism of kanzen chōaku remained the keystone of Buddhist social thought throughout the early Meiji period.

To a large extent, the charities that the Buddhists established in the early Meiji period represented a defensive response to the competitive challenge of Protestant charitable institutions. Yet, the need for charity was a "godsend" for them. In the face of criticism and persecution, it gave them an opportunity to demonstrate their "usefulness" to the nation. The Ōtani sect's involvement in road building and reclamation projects in Hokkaidō was undertaken explicitly "for the national benefit" (*kokueki*). Buddhists were also active in campaigns to curtail abortion, the abandonment of children, and child exposure (*mabiki*, literally, "thinning out"). They sent money and aid to the victims of the Seinan uprising of 1877. In the same year the Philanthropy Society

(Hakuaisha, forerunner of the Japanese Red Cross) was founded, with the omnipresent Shimaji Mokurai as its head.[54]

Because it was based on the ideal of the "interdependence of rich and poor," Buddhist charity was an impediment to the concept of social or economic rights. As time went on, however, Buddhists began to realize the need for a new concept of charity, one free from the simplistic Confucianism of the past. The New Buddhist Movement, which had self-consciously broken with the philosophy of "Buddhism for the national benefit," pioneered in what could be called "the Buddhist discovery of society." Buddhists involved in charitable activities began to think of their work as something done for society and not simply for the emperor or the state.

In the end, Buddhist charity outgrew the competitive attitude it previously had vis-à-vis Christian social activism. Thus "charity work" (*jizen jigyō*) became the "reform and the relief activities" (*kanka kyūsai jigyō*) of late Meiji. In spite of its "modern" and "scientific" packaging, the new social work perpetuated most of the traditional ideals of class harmony, and saw Buddhism as a Middle Way between capitalism and labor. Throughout the Meiji and Taishō periods, Buddhist pronouncements on social questions invariably followed the line set forth by the state. In effect, "reform and relief" fell in line with the ideal of "national prosperity and popular welfare" (*kokuri minpuku*).

Conclusions

The Religious Construction of a Rhetoric of Development

I should begin my concluding remarks by saying that I have not found in Buddhism the "mighty enthusiasm" that Max Weber thought was necessary for the rationalization of economic and social life.[55] I have tried to show that Japanese Buddhists were primarily *reacting* to the momentous changes going on about them in the Meiji period and that the changes they did initiate were limited primarily to sectarian politics, the religious press, and the academic world.

In a more positive vein, I have shown that institutional Buddhism finally did lend its support to a Japanese-style "rhetoric of development." The creation of a Buddhist rhetoric of development was brought about not by the direct imposition of religious ideas on society but "dialectically," through the mediation of religious institutions. This means that the history of Buddhism and the history of economic development converge not at the level of the history of ideas but at the level of social history. It also means that one cannot understand this history simply by dilating on the "impact" of "the central value system" on society in any abstract way.

Our historical investigation into the points of contact between religion, rhetoric, and ideology suggests that the Weber thesis is of limited value as a paradigm for Japanese development. More helpful parallels might be found in studies of the "penalization" of minorities or the status deprivation and/or status inconsistency of such economically active groups as Jews, Mormons, Nonconformists, and Dissenters.[56] The odd thing about Japan is that Buddhists were neither an ethnic nor a religious minority. They found themselves similarly threatened because, after 1868, their teachings, already tainted by the patronage of the previous regime, failed to mesh with the outlook of the country's new "developers."

Buddhists first reacted to the contradictions of modernity with silence and indifference. Historians find such otherworldly responses particularly recalcitrant to work with. Evidence usually comes not from the religion itself but from cultured despisers who look on religion in general as a quagmire of magic and metaphysics having little to do with "social reality." Ironically, silence—especially moral aphasia in the face of suffering and injustice—may have been the major contribution ("passive enablement") Buddhism had to make to the development of Japan. At least one could launch the ironic argument that if rapid development rests on "pyramids of sacrifice"—to use Peter Berger's crushing expression—silence about the fate of those caught beneath the pyramids may contribute indirectly to efficiency itself. Social protest, on the other hand, slows things down and diminishes productivity. Whatever the case, the Meiji government cultivated silence about some of its policies with a heavy hand. We have seen how it silenced Buddhist discussions of the Ashio copper mine affair. In the 1880s and 1890s, it began to suppress political discussion of all sorts. In 1880, it barred military men, police officers, teachers, students, and agricultural and technical apprentices from attending political meetings. State Shintō was turned into a mute, patriotic cult. In 1899, the government ordered that religion and politics not be discussed in the public schools. Thus, by the beginning of the Taishō period, public interest in formal politics had been considerably curtailed.[57]

Structurally related to silence is ambiguity, another of the survival tactics of institutional religion. While ambiguous preaching is not heard in faith's finest hour, it unquestionably has a *structural* role to play in the adaptation of religion to social change: it allows religion the flexibility it needs to survive and flourish. Weber might well have characterized Buddhism, as he did Anglicanism, as a "religion of gentle moods." Instead, he heavy-handedly described it as a religion of "moody inwardness" incapable of generating economic rationality on its own.[58] When we look carefully at Buddhist social teachings, however, what strikes us is not their moodiness but their intrinsic ambiguity. This owed much to the internal structure of the religion itself, which had always been tolerant, forbearing, and broad-minded. We have seen that ambiguity also had a more immediate source: institutional self-interest. In Meiji Japan, it was difficult to say exactly *what* the Buddhists' social ideals were or *how* they hoped to achieve them. Even the progressives were irritatingly vague. Buddhist social maxims seemed to be infinitely plastic. The idea of nonego, for example, was used to whip the female factory operative into submission to her industrial masters. In the Taishō period, it was the doctrinal foundation for Nishida Tenkō's tendentious idea that one should work not for money—"money is unnecessary"—but out of gratitude.[59] The ideal of nonego could be invoked by Buddhist socialists in their attack on the "egoism" of the capitalist system. Later, it was used, and certainly corrupted, to generate a spirit of absolute military discipline. The ideal of noninjury was surrounded with the same fuzzy hermeneutical halo. Meiji officials used Buddhist priests to persuade farmers that, since the nation was dependent on silk for exports, the rule of noninjury did not apply to the killing of silkworms. But noninjury could be safely set aside in time of war against other human beings. As these examples suggest, the flexibility of Buddhism's basic ideas and symbols enabled secular movements of all sorts to use the religion as they saw fit.

While equivocal systems of thought provoke the disdain of philosophers, historians and sociologists should regard them as objects of great curiosity. I say this for the simple reason that ambiguous ideas are flexible, and flexible ideas are ones *especially open to change*. If so, those interested in the problem of religion and social change should concentrate on the inherent vagaries of a religion's social message. If the ideas of institutional religion are as fluid as I think they are, one is led to expect three things: 1. that religious notions will usually be involved in social and historical change not as the initiators of that change but as bystanders or collaborators, 2. that religion will respond to change by modifying its own ideas and practices, and 3. that this modification will take place primarily in response to the needs of religious *institutions*.[60] All of these expectations seem to have been borne out by the present study of the role of Buddhism in the development of Meiji at Japan.

Positive Enablements, or Does Religion Really Matter?

While I have stressed the nebulousness of the social teachings of institutional religion in this chapter, I do not want to belittle their obvious historical importance. One should however be deeply suspicious of those who talk glibly about the "impact of values on society" or about the "cybernetic control" of society by "*the* central value system." For generations, thinkers as different as Machiavelli, Mandeville, Nietzsche, Marx, and (more recently) Alasdair MacIntyre have repeatedly demonstrated that complex societies have no integrated, "central value system" but that they rest, or float on, ambiguous, incompatible, and contradictory values. Nevertheless, values and the religions that spawn them obviously *do* make a difference.

Although religious ideals seem to be infinitely malleable, or nearly so, they impose some restrictions on what can and cannot be said or done in a given culture. Thus, even if religion contributed to industrialization primarily by getting out of its way, its internal logic yields important clues about the *shape* industrialization has taken in different countries. Here I would like to draw the reader's attention to three cases in which different religious structures seem to be related to different patterns of secular development. In the following paragraphs, I am primarily interested in comparing Britain, the first country in the world to experience the Industrial Revolution, and Japan, the first non-Western country to become an industrial power. Because of the magnitude of the problem and the vast number of variables involved, I am forced to speak rather vaguely about the parallels, correlations, and anticipations that link religion and development, and not about historical causation per se. What follows is therefore admittedly speculative and is based only in part on the research presented in this chapter.

Rhetoric and Ideology.

In both England and the United States, the spiritual individualism nourished by Protestantism proved to be congruent with the economic individualism of the classical economists. Adam Smith, one of the chief architects of the morals and mechanics of the new economy, recognized that love, gratitude, friendship and mutual esteem help society to flourish. Nevertheless, he went to great lengths to describe an economic system that would work *without* ascribing to humankind any natural "togetherness" (*appetitus societatis*). His system was explicitly guaranteed to work—by the Divine Utilitarian who allegedly designed it—without the help of love, benevolence, loyalty or gratitude.[61] In the late nineteenth century, the Social Darwinists devised a still harsher economic philosophy by mixing Smith's relatively benign doctrine with the principles of biology. The result was a moral legitimation—in terms of the "survival of the fittest"—not only of competition, but of the class system itself. In Britain (and a fortiori, the United States) this culminated in a rhetoric of development characterized not just by individualism but also by an antisocial *ruthlessness* seldom witnessed in other countries. The abstract theory of laissez-faire was eventually supplemented with a grass-roots, religiously based aversion to state interference. Dissenters and Nonconformists were not about to turn to the state to make the country rich or to solve "the social question." Why should they expect such things from the state when the state had taken so long to grant them their own civil rights? They would sooner do the job themselves—by bringing the Gospel to the poor, giving them jobs, and, of course, sobering them up. Only when the power of Dissent began to dissipate (around the end of the nineteenth century) did Protestants turn to the government to solve the problems of the day.[62]

In Japan, where translations of Friedrich List and other protectionists appeared even before the works of Smith, Ricardo, and Bentham, a vastly different rhetoric took shape. Japanese entrepreneurs initially failed to create a business ideology that could deflect Confucian prejudice against commerce.[63] Consequently, they found themselves in a defensive position not unlike the Buddhists. It is not surprising that the ideology they finally came up with was not very different from the Buddhist outlook discussed in this chapter. Religiously reinforced *Gemeinschaft* ideals prevented them from explicating business in terms of Social Darwinism. After unsuccessfully experimenting with the practices of the Anglo-American sweatshop, they learned to apply—with far greater effect—the archaic symbols of "hierarchical complementarity" (family, village, and imperial parent) to the economy. For example, in 1908, Soeda Jūichi, president of the Kōgyō Bank declared: "The master—the capitalist—is loving toward those below, and takes tender care of them, while the employee—the worker—respects those above and will sacrifice himself to his work. The spirit of loyalty and love of country . . . is by no means limited to the relationship between the sovereign and subject."[64]

To these images were added the totalistic (if not totalitarian) slogans of Buddhism: the "nonduality of self and other," "harmonious unity," "the mutual reliance of rich and poor," and so on. Armed with these values, symbols, and slogans, the Japanese took their first ideological steps toward the creation of their now celebrated system of economic nationalism, or "neo-mercantilism."

MORNING DISCUSSION IN A JAPANESE BANK. Japanese firms often begin the day with a "pep-talk," exercise, or a ritual affirmation of the ideals of the company.

The Role of the State in Development.

Although Japanese Buddhists and the English Dissenters and Nonconformists were all persecuted, they did not respond to tribulation in the same way. We have seen that the Buddhists had a long tradition of subordination to the state. While Caesaro-Papism had a long history in the west too, other models for relating church, state, and society were available to the English sectarians. These included *ressentiment* (as Nietzsche showed) and an anarchistic longing for the overthrow of established wealth, rank, and power. Discrimination naturally exacerbated the entrepreneurial Nonconformist's mistrust of the state. An adversarial relationship between government and business therefore seemed as natural to the churches as it did to the Manchester economists. The contrast with Japan could hardly be more pronounced. While the British bourgeoisie had a deep suspicion of all unelected officials, in Japan, as far back as the seventh century, bureaucrats were highly respected. With their ancient tradition of mutual support between state and Sangha, Japanese Buddhists were more than willing to follow the lead of the state. These contrasting patterns of trust and mistrust seem to have an obvious correlation with the development of a negative, regulatory bureaucracy in Britain (and the United States) and a positive, developmental one in Japan.

Enfranchisement, De-alienation, and the Work Ethic.

In the last chapter, we saw that there are libertarian forces at work in Japan (and other industrial nations) that seek to reverse the traditional relationship between society and the economy by subordinating the former to the latter. The relentless pursuit of productivity and profit in Japan has entailed *and legitimated* the suffering of those unable to control their own destinies, e.g., the exploitation of school children and the female members of the work force, the torture of students during "examination hell," and the restrictions on personal freedom in general (at least from an outsider's point of view).

In spite of the kaisha culture's negative internalities, on the moral front it seems to have accomplished two major feats. In the first place, it has created *a sense of inclusiveness* embracing all Japanese—except, of course, the Burakumin, Korean-Japanese and other minorities. Since the Heian period, there has been a progressive social "enfranchisement" of the population. In religion, for example, this process can be traced in the breakdown of monopolistic parish guilds (the *miyaza* discussed in chapter 1), the rise of vernacular, evangelistic religions (from some of the Kamakura Buddhist sects to the New Religions), the development of an inclusive prewar civil religion, and the postwar resurrection of civil-religious self-images in "Japan theory" (see chapter 8). The same kind of enfranchisement took place in the country's economic history from the spread of competitive markets and the breakdown of commercial guilds (*za*) in the Tokugawa period to the creation of a meritocratic system in modern times in which—for all its faults—careers generally are open to talent. Considering the fact that Japan is less than a century and a half removed from feudalism, the nation has truly done a revolutionary job of destroying most of the ascriptive restrictions tradition had placed on ability and ambition.

The second major achievement of the system is this: the new meritocracy—and the kaisha culture which it serves—have generated within the workforce *a sense that the system is fair*. While labor in Japan traditionally was as badly exploited as labor in nineteenth-century England, during the postwar years Japanese industry learned the value of "human resources" and put into operation highly effective management programs which seemed to create a sense of personal and moral satisfaction. I must hasten to admit that beneath these positive feelings often smolder the negative ones of alienation and resentment, and that often what passes for fairness is really the "false consciousness" concocted by the captains of industries. Nevertheless, personal gratification seems especially high among those lucky enough to belong to an "upper-tier" firm which is large, powerful, and "caring." Feelings that the system is fair cannot be divorced from the attractiveness to most Japanese of the image of a company in which human relationships are personal and paternalistic. Generally, they like to feel that the kaisha, like Amida Buddha, has embraced, and will never forsake them. Whatever it is, however real it may (or may not) be, the Japanese sense of fairness is not to be confused with the western notion of fairness as the successful assertion of adversarial rights. While the Japanese management system owes much to western advisors, its publicly espoused *tatemae*-values, at least, seem fundamentally congruent with the Buddhist and Confucian values of paternalism, cooperation, and loyalty. Some of the heart-felt *honne*-feelings of the workers themselves may not be as far removed from the public ideals of management as some of us in the west would like to believe.

While Japanese intellectuals often fault their culture for producing no Reformation or bourgeois revolution—and therefore no indigenous concepts of individualism, autonomy, rights, or loyal opposition—in the long run this failure *may* have been an ideological boon. Early capitalism in the West *may* have been based on individual rights, but "individualism" is not necessarily a prerequisite for capitalism in all times and places. As I suggested above, individualism and absolute property rights may even be negative factors in advanced capitalism. At least an ironic argument could be made to this effect.

In England, a similar process of religious enfranchisement began at the time of the Reformation but soon degenerated into sectarian factionalism inspired, in part, by the country's well-entrenched class system.[65] In the crucial years of the late eighteenth and early nineteenth centuries, the working classes were excluded not only from the Anglican establishment but also from the middle-class chapels of Dissent and Nonconformity. The result was the "de-churching," if not the absolute secularization of manual labor.[66] These religious developments seem to have foreshadowed the general alienation of British labor. They may even be part of the long-term historical process that culminated in the *de*industrialization of Northern England, Scotland, and Wales. One wonders whether contrasting patterns of religious and cultural enfranchisement in Japan were not related to the (relative) *de*alienation of labor in that country during the postwar period; to the (relatively) high sense of fairness characteristic of many Japanese firms today, or to the development of the (absolutely) fabled Japanese work ethic. While the Japanese obviously have not resolved all of the "cultural contradictions of capitalism," they seem to have developed a genuine work ethic, and not just a work ideology. Some Japanese industries—not all—have shown that a work ethic does not necessarily rest on religious anxiety and economic insecurity, hobgoblins imposed on labor by Max Weber and orthodox economics. Rather, the postwar Japanese experience seems to imply that workers can best be inspired by perceptions of "this-worldly" fairness and mutual trust.[67]

Perceptions of inclusiveness and feelings of fairness are not, of course, the same as genuine enfranchisement and economic justice. Like the west, Japan has yet to discover the perfect formula for an economy which is both productive and just. Nevertheless, the sense of integrity which the kaisha culture *has* achieved seems to be due, in some measure, to the ability of the Japanese to tap the root-values of their own religious and moral traditions. In this chapter, I have simply tried to argue that positive enablements of this sort do not provide a complete explanation of the role of religion in the rise of capitalism.

CHAPTER 6

Ittōen: The Work Ethic of a Buddhist Utopia

The Community: Its History, Myth, Life, and Ideals

We turn next to a detailed case study of the Buddhist idealism discussed in chapter 5. Ittōen (or Kōsenrin Village) is a utopian community in Kyoto which, to this day, bears witness to the religious idealism of Meiji and Taishō Japan. One might even say (with no disrespect intended) that, having lovingly preserved the memory of its founder, Nishida Tenkō (1872–1968), in its own myth, ritual, and praxis, Ittōen has become a living fossil of the Buddhism of this period. Needless to say, this gives us a unique opportunity to study the traditional social and economic notions of Buddhism in a contemporary setting.

Stalwart members of the community see little difference between the history and the myth, the reality and the ideals of Ittōen.[1] For them, the significance of the community is still intimately related to the founder's own personality and thought. Born in Nagahama in Shiga Prefecture, Tenkō san (as he is known in the village) was concerned from childhood about the problems of social conflict. Throughout his life, he tells us, he hated quarreling and pondered how men could live without "struggling for existence."[2] When he was twenty years old, in order to avoid conscription he agreed to take charge of a land reclamation project in Ishikari on the northern island of Hokkaidō. During the eight years he spent there directing the activities of one hundred families of tenant farmers, he immersed himself in a biography of Ninomiya Sontoku, the agrarian moralist of the late Tokugawa period. Because of selfish demands made by both the investors in the project and by his tenant farmers, Tenkō san found himself unable to put Ninomiya's ideals into practice.[3] Finally, when both the farmers and their capitalist patrons insisted on their "rights," the whole enterprise came to deadlock (*iki-zumari*). Caught between the conflicting parties, Tenkō san signed his position and returned home to meditate on the sources of conflict in modern society. Some time later a friend gave him a copy of Tolstoy's book, *My Religion.* Cloistering himself for two days in a hotel in Kyoto, Tenkō san studied the book and fasted. Tolstoy's dictum, "Die if you want to live," made a deep impression on him. With these words still ringing in his ears, Tenkō san left the hotel and, throwing himself into the hands of the Light (deity), set out on a life of wandering "social service." Knocking on the doors of complete strangers, he offered to clean the storehouse, straighten up the house, do the dishes, or clean the toilet. No chore was too menial for him.

It was at this time that a telegram came from his family in Shiga Prefecture informing him of their impending bankruptcy and asking him to return home. Taking the train as far as Maibara, he set out to finish the rest of the journey on foot. Along the way he stopped and sat down to rest by the side of the road. He must have looked like a bent-over corpse, wrapped in a white shroud, he later reflected. Yet, in spite of appearances, Tenkō san was happy. The financial "deadlock" faced by his family now seemed a distant problem.[4] When he finally arrived at the family gathering, he advised his relatives to pay off their debts even if it ruined them. "Even if we die," he admonished them, "isn't it best to do the right thing?"[5] The head of the family, of course, thought

STATUES OF NISHIDA TENKŌ AND HIS WIFE.

that Tenkō san had lost his mind. Seeing their reluctance to take his advice, Tenkō san declined all refreshments and abruptly took his leave. That night, unwilling to stay with relatives, he slept under the eaves of a Shinto shrine. There he stayed for three days and nights, fasting and doing *zazen* (meditation). Before long, he became dizzy from hunger. His body began to waste away and even his eyesight grew dim. Then, just as dawn broke, on the morning of the fourth day, he suddenly heard a baby cry.

> What's this, I wondered. What if I too were to cry like this baby . . . ? The baby is crying now. . . . Its Mother's breasts must be filled with milk. Holding her swollen breasts in hand, the Mother probably is overwhelmed by her responsibilities. But if the baby didn't cry and were to starve to death, how the Mother would grieve! By crying, the baby is doing its Mother a favor. Breast-feeding, which delights Mother and baby alike, must be the opposite of competition, conflict and the "struggle for existence." Before the baby was born, the Mother's breasts were not developed. Milk appears only after birth. The baby makes not the slightest effort to get the milk. Nor does the Mother. The two of them, together, are saved by the blessings of Nature. Actually, mankind should be nourished in this way! But because of our *unnatural* actions, we lose these blessings which we ought to be receiving. Perhaps, like this baby, someone is waiting and preparing food for *me!* From now on, I will not strive to live. I will live if I am allowed. And if I'm allowed to live, in what way should I "cry"?
>
> Just then I saw a sunflower [*himawari*]. The sunflower bends its head, following the movement of the sun. That's it! In the same way, I'll just go where there's food! It's not "struggling for existence" if I just honestly admit to someone that I'm hungry. This resolved, I got right up and went off to the town. Since it was early, most places were still closed. Not too far away, I noticed some spilt rice, running like a thread across the street. It must have spilled out of someone's sack. Thinking that there would be no harm in gathering it up, I carefully picked it up, grain by grain.[6]

After eating the gruel he made from this rice, he went to the home of an old acquaintance. There he was offered food, but would eat nothing but the rice that stuck to the bottom of the pot. "After that, for the first time (since my "Three Day Metamorphosis" in the shrine) my stomach was full. I, who had died, now had no obligations [*gimu*]. I was full, free, and had no responsibilities [*nan no nasubeki shigoto mo nai*]. Suddenly I realized I was free. I began to *move*!"[7]

He stayed in this house for three days, doing the dishes, cleaning the yard, and even cleaning the toilet; in short, "doing the lowly tasks of the maids and apprentices." Finally he could say that he had "overcome the world."[8] But overcoming the world by doing lowly tasks was not only a solution to his own problems.

> It unexpectedly turned out to be a twofold victory. On the one hand, without premeditation, my spontaneous activity [*mui no dōsa*][9]—quite naturally—brought strength to other people. On the other hand, a family was rescued which had been on the brink of financial ruin.
>
> The result of my seven or eight years of searching was that, first, a whole family was revitalized by going through the depths of a Great Negation [*daihitei*] and, secondly, there was this completely unexpected occurrence: I, a mere nobody, was sent into the world relying on a New Livelihood. Just by moving about in a natural way, I had this remarkable influence on those around me.[10]

For about ten years Tenkō san led this life of wandering service, or *rotō*. Persuaded by some friends to allow himself at least the comfort of a roof over his head, Tenkō san and his wife settled down in what was called the Jōhanryō, a tiny dwelling of only three mats (the measure of rooms in Japan). According to Tenkō san, a person needs only the space of one and a half mats—one for sleeping and a half a mat for sitting while awake. Thus, he and his wife needed only a three-mat house. In 1913, one of Tenkō san's patrons gave him a building in Kyoto's Shishigatani to use as a seminary and as a temporary dormitory for his followers. Generally, however, his followers worked and slept outside of the community. Influenced by a lengthy friendship with a Zen master, Tenkō san used Buddhist words to describe his community's activities. In addition to the word *rotō* just mentioned, there was *takuhatsu:* work done in or outside the community in the spirit of selfless service.[11] In 1919, Tenkō san started what he called the Rokuman Gyōgan Movement.[12] While the term *Gyōgan* has come to be a euphemism for toilet cleaning, it also refers to a community prayer:

> Oh Light of Heaven and Earth!
> Accept this humble act of service
> As a means to worship Thee.
> I have nothing else to offer,
> For I have no virtue of my own.
>
> I have searched for the root
> Of all troubles of the whole wide world,
> And I have found that it lay within my own heart.

It was from this knowledge
Sprang this act of worship.

I therefore entreat
That I may serve in this manner,
And that this service may make
For the strengthening
Of the moral foundations of our land.

May this act of mine help to fulfill
The desire of the great Emperor Meiji,
Who sang that all men the four seas over
Are one brotherhood.[13]

In 1921, Tenkō san published a book, *The Life of Repentance.*[14] This book quickly became a best-seller in Japan and greatly assisted in spreading Tenkō san's ideas and in increasing his following. Suzuki Gorō was one of those who joined the community after reading the book. In a personal communication he writes that when he joined in 1921 there were fewer than twenty men and women in the group. After a month their number had doubled. By the next year Tenkō san had collected about two hundred followers. Almost all of these charter members were single people, the men being generally about twenty-five years of age, the women twenty.

In 1923 a national auxiliary group was formed called the Friends of Light (Kōyūkai). In the same year Ittōen was able to establish an outpost in Manchuria. From this time forward Tenkō san was to become one of Japan's most active religious leaders. Between 1924 and 1943 he went on numerous teaching tours[15]—three trips to Taiwan, seven to Korea, fourteen to Manchuria, two to America, and one to Java.[16] In 1930 the community moved to the southeast side of Kyoto, to a place called Misasagi. In 1936 they moved once again to forty acres of land in nearby Shinomiya, where they are found today.

Although Tenkō san was suspected of harboring "dangerous thoughts" during the ultranationalist period, Ittōen did its best to support the nation's military policy. In 1944 crisis conditions forced the temporary suspension of the community's magazine, *Ohikari* (Light). The same year saw community members doing takuhatsu in a textile factory as their contribution to the war effort. In 1946 the dōnin (comrades) returned to the village. In the following year Tenkō san was elected to the House of Councilors of the Japanese Diet. After failing to get a bill passed which called for nationwide "repentance," Tenkō san contented himself with a passive role in the Diet. Compared with internal, moral reform, political activity had little meaning for him. Occasionally he cleaned the toilets in the government buildings.

In the postwar period the financial ventures of the community continued to prosper. In 1955 the Ittōen Agricultural Research Center was begun. This firm, specializing in the mail-order sale of rice seed, is the community's most valuable asset. A construction company, a small publishing concern, a thriving preschool for outside children, forestry, and farming are the dōnins' other means of support.

In order to pass on the ideas of Ittōen to the second generation, an educational system (including a three-year college program) was established. In the Ittōen schools, children call their teachers "auntie" and "uncle" rather than the more formal sensei. Since Tenkō san believed that grades encourage an unnatural spirit of competition, grades are shown to parents only upon request. Children begin to do *gyōgan* (ritual toilet cleaning) in middle school—before they are able to understand intellectually the relationship between toilet cleaning and the "world peace" which it is supposed to bring about.[17]

Today the community continues to be governed by a "man-in-charge" system (*tōban seido*).[18] In spite of the egalitarian sound of its name, this system relies rather strongly on hierarchical principles. Beneath the head tōban there are subtōbans chosen by him to take charge of the community's major activities: one each for the agricultural research center, the school system, the printing shop, and so on. These tōbans constitute the heart of the management (kōsenrin) of the community. O san, one of the stalwart members, has written a brief description of the tōban system in English. He calls the system "perfectly autocratic in form." "Each member of Kōsenrin's society voluntarily abandons his decision-making powers and entrusts himself to the tōban." "Entrusting all to the present tōban is equivalent to entrusting all to God," he writes. In other words, "in this autocracy we are ruled by the tōban formally, but by God (Light) essentially." Saying yes to the tōban is regarded as obedience to the Light. O san recalls in his little treatise that Tenkō san once said that even if a tōban is mistaken, by obeying him unconditionally the dōnin are able to achieve an egoless state (*muga*, another Buddhist term). All marriages between dōnin must be approved by the tōbans.

After his death in 1968 Tenkō san was succeeded by his grandson, Nishida Takeshi. Although an able administrator, Takeshi san (as he is styled) is unable to claim the charisma or authority of his grandfather. One dōnin told me that Tenkō san was able to hear the whispering (*sasayaki*) of the Light. When I inquired whether Takeshi san too received such divine counsel, his answer was evasive ("*sore wa daimondai desu yo!*"). Obviously aware that the older dōnin can never forget Tenkō san, Takeshi san is the first to admit that at Ittōen the word tōban means Tenkō san, even to this day. Outranked in age by a large number of dōnin, Takeshi san is wisely humble about his role, stressing the importance of consultation and consensus in the decision-making process of the community. When important decisions are made—for example, when they decided to build a new school or when plans were drawn up to build a new crypt—communitywide discussions are held. A "four-man group" (*yonningumi*) consisting of four elderly dōnin, formerly intimates of Tenkō san himself, acts as Takeshi san's board of advisers. Nevertheless, he stressed that he himself has the final responsibility for all decisions. At the same time, since each of the financial enterprises of the community operates on a separate budget, the head tōban seems to delegate to the subtōbans a considerable amount of responsibility. Takeshi san hopes that the community will not grow any larger than it now is, fearing that with greater numbers voting would eventually replace the tōban system. He also believes that when the time comes to pick his successor his own son should be selected as head tōban, even if there are equally qualified candidates at hand.

In spite of the hierarchical nature of the tōban system, not all dōnin agree with O san that it is autocratic. Kōsenrin's hierarchy is complemented by informal consultations and consensus. At Ittōen, as in nearly all Japanese groups, vertical relationships are reinforced by less formal horizontal ties. This subtle form of social integration is made possible, not by dilating upon the autocratic character of the system, but by stressing the tōban's suffering and humility. Tenkō san, for example, once retired to his old home, the Jōhanryō, and made a friend temporary tōban. In imitation of the humility of Christ he even washed his disciples' feet. One can say therefore that in general relationships between dōnin and the subtōbans are inoffensively hierarchical.

In recent years approximately seventy families have been living at Ittōen. Their day begins when the bell rings at five in the morning. As soon as they are dressed members scurry to various parts of the community where they clean, scrub, and sweep for about twenty minutes. This is followed by religious services (*otsutome*) held in chapels called the reidō and muendō. The morning and evening services are completely voluntary and are generally attended by only between twenty and twenty-five people. The morning service begins with what looks like some unusual spiritual calisthentics. First, the leader—a male stalwart, and often an elder—offers incense before the round, open window of the reidō. Nothing is enshrined here, but the garden and stone lantern which are visible through the window remind the worshiper of the presence of Great Nature (*daishizen*) or Light. Standing erect, the leader intones the powerful word ōun[19] and makes a complete circle above his head with outstretched arms. This is repeated three times by all. This ritual gesture is an affirmation of the spiritual wholeness of life. After singing the Rokuman Gyōgan song and praying in silence for a few moments they resume their places, all sitting with feat beneath them (*seiza*). There follows a recitation of part of the *Vimalikīrti Sūtra*[20] (stressing the Bodhisattva role of the Buddhist layman) and Tenkō san's *One Fact of Life* [*Ichi jijitsu*], a sutralike prose-poem composed in 1955:

> A man is standing at the roadside. Although he is an ordinary man he seems to be illumined by Light. At times he holds his hands prayerwise as if worshipping the Invisible. At other times he enters homes to straighten the footwear at the door, sweep the garden, clean the toilet, or tidy the storeroom. If he is hungry he stands near the kitchen his hands prayerwise. If he feels that the giver's heart is not sincere he does not accept what is offered. When he does accept he meditates momentarily and the giver's heart is purified. . . . Being neither priest nor layman,[21] he has limitless resources of *Fukuden* (the purified wealth of non-possession), but he is also a labourer. He is nurtured by Light and does not work in order to live but to express gratitude for the blessings he has received. . . . When one who believes in him asks him the way to truth, he answers that he is ashamed because of his lack of virtue. When pressed for a fuller answer he replies that he is led by Light and walks and acts in accord with the Formless Form. He does not believe exclusively in either God or Buddha or Confucius but regards all these as within the gate of *Funi-no-Komyo* or the Light of Oneness. . . . Gentle, modest and diligent, he has no desire to compete with others, neither has he desire for possessions though he delights in producing plenitude. He neither affirms nor denies any of the world's ideologies, but with innocent heart trusts all things to the operation of natural law. A mortal man? The Light Itself? Or maybe an idiot? He himself does not know. How much less do others! Nevertheless here is one fact of life.[22]

After this recitation, those who have attended the service in the reidō walk in a procession to the refectory, chanting the words of a sutra (the *Shigu seigan*).

In the refectory the recitation of sutras continues for a few minutes. The breakfast is simple fare, generally consisting of miso soup with eggplant or cabbage, unpolished rice, pickles, and tea. Those who do not wish to eat in the refectory send their wives to pick up the food from the community kitchen. In the refectory all meals are eaten in silence. As in Zen monastaries, rice bowls and chopsticks are wrapped in a cloth and stored on shelves along the wall. At seven thirty each able-bodied member appears at the place assigned to him by the tōban and begins his daily chores. Those not assigned a regular (skilled) job, say, at the agricultural research center or in the school, find their assignments posted by the tōban on a blackboard next to the refectory. At ten o'clock and at three in the afternoon, there are brief rest periods. At noon lunch is served in the refectory and at five the workday ends and supper is served. At six o'clock an evening service is held, a slightly longer event than the morning service. It consists entirely of the recitation of sutras, including the *Heart Sutra* and part of the *Lotus Sutra*. One sutra is even recited, by rote, in Sanskrit. At nine the bell rings and all clasp their hands in prayer even if they are in the *ofuro* (communal bath). By ten o'clock nearly all have gone to sleep.

Ittōen does not call itself a religion and is uncomfortable about being ranked among the so-called New Religions. It does claim, however, to be the practice which is the basis of all religion (*shūkyō no moto*). Tenkō san himself denied that he had a philosophy. When asked a difficult or philosophical question he used to say, "just practice and you will see!" This attitude lingers on in the community's subtle, but still perceptible anti-intellectualism and antagonism to all ideology. "Is Ittōen a religion or a way of life? To this question we must answer, it is nondual [*funi*]. Is it for householders or for monks? Answer: it is nondual. Is it based on Self-Power or Other-Power? Is it a form of Christianity or of Buddhism? Is it internationalist or nationalist? Is it bourgeois or proletarian? To just about all such questions the answer is simply: it is nondual."[23] By giving its allegiance neither to capitalism nor to communism, Ittōen seeks to avoid arguments.[24] Unfortunately, it pays for this irenic stand by a loss of clarity regarding social questions. This can be seen in its attitude toward questions of war and peace and in its relationship with capitalism.

One must admit that, even before the war, Ittōen did have a pacifist tendency. Tenkō san originally went to Hokkaidō to avoid conscription. During the ultranationalist period he was occasionally interrogated by the police who suspected him of harboring leftist ideas. When someone pointed out that the Chinese character *ten* in his name was the same as the *ten* in *tennō* (emperor), he began to write his name with the letters of the Japanese syllabary. The community later interpreted this as an antiwar gesture.[25] On the other hand, Tenkō san's gospel of radical obedience was welcomed by the Japanese government and industry alike. Mantetsu, the government-sponsored railway in

Manchuria, invited him to the Japanese-occupied mainland to give lectures. Ittōen's training sessions (kenshūkai) were begun in 1941 in order to produce men of character in the hour of national crisis. Suwaraji, the Ittōen drama group, played before the troops during the war, traveling as far as Manchuria to boost morale.[26] When members went to work in wartime factories, they regarded their activity there as sanctified labor (*takuhatsu*). After the war, however, Tenkō san's voice was added to those of leaders from other New Religions proclaiming his way of life as the key to world peace.

The basic ideals of Ittōen appear to be a mixture of Buddhist teachings about selflessness and the ascetic wisdom of the peasant sage, Ninomiya Sontoku. More important than the philosophical elaboration of these ideals by Tenkō san and his stalwarts was their incarnation in Tenkō san's own life and hagiography. His own life of voluntary poverty, fasting, and service was a good example of what I like to call the "suffering of the founder," a theme that runs throughout Japanese religion and society.[27] To this day the stalwart commonly refer to his example when explaining the ideals of the community to outsiders. They tell, in detail, the story of his "metamorphosis" or conversion in the Hachiman shrine. In particular they like to recount his story of the crying baby and its mother. They also like to tell how Tenkō san used to wash his disciples' feet and how he cleaned toilets wherever he went to lecture. In the life of their founder the stalwart see a reflection of the lives of Christ, Buddha, and Gandhi. (Abraham Lincoln, Albert Schweitzer, and Ralph Nader are also said to have lived the Ittōen life.)

Although Ittōen claims not to be a religion, its stress on self-denial grows directly out of the Buddhist tradition and can be associated with Zen in particular. Religion itself is identified with practice, especially with the act of "throwing away the self" (*sutemi*). "Worship is doing away with the self. When one does away with self the All becomes the self."[28] Needless to say, the best example of sutemi and self-denial (*jiko hitei*) was Tenkō san's own metamorphosis, an experience modeled at several crucial points on the death and resurrection of Christ. One might even call the story of the baby-at-the-breast a *haggadah* on *muga*. Another religious image used by Tenkō san and Ittōen to express these ideas is Death. "Death solves all problems. If you have any problem, assuredly it is because you have not completely died."[29] This image is obviously borrowed from both Chrisitianity and Buddhism and goes back to Tenkō san's discovery of Tolstoy's words, "Die if you want to live." "Knowing that the Whole will live even if the self dies is a source of great satisfaction. Oneself and others are like bubbles which accidentally develop on the surface of water. Our attachment to bubbles is due to the fact that we do not recognize the water—i.e., the 'Whole'—beneath them."[30] Paradoxically, however, self-denial is the way to freedom and self-expansion. Tenkō san liked to say that "any number divided by zero is an infinity."[31] Zero is man's true body, the point at which he becomes one with the Light. According to this arithmetic, number is associated with the world of attachment and strife. Ittōen's ideal is for all men to return to zero through repentance.[32]

Kenshūkai: A Work Ethic and its Propagation

In the postwar period, many Japanese companies have assumed the responsibility for inculcating morality which, before the war, was largely a function of the public schools. In order to enhance the spirit of harmony within the firm, many companies sponsor spiritual education programs in Zen temples and other appropriate centers. Some even teach their employees a quasi-military discipline by sending them to retreats on bases operated by the self-defense force. Ittōen provides such a training session, called the kenshūkai, held every month except January. Two-thirds of the participants in these sessions are sent by their companies, which pay Kōsenrin a set fee for instruction in the Ittōen way of life. The majority of these participants are young (generally in their early twenties), unmarried factory workers without a college education or specialized skills.[33]

The most important of Ittōen's training sessions is held during the summer assembly in August, coinciding with the Japanese festival of Obon. Participants are instructed in some of Ittōen's basic ideals: that one should work out of gratitude in order to repay one's benefactors (*hō-on no gyō*) and not in order to make money. *Money is not necessary.* Therefore one should not try to translate labor into its monetary equivalent. Rather, people should work with all their might, giving themselves to their firms in free service (*mushō hōshi*). Happiness can never be discovered by the individual seeking exclusively his own benefit. In these lectures Ittōen's ideals are mixed with practical wisdom. One speaker, for example, maintained that Japanese youths should go to Southeast Asia to help develop those underdeveloped countries so that, by building up a sense of gratitude among these peoples, Japan never again need fear an invasion. Another speaker stressed the importance of smiling for the sake of the company. At least one of the speeches is regularly devoted to the meaning and techniques of toilet cleaning. The participants are told that the toilet-cleaning expedition which they will take part in will help them overcome self and will lead to world peace.

The morning of the second day is devoted to *gyōgan*. After breakfast the group is divided into squads, each with its own leader. After a brief service—held out-of-doors before the bronze statues of Tenkō san and his wife—the leaders take their groups to a preselected neighbourhood in downtown Kyoto and assign each person a specific street or area. The experience is often disappointing. Embarrassed housewives usually reply to their offer to clean the toilet: "No thank you, I have just cleaned it myself," or, "Oh, it's not really necessary. We have a modern flush toilet and there's no need to bother!" A lucky participant will be able to clean about three or four toilets in one day, although he may knock on as many as forty doors.[34]

The third day of the kenshūkai is devoted to rotō. At half past seven the group is again divided into squads. After another brief service, the participants march into the town and go from house to house offering to do any kind of free service—cutting grass, painting fences, and other odd jobs around the house. Although they are not supposed to think about lunch, since they will be "on the roadside" until three in the afternoon, it is hoped that someone will offer them a meal "out of gratitude." This experience is meant to demonstrate the new kind of purified economic relationships Ittōen seeks to cultivate—free service rewarded not by wages but by the generosity which grows out of grat-

RETREATANTS LEAVING TO CLEAN TOILETS.

itude. This, it is said, is a *natural* and *spontaneous* way of living, for it is based on the experience of "entrusting oneself to the Light (or, Great Nature"). At three o'clock the participants return to the village, where they are free to take a bath or a swim in the pool until dinner.

Participants who have intellectual doubts about Ittōen's ideals usually ask such questions as: How can I get along without money? Even if I can get along without money as a single person, what will happen when I marry? How can I support a wife and a child without money? What will happen when I become old and sick? On the other hand, when one asks participants whether they accept Ittōen's ideas, their professions of approval rival the zealous testimonies of the community's own stalwarts. Participants often criticize themselves for having been too self-centered. They are not usually bothered by the questions which seem to be most obvious to the western observer. The following excerpt from a conversation I had with one participant is typical:

> In what way do you hope your life will be different when you return to your job?
>
> I hope to be more easily used (*tsukaiyasui*).
>
> In that case, would your company not take advantage of you and the other employees?
>
> I am willing to take that risk. But even if I did not protest, other employees would. And so there is no danger in espousing these ideals.
>
> What would happen if the men in your company did not want to come to the training session?
>
> They would not be regarded as real employees.

When I asked Ittōen stalwarts whether companies might not exploit the Ittōen ideal of not working for money, I was told that since employers were also expected to attend the training session this simply would not happen. (While managers and entrepreneurs are *expected* to attend the sessions with their men, I met only one person in management and no owners in the two training sessions I participated in). Employers are urged not to be selfish. But service (*hōshi*) in their case seems to be of a special sort. Harakawa Yoshi, Ittōen's business consultants, urges companies to provide more free installations and other free services (*sābisu*).[35] By means of such hōshi or sābisu the company is bound to prosper.

Before discussing the contradictions which seem to arise among Ittōen's ideals, let us look more closely at the religious foundations of the asceticism taught in the kenshūkai. It is, in many respects, a system based on the ideals of Ninomiya Sontoku: diligence, thrift, living within the limits of one's talents (through allegiance to the tōban), and "giving way," that is, working for the group rather than for self. Complete realization of these ideals was possible only after Tenkō san "threw himself away" and entered the life of rotō. From this experience he learned that "any vexatious problem whatsoever becomes simple if only one handles it by becoming like a baby."[36] This is the starting point of the asceticism of Ittōen.

Max Weber has taught us to look for the origins of asceticism in a group's style of suffering or theodicy. If we apply this concept to Ittōen, we find that there is some correlation between the community's ideal of self-denial, its general world view, and its attitude toward suffering. But the picture is far from clear. For some dōnin the asceticism of Ittōen has a clear religious base. One elderly stalwart, formerly a priest in the True Pure Land Buddhist sect, no longer feels the need to chant the name of the Buddha (*nembutsu*) since, at Ittōen, "work is *nembutsu*." Others explain the severity of the Ittōen life as a road to world peace. Looked at from this perspective, the community's asceticism seems to be based on a voluntary acceptance of suffering. One of Tenkō san's better-known sayings was: "genuine religious ecstasy (*hōetsu:* a Buddhist term) will come only after you have borne your Cross."[37] The community's ethic of radical obedience to the Light (saying yes to the tōban), which has become the cornerstone of its social solidarity and economic well-being, is based on a form of self-denial which comes close to what Peter Berger technically calls "masochism."[38] Elements of this spirit also are evident in the training sessions. Enduring the pain of sitting in the traditional Japanese fashion during services and meals is deliberately made into an integral part of the participants' spiritual education.[39] In some cases, however, the Weberian formula seems to be reversed: the work ethic becomes the explanation for suffering. Takeshi san once remarked to me that the work of a sick man is to recover his health. One dōnin, dying from cancer, testified that his pain was his "last takuhatsu." (At Ittōen, death itself is regarded as "returning to the Light" [*kikō*].)

Unfortunately, we cannot draw any general conclusions about the relationship between Ittōen's theodicy and asceticism since the dōnin are not consistent when they speak about their thoughts on suffering and work. I was once told by a stalwart that cutting the grass—which he was doing as we talked—was really play (*asobi*) for him. For this reason, he did not need extra money for entertainment. According to Takeshi san, work can be a pleasure in itself. Suzuki Gorō, however, points out that the aim of takuhatsu is not just "work-for-work's-sake." Rather, it is the means for achieving selflessness. Tenkō san himself used to stress that true service is not pain (*kutsū*), but rather is a kind of revitalization or rebirth (*yomigaeri*).[40]

Tenkō san's solution to the problem of economic conflict was basically a pietistical (or masochistic) obliteration of the self. Rather than trying to change working conditions, he sought to change men's attitude toward work. "If you can selflessly do monotonous work, you will be doing a great work indeed."[41] Economic fastidiousness had an obvious religious base for Tenkō san. Because everything is "on loan" from the Light we should have a more respectful attitude (*keiken na taido*) toward things.[42] Frugality thus grows out of the recognition that all entrusted things are "soul blood" (*tamashii no chi*).[43] Waste is simply impious.

Liminality: An Ideal and its Nemesis

Contradictions and Nostalgia

The original myths, symbols, and ideals of Ittōen are good examples of what Victor Turner describes as "liminality." Enlarging upon Van Gennep's analysis of *rites de passage*, Turner writes:

> Liminal entities, such as neophytes in initiation or puberty rites, may be represented as possessing nothing. They may be disguised as monsters, wear only a strip of clothing, or even go naked, to demonstate that as liminal beings they have no status, property, insignia, secular clothing indicating rank or role, position in a kinship system—in short, nothing that may distinguish them from their fellow neophytes or initiands. Their behavior is normally passive or humble; they must obey their instructors implicitly and accept arbitrary punishment without complaint. It is as though they are being reduced or ground down to a uniform condition to be fashioned anew and endowed with additional powers to enable them to cope with their new station in life. Among themselves, neophytes tend to develop an intense comradeship and egalitarianism. Secular distinctions of rank and status disappear or are homogenized.[44]

Turner notes that "liminality is frequently likened to death, to being in the womb, to invisibility, to darkness, to bisexuality, to the wilderness, and to an eclipse of the sun or moon."[45] While the category of liminality was originally developed by Van Gennep in his study of ritual initiations, Turner has shown its wider usefulness in understanding "such seemingly diverse phenomena as neophytes in the liminal phase of ritual, subjugated autochthones, small nations, court jesters, holy mendicants, good Samaritans, millenarian movements, 'dharma bums,' matrilaterality in patrilineal systems, patrilaterality in matrilineal systems, and monastic orders."[46]

There is no doubt that the original members of Ittōen's Shishigatani community belong to this far-flung and motley band of "edgemen."[47] They shared with other liminal men the ideals of spontaneity, immediacy, nakedness, poverty, obedience, passivity, egalitarianism—not to mention a knowledge of the symbols of death and rebirth. One might even compare the stress on muga at Ittōen with the mind of the neophyte which must be a *tabula rasa,* a blank slate, on which is inscribed the knowledge and wisdom of the group."[48]

According to Turner, liminality (or "communitas") is a constant dialectical relationship with "society as a structured, differentiated, and often hierarchical system of politico-legal-economic positions with many types of evaluation, separating men in terms of 'more' or 'less.' "[49] "No society," he believes, "can function adequately without this dialectic."[50] Quoting here only those polarities which describe the relation of Ittōen and its structured counterpart, Kōsenrin, this dialectic is described by Turner as follows:

Figure 8

Turner's Structure and Antistructure

Structure	*Antistructure*
state	transition
partiality	totality
heterogeneity	homogeneity
structure	communitas
inequality	equality
property	absence of property
distinctions of rank	absence of rank
complexity	simplicity

The paradigmatic dichotomy of structure and antistructure (liminality) was expressed clearly, albeit in rather curious jargon, by Tenkō san himself. The need for structure was felt first and foremost in the managing of the "purified wealth" (*fukuden*) which was entrusted to the community by the Light—what outsiders would simply call property. Because of Tenkō san's stress on nonduality, the management of purified wealth was not simply the material side of Ittōen's spiritual ideals. It too is an ideal, an essential complement to the Ittōen ideals of service and trust.

A group which is set up to oversee the use of entrusted things (*azukarimono*) is called a *senkōsha*, a "Society for the Propagation of Light." Tenkō san defined it in terms which have a social-scientific ring as: "On-the-spot research of various matters as reference materials for the reconstruction of economic organizations."[52] The particular senkōsha which was set up by the Ittōen community in 1928 was called "Kōsenrin," the "Forest of the Light." The relationship between the ideals of Ittōen and Kōsenrin is explained by some dōnin as the same as the relationship between Truth and the proof (*akashi*) of the Truth. Tenkō san himself explained it in this way: Ittōen is saying yes to the Light. Kōsenrin is a way of "entrusting" things (*azukarikata*). Using the language of Pure Land Buddhism, he maintained that Ittōen was the "going to the Pure Land" (*ōjō*), while Kōsenrin was the "return (as a bodhisattva) from the Pure Land" (*gensō*).[53]

Kōsenrin is the community's hierarchical tōban system acting as overseer of a distributionless economy (*fubunpai no keizai*). According to Harakawa Yoshio, what Japan herself needs above all else is to accumulate capital. This, he believes, is why industrialists and entrepreneurs are interested in Ittōen.[54] Writing in 1954, Tenkō san saw senkōsha/Kōsenrin as a model for national reconstruction. Just as Ittōen grew out of nothing, so, he hoped, Japan could rise from the ashes of defeat.[55] (He believed that the reason why Japan at that time had not yet made an economic comeback was that the country had not heeded his plea for general repentance. It had not yet cast off the self.)[56]

Durkheim may have been right when he said that the most important conflicts in a society "are not between the ideals and reality, but between two different ideals that of yesterday and that of today."[57] The tension among the ideals of the Ittōen community are both of this historical sort and of a more basic, structural nature. Most obvious are those tensions between the Ittōen ideal of being absolutely without property and the Kōsenrin ideal of managing purified wealth.[58] Needless to say, members of the Ittōen community do not regard this tension as a contradiction. The history of the change of this "dialectical tension" into an outright contradiction among ideals is the story of the transformation of liminality into security. Here our best witness is Tenkō san himself. "During the fifty years I spent straying not an inch from this 'empty-handed life at the roadside,' believing that one does not need money at all, our property [*mono*] began to increase."[59] Forty years after the founding of Ittōen, Tenkō san looked back to the days in Shishigatani as a time of absolute simplicity. In those days the humble work (*geza*) of the community was perfect. After Tenkō san finished the morning service, all members went out to do their takuhatsu and returned late at night, if then. Only three days at New Year's and two at Obon were not devoted to doing social service. Because their takuhatsu was uninterrupted in those days, the "virtues" of the community began to "pile up."[60]

Today, however, most of the members do their takuhatsu not outside, but within the community. (For this reason, it is not clear to the outside observer who is the beneficiary of this activity: Ittōen or the greater society.) Compared with the risky way of living in the Shishigatani days, today's Kōsenrin is easygoing (*raku na mono*) by Tenkō san's own account.[61] In the early days neighbors thought that Tenkō san and his followers were mad. They were even shadowed by the police—not an unusual experience among the liminal of this world! Tenkō san believed that the purity of the Shishigatani period was of fundamental importance in the genesis of the Ittōen way of life. "One could say that had there been no Shishigatani period, the present Kōsenrin would not exist."[62] Suzuki Gorō divides the community's history into two dispensations: the Ittōen period (when the community was in Shishigatani) and the Senkōsha period (after the move to Yamashina).

What Tenkō san and his older followers felt seems to have been a *nostalgia for a lost liminality.* Compromising with economic reality and human frailty, the community gradually bartered away its marginal existence for security. While even today the individual dōnin may not have much pocket money, he does have an economic, social, and psychological security which few Japanese outside the village enjoy. Gradually, the main burden of rotō and gyōgan has been shifted to the shoulders of participants in the training session—to outsiders. Most members of the community go outside to do rotō or gyōgan only a few times a year. The January rotō of the members has gradually been reduced from two weeks to ten days, and finally in recent years to five days. The discipline for outsiders has also undergone significant changes. Professor A, a well-known philosopher in the Kyoto area, recalls how he spent ten days doing rotō at Ittōen before the war. Dissatisfied with both the Pure Land Buddhism in which he had been raised and with academic philosophy, he was looking for a deeper religious experience. Going to Kōsenrin Village, he entrusted his wallet and other belongings to the office and went out to do rotō on his own. He was told that he could not return to the village to sleep and that he was to tell no one that he was from Ittōen. Today things are different. Rotō has become a fixed routine, a religious ritual. Going out to the roadside for about six hours, participants in the Kenshūkai risk only the loss of their noonday meal. When they return at three in the afternoon, a sandwich and a glass of milk are waiting for them. Today participants are specifically instructed to tell people that they are undergoing religious discipline at Ittōen. And, needless to say, they need not worry about sleeping "on the roadside" at night.

Major historical changes have also taken place in the spiritual nurture of the children of the village. To use the terminology we developed in chapter 1, we can see in the attitudes of the younger generation the familiar transformation of purposeful ('in order to') *motives* into less-than-zealous *obligations* (or 'because' motives). While a few classes in morals are included in the curriculum of the schools, there seems to be no single, authoritative voice which can explain to the children the meaning of Ittōen. For this reason, many young people feel that what was once a true way of life is degenerating into custom and habit. They are also aware of a creeping eudemonism and hedonism in the village, as evidenced by new refrigerators, electric fans, and televison sets.[63] Commercialism and the "struggle for existence"—evils the Ittōen school system was designed to combat—now slip into the village via television. Frustrated by being unable to make something of themselves within the community, nearly all of the graduates of the Ittōen high school leave to seek their fortunes in the outside world.

What the youth of the village sense is nothing short of a structural tension or contradiction. Ozaki Sensei, founder of the Shinkyō Buraku community in Kasama put it bluntly: "Show me a 'utopian' group that gives a damn about its neighbors!"[64] I take these words as a challenge to go beyond Durkheim's theoretical limitation of conflict to the realm of ideals to a consideration of even more fundamental contradictions between Ittōen's ideals and *reality*.[65] From this point of view, Kōsenrin, regarded *ideally* as "a way of entrusting things to the Light," is *really* an employer in a capitalist economy. The agricultural research center, the printing and construction companies, all employ outside help. Donations to the community are actively solicited both by the Friends of Light and by itinerant members of the village. About thirty outside teachers conduct classes in Ittōen schools as a form of "religious practice" (i.e., gratis). Participants in the monthly training sessions are also asked to do work around the grounds of the community "in order to express their graditude." Retreatants are charged a set fee even though they are also expected to work long and hard hours on behalf of the village. While such contributions may be regarded *ideally* as offerings to the Light, they seem to be of *real* benefit primarily to members of the village.

Hōshi clearly does not mean the same as "charity" (*jizen*). According to Takeshi san, jizen demands only a part of one's time or substance, while hōshi is an offering of one's whole self. Thus it is not surprising that the community's charitable projects are few in number. The village maintains a small house near the railroad tracks for the indigent. Free meals and lodging are provided in exchange for a gift of free labor around the grounds. While the community does make contributions to Lighthouse (a fund for the blind), UNESCO, and other charitable foundations, such gifts do not get to the heart of hōshi. The more symbolic hōshi is, the more meaningful it seems to become. Even young people within the village point out that in the day of the flush toilet, gyōgan is hardly more than a dramatic gesture. Another equally theatrical demonstration of Ittōen's piety takes place once every summer. On this day, dōnin put on their Ittōen headbands and, instead of holding their customary morning service, go to the cemetery which borders on the village and clean up the graves for Obon. Since the cemetery does not belong to the village, this activity seems to be "social service" par excellence.

Plausibility Structures: How to Maintain a (Lost) Liminality

There are several ways (technically, plausibility structures) by which the community tries to maintain yesterday's ideals in the face of those of today, or against what some outsiders would call "reality." One of the most obvious ways is to deny there has been any change in the community's ideals. One elderly stalwart maintains that Ittōen is exactly the same as the day he first met Tenkō san. Another told me that the ideals and reality of the village today are the same as those of the Shishigatani period. Every day, members have the feeling that they have been "called from the roadside" to work in the village. Suzuki Gorō maintains that Ittōen is different from other Japanese utopias (such as Atarashiki Mura) in that the dōnin do not take the village itself as their base. Their base is the roadside itself.[66] In return for their services, they receive food and shelter in the village. Once, when I began to question O san about the apparent security of the dōnins' lives, he replied that, far from being secure, they never knew from one day to the next where their next meal would come from. Perhaps the best way to understand this conviction among the orthoprax was suggested by a young retreatant who said that there is no contradiction between the ideals of Kōsenrin and Ittōen because "not having things is a *feeling* (*kimochi*)."

A community the size of Ittōen can maintain itself only by using a set of controlling symbols, key terms freighted with special emotional nuances. Words are gerrymandered until, as Geertz might put it, "ethos" becomes blended with "world view."[67] At the same time these specially nuanced concepts help to stave off a confrontation between the community's ideals and reality. We have already seen examples of this in the borrowing and redefining of Buddhist terms.[68] Language is also used in a special way in order to emphasize that Ittōen's activities are all a form of service to the world. The ideal of the community is to be ready to do any task "when called upon."[69] Tenkō san was "called" to Manchuria and Korea. He was "called" by various companies to restore internal harmony and peace. Kōsenrin was "asked" to build itself a new school. Members are "called" to take jobs outside the village. This manner of speaking makes all community activities a form of social service—even when the only visible beneficiary is the village itself.

The most important of these rhetorical plausibility structures is the concept of entrusted things (*azukarimono*). Because all purified wealth is a trust from the Light (or something entrusted *to* the Light through the good offices of Kōsenrin) the community can seriously maintain the myth of its own poverty. When new buildings are erected, or new equipment purchased, a special service of entrustment is held. Through this careful use of words, Kōsenrin Village completely avoids the idea of possession. I was once corrected when I said that Kōsenrin *has* a lot of *azukarimono*. "If you say we *have* 'entrusted things' you completely misunderstand us."

In spite of the liturgical impoverishment of the village—there being only one hymn and a smattering of sutras which are used in services—ritual plays an important role as a means of maintaining the community's pristine ideals. The services in the reidō and muendō daily re-create the somewhat mysterious image of "a man standing at the roadside," the ideal man of the community.[70] This figure is Ittōen's version of Turner's "edgeman" or "dharma bum"—"a mortal man? The Light Itself? Or maybe an idiot . . . ?" For the dōnin, these images doubtlessly bring to mind the memory of Tenkō san himself.

Frugality itself can be regarded as a ritual reenactment of the myth of the man at the roadside. Living in small quarters scattered here and there about the grounds and subsisting on simple fare doled out by the community kitchen are, in effect, ritual affirmations of the mythical idea that money is unnecessary. The ritual nature of rotō and gyōgan has already been suggested. Work itself, especially the perfunctory morning cleaning routine, seems often to have more importance as a ritual than as a means of keeping up the community's property or increasing its wealth.

The two most important rituals for preserving the original ideals of Ittōen are "the general rotō of the members" (*dōnin no sōrotō*) and "the leader's rotō" (*tōban no rotō*, otherwise known as *kirotō*). These

ITTŌEN MEMBERS LEAVING THEIR HOMES. During this ritual, all members of the community leave their homes and "return to the roadside".

events, occurring during the summer assembly in August and on New Year's Eve, respectively, ritually reestablish the now lost liminality of the Shishigatani days.

Because the general rotō of the members takes place during the summer assembly, participants in the August training session and visiting members of the Friends of Light are able to take part in the drama. In this ritual, the residents of Kōsenrin Village entrust the entire village to the participants in the training session and to the Friends of Light and return to a state of pure rotō. At breakfast, all participants in the training session are assigned to various buildings on the grounds. There they will clean or stand guard until the experience is over. The agricultural research center, the printing and construction companies, and all other buildings are turned over to these young people and to the Friends of Light (who are much older). Then, at eight o'clock, all able-bodied dōnin go to the refectory to get their *jihatsu* (rice bowls and chopsticks wrapped in a cloth). With jihatsu in hand, they assemble in the schoolyard. After a few words from Takeshi san, they march in solemn procession to the front of the compound. On the bridge in front of the village the tōban stops and turns over to the president of the Friends of Light his seal (*hankō*) and keys, in this way symbolically entrusting the village and all of its *azukarimono* to him. Starting out once again, the dōnin silently follow their tōban in single file to a nearby Shinto shrine. At the shrine, after briefly worshiping the kami, they set down their jihatsu and begin to do takuhatsu by cleaning up the shrine precincts. After working about an hour, representatives of the training session and the Friends of Light appear and have a few words with Takeshi san. They tell him that, after discussing the matter among themselves, they have decided that taking care of Kōsenrin is too much for them. They praise the dōnin for their diligence in maintaining the village and invite them to return "from the roadside" to their homes. Once again the members line up in front of the shrine and clap their hands in worship. Then they march back to Kōsenrin led, this time, by the representatives of the Friends of Light. When they are once again back in the schoolyard, the president of the Friends of Light returns the purple box containing Takeshi san's seal and keys. And with this the general rotō comes to an end, about an hour and a half after it began.

Closely related to this ritual is the leader's rotō on New Year's Eve. On that evening, Takeshi san, following his grandfather's example, goes to the Heian Shrine in Kyoto and picks up the litter scattered by the thousands who go to the shrine for their first visit of the year. Next

RECEIVING A TRUCK FROM THE LIGHT. To Ittōen members, all possessions are things entrusted to them by the Light.

morning, at about four o'clock, after receiving a free bowl of *toshikoshi soba* for his efforts, the tōban goes to a shrine in the Keage district. There he is customarily met by a group from the village which invites him to return to the community.

What is the meaning of these rituals?[71] According to one young stalwart, B san, the purpose of the general rotō is to test oneself in order to see whether one can really lead the Ittōen life. It is a "proof" or a "demonstration" which proves to one's own satisfaction that he has in truth given up everything and is living at the roadside. This knowledge reassures the members that their "hometown" is rotō. While he acknowledges that this experience could become a mere routine, B san insisted that if one participates in it "with the spirit of Tenkō san"—not knowing whether he will ever be allowed to return to the village—he will be able to return to a *pure* life "at the roadside." This, he said, is the original form of life, the "place of life" (*seikatsu no ba*) where man is given life by nature. In other words—if I may translate B san's thought into Victor Turner's paradigm—through these rituals of rotō which symbolically reenact the original purity of the Shishigatani community, the present community is able to recover its now lost liminality.[72]

According to Takeshi san, the meaning of his rotō is to demonstrate to the dōnin that the leader himself is penniless and without any property. It is an experience which demonstrates that he is not attached to the entrusted things of the village.[73] Professor Turner's notion of the dialectic between "structure" and "antistructure" also seems to clarify the meaning of the leader's rotō, for it is by means of this ritual that "structure and the high offices provided by structure are thus seen as instrumentalities of the commonweal, not as means of personal aggrandizement. The chief must not 'keep his chieftainship to himself.' "[74]

Pure Activity: The Foundation of Liminality and Community

Tradition and the "Moral Entrepreneur"

Moral entrepreneurs like Tenkō san are purveyors of spiritual casseroles, the ingredients of which are so well mashed and blended that they defy all recognition. If the origins of the concoction cannot be reconstructed one by one, from the general flavor and aroma of the whole dish one gets some idea about what was in the pantry. I propose here not merely to trace Tenkō san's religious ideas back to their classical origins in the pantry of history, but to draw the outlines of a religious modality which, spreading across several established traditions, flavors both the liminality and the collective unconscious of Ittōen. This I shall call "Pure Activity."

The dream of Ittōen is a universe of unrestricted freedom (*jizai*) and no deadlock.[75] It is an aspiration to live naturally as children of the Light, according to a vision which calls men to return to a spontaneous, ingenuous, if not naive, way of life. Tenkō san insisted that Ittōen was not merely a development of Japan's established traditions. Nor was it an artificial ideology or, worse, something imported from abroad. Rather, it had welled up from Mother Earth herself.[76] He explained his discovery of the Ittōen life in many ways, always emphasizing its naturalness. "*Sange-hōshi* (repentance and service) is not something one thinks about and then does. It is like taking a stroll—a 'formless' activity (*musō no yūho*). I cannot explain it in words. In Buddhism it is meditation. For now, I can only call it *sange-hōshi.* It implies that one is absolutely absorbed in relaxed, effortless activity under the inspiration of the Light (*musakimui no yūgi zanmai*)."[77]

It is precisely this kind of activity that I shall call "pure." Pure Activity represents a realm of spontaneous, free, and natural movement far surpassing all mundane efforts to control one's destiny, secure one's livelihood, digest one's food, or hit one's target. In short, it transcends all attempts to live 'according to plan.' It defies all of life's 'in order to' motives (see chapter 1). Since it transcends the domain of the deciding self, it naturally goes beyond the realm of good and evil (the sphere of principles, rights, obligations, and decisions). While entrée into the world of Pure Activity may be traumatic, once one has rid oneself of the deliberating self and the scrutinizing other he finds that for the first time one can live naturally, without even "taking thought." It is, as one Ittōen stalwart puts it, like "floating on one's back while swimming."[78]

Pure Activity is a theme that runs throughout the religious traditions of Japan. It is a mode of activity found among the kami, the Buddhas and man alike. The theme of Pure Activity can be discerned in the nativism of the School of National Learning, especially in Motoori Norinaga's attempt to rid the Japanese tradition of "Chinese principles." More important than Confucian principles was *musubi,* the spirit of creativity, a "miraculously divine act the reason for which is beyond the comprehension of the human intellect."[79] While purity and divine activity were both stressed individually by Shinto, the ideal of Pure Activity per se seems more clearly articulated (mutatis mutandis) in China and Japan by philosophical Taoism, Zen Buddhism, and the Wang Yang-Ming (Ōyōmei) School of Neo-Confucianism with its emphasis on "intuition" and the "unity of knowledge and action." Even in Pure

Land Buddhism, "to do what is natural, what is uncontrived, and spontaneous has the highest significance."[80]

These religious traditions differed widely in their understanding of the ultimate state of Pure Activity—whether it was one of mystical illumination or one of enhanced sensitivity, or whether it entailed political activism or indifference. They also differed radically as to the means for achieving this end, stressing a variety of ritual techniques from alchemy to meditation. Nevertheless, there is in general surprising agreement on four points: Pure Activity is 1. natural, 2. spontaneous, 3. superior to mere cogitation about good and evil, and 4. capable of setting men free from the obstacles and deadlock of their lives.

While the most immediate and obvious religious influence on Tenkō san's thinking was Zen Buddhism, parallels can easily be drawn between the Ittōen ideal and philosophical Taoism. Even during the Tokugawa period Taoism inspired an interesting genre of utopian fiction centering around Lao-tzu, Chuang-tzu, and Lieh-tzu.[81] Thus it is not surprising that some of Tenkō san's utopian ideals would be redolent of these Taoist teachings. It was one of the stalwarts of Ittōen, M san, a teacher in the Ittōen high school, who first drew this to my attention. When I inquired about the meaning of a passage in *The Life of Repentance* where Tenkō san stresses the importance of digesting one's food "without taking thought," M san replied that this was merely an application of Lao-tzu's concept of *wu-wei* (spontaneous activity). M san went on to point out, as do all Taoist masters, that this is an ideal which is as applicable to intellectual and artistic activities as it is to the performance of the alimentary canal.

The similarities between Taoism and Ittōen are of two sorts: primary resemblances based on the concept of activity and secondary ones having to do with the use of similar images and metaphors.

The Taoist concept of activity is best expressed by the two concepts *wu-wei* and *tzu-jan* (being so of itself). *Wu-wei*, as all commentators point out, does not mean "inactivity," in the usual sense of the word. Rather, as H. G. Creel puts it, it means "doing nothing that is not natural or spontaneous."[82] In the words of the *Tao te ching*, it is an inactivity whereby "everything can be activated."[83] Like Tenkō san's own thought, the Taoist concept of activity seems to be structured around the existential and ontological polarities of obstructed activity versus liberated or natural activity. In order to overcome obstructions, the sage returns to a life which is in harmony with "natural law,"[84] Taoists regarded this as something surpassing Confucian morality and ethical or pragmatic calculation. It calls for a return to the "Great Form without shape,"[85] to that point where "Being and Not-being grow out of one another."[86]

For both the Taoist and Tenko san, man's most serious spiritual problem is obstructed activity, or deadlock as Tenkō san would put it. From this both seek liberation and the ability simply "to move." Such movement was what Tenkō san, after his metamorphosis, referred to as his "*wu-wei* activity" (*mui no dōsa*). The activity of the Ittōen dōnin seems always surrounded by the nimbus of the "magical passivity" of the Taoist.[87] The "limitless resources of purified wealth" seem to accumulate quite naturally wherever he goes. Trusting "all things to the operation of 'natural law' " and acting "in accord with the Formless Form," neither dōnin nor Taoist is concerned about ideologies. "The power of civilization has no meaning for this truth seeker. Civilizations are built up by men and by men they are destroyed. These men sorrow for what they lack and suffer for what they have" (Tenkō san's *Ichi-Jijitsu*).[88]

Ittōen's use of images and metaphors is also similar to those of philosophical Taoism. Most obvious are those of the mother and child. According to the *Tao te ching:*

> He who knows the male, yet cleaves to what is female
> Becomes like a ravine, receiving all things under heaven,
> And being such a ravine
> He knows all the time a power that he never calls upon in vain.
> This is returning to the state of infancy.[89]

Tenkō san could easily have used Lao-tzu's words to express his own visionary experience in the shrine: "Wherein I am most different from men is that I prize no sustenance that comes not from the Mother's breast."[90] Kaltenmark points out that in the *Tao te ching* "this 'nourishment' yields, if not immortality, at least long life."[91] Thus, while it may be coincidental, it is nevertheless curious that Tenkō san discovered his own "eternity" immediately after his vision of the nursing child.[92]

Even Ittōen's economics seems to have points in common with the Taoist viewpoint. Both condemn greed. According to the *Tao te ching:*

> No lure is greater than to possess what others want,
> No disaster greater than not to be content with what one has,
> No presage of evil greater than that men should be wanting to get more.[93]

Still more remarkable is that in both cases, Pure Activity seems to result in "purified wealth."

> The Sage has no need to hoard;
> When his own last scrap has been used up on behalf of others,

> Lo, he has more than before!
> When his own last scrap has been used up in giving to others,
> Lo, his stock is even greater than before.[94]

What do these parallels mean? Admittedly they do not show that Tenkō san was a Taoist or prove that his disciples—in spite of the magical nuances of rotō and gyōgan—are wizards. The very idea of founding an intentional community like Ittōen would run counter to most Taoist teachings. Also contrary to the teachings of the *Tao te ching* is Tenkō san's moralism, based on the traditional Japanese ethics of "benefits" and their "return." The techniques which Taoism and Tenkō san used in order to return to Pure Activity also differed greatly. Instead of the Taoist stress on "breathing exercises, sexual gymnastics, herbal drugs, alchemy,"[95] Tenkō san's method was simply humble work and toilet cleaning.

While we cannot trace Tenko san's ideals back to the *Tao te ching,* we can say that his thoughts and ideals took shape within a diffuse religious tradition which, like this Taoist classic, put a premium on natural, spontaneous activity. The ultimate state of Ittōen's version of Pure Activity was not merely the heightened sensitivity of the *Tao te ching,* but the Buddhist experiences of nonego, self-abandonment, and awakening.[96]

One of the first western scholars to discuss what I call Pure Activity in the Japanese tradition was Ruth Benedict. In her discussion of Zen, she points out ways in which the split between actor and observer, and between the observing self and the observed self, are overcome. This is done by getting rid of the everyday self, thus removing it from the immobilizing gaze of both self and other. In this way, one is able to "eliminate the self-censorship of shame (*haji*)."[97] In Zen archery, for example, self, arrow and target become one. Since the observer is forgotten there is no longer a fear of missing the mark (and losing face). The act is pure.

Since man and nature are both involved in Pure Activity, the phenomenon has both an existential and an ontological aspect. Suzuki expressed the ontological side of Pure Activity in Zen when he wrote: "Nature is always in motion, never at a standstill; if Nature is to be loved, it must be caught while moving. . . . To seek tranquility is to kill nature, to stop its pulsation, and to embrace the dead corpse that is left behind."[98] The traditional Japanese view of nature has been one of spontaneous growth and development: *natura naturans*. The sacred and the human are regarded as currents within the flowing stream of nature. Related to this is a general way of thinking "with emphasis upon the fluid, arresting character of observed events [which regards] the phenomenal world itself as Absolute and rejects the recognition of anything existing over and above the phenomenal world."[99] "Impermanence is the Buddhahood."[100] Thus nature is generally regarded as process and not stasis (*natura naturata*).

Looking at the existential aspect of Pure Activity, it is clear that for man to live "at one with nature" means that he must participate in its flux. Rather than trying to arrest or control its course, he must enter into it with the spontaneity of a child: "When we speak of being natural, we mean first of all being free and spontaneous in the expression of our feelings, being immediate and not premeditating in our response to environment, not making any calculation as to the effect of our doings either on others or on ourselves, and conducting ourselves in such a way as not to leave room for thought of gain, value, merit, or consequence. To be natural means, therefore, to be like a child."[101]

Because Pure Activity is uncalculating, it can have nothing to do with the calculus of good and evil, that is, with the 'in order to' world of ethics. "Zen finds its inevitable association with art but not with morality. Zen may remain unmoral but not without art."[102] Purpose itself runs contrary to the flux of natural experience. "When teleology enters into our life, we cease to be religious, we become moral beings."[103] Dōgen (1200–1253), the founder of Japan's Sōtō Zen sect, emphasized the "flowing" and transmoral aspects of Pure Activity, which he contrasts with "attachment": "Free yourself from all attachments and bring to rest the ten thousand things. Think neither of good or evil, and judge not of right or wrong. Maintain the flow of mind, will, and consciousness; and bring an end to all desires, concepts, and judgments. Do not even think of how to become a Buddha."[104]

An example of the diffusion of this religious modality throughout Japanese culture is the role of Pure Activity in military history. Pure Activity has long manifested itself as a fanatical and irrational ethic of loyalty. Since Zen was the faith of the Japanese warrior, the appearance of Zen-inspired ideas such as muga in the cockpit of a modern aircraft during World War II comes as no surprise: "A bombing pilot approaching his goal has 'the sweat of muga' before he releases his bombs. '*He* is not doing it.' There is no observer-self left in his consciousness. An anti-aircraft gunner, lost to all the world beside, is said similarly to have 'the sweat of muga' and to have eliminated the observer-self. The idea is that in all such cases people in this condition are at the top of their form."[105]

The role of Pure Activity in military history is also instructive because it helps us grasp the opposite kind of activity: the Mundane. By this, I mean a mode of activity which is plodding, unheroic, and apt to be arrested by the scrutiny of the public eye or the private purse. From the traditional Japanese point of view, Mundane Activity results from calculation and hidden interest. In the ultranationalist period when all political parties were coming under attack, politics itself was regarded as Mundane Activity par excellence. The nemesis of such calculating behavior was thought to be a paralysis of soul and body. For this reason, the *Imperial Rescript to Sailors and Soldiers* warned military men (members of the emperor's "body," and hence "pure") not to "be led astray by current opinions nor meddle in politics." "If you . . . tie yourself to unwise obligations, you may find yourself in a position *where you can neither go forwards nor backwards*."[106] In short, the risk of political involvement, or Mundane Activity, was immobilization.

War itself was regarded as a pure and liberating act, and was often contrasted with the temporizing activities of politicians and diplomats. For Tokutomi Sohō, the outbreak of the Sino-Japanese War was a spiritual release (*seishinteki gedatsu*).[107] Itō Sei, the critic and novelist, wrote in the *Miyako shinbun* shortly after the beginning of World War II, "This war is an *absolute act*. It is not merely an extension of politics or the reverse side of politics."[108] Honda Akira, a specialist in English literature, expressed a similar feeling. "Now the meaning of the words 'holy war' is obvious, and our war goals are pellucidly apparent. A new courage has welled up, and *everything has become easier to do*."[109]

I point out the role of Pure Activity in Japanese political and military history not in order to condemn it, but 1. to demonstrate its deep penetration into the vitals of the culture, and 2. to show how widespread, even in popular thought, was the dichotomy between obstructed activity, on the one hand, and liberated or spontaneous activity, on the other.

Before looking more closely at Ittōen as an example of Pure Activity, let us summarize what we have already said regarding this phenomenon. We have seen that Pure Activity is a religious modality, a way of moving—or even flowing—possible in the realm of nature, as well as among the gods, the Buddhas, and men. Both existentially and ontologically, its accent is upon immediate, fluid experience. Because of its free, spontaneous orientation, Pure Activity can abide no fetters whether moral, legal, or political. Even if learned, it is like a natural skill, or a knack. One versed in its magic can be active while at rest, running while standing still, hitting his mark without lifting a finger. Because he has overcome the dualism of subject and object, he never interferes with "others." Nor is he hampered by "them." He is what he does. Form without content, Pure Activity is bound neither by tradition nor by reason. From its sublime heights, one can only be impatient with action that is finite or mundane. Where Pure Activity is absolute, unconditional, free, natural, ingenuous, Mundane Activity is relative, contioned, bound, artificial, and contrived. Pure Activity is marked by effortless, quick, supple, but decisive behavior; Mundane Activity by plodding, hesitation, and deliberation. Pure Activity has to do with creating, intuiting, doing, and daring; Mundane Activity with maintaining, calculating pondering, and caring. With these ideal-typical distinctions in mind, let us return once again to Tenkō san's dichotomy between Ittōen and Kōsenrin.

Ittōen as Pure Activity

The tradition of Pure Activity provided Tenkō san with a basic orientation within which to ask his questions and frame his answers. For him, the fundamental dichotomy of Pure versus Mundane Activity was a tension between a flowing, spontaneous activity on the one hand, and paralysis and deadlock on the other.

If we turn back to his own conversion experiences, we discover that they have the basic structure of most rites of passage. They mark a transition from the paralysis of *ikizumari* to a state where he could, at last, *move*. The symbols embedded in these experiences are clearly of a religious sort. First of all, there was Tolstoy's challenge: "die if you want to live." We have seen that he responded to this by reducing himself to a state where he could be mistaken for a corpse swathed in white. He challenged his family to die with him. He was rejected as a fool. The crowning event, of course, was the metamorphosis itself, an event which occurred in his thirty-second year and which was modeled after the death and resurrection of Christ. In connection with this experience he even cites Jesus' promise to rebuild the temple in Jerusalem in three days.[110] He also identified his experience with the story of Shakyamuni giving up his throne in order to "go begging." Through this religious experience he was able to make sense of all that had happened to him, even his failure in Hokkaidō. "The baby of my New Life, which had been conceived by reading the biography of Ninomiya Sontoku [in Hokkaidō] no doubt raised its birth-cry at that time [in the shrine]."[111]

The metamorphosis itself was filled with obvious, religious symbolism. Because he was fasting, he nearly lost his sight. This near-blindness seems to be deliberately contrasted with the Light which appears with the dawning of the fourth day. He notices a *sunflower* which, always following the Light, gives him the idea that he should imitate the crying baby and simply go where there is food. From the

Figure 9

Nishida Tenkō's Transformation Scenario

Mundane Activity	***Mediating Experiences***	***Pure Activity***
Death		Life
Ikizumari (deadlock)	*Symbols of Liminality:*	"Everything going smoothly"
Unnatural actions (search for money, power and knowledge)	Nature	Natural action
	Light	
	Dawn	
Inability to receive Nature's blessings	Milk	Ability to receive Nature's blessings
	Breasts	
Blindness	Mother-Child	Sight
Hunger	Sunflower	Satiation
Obligations and responsibility	Happy White Corpse	No obligations or responsibilities
Self	*Rituals of Liminality:*	Egoless communitarian personality
Assertion of "rights"	*Rotō*	Obedience to the Light
Wages	*Gyōgan*	"Money is not necessary"
Conflict:	*Geza* (humble work)	Harmony:
Industrial (strikes)	*Takuhatsu* (sanctified labor)	Industrial
Domestic		Domestic
Bankruptcy		*Fukuden:* purified wealth

point of view of symbolic structure, the Light and the sunflower seem to mediate between the deadlock and hunger of his fast and the movement and fullness he experiences after he leaves the shrine. Another structural contrast is between the starvation he experiences in the shrine and the flow of milk from the mother's breasts. These images of the shrouded (happy) corpse, the sunrise, the sunflower, milk, and breasts seem to combine the symbolisms of whiteness and flow.[112] Taken together, they constitute a bridge over which Tenkō san was able to pass from the *ikizumari* of his former life—and ultimately from all the "unnatural actions" men engage in in their search for money, power, and knowledge—to pure, unfettered *movement.*

If we incorporate into this conversion experience his whole comunitarian outlook, the transformation scenario shown in figure 9 seems to emerge.

With the complete scenario before us, we are in a better position to understand the significance of Ittōen's myths and rituals of liminality. Here again, the work of Victor Turner is of great importance, above all his discovery of the connection between the symbols of light, flow, and *community.* One might say that in such symbols

> what is sought is unity, not the unity which represents a sum of factions and is susceptible of division and subtraction, but an indivisible unity, "white," "pure," "primary," "seamless," expressed in such symbols as the basic generative and nurturant fluids such as semen and milk, as "running water," as "dawn," as "light," and as "whiteness." Homogeneity is sought, instead of heterogeneity. The members of the religious community are to be regarded, at least in rite and symbol, as a simple unit, not as a sum of segments or the ultimate product of some mode of social division of labor. They are impregnated by unity, as it were, and purified from divisiveness and plurality. The impure and sinful is the sundered, the divided. The pure is the integer, the indivisible.[113]

The pivotal symbols of Pure Activity seem to underlie both the social boundaries of the Ittōen community and its collective unconscious.[114] As images of unity, such symbols help to integrate the community, setting it apart from the outside world. Collectively, these symbols seem to be woven into the fabric of the community's "mythological charter."

Capitalism and the Buddhist Utopia

Earlier in this chapter, we saw that Ittōen was begun by the young Nishida Tenkō after he found himself trapped between the capitalists and workers engaged in a reclamation project in Hokkaidō. Like the Buddhist factory chaplains mentioned in chapter 5, Tenkō san sympathized with the working classes, but preached a message which seemed designed to keep them in their place. Like the Buddhist preachers, he seemed to see nothing wrong with the ideal of "discriminating equality" (*shabetsu-soku-byōdō*). While he occasionally made antiestablishment noises, his community was anything but a utopia of dissent. Does this mean that Ittōen was one of the creators of Japanese capitalism? Hardly. I see no reason to believe that Tenkō san's economic ethic generated the kind of "mighty enthusiasm" Weber associates with the spirit of capitalism. There is, for example, little in his way of thinking that encourages risk taking or innovation. On the contary, it is monotonous, lowly, even meaningless toil that he praises. Thus, the Ittōen spirit seems to have been a factor indirectly (but passively) enabling capitalists to move forward. Why else would they pay to have their operatives trained in the ideals of the community? If Ittōen is not a positive enablement of capitalism, it is at least *useful* to the capitalists insofar as it creates an ethos of obedience among those who toil at his behest. In effect, Tenkō san was doing what the Buddhists of the Meiji and Taishō periods promised to do: deflect the threat of the political left by inculcating a conservative spirit of loyalty to state and industry alike. His tours of the outposts of the Japanese Empire suggest that he himself was used by the government in its program of religious "pacification." In short, the idealism of Tenkō san's Buddhist utopia seems basically congruent with the strategy of accommodation of the Buddhist temples and their determination to demonstrate in all ways possible the "usefulness" of the dharma to the state (*buppō kokueki*).

When Tenkō san published his book, *The Life of Repentance,* in 1921, he did not invent utopia. On the contrary, throughout the Japanese middle ages, sectarian reformers, fired by the cargo cult-like visions of the Lotus and Pure Land sutras, had repeatedly founded religious sects which embodied utopian dreams. Nevertheless, it was not until the twentieth century that such visions resulted in the founding of intentional, residential communities for both sexes. During the Tokugawa period, utopian tales were often spun out of the Buddhist sutras. Others were written about such Taoist figures as Lao-tzu, Chuang-tzu, and Lieh-tzu. After the Meiji Restoration western utopias became the model for this literary genre. In 1882, Sir Thomas Moore's *Utopia* was translated with the Japanese subtitle, "On Good Government."[115] Even before this, utopian books by Dutch authors dealing with the "scientific age" of the twenty-first century had been translated. While traditional Japanese utopian tales were generally set in the past, this new literature, like our own science fiction, was about the future. Its picture of utopia was one of men in society and not one of Buddhas and heroes. Yanagita Izumi points out that at the beginning of the Meiji era all Japanese, in a sense, were utopians, each with his own plan for rebuilding Japan.[116] These early Meiji schemes were inspired by the culture of the western Enlightenment, but also by a deep faith in the Japanese emperor's Five Articles Oath of 1868. Since the government was not sure of its own course, the leadership itself was prone to utopianizing. Such utopian schemes were mostly political. After the establishment of the constitution and the opening of the Diet, the focus of utopian thought gradually shifted from politics to society itself—to the problems of women's rights, labor unrest, poverty, education and science, and the challenge of socialism and the Freedom and People's Rights Movement. By the time of the Sino-Japanese War, social issues had outstripped political ones in the utopian imagination of the Japanese. At the same time, a robust literature on how to get ahead (*risshin-shusse*) was competing for the attention of the reading public. When Tenkō san first published his best seller, the air was therefore filled with utopian schemes of every conceivable sort. The Russian Revolution had occurred just four years previously, causing discussions of socialism to take on a new and more dangerous note of realism. The writings of Karl Marx were being translated by Takahata Motoyuki and were being devoured by a voracious reading public.

The dramatic growth of the Ittōen community after the publication of Tenkō san's book coincided with a period of economic recession and labor unrest. The Japanese economy, which had reached maturity after the Russo-Japanese War, was greatly stimulated by World War I. The period from 1900 to 1930 was one of unprecedented growth, in spite of the unspectacular 1920s. During this period, manufactured goods increased twelvefold, while export trade multiplied by a factor of twenty. In spite of this *Wirtschaftswunder*, economic prosperity was not equally shared. The financial boom occasioned by World War I widened the gap between rich and poor. The rice riots of 1918 were the prelude to widespread labor unrest in 1919 and 1920.[117] From March 1920 until 1922 Japan suffered a serious economic recession. Under these circumstances, books like *Shisen o koete* [Across the deathline] by the Christian socialist Kagawa Toyohiko (1920) and Tenkō san's *The Life of Repentance* (1921) became instant successes.

As disturbing as these events must have been, the gradual transformation of Japan's traditional, feudalistic, agrarian economy into a more highly rationalized, capitalistic one was more important. The invasion of a cash nexus into even the smallest hamlets transformed labor—heretofore embedded in an unbroken network of religious and social obligations—into an independent commodity which could be conceptually isolated from one's other devoirs, weighed, bought, and sold. With these severe strains on the traditional way of life, it was no wonder that "Japanese utopianism first appeared in the burned-over region between Nagoya and Osaka, the region where modern industry first took root and where there had been a highly commercialized economy even before industrialization began."[118]

There is little doubt that the Ittōen community was what Anthony F. C. Wallace calls a "revitalization movement."[119] It is also clear, however, that Tenkō san's revitalization was of a reactionary sort which, in effect, revived the spirit of the traditional Japanese village. After all, in the traditional village money was quite literally "not necessary." It was a society in which reciprocal, vertical relationships formed the basis of an ethos of obedience, protection, and gratitude. Such ties were reinforced by horizontal relationships which stressed unitive, community values. In this traditional society, as in Kōsenrin Village today, labor was thought of as an expression of gratitude for the benefits one had received (*hō-on no gyō*). Economic relationships were infused with diffuse emotional dependency and religious duty. In other words—to use the terminology developed in chapter 4—the economy continues to be "embedded" in communitarian structures. The importance of the village mentality, both in the formation of "modern" values and ideological images, can hardly be exaggerated. As Nigel Harris aptly put it, "Almost all societies dragging themselves out of a predominantly agricultural state have experienced a pervasive and romantic sense of loss about the village."[120] Tenkō san transformed this nostalgia into community. For him, the process of modernization (which destroyed the village) was primarily one of "cultural distortion" (Wallace). It was characterized by competition, a struggle for existence, a clamor over individual rights, and conflict between employers and employees. In other words: deadlock and Mundane Activity. Rather than rejecting modernity out of hand, Tenkō san sought to resolve its dilemmas by an atavistic revitalization of the traditional values of rural Japan. Like the ethical outlook of the peasant, the cornerstone of his moral reflection was gratitude. As he once put it: "I don't understand difficult matters. I'm just *thankful*, and I don't dare to hide it. I'm not thankful because somebody told me I should be. Sometimes I'm too busy to remember to be grateful—something I'm also thankful for! Because I'm thankful, I feel that it's wasteful not to be working. I must do anything I can to be useful."[121]

In the traditional Japanese village before the introduction of wage labor, such feelings of gratitude to one's benefactors—both human and divine—constituted the religious rationale of labor relations. Thus, Ittōen's hōshi is only a step removed from the ethic of *hō-on* (paying back favors) of pre-modern Japan. Even the theatrical quality of Ittōen's "public service" is traditional, for as David Plath points out, "Conspicuous contribution seems to be as much a feature of rural life in Japan as conspicuous consumption."[122] The Kōsenrin ideal of a distributionless economy not only goes back to the asceticism of Ninomiya Sontoku; it is taught by Confucianism itself.[123] Its solicitation of donations, its emphasis on acts of ritual labor, and its stress on not spending money (rather than on making it), are all examples of the comparatively low level of rationalization of a premodern economy. The economics of Kōsenrin is, in short, a sublimation of what Norman O. Brown calls the "psychology of precapitalist hoarding."[124]

Another traditional item in Ittōen's value system is the high premium placed on passive virtues. One of Tenkō san's most widely quoted phrases is "to live if allowed." Among his followers this inspired a nondialectical, or nonadversarial spirit of acquiescence and obedience. We have seen how Tenkō san used the image of the nursing child—a vivid symbol for what Japanese psychologists call "intimate dependency relations" (*amae*)[125]—as a model for labor relations. According to Tenkō san, "the more we avoid the cause of economic conflict, the better society will be."[126] Closely related to this is his use of the Buddhist concept *muga*. This ideal was also highly regarded in the traditional Japanese village, as, in fact, it is throughout Japanese culture today.[127]

The logic of utopia is one of frustration, hope, exaggeration and daring. For this reason, it may be expecting too much to ask that the first principles of its philosophy be based on clear and distinct, let alone critical or dialectical, ideas. As Marx pointed out in his criticism of other utopian dreamers, "To realize all these castles in the air, [utopians] are compelled to appeal to the feelings and purses of the bourgeois."[128] Ittōen's reliance upon industrial patrons certainly seems to bear this out. In his Rauschenbusch Lectures, Kagawa Toyohiko criticized Ittōen from the laborers' point of view: "The members of this group undertake the most menial service with a willing spirit and without compensation. They do not realize, however, that their well intentioned service has thrown out of employment many who depend upon service in these homes as a means of livelihood."[129]

While dōnin maintain to this day that Ittōen is a spiritual communism whose ideals are closest to those of Japan's Communist party, the ethic taught in its training sessions owes little to Marx or Lenin. The impropriety of preaching a feudalistic morality in the context of a capitalist economy, while quickly noticed by outsiders, obviously is not evident to the stalwart of the village. While their life-style differs in many ways from that of their neighbors, as a cultural alternative Ittōen appears to be no more than a revitalization of the values and outlook of premodern Japan. Having lost the creative tension between structure and antistructure, Ittōen's myth of poverty threatens to degenerate into an ideology of a limited social nexus. Before long, its original idea of liminality may be completely transformed into a private, annual ritual. After this, Kōsenrin village will become a quiet and secure retirement home for the aged disciples of Nishida Tenkō.

PART IV

Secularization and National Identity

CHAPTER 7

The Secularization of Japanese Religion

For historians and sociologists of religion one of the most important spinoffs of modernization theory has been a subset of problems concerning secularization. While definitions of the phenomenon differ, the concepts of secularization which have grown out of theoretical studies of modernization fall between two extremes.[1] The first sort declares that the decline of religion is *inevitable*. The original statement of this position pictured religion as the unhappy victim of the advance of science and reason. As continental scholars liked to put it, Mythos was dethroned by Logos. This idea was conventional wisdom for many of the thinkers of the 18th and 19th centuries. A corollary of the doctrine of social progress, this notion has yet to be exorcized from the catalogue of academic obsessions. The decline of religion for Auguste Comte was part of the general law of evolution of society and corresponded to the development of individuals from infantile theologians to mature natural philosophers or scientists.[2] Max Weber's discussions of *die Entgötterung* and *Entzauberung der Welt* link the decline of religion and magic to the overall process of the rationalization of society and ultimately to the destiny of modern civilization itself. More recent versions of the inevitable decline theory treat religion as part of a syndrome of social, economic, political and psychological changes which, collectively, make up "the modernization process."

The other extreme makes the decline of religion ultimately *impossible*. Scholars working in the *Religionswissenschaft* tradition are the first to come to mind. G. Van der Leeuw, for example, declares that "religion exists always and universally."[3] Rudolf Otto's stress on "divination" as an a priori category of the human mind and Mircea Eliade's emphasis on the essential religiousness of man (*homo religiosus*)[4] both seem to imply that secularization just cannot take place. This position seems to rest on the historical generalization that religion has existed de facto in all cultures up to the present and concludes, falsely I think, that it therefore will continue to do so in the future *de iure*. In its more philosophical versions, this theory seems to be based on analysis of the "essence" of human nature. Otto, for example, believed that the experience of the numinous is a "fact of our nature." The history of religions therefore presupposes man's eternal capacity for apprehending the Holy. Implied in this argument seems to be the intimation that man achieves maturity only when he develops these religious sensibilities.[5]

Some sociologists also have stressed the ultimate impossibility of secularization. Emile Durkheim, while believing that religion continually embraces a smaller part of social life, saw in what he called "the cult of the individual" a quasi-religious integration of modern society. The structural-functionalist school which took its inspiration from him has been deeply imbued by a piety which, as Nisbet puts it, "represents a conviction that full understanding of social phenomena is impossible save in terms of a recognition of the unalterable, irreducible role of the religious impulse."[6] This tendency is quite apparent in the works of Talcott Parsons who, elaborating Durkheim's fundamental postulate that collective representations are symbols for the integration of society, has consistently sought to ground both ethical norms and culture per se in the templates of religion. What others took to be the enervation of religious institutions, Parsons has regarded as instances of "value-generalization."[7] His seminal essay, "Christianity and Modern Industrial Society," was cast as an alternative to Pitirim Sorokin's view of secularization as an inevitable consequence of the transition from an "ideational logico-meaningful sociocultural supersystem" (*sic*) to a "sensate pattern" of culture in which "the World takes flesh." Following Parsons, Robert Bellah in his development of a neoevolutionary analysis of religious history adopts a modified Eliadean position and insists that "neither religious man nor the structure of man's ultimate religious situation evolves, then, but rather religion as a symbol system."[8] Thus he seems to imply that homo sapiens is essentially homo religiosus. While the notion that secularization is ultimately impossible is more sophisticated than the inevitable decline theory, it too has a built-in theoretical bias. It tends to transform instances of religious decline (however defined) into simple cases of religious change.

The two general theories I have mentioned stand at the antipodes of the study of secularization. Both rely heavily on specific modernization theories for their underpinnings. There is a tendency in both theories to presuppose that cultural change, and religious change in particular, is synchronic with the overall transformations of society. This bias is especially strong in traditional functionalism, which saw in religion a symbolic means for effecting social solidarity.[9] Proponents of both types of theory have tended to analyze modernization by drawing up two lists of predicates, one under the heading "tradition," the other under "modernity." Modernization for these scholars means simply the movement from the first to the second list. Such dichotomous configuration theories of modernization have the tendency to smother the historical specificity of religious change under the soft pillow of sociological abstraction. Like functionalism in general these theories assume that religious change is eurhythmic, i.e., that the transformation of religion always keeps step with other changes in society.[10] One of the dangers in this double list approach is that tradition and modernity easily become falsely reified and artificially contrasted. As Joseph Kitagawa points out, "we are often presented with a stereotyped dichotomy between a supposedly irrational worldview in which tradition-equals-religion-equals-premodern-thinking, on the one hand, over against a modern-equals-secular-equals-rational scientific mode of thinking on the other."[11]

I offer no full-blown paradigm or alternative to these theories. Instead, I would simply point out the importance of the kind of analyses careful historians of religion have been doing, perhaps intuitively, all along. Rather than assuming that the decline of religion, however defined, is either inevitable or impossible, I shall assume that it is possible, not necessarily unilinear, and therefore reversible. Such is my hypothesis. I shall try to demonstrate by statistical and historical examples that there is no universal measure for "*the* secularization process"—whatever that means!—and that even within a single religious system "the *general* decline of religion" is a meaningless jumble of words. It is my position that the concept of secularization can be rehabilitated only if we take a more nominalistic approach to the subject. This entails 1. breaking religious systems into their component parts, e.g., belief, emotion, and modes of expression and behavior, 2. determining which of these parts is dominant, which recessive, 3. defining and operationalizing the concept of decline within each part, and 4. investigating specific cases in the history of religions in this way by looking at the behavior of specific churches, sects, and social or ethnic groups. In this chapter, I shall concentrate on the first two points and their application to the alleged decline of religion in modern Japan. Following Larry Shiner, I shall assume that the meaning of secularization includes the complementary notions of desacralization, differentiation, and the transposition of religious beliefs and behavior to the "secular" sphere.[12]

Some years ago, I had a mid-air conversation with a Japanese banker who was flying home from a seminar in the United States.

When he learned that I was studying Japanese religion he shook his head and sadly assured me that there no longer was such a thing. I was later to hear the same thing from many other Japanese. While I suspect that this opinion is, in part, a reflection of the this-worldly work ethic of upper-middle-class white collar workers (the so-called "economic animals"), statistics seem to bear this position out. A recent Gallup survey of religious beliefs around the globe produced the results summarized in figure 10.[13]

The survey concludes that "the United States stands at the top of the industrial societies in the importance religion plays in the lives of its citizens. Japan, which also has a high level of education, stands at the opposite extreme."[14]

I present this information not because I think it solves our problem, but because it brings out the difficulty, or rather the impossibility, of measuring overall, cross-cultural religiousness or secularity by such simple sociometric techniques. Beneath the superficially simple questions asked in the survey are such unquantifiable problems as the relative importance of belief per se in each religious system and the relationship between religion and national identity. The poor showing of the Japanese in this survey is not, of course, explained by the figures themselves. The fact that religious beliefs are "fairly important" to more Japanese than to any other group, while they score lowest among those holding these beliefs to be "very important," could very well be attributed to the notorious capacity of the Japanese for self-effacement. Furthermore the Japanese, who have a deep appreciation for ambiguity both in literature and in daily conversation, dislike committing themselves in a public way to any political, ideological or religious opinion. The low incidence of belief in God can be attributed in part to the fact that Japanese religions do not school their adherents in the abstractions of theology—not even in "belief." Finally, the poor showing of the Japanese in answers to the last question (about life after death) has to be counterbalanced by the importance Japanese place on ancestor worship.

Turning to Japanese surveys, there does seem to be evidence of a decline of religious belief since World War II. During the war itself, when religion was one of the tools of national ideology and thought-control, 72 percent responded positively to the Nishitani survey which asked "do you believe in the *kami* and Buddha?" In 1946, 56 percent of the respondents in the Jiji Tsūshinsha survey said that they were "inclined to believe in religion." While the same survey uncovered a wide range of negative feelings towards religion, only 1.5 percent said they thought religious teachings are a "lie." The Nagamatsu survey of the same year showed 77 percent replying that they had a "religious atti-

Figure 10

Gallup Survey of Religious Beliefs

QUESTION: "How important to you are your religious beliefs?"

RESULTS (abbreviated; percentage of those surveyed):

	very important	*fairly important*	*not too important*	*not at all important*	*don't know*
India	81	14	3	2	—
United States	56	30	8	5	1
United Kingdom	23	26	26	20	5
Scandinavia	17	28	39	13	3
Western Europe (av.)	27	32	26	13	2
Japan	12	34	44	10	—

QUESTION: "Do you believe in God or a universal spirit?" (Those who said "yes" were also asked the following questions: "Do you believe that this God or universal spirit observes your actions and rewards or punishes you for them?")

RESULTS (abbreviated; percentage of those surveyed):

	believe in God	*don't believe*	*don't know*	*God observes*	*doesn't observe*	*don't know*
India	98	2	—	90	6	2
United States	94	3	3	68	19	7
United Kingdom	76	14	10	34	28	14
Scandinavia	65	25	10	28	27	10
Western Europe (av.)	78	16	6	43	22	13
Japan	38	34	28	18	7	13

QUESTION: "Do you believe in life after death?"

RESULTS (abbreviated: percentage of those surveyed):

	yes	*no*	*undecided*
India	72	18	10
United States	69	20	11
United Kingdom	43	35	22
Scandinavia	35	44	21
Western Europe (av.)	44	39	17
Japan	18	43	39

tude" (*shinkō-shin*). Since this was a broader question than the one asked by Jiji Tsūshinsha, a larger number of positive responses might have been expected. Nevertheless, the Jiji Tsūshinsha survey of 1947, using its original question, likewise showed an increase of believers, rising from 56 percent to 77 percent. Believers in Buddhism went up from 33.2 percent to 54.3 percent and Christians increased from 1.3 percent to 6.0 percent. Shintō, discredited by the surrender, decreased from 8.7 percent to 6.8 percent. The dramatic shifts indicated by these surveys in the immediate postwar period are difficult to interpret. What is clear is that much of the hyper-ventilated *overbelief* of the war years continued to exist during the immediate post-war period and was sustained through the early 1950s. A Yomiuri newspaper survey of 1952, for example, found that 65 percent of the Japanese believed in a religion.[15]

Our data thus far is "soft," based as it is on different survey techniques and questions. Evidence becomes much better after the beginning of the government's *Survey of the National Character of the Japanese* conducted every five years beginning in 1953. By using the same questions and sampling methods over an extended period of time, the findings of this research project can be regarded as comparatively "hard" evidence. One of the questions posed by this survey is: "Do you have some kind of religious faith or attitudes?" (*nani ka shinkō to ka shinshin*). The percentage of positive replies made every fifth year are as follows (a dash indicates that the question was not asked in that year):

—/35/31/30/25/34

Over a fifteen-year span, religious beliefs and attitudes seemed to decline about 10 percent before returning to their (relative) high-point.[16] The description of Japanese religious beliefs in the *Survey of the National Character* is therefore no more flattering than that found in the international Gallup poll. But, before we draw any final conclusions, we should look at other evidence from the same survey. This will make the picture more complicated, but perhaps also a bit more realistic.

The number of Japanese who believed that a religious attitude (*shūkyōshin*) is important has remained about the same throughout the duration of the study:

—/72/77/76/69/74

In the 1973 survey, 63 percent said "revering one's ancestors" is "*extremely* important," while 76 percent held "filial piety" in similar esteem. These feelings—which one naturally associates with "ancestor worship"—seem to be divorced from "religion" (*shūkyō*) by the Japanese. At least, only 28 percent indicated that religious feelings (*shūkyōteki na kokoro*) were "*very* important."[17] These figures seem to show that while individuals are hesitant to commit themselves to any specific religious belief, they believe that in principle religion is important for people. The unbelief revealed in this study therefore cannot be equated with a principled disbelief.

The findings of this government survey incline one to wonder whether belief should be the measure of Japanese religiousness and secularity at all. This suspicion is underscored by Basabe's study (1967) of the religious attitudes of Japanese men aged twenty through forty living in metropolitan areas.[18] In this study, 14 percent said they believed in some religion; 22.1 percent said they did not believe; 59 percent were indifferent. The lines between these groups were by no means clear. For example, the traditional Buddhists (who constituted 35 percent of the believers) displayed what a westerner might think was a high level of theological nonchalance. Eighty-three percent believed that since "religion is something depending on man's moods and feelings, it is perfectly right for him to accept or reject it." Forty-four percent believed that "God is nothing more than a yearning existing in man's heart." Forty-two percent thought that "there is no such thing as an afterlife, but because people want an afterlife, they believe in it." In spite of the fact that customs like *Obon* (All Souls Day) are important for these traditional believers, only 34.6 percent agreed that "at *Obon* time, the spirits of the ancestors return to their homes." Still more revealing was the finding that of those styling themselves "unbelievers," 32.5 percent have Buddhist and Shintō altars in their homes, 57.6 percent participate in festivals and pilgrimages, and 27 percent carry an amulet. Of those "indifferent" to religion, 59.3 percent have Buddhist and Shintō altars and 34.5 percent offer prayers before these altars. Six percent do so daily, while 28.4 percent do so occasionally. Sixty-one percent now and then participate in pilgrimages to shrines or temples and 43.1 percent carry amulets. In short, Basabe found that even among believers there is a low level of commitment to specific beliefs. On the other hand, he found that those calling themselves "unbelievers" or "indifferent to" religion *continue to do religious things*. The *Shūkyō chōsa* study (reported in the *National Character of the Japanese*, No. 2) which investigated feelings of reverence likewise found that the number of Japanese having religious feelings far exceeds the number willing to call themselves believers. While believers in this survey stood at 28 percent, those who claimed to have "experienced feelings of reverence before a Shintō shrine" were 71 percent. Sixty-nine percent said that they had "experienced feelings of reverence before a statue of the Buddha or while listening to a sutra." Only 25 percent clearly deny ever having such feelings.[19]

What these findings indicate is that "in Japan, the criterion of 'believer' and 'non-believer' does not suffice to make an adequate distinction between those souls that are truly religious and those which are irreligious or indifferent."[20] While belief naturally seems to be an appropriate index of religiousness to the westerner (and to the Japanese sociologist trained in western sociology), by itself it tells us only part of the story. The reason for this is that religious praxis (*shugyō*) and feelings (*kimochi*) and not belief per se form the core of Japanese religion. The best way to understand the real genius of this religion (and its putative decline) is to turn from what the Japanese believe or think about religion to what they feel and do. This, of course, takes us from statistics to a more humanistic examination of religious behavior.

Without a doubt, the greatest secularizing influence on Japanese religion was the growth of a money economy. A process at work in Japanese history even before the Tokugawa period, the growth of market relationships disrupted both class relationships and family ties.[21] During this period of economic development a group of writers whom Smith calls "technologists" appeared with the express purpose of showing the farmer how to increase the prosperity of his own family. Not only did the opinions of these technologists run counter to the ascriptive hierarchy and Confucian principles of Tokugawa society; their utilitarian, functional rationality inspired a vehement attack on religion. Farmers should rely upon themselves and not just on the gods. The following passage is taken from a contemporary book on sericulture:

> Let two men be equally lucky, one will succeed and the other fail by reason of differences in skill. Even in good growing years when everyone prospers, yields nevertheless vary with skill. Although everyone is the same distance from heaven, it is plain that there are differences in ability [*jinriki*]. People who do not recognize this fact stupidly pray to the Buddha and *kami,* or they blame the eggs for their bad results and envy the success of others. The Buddha and *kami* may help ever so much, but if one's sericultural methods are slipshod [*orosoka*], one is not going to get good results. But if one's methods are made sound by inquiring tirelessly about methods from experts, one will get good results even in bad years.[22]

Changes in the economy weakened groups which traditionally had been in charge of local festivals. The result was often the formation of rival festival factions within the villages.[23] As time went on "sacred time and space" within many of these villages began to shrink. For example, in premodern Japan, *sakaki* branches, sacred festoons and yin-yang symbols (actually images of male and female genitalia) often bedecked the gates of a village, marking off the village as, in some sense, sacred space. All adult males in the village were regarded as "children of the clan" and were collectively responsible for the abstinences and taboos imposed by the local clan god (*ujigami*). Because the village was in a state of perpetual ritual purity, its residents often could dispense with special purification rites before the spring and autumn festivals. When special abstinences were performed by the Shintō priests of the village they were considered rituals carried out on behalf of the entire community, and not a means of raising the level of purity of the individual celebrants themselves. Gradually all of this changed. The symbols which once had been hung from the village gates were withdrawn to places inside the village and were fixed to the entrance to the shrine precincts, or above the altars of individual houses. (The spread of domestic altars was a reflection of the growing sense of independence among smaller-scale families.) As sacred space was constricted, sacred time was curtailed. Throughout Japan the demands of more "rational" work schedules made it increasingly difficult to spend much time on festival celebrations or in mourning. Originally, festivals were not conceptually distinguished from their preparations or postludes. Later on, however, the preparatory abstinences and the ceremonies held on the eve of the festival (*yoimatsuri*) and the night after (*uramatsuri*) were separated from the festival itself.[24] This degraded both. Sacred time was reduced to a fraction of the festival day itself, often to the parade to and from the shrine. These changes naturally destroyed the continuity and unity of traditional festivals. Taboos which interfered with people's work were gradually eliminated. The number of "sacred people" connected with festivals also declined. First, lay celebrants and oblationers took over from the community the responsibility for the preparations and abstinences of festivals. Later on, their roles were taken over by hereditary or professional priesthoods. With the decline of a purely lay priesthood the religious interest and involvement of many people began to wane.[25]

The folklorist Yanagita Kunio points out many other subtle changes which took place in the festival faith of the common folk.[26] In the Meiji period the government itself, in its frantic efforts to modernize the country, played a major role in the secularization of folk practices. Local customs such as ritual transvestism and orgies, dressing up as ghosts at *Obon*, and cutting down trees for making New Year's decorations were prohibited in the name of decorum and frugality. After the Tokyo dialect was declared the standard language, country folk suddenly realized that the words of religious chants and traditional songs were now considered "dialectical" and crude. Those who moved to the cities usually forgot them. Another secularizing item introduced by the government was the occidental solar calendar which was first put into use in 1873. On 4 January of that year five traditional religious holidays based on the lunar calendar were abolished, and on 14 October various imperial festivals were promulgated. Even the equinoxes were decreed sacred to the memory of the imperial ancestors. These changes worked havoc with local custom. Even when festivals were not abolished outright, the new calendar made them come at the wrong time. The association of religious celebrations with specific seasons had aesthetic connotations which were extremely significant to the people. Special kinds of food offerings were no longer available when festivals were celebrated according to the new calendar. After the introduction of the solar calendar many villages simply gave up their festivals. On 22 March, 1876, Sunday was made the national day of rest at the suggestion of foreign teachers. In 1877, Christmas, which has virtually no religious meaning in Japan, was introduced in Tokyo by the Maruzen department store. In that year the store began to sell *Kurisumasu purezento* as they do even now. In 1888 Christmas cards were introduced. European-style Christmas cakes, carefully embalmed to ensure a long shelf-life, continue to fill the stores in December and January. In the Meiji period, a new postal service made it possible for people to send cards to one another at New Year's instead of visiting each other in person. This tended to break down the high level of social interaction—an important aspect of genuine religious festivals.

In the days before the introduction of the solar calendar there had been a saying "when whores are faithful and eggs are square, the moon will come up on the last day of the month." After the imposition of the new calendar there were times when the moon *did* come up on the last day of the month, apparently without the help of whores or eggs.[27] Naturally, not all Japanese were willing to accept this state of affairs. Most farmers continued to follow the lunar calendar for all practical purposes. An article in a periodical published in 1915 complained:

> Ask any child and he will tell you that the 8th day of the 4th month is the Buddha's birthday, and that during the Obon festival the boiling caldrons of hell are opened for the condemned souls to escape. But even an old fellow like myself will not be able to tell you why the (new fangled) Foundation Day and the Emperor's birthday need to be

> commemorated. To exalt these days that the people care nothing about, the government makes everybody put up lanterns, and a flag that looks like an advertisement for red pills. The old holidays were celebrated because the people felt them to be festive occasions. It is asking too much to make the people celebrate days they do not feel to be festive.[28]

While the word *hare* today is generally thought of in connection with the weather (meaning "clear," or "bright"), it has broader connotations. It also refers to something which is public, open, common, or even to society itself. It is associated with formal occasions, but also with refreshment and novelty. Festivals themselves were therefore associated with *hare* conditions. They were traditionally regarded as extraordinary days when people could eat special food, wear special clothing, and enjoy special activities and events. The opposite of *hare* is *ke,* a term referring to what, instead of clear and bright, is dark or gloomy. Rather than something public, *ke* is private. Accordingly, *ke* is associated with informal things, such as an old kimono one might put on when at home. *Ke* therefore can be thought of as "the grind," or to use H. G. Wells' word, "everydayishness." Thus the cheap millet that farmers used to eat as everyday fare was called *ke-shine*. Festivals, on the other hand, were an opportunity to indulge the palate in "something different" (*kawarimono*) or what sometimes was called "occasional food" (*tokidoki*). Before the Meiji period peasants thought of rice, fish, tea, and sake (which one thinks of today as the "typical" Japanese diet) as festival fare. The custom of eating rice every day was spread through the countryside by young army conscripts returning from urban camps where they had grown accustomed to a better diet. Before this, rice had been grown primarily to pay taxes. Drinking customs also changed during this period. In 1872 the government prohibited the private brewing of sake. This brought to an end the tradition of making sacred rice wine (*miki*) which was drunk in the presence of the local kami. After this, wine for festivals had to be purchased. Drinking alone, instead of from a common jug, also became more common in the Meiji period—although even nowadays it is regarded as a sign of alcoholism. (Only in the recent past have small bottles of beer become common in Japan). Eating alone on separate trays also became widespread in the Meiji period. Before this, such a way of eating was seen only at funerals. The Japanese also used to make a clear-cut distinction between work and festival dress. Although, after the end of the sumptuary legislation that had been in force during the Tokugawa period, commoners were free to wear whatever colors they chose, traditional dark blues and greys continued to be favored for everyday use. Gradually, however, people began to wear throughout the week the brighter colors which formerly had been worn only during festivals. Rouge and other cosmetics, which also had been used only at festival times, became part of a woman's daily makeup. What we see in these changing customs seems to be indicative of a leveling of the traditional distinctions between *hare* and *ke,* or between festival time and ordinary time.[29] This growing indifference to the uniqueness of festival customs might well be regarded as a symptom of secularization.

The Japanese festival was originally a ritual performed within the local community by local people. To worship the kami therefore meant serving and waiting upon them in a specific place. Demographic mobility and travel (including pilgrimage itself) therefore tended to disrupt the age-old festivals of the local community. Urbanization, and later suburbanization, greatly weakened the obligatory motivations binding families to the Shinto parish, the Buddhist family temple, and other "locative" religious routines.

In ancient Japan, festivals had been held in the dark. Conducted by the local inhabitants, the rituals and festivities centered around a bonfire built in a family courtyard. So far removed were these *matsuri* from the spectacles we nowadays call festivals that in some parts of Japan it was believed that if a stranger watched these secret rites he would die.[30] Today, fire festivals have been transformed into daytime festivities in order to attract larger crowds. This is especially obvious in events like the Kumano Fire Festival which these days features the burning of enormous pine torches in broad daylight.

Since Yanagita seemed to equate the authenticity of a festival with its indigenous or locative nature, he naturally had a rather critical attitude towards pilgrimage. He felt that the mass pilgrimages of the Tokugawa period played an important part in the degeneration of traditional festivals. So numerous did pilgrims become that temple inns (*shukubō*) could no longer hold them. Putting up in secular *ryōkan,* the pilgrims could go on pilgrimages without coming into direct contact with priests, and could even avoid the maigre fare of the *shukubō.* Pilgrimage finally became the kind of recreation it is to this day. Yanagita was especially critical of the custom called *sensharei,* which literally meant pasting pieces of paper bearing one's name to a thousand shrines. Some people spent so much time and money indulging in "pilgrimages" of this sort that they were criticized by contemporaries for pestering the kami.[31] Still another symptom of the degeneration of festival traditions was the development of the collection boxes (*saisenbako*) placed in front of shrines. In many out-of-the-way places such boxes still do not exist. He notes, with delightful humor, that when a *saisenbako* is placed before the shrine of a small village, the scattered offerings of rice are quickly devoured by sparrows and neighborhood urchins see to it that nothing glitters in the offering box too long. Originally, gifts made to the shrine consisted of land, cloth, sake, or rice. As travel and pilgrimage increased, strangers began to visit festivals in which, because they *were* strangers, they were not allowed to participate. Not knowing how to worship the local kami properly, they would offer a few coins before the shrine. Money offerings thereby became substitutes for real participation in the worship of the kami. In ancient times it had been an insult even to mention the word "money" in the presence of a nobleman, let alone a god. Yanagita concluded that throwing coins into the *saisenbako* was not much different from the westerner's demeaning custom of tipping servants and underlings.[32]

Yanagita also believed that the decline of religious custom could be measured in terms of the roles of and attitudes towards children. Since infant mortality was as high in Japan as it is in other premodern societies, there were many magical spells used to ensure the health and safety of children. After the spread of modern medicine in the Meiji period, these spells began to be rejected by many people as

SENSHAREI. Pasting one's name under the eyes of shrines is an example of the custom of establishing temporary, ad hoc affiliations with religious institutions.

superstitious.[33] Childbirth itself had been surrounded by numerous taboos. In some parts of Japan parturition huts were used to sequester new mothers and women who were having their menstrual periods. To avoid contaminating others with their "red pollution" these women were expected to eat food which had been prepared in a separate place. In modern times, it became simply too expensive for women to spend long periods of time in ritual seclusion and the custom died out.

As adults became less involved in local religious customs they often turned their own festival roles over to children. Today children's festivals abound in Japan: the festivals of the road-god, *Tanabata, Jizōbon,* the chrysanthemum festival, and rites to drive away birds, moles, and other pests. In one city in western Honshū I watched a children's festival which featured a parade of *omikoshi*[34] in which had been "enshrined" such juvenile deities as Snoopy, a longtime favorite of Japanese children, and Taiyaki-kun, a fish (actually a fish-shaped, bean-filled cookie) who figured as the tragic hero of a popular children's song. The streets resounded with the same "*wasshoi, wasshoi!*" that welcomes the kami in more solemn processions. Even the celebrations of New Year's Eve are entrusted to children, something Yanagita considered a sure sign of secularization. Only in more conservative villages where religious traditions persist do elders continue to dominate festivals. In some places, however, children have always played an important festival role. Divine children (*ochigosan*), who were sometimes the children of Shintō priests, were often treated as gods and were expected to deliver oracles. Nowadays these children merely distribute amulets and dance, their oracular powers having vanished. Only in one remote fishing village in Wakayama prefecture have I seen people actually worshiping divine children.[35]

As in contemporary America, the handling of death is still another index of secularization. Since it was one of the greatest pollutions, death was traditionally surrounded by taboos. It even contaminated the fire in the family hearth. A bereaved family was cut off from all neighbors lest its pollution contaminate them too. Only the members of the family could carry the coffin. Special huts were set up for mourners in some parts of the country where they had to live for forty-nine days after the funeral. It was taboo to eat with members of a family in which there had been a death. Families often divested themselves, at least temporarily, of their herds, crops, and crop seed when a death occurred. Because such customs were financially disadvantageous they have disappeared in modern times. The period of mourning decreased from the maximum of forty-nine days to twenty-one days, and then to seven days. Nowadays very little time is spent on mourning in an official way.

TAIYAKI-KUN PALANQUIN. This god-cart was carried by children during a festival.

Contrary to the fears of the pious, secularization is often a necessary condition for the development of a more humanistic culture. What happened to the Japanese way of handling death during the Meiji period is, in some ways, a case in point. While there had always been taboos against coming into direct contact with the bereaved, cooperative groups had long existed which dug the grave and helped the family in whatever way they could. But as death taboos grew less important, more humane attitudes made their appearance. Members of cooperative funeral associations began to assume the duty of carrying the coffin. We even find people willing to put taboos aside and eat with the bereaved family.

There was still another side to the treatment of death. In the 1870s professional undertakers began to appear in Tokyo. This was about the time when the profession became widespread in the west. Needless to say, the undertaker seriously altered traditional ways of dealing with death. Funerals became not only professionalized but commercialized. According to Yanagita, even total strangers would come to see the large funeral processions staged by an undertaker. In the end, like religious festivals themselves, funerals threatened to become a spectacle.[36] Incidentally, after the Russo-Japanese War, individual grave markers became quite popular. Families began to compete among themselves to see which could rise the largest monument.

In view of the central place of feeling and emotion in Japanese religion, the slightest change in the aesthetic nuances of a festival can affect its total impact and religious significance. No one who has visited Kyoto's famed temple gardens, originally designed as landscaped catalysts for the awakening of the mind, can fail to notice the disturbing effect of the "explanations" which periodically blare forth from loudspeakers around the grounds transforming one's pilgrimage into a superficial, and often silly, history lesson. Some of these changes, I suspect, may be more apparent to the foreigner than to the Japanese themselves. This is especially true in cases of cultural incongruity. For example, once, while attending the Buddha's birthday celebration (*hana matsuri*) in Gobō, a town in the middle of Wakayama prefecture, I was appalled to see a statue of the infant Buddha carried through the streets of the town while a brass band played "Anchors Aweigh My Boys."[37]

The lantern festival which takes place at *Obon* at the Kōkokuji temple near the same town provides another example of this kind of aesthetic secularization. Soon after sunset crowds of people begin the long walk up the steps of the temple. The religious rites begin in the temple at the top of the hill. After a recitation of the Heart Sutra, a well-known band of *shakuhachi* (Japanese flute) players wearing basket-like hats circumambulates the temple three times and begins to march slowly down the hill. Behind them comes a procession of lovely paper lanterns held aloft on long bamboo poles, each illuminated by a small candle and decorated with paper streamers attached to the bottom. In the paper walls of each, the words *Namu Amida Butsu* have been cut out with exquisite care. Families which have lost loved ones during the past year carry all-white lanterns; the others are brightly colored. After the procession reaches the clearing halfway down the hill, the lantern bearers take their places on the sloping hillside.

The action which followed had the essential ingredients of all Japanese festivals, mixing sport and ritual. First, four strong young men came into the arena one by one, staggering under enormous, smoldering torches. Each torch, measuring about a yard and a half in diameter and seven feet in length, was said to weigh over eight hundred pounds. Made of half-dry branches, the ends of these torches were set ablaze before they came into the arena. Each man was expected to circle the arena three times, hopefully without incinerating himself, before putting down his burden. All of the details of the performance—the measurements of the torches, the names of the participants, and so on—were announced over the loudspeakers, which as usual in Japan were set too loud. In the meantime, the *shakuhachi* players had taken their positions at the end of the arena behind other microphones which—as though in competition with the clamor of the announcer's loudspeaker—magnified the ancient plainsong of the instruments into deafening shrieks throughout the evening. The climax came when the four torches brightly burning beneath the full August moon were leaned against each other to form a large bonfire. The large white paper lantern representing the temple itself was then carried down the hillside and lowered into the fire. As its streamers and delicate frame caught the flames, the whole area was suddenly illuminated. The contest had become a sacred drama. After this the rest of the lanterns began to move towards the fire. One needed no official "explanation" to sense what was going on. The ancestors who had come back to be with their families for the *Obon* festival were now returning to the Great Majority. The torches with their enormous weight and all-consuming fire had become a pyre waiting to consume the frail lantern-bodies of the ancestors. As they moved down the hillside, each lantern seemed as delicate and finely wrought as the soul of the ancestor it symbolized. The idea of destroying such fragile beauty in this way suddenly became totally repugnant. As I watched, the words of Dylan Thomas came to mind: "do not go gentle into that good night. . . . " Yet down the hill they came, one after another, the ancestors themselves gliding gently to their own recremation. I should think, though I do not know, that many in the crowd perceived these things as I did, as an acted-out parable not merely about the frailty of life and the crushing inevitability of death—these themes were only too evident—but about the still deeper Buddhist truths of extinction and detachment.

After all of the lanterns had been cast into the fire the crowd began to melt away into the night. Only a handful of us stayed to watch the fire die down into embers. As the field became quiet we became aware of something remarkable that had been going on in front of us for some time. A group of six elderly men were standing together at the end of the field chanting the *rokusai nembutsu*. Throughout the evening they had been standing there chanting the name of Amida Buddha, imploring his mercy on behalf of the returning souls. Yet, in the din of the loudspeakers and the excitement over the lighting of the bonfire, they had been completely obscured. Only after the microphones had been disconnected and the crowd had gone home did we even notice *this very religious event*. The unnatural electronic amplification of the events of the evening had effectively silenced this small choir which, in an earlier day, had probably been the chorus for the drama unfolding before our eyes.

None of the examples I have given of the secularization of feelings and customs is sufficient by itself to *prove* that Japanese religion as a whole has "declined." Each example is open to question and further interpretation. The critical reader will have noticed that the concept of secularization running through them is by no means univocal. Hopefully, however, these meanings complement and do not contradict each other. At best, these examples can be taken as the *kind* of material one needs to investigate before pronouncing upon the health of Japanese religion. Even this kind of approach is bedeviled by the problem which until now we have set aside: how to conceptualize secularization in a culture in which the sacred and the profane are not understood as categorical opposites.

Throughout Japanese religious history the radical disjunction of the sacred and profane found in some cultures has been replaced by a continuum of sacred and profane experiences and feelings. In traditional Japanese shamanism, the shaman was closely identified with the god he served. Japanese ancestor worship itself breaks down the distinctions between the earthly and the heavenly realms. The Japanese are probably one of the few peoples who maintain that man becomes a kami automatically when he dies. To "become a Buddha" (*hotoke ni naru*) has become a euphemism for the verb "to die." The Shintō tradition is filled with hierophanies taking place *in hoc mundo*. The great Shintō scholar Motoori Norinaga wrote that the concept of kami included human beings. "It also includes such objects as birds, beasts, trees, plants, seas, mountains and so forth. In ancient usage, anything whatsoever which was outside of the ordinary, which possessed superior power, or which was awe-inspiring was called *kami*. Eminence here does not refer merely to superiority or nobility, goodness or meritorious deeds. Evil and mysterious things if they were extraordinary and dreadful, were called *kami*."[38] Likewise, throughout Japanese Buddhism, the Mahayana teaching of the Original Enlightenment (*hongaku*), derived initially from the *Awakening of Faith*, identifies the essence of this samsaric world with Buddhahood itself.[39] As Dōgen put it, "impermanence is the Buddhahood. The impermanence of grass, trees, and forests is verily the Buddhahood. The impermanence of the person's body and mind is verily the Buddhahood. The impermanence of the country and scenery is verily the Buddhahood."[40] The entire world thus became a "predisposition" for a Buddha. The ontology (or mē-ontology) established by these teachings quite naturally coalesced with the indigenous religious sensibilities expressed by Motoori. The effect was to locate the sacred within the profane. What we commonly call the sacred is therefore "dehypostatized" by the Japanese and made an adjective qualifying even the most mundane activity. One could say that in Japan perhaps more than elsewhere, "technique and ritual, profane and sacred, do not denote types of action but aspects of almost any kind of action."[41]

Itō Mikiharu concludes from this collapse of the sacred and profane that secularization is ultimately impossible in Japan. Unlike Durkheim's Australians, from whom this dichotomy was originally taken, the Japanese do not divide their year between sacred and profane time. Categories like *hare* and *ke* intermingle throughout both the busy agricultural season and the months when the farmer is idle. The relationship between *hare* and *ke* is therefore complementary. Space which is *hare* may soon be treated as *ke,* and vice versa. Unlike the absolute either/or dichotomies of western logic, Japanese culture—at the *implicit or structural level*—is based on a "logic of relative contrasts." Even when religious customs change—at the *explicit level of culture*—there is a tendency for the original implicit categories to reassert themselves in a new guise. Thus, even if many Japanese no longer visit Shintō shrines at New Year's, the old festival spirit (*hare*) can still be felt in the "secularized" parties held at that time of year.[42]

The difficulty with this position (based on the distinction between implicit and explicit culture in the works of Boas, Wissler, and Murdock) is that it encourages a schizophrenic break between the history and structure of culture. If Itō is right, we have wasted our time in seeking evidence for secularization in diachronic statistics, economic history, folk customs, and the aesthetics of rituals. The issue is to be settled by theory and definition. Historical changes in religious ideas, institutions, and behavior have no effect at all on the basic structures of religion. But can the problem of secularization be solved so easily? The criteria Itō uses to distinguish between the explicit and the implicit elements of a culture are something of a mystery. He seems to have two alternatives. Either implicit culture (structure) is to be identified with a society's archaic mazeways, or it is discovered through an act of ("phenomenological"?) intuition. Both of these solutions have obvious drawbacks. History changes even the oldest of customs, and intuition is notoriously fallible. While I therefore cannot agree either with Itō's definition of the problem or his solution, his emphasis on the "logic of relative contrasts" is important to bear in mind. This way of thinking—and feeling—may even help to account for the unexpected overlap between religious behavior and unbelief pointed out by Basabe.

Itō's research serves to underscore the importance of the persistence of religious and quasi-religious activities in contemporary Japan. The period when our "hardest" statistical evidence indicates a decline of religious belief in Japan coincides paradoxically with the phenomenal growth of the so-called New Religions. Most of these organizations, can be regarded as atavistic revitalization movements based on religious and magical practices such as shamanism, ancestor worship, purification rituals, and exorcism which can be traced back to prehistoric times.[43] In addition to the New Religions, new magazines such as Matsushita Konosuke's *P.H.P.*, *The Light of the House*, *Women's Friend*, and *Inner Trip*, all deeply imbued with practical, religious idealism, sell hundreds of thousands of copies each month. Biographies of the founders of the Kamakura sects of Buddhism have become enormously successful. A large proportion of the population continues to visit shrines and temples at New Year's. Many people still observe religious (or magical) taboos even though they no longer explicitly believe in the retributive powers of ghosts and kami. We have seen in chapter 6, that many Japanese firms provide weekend retreats for the "spiritual education" of their employees, a function performed by public schools in prewar Japan. One could, of course, argue that this persistence of religious behavior is merely the "implicit structure" of Japanese culture reasserting itself. If all that were meant by this was the recrudescence of *historic* religious tendencies, Itō's formulation would be perfectly acceptable. In any case, there is no doubt that the paradoxical coincidence of the decline of religious belief measured by the opinion polls, on the one hand, and the rise of the New Religions, on the other, can be understood only by supposing that statistical unbelief is largely *situational*. It is symptomatic of that existential drift for which the Japanese have such talent, rather than any disciplined, philosophical commitment to atheism.[44]

The statistics themselves seem to bear this out. In addition to the evidence we have already seen, in an admittedly small survey of the religious opinions of 270 people, 43 percent said that they were "too busy," to believe, "didn't have the opportunity," were "too young," or simply were not believers *at the present moment*. Another 14 percent thought that religion was necessary for others but not for themselves.[45] These figures, together with the evidence from Basabe and the *Survey of the National Character of the Japanese*, seem to indicate that much unbelief grows out of social situations in which there is little or no social opportunity or incentive to believe. On the other hand, Japanese continue to respond quite readily to formal situations which call for "religious" behavior, e.g., weddings, funerals, and ground-breaking ceremonies. Well educated people from higher income families who may score badly on religious belief are generally the most scrupulous in their performance of these public rituals.[46] Religious activity of this sort, carried out as a matter of social principle (*tatemae*), contrasts strongly with the kind of zealous devotion and commitment demanded by the New Religions of their devotees.

Another area of Japanese culture where the "logic of relative contrasts" is clearly in evidence is the relationship between magical attitudes and the goal-rationality (Weber: *Zweckrationalität*) one commonly associates with modern industrial societies. While I believe the "overall secularization" of different cultures cannot easily be compared, here we do have an example of a striking contrast between Japan and the west. Contemporary research on sixteenth and seventeenth century England, for example, has gone far beyond Weber in demonstrating the rationalizing effect Puritanism had upon society. Keith Thomas in his monumental study, *Religion and the Decline of Magic* (already mentioned in chapter 4), shows that:

> . . . in England magic lost its appeal before the appropriate technical solutions had been devised to take its place. It was abandonment of magic [under the influence of Puritanism] which made possible the upsurge of technology, not the other way around. Indeed, as Max Weber stressed, magic was potentially "one of the most serious obstructions to the rationalization of economic life." The technological primacy of Western civilization, it can be argued, owes a sizable debt to the fact that in Europe recourse to magic was to prove less ineradicable than in other parts of the world.[47]

Although the examples of Ishida Baigan, Suzuki Shōsan, and various Confucian thinkers of the Tokugawa period could be cited to the contrary effect, in general, popular Japanese religion had no comparable disenchanting effects upon society or nature. The voice of the "technologist" was seldom heard in religious circles. Popular religion in Japan continues to be deeply colored by the magic of charms, fortune-telling, amulets, omens, and taboos. Even today statistical studies have shown that while religious faith which is *low* in utilitarian content declines as individuals advance from junior high school (20.5 percent) to college (10.9 percent), a *more* utilitarian, (magical) faith actually increases (from 7.6 to 14.3 percent).[48] Magic, like Japanese religion itself, is highly situational and quickly learns to adjust to new conditions. Neither in the village nor in the new cities were there synods or bishops to enforce the mores and taboos of the local ujigami. The "disenchantment of the world" which is said to be both the prerequisite and the byproduct of industrialization therefore did not take place in Japan as the result of a head-on confrontation between a secularizing religious ideology and gross superstition (or magic), as it did among the "hot Protestants" in England. In chapters 4 and 5 we saw that the greatest contribution of Japanese religion to the "modernization" of the country was a passive one: the barriers it put in the way of industrialization were negligible. Its contextual "logic of relative contrasts" enabled religious taboos to make a graceful and judicious retreat. On the positive side, popular religion provided the modernizing elite with some of its most powerful ideological tools, e.g., the ujigami. Absorbed and revalorized by the "imperial system," these symbols became a means for extending the particularistic social nexus of the village to the nation itself. The sacred space which disappeared in the local community as a result of the development of a market economy thus reappeared in the nationalistic mythology of Japan, the divine land. While amulets may have been discarded by many Japanese, the political slogans of the prewar regime had, themselves, a hypnotizing, amuletic effect.[49]

In this chapter I have suggested that while it is possible to study secularization, it is not productive to treat the problem as the overall decline of religion per se. Instead, depending upon the culture one is dealing with, it is wiser to use a less ambitious, and more cautious, approach, e.g., a "multiple scoring" to assess changes in beliefs, aesthetics, feelings, morals, and customary behavior. In other words, while it is virtually meaningless to talk about the *general* secularization of religion in a society, and even more obscure to discuss the comparative levels of secularization in different societies, it may be possible to take the measure of the well-being and/or decline of the various *aspects* of religion in a specific society. Even then, not all of these aspects will carry equal weight. I have tried to show that in Japan, where praxis, aesthetics, and feelings are the core of religion, the problem of secularization can be more fruitfully studied by examining changing religious customs rather than by dilating on the decline of religious beliefs. I have suggested that the lack of clear-cut distinctions between the sacred and the profane in Japan does not make the concept of secularization (in my limited sense of the word) impossible. It merely reminds us that, even after we have discarded the idea that secularization is a logical impossibility or part of some inevitable *Weltplan* of history, we are still left with a set of complex problems of interpretation and proof.

I have concentrated in this chapter on some of the more difficult issues at stake when one tries to answer the question, "Has religion in Japan declined in recent decades?" Concern for the subtleties implied in this question may have prompted me to overemphasize the continuities and to underplay the corrosive changes in contemporary Japanese religion. In my determination to correct the theory of the absolute decline of religion, I may have placed too much emphasis on the simple metamorphosis or transformation of religion. But, obviously, concern for the complexity of the problem should not cause one to deny the obvious fact that *in some crucial aspects* Japanese religion *has* "declined." In conclusion, I would like to violate my own moratorium on comparative judgments about secularization and hazard one, quite limited proposition which does seem to hold true: namely, that today, *as an institution and as a set of beliefs*, religion plays a less decisive role in Japanese society (and *a fortiori* in politics) than it does, say, in the United States. Educated, middle-class Japanese seem to entertain fewer specific religious ideas (and perhaps ideals), and commit themselves to religious institutions with less enthusiasm than do their social counterparts in this country. The religion to which this stratum is committed seems to be primarily the decorous proprieties of family and society, e.g., the rituals of weddings, funerals, festivals, and the rites of the omnipresent business culture in general. While—as we have repeatedly seen in this chapter—belief is only one dimension of religion, the decline of religious belief is an extremely interesting and important aspect of secularization. Again, one might hypothesize (as I did in chapter 4) that a nation not encumbered by specific religious commitments might be freer to change and respond to the challenges of modernity (or postmodernity) than a nation tied to the past by religious conviction.[50] The relative secularization of a nation's middle-class and elite strata may therefore even fuction as a "passive enablement" in the development of that country. This, of course, raises the questions: to what *are* these people committed? What *are* their basic principles? What *is* the source of their identity as a nation? To these questions we turn in our final chapter.

CHAPTER 8

Japan Theory and Civil Religion

In chapter 7, we saw that in many respects (but not in all) postwar Japan has become a *relatively* secular culture. While Shinto festivals are celebrated with gusto throughout the country, while Buddhist rites continue to usher the dead into their new homes in the Pure Land, by and large the old religions have failed to provide the Japanese with a philosophy adequate for life and death in the modern (or "postmodern") world. Most shrines and temples are more concerned about assisting members to fulfill their religious obligations to kith and kin than they are with developing an articulate worldview. This, of course, has been one of the "selling points" of the New Religions—they *do* try to provide their devotees with an explicit *Lebensphilosophie,* however primitive it may seem to outsiders. But even in this case, the Japanese thirst for things religious seems to have been slaked. The recent appearance of so-called New New Religions (*Shin-shinshūkyō*) probably will not change the growth pattern of the New Religions as a whole. While they continue to catch headlines—often because of their unusual, tasteless, or even illegal antics—few New Religions are catching new members at the rate they were a decade or two ago. What is more, institutional religions, old and new alike, seem to have relatively little direct, serious impact on Japanese society. In politics, Japanese religion seems to have very little direct influence, especially compared with religion in the United States. While the Clean Government party continues to get indirect support from one of the New Religions (Sōka Gakkai), its opportunistic, right-of-center policies seem far removed from its original ideal of establishing a Buddhist socialist state.

Assuming, then, that secularism (however defined or measured) has deeply influenced the Japanese way of life, the question arises: what has happened to the Japanese sense of identity which, until 1945, rested explicitly on *religious* foundations? If the Japanese no longer think of themselves as distant relatives of the sun goddess (via her direct descendant, the emperor), who *do* they think they are? If they no longer get their sense of identity from religion, to what, or to whom, do they turn to discover who they really are?

Since the early 1960s, the Japanese press has been glutted with books and articles searching for a national identity. Known rather grandly as Japan theory (*Nihonron*), this literature includes ruminations on culture, society, and national character. Needless to say, each of these subdivisions is also a "theory". The "theory of Japanese culture" is a study of the uniqueness of Japanese consciousness as expressed in literature, language, religion and the arts. The "soft-shelled" side of the theory, these studies cover roughly what a Marxist calls ideology. The "theory of Japanese society" attempts to simplify the confusing details of local history, changing family and political structures, and other historical and sociological complexities, reducing them to a set of easily grasped, intuitively convincing patterns. At best, the theory of Japanese society helps one see basic, shifting trends in the development of the country; at worst, it degenerates into a confluence of modernization theory and collective narcissism.[1] Finally, the "theory of the Japanese people" deals with who the Japanese themselves are, their national character and personality. Many of these theories seek to delineate an idealized, unimodal personality at the expense of the rich variety of personality types. Although bibliographies have been compiled of these theories, both their diversity (ranging from the banal to the academic, categories that are not always distinguishable) and their sheer volume make describing the parameters of the movement a difficult task.[2]

While the names of the authors of the theory may not be recognized by many western readers, one could describe the phenomenon ostensively by listing some of the principal theorists, people such as Nakane Chie, Yamamoto Shichihei, (*alias* Isaiah Ben-Dasan), Doi Takeo, Kawai Hayao, Okonogi Keigo, Hamaguchi Esyun, Yoneyama Toshinao, Sera Masatoshi, Sakuda Keiichi, Aida Yūji, Mita Munesuke, and many others. Since national self-images, like identity itself, are socially constructed through a process of interaction with "significant others," what foreign scholars have written about the Japanese also figures in the creation of Japan theory. Names like Ruth Benedict, Edwin Reischauer, Robert Bellah, and Ezra Vogel come to mind. All of these writers have tried, in one way or another, to spell out the essence of Japanese culture or the unique significance of Japan and her people in the modern world.

Needless to say, Japan theory has its own history going back well before the Pacific war.[3] Since the war, its development can be divided, roughly, into three periods. In the years immediately following the defeat of Japan (c. 1945–1952), writers tended to blame the failure of

Japanese democracy and the rise of the imperial system on the "unique" features of Japanese culture: its village ethos, family-ism, and the "feudalistic," hierarchical relationships that infused all institutions. Above all, the undialectical, indeed mindless, ethos of obedience instilled by the authoritarian state after 1868 came in for a beating. The magisterial writings of the learned political scientist, Maruyama Masao, are probably the best examples of the self-critical spirit of the Japan theory of this period. The following decade (c. 1953–1963), our second period, was a period of growing self-confidence. The nation regained its independence and, with the economic stimulation of the Korean War, began its economic recovery. Japan theorists moved away from self-criticism and became interested in situating the history of their own country among the histories of the other world powers. Umesao Tadao, now head of the National Ethnological Museum in Senri, described Japan as an autonomous "Great Civilization" (*daibunmei*), on a par with China, India, and Europe. Even though Japan was geographically located in Asia, Umesao ("theoretically") tried to show that the country had more in common with its industrial competitors in the west than with the underdeveloped countries of Asia to which it *seemed* to be related by history. The third period of Japan theory began around 1964 and continues to the present. By this time, Japan, thanks to her remarkable economic growth, had indeed risen to first world status. Once again emphasis was laid on the "uniqueness" of the Japanese modal personality and the "homogeneity" of the country's culture and society. But, unlike early postwar theories, the country's uniqueness became once again a source of pride. Indeed, the salient feature of the Japan theory of this period is the way the theorists transformed the critical or negative images of Japanese uniqueness found in writers like Maruyama into positive cultural assets. The confident Japan theory of this period is typified by Nakane Chie's classic, *Human Relations in a Vertical Society* (*Tateshakai no ningen kankei,* 1967), a book that stressed the hierarchical structure of Japanese institutions and the group-orientation of all Japanese behavior. Others, such as Doi Takeo, Kimura Bin and Hamaguchi Esyun, explored the "uniqueness" of the Japanese psyche and its relation to various social institutions. The traditional lack of personal autonomy (*shutaisei*) bemoaned by Maruyama and the earlier theorists was now celebrated as a mark of the cohesiveness of Japan's unique society, if not one of the secrets behind the country's industrial success.

The third period of Japan theory gave rise to two new sub-theories. The first is the "theory of Japanese management," i.e., literature purporting to explain the Japanese *Wirtschaftswunder* in terms of the country's unique culture, values and manners. Typical of this literature is Yamamoto Shichihei's *The Spirit of Japanese Capitalism* (*Nihon shihonshugi no seishin*, 1979), a popular title echoing Max Weber's own *Protestant Ethic and the Spirit of Capitalism.* Both books try to prove the uniqueness of the *Geist* (*seishin*) of their respective turfs in terms of religion—Weber in terms of the spirit of western Protestantism, Yamamoto in terms of the allegedly unique, secular and diffuse religiousness of the Japanese. Japanese capitalism itself was "founded," Yamamoto says, by Suzuki Shōsan, the warrior-turned-monk of the early Tokugawa period. Secular occupations, Suzuki taught, are manifestations of Buddhist religious practice (*butsugyō*) and provide the means for becoming a Buddha (*jōbutsu*) oneself. The second sub-theory appeared in the 1980s when Asada Akira and other young Japan theorists turned the oracles of Europe's deconstructionists, poststructuralists, and "postphilosophers" into a new "theory of Japan as the world's first postmodern society." The gameplan of these theorists seems to have been to let the west walk off with the prize of the modernity that *its* theorists had always claimed, while seeing to it that the Japanese themselves picked up all of the trophies of *post*modernity. Since postmodernity seems to be the logical historic successor of modernity, this meant that the wartime goal of "overcoming the modern" (*kindai no chōkoku*) had been achieved. Since Japan has already surpassed the west, the twenty-first century promises to be the "century of Japan." In short, postmodern Japan theory has transformed the agenda of western postmodernism—which originally was concerned with artistic, literary, and hermeneutical problems—*into a set of highly competitive, nationalistic self-images.*

As the memory of the lost war recedes—a process helped along by the government's "textbook revisions"—and as economic recovery turns into a worldwide conquest of an unprecedented magnitude, the Japanese have understandably taken greater pride in their country and in being Japanese. Throughout the history of postwar Japan theory, one can therefore see a steady growth in self-confidence, a tendency to disown the past, and, in some cases, even a new arrogance. Two events stand out as especially representative of this transformation. The first was the pronouncement by former Prime Minister Ōhira that America is no longer a superpower. While greatly exaggerated, this statement by America's foremost Asian ally seemed to reflect a new Japanese perspective on international relations, a new readiness for independence and, perhaps, a new sense of vulnerability.

The second event which symbolized the emergence of a new Japan was a short television series aired in Japan late in 1979. At that time,

Suntory Whiskey Company sponsored a series of seminars called "Japan Speaks" (or more accurately translated, "Japan Insists"). The seminar was graced by the presence of Claude Lévi-Strauss, Robert Jay Lifton, and Daniel Bell, western scholars of worldwide reputation who took their places with lesser luminaries from Japan. Ezra Vogel, whose book *Japan as Number One* is, itself, symbolic of the new Japan, introduced the series, addressing his TV audience in fluent Japanese, standing on the White House lawn. Since Harvard, where Professor Vogel teaches, is nowhere near Washington, I presume that either Suntory flew him to Washington to tape the interview, or that the White House scene was dubbed in behind him. In either case, what was striking was the symbolism: a Harvard professor standing in front of the White House talking about (as I recall) Japan as Number One. Since the Japanese had long believed that America was Number One, symbols of American legitimacy—a Harvard professor and the White House itself—had to be trotted out to make the message credible. (One can imagine how ridiculous the Japanese would have found all of this had the same monologue been delivered, say, by an assistant professor at the University of Florida from the beaches of the Sunshine State). The commercials from the sponsor were also revealing. One showed New York's Statue of Liberty holding a bottle of Suntory whiskey in her uplifted hand. Another featured the I Musici ensemble playing Bach melodies. In English, beneath the picture, were the words "I Musici plays J. S. Bach for Suntory." Here, in short, was a magnificent array of potent, legitimating symbols—Harvard, the White House, the Statue of Liberty, and Bach—symbols of the educational, political, and artistic excellence of the west. All were now pointing eastward, to Japan—or at least to Japanese whiskey. And all were drawing attention to a Japan which now could "speak" and even "insist."

The consciousness of the new Japan is being distilled today not just by the Suntory Foundation, but by the various authors of Japan theory. The general drift of this literature can be summarized under the following five points:

1. The first and most important characteristic of the Japan theory movement is that it is *not* comparative research. This may sound contradictory because these books are filled with comparisons of Japan and other countries. The reason why I maintain that it is not comparative research is that the authors generally take the uniqueness of Japan as their starting point or fundamental presupposition. Truly comparative research is interested in contrasts, degrees of difference, and the continua of human experience which makes the study of foreign cul-

tures so interesting. Japan theory will have none of this. It assumes the uniqueness of Japan and sets out to prove it by a random selection of data. A related point is this: the so-called comparisons which one does find in Japan theory almost always compare Japan with America and western Europe, i.e., with Japan's so-called trade partners. Few have tried to compare Japanese customs in an unbiased way with, say, those of an African tribe. I mention this because, in my own research on Japanese religion, comparisons with African or Indian customs have often seemed both helpful and revealing. This unwillingness to engage in comparative studies which are truly comparative is, I think, indicative of the subliminal ethnocentric tendency of much of Japan theory.

2. The positions taken by the various theorists are complementary or supplementary ones. That is, the images they develop of Japan are not clear-cut alternatives to anything in particular. Instead, they tend to generate lists of typically Japanese characteristics—i.e., the Japanese are hard working; they understand each other by a mysterious form of nonverbal communication; their society is based on groups and not on individuals; they indulge (*amayakasu*) and accept indulgent relations (*amaeru*); they make clear distinctions between in-groups and out-groups; they have a vertical social structure; and they are inept in foreign languages. To make sure that analytical levels are thoroughly confused, the fact that they live in a small, island country is generally thrown in, somewhat gratuitously. (Actually, how gratuitous the last point is can be questioned. G. K. Chesterton, for example, once pointed out that " . . . the patriot never under any circumstances boasts of the largeness of his country, but always, and of necessity, boasts of the smallness of it."[4] After giving this pinwheel of national characteristics a good spin, an author brings it to a halt at the place he feels is most propitious for unlocking the mystery of the whole society. Often, this leading characteristic will be given a catchy name that will appeal to the mass media. It is important to bear in mind that the theorists are competing nowadays in a literary marketplace filled with readers whose appetite for new self-images is already satiated, if not quite jaded. For this reason, theorists in search of the national essence (and a publisher) are forced to concoct a steady stream of new appellations for Japan. Like the names of God in theology, the names of Japan never exhaust their divine subject: the society of protean man, the society of moratorium man, the vertical society, the miniaturizing society, the society of the eternal child, the maternal society, and—my favorite—the hollow onion. Each one of these characteristics becomes a prism or a lens through which the whole society can be viewed.

3. Closely related to my previous point is the third aspect of the theory: Japan theory is vague. Because the images it generates are am-

biguous, there is no way to select or judge between them. The theory gives us no way to select the most adequate or accurate characterizations of the Japanese people. For this reason, Japan theory cannot be said to be a *theoretical* discussion at all. Nor has it given rise to truly academic (i.e., "dialectical") discussions (*ronsō*). The prose of many of the theorists is so nebulous that one does not know whether they are celebrating the status quo or whether they would like to reform the country and its national character in some way. Although it is difficult to decode the political persuasions of theorists, I suspect that in most cases it is well to the right of center.

Although theorists assume a descriptive posture, their writings have clear normative overtones. By telling the reader who the Japanese are, they are, indirectly, telling the Japanese who they *ought* to be and how they *ought* to behave. One cannot dismiss such literature lightly simply because it tends to be platitudinous. Platitudes, when they describe the life of a people, tend to become norms. As such, Japan theory may someday—perhaps even today—play an important role in social control. In this connection, the favor which the Japanese government has bestowed upon the theory of Nakane Chie seems to be of singular importance. According to Mouer and Sugimoto, "The Foreign Ministry had Nakane's *Japanese Society* rewritten for its 'official' presentation on Japanese society. Entitled *Human Relations in Japan*, it was first published in 1971 and serves as the volume in the ministry's public information series on Japan for distribution overseas at its embassies and consulates."[5] Obviously the government finds something gratifying in the image of Japan which she creates—that of a unified, consensual, classless society in which all work and cooperate (under benign "vertical" supervision) for the good of all.

4. The fourth characteristic of Japan theory is that it tends to grow out of the author's own experience in foreign countries, or his own encounters with foreigners in Japan. Doi Takeo and others are quick to inform their readers that their books originated in some kind of international exchange or culture shock. The degree to which the author has an international or a "truly Japanese" self-image becomes a serious issue when the Japanese try to evaluate his work. For example, "Professor Tanaka is too international to understand us," some might say. Others will retort, "But Mr. Yamada has no international experience, so how can *he* say anything about Japan's uniqueness?"

One suspects that Japan theory is aimed primarily at a reading public with some international experience—from the seasoned world traveller to young honeymooners fresh from a five-day JAL-PAK tour of Honolulu, Los Angeles, and San Francisco. It is significant to remember that the boom in Japan theories in the 1960s and 1970s coincided with a period of growing trade rivalries with the west and unprecedented contacts with other peoples. The shock of encountering unfamiliar values and world views, coupled with a growing pride in Japan's own economic tour de force, seems to have provided stimulus for pondering anew the old question: Who am I and who are my people? This, at least, I would allege, is the primary factor in the burgeoning of this by-no-means-new genre in recent decades.

5. Taken collectively, Japan theories seem to play a number of roles. I have already suggested that they can function as an agent of social control reinforcing the norms of the society (or the values of a particular author). Another function is self-defense. The symbolic defense, justification, or legitimation of a society is, of course, one of the major roles of a "civil religion," a point not to be forgotten when we later examine Japan theory as a secularization of the civil religious sentiments of the prewar period.

The defensive function of Japan theory emerges rather clearly in books and articles which use feminine and maternal images to describe the psychology of the Japanese. For example, Kawai Hayao, in his book *The Pathology of Japan's Maternal Society*, draws a contrast between maternal and paternal principles, a mixture of which, the author believes, constitutes the psychological foundation of all societies.[6] In a maternal society like Japan the individuals of the society are treated like children on a mother's lap. All of these citizen-children are regarded equally as belonging to the "national mother" regardless of their own individual achievements. All participate in the same "unity with the mother" and share the same place (*ba*) on her lap. Among these children, social relations are governed by an ethic of place (*ba no rinri*), a locative morality in which each surrenders his claim to justice in order to preserve the subtle equilibrium of the group. For example, in Japan the guilty party in a traffic accident will usually visit the victim's home to apologize. The latter, however, customarily will not demand reparations because this would upset the ba. In paternal societies (i.e., the west), children must prove themselves to their father on the basis of their own merits and achievements. That is, the father does not accept his own children until they have performed adequately and rightly. This, of course, makes for a highly disciplined, strict society. From this (stereotypical) contrast, Kawai concludes that the Japanese exemplify Jung's archetype of the "eternal child," a mythological infant enshrined forever upon the lap of the eternal feminine or great mother.[7] The political consequences of this organic model of society are, as one might expect, profoundly conservative. Kawai follows Nakane in describing

Japan as a highly unified, consensual society. It is a society in which serious reforms or rebellions ultimately are futile. Reformer and rebel alike inevitably slip back into the great mother's lap. Thus the locative ethic seems to fuse the ambitions of the eternal child (a symbol of the limitless possibilities open to all regardless of their ability) with a passive acceptance of existing relationships of power, wealth, and prestige. Finally, Kawai argues, because different principles govern Japanese society, one cannot measure Japanese maturity by western psychological standards. Given the maternal foundations of the Japanese psyche, the periodic return to the great mother's womb by the Japanese adult does not count against his maturity.

Okonogi Keigo has extended the mythological foundations of this psychological portrait of the Japanese in his study of the decline of the highly regimented Japanese work ethic. Building on Erik Erikson's notion of the "adolescent moratorium," Okonogi points out that in traditional societies adults allowed young people a period of time during which they could acquire the necessary skills and habits for maturity. During this time they were expected to remain single and defer to the power and status of their elders. After completing his apprenticeship, a young man would choose a wife, find a job, and assume his various social responsibilities. Today, however, young people find the moratorium period too comfortable to leave. Furthermore, "moratorium man" has moved beyond adolescence and has become the modal personality of the society.

Moratorium man is characterized by an inability to join institutions of any kind. All of his roles are temporary and therefore not expressive of his true self. His life style is hypothetical, hedonistic, and self-centered. In his never ending search for novelty, moratorium man is practically identical with protean man as described by Robert Jay Lifton.[8] Okonogi imputes the development of moratorium man to various historical influences: the rising demand for educational credentials in technological societies, the diffusion of authority in modern corporations, the shifting of personnel from place to place, upward social mobility, consumerism, and (originally) the occupation of Japan by the United States. The society which gave rise to this kind of national character is not one split between haves and have-nots, right and left, but between those who display a "host mentality" and those with a "guest mentality," i.e., joiners and nonjoiners. Those who have committed themselves to the bureaucratic, competitive structures of modern society have become the protectors of society as a whole. The others—students, members of the service professions, the unemployed, the retired, and even many who *seem* to take part in social institutions—are, in fact, comfortably alienated moratorium men dependent upon the more responsible members of society for their protection and nurture.

While moratorium men can be found in all advanced industrial societies, Okonogi's theory of the Ajase complex seems to apply best to Japan's "maternal" society. The Ajase complex was originally put forth in the 1930s as a Japanese alternative to the Oedipus complex by the psychologist Furusawa Heisaku. A devout member of the Pure Land sect, Furusawa developed his theory in order to "internationalize" his own experience as a Buddhist and as a Japanese.[9] Without going into detail, his so-called Ajase complex, derived from a Buddhist legend about the Indian prince Ajase (Ajātaśatru), focuses on the mother-child relationship, rather than on the father-child axis which Freud had stressed in his Oedipus complex. The Ajase complex begins with the idealization of the mother, but results in disillusionment and even in acts of violence against her. The mother, for her part, endures the child's misbehavior. Thanks to her acceptance or forgiveness (*yurushi*) the rebellious child is reconciled, and the primordial unity between mother and child is restored. Thus, while the western conscience is formed by the fear of the father's wrath (specifically his threat of castration), the Japanese conscience is molded by the mother's yurushi. Unlike Freud who tried to deduce universal psychological mechanisms from the myth of Oedipus, Okonogi—like Doi in his description of *amae* and Kawai in his treatment of the "eternal child"—is looking for something uniquely Japanese. The masochism that Freud thought was an illness is regarded by the Japanese as a primary virtue. It is precisely this masochism and the yurushi growing out of it that make possible the sense of oneness (*ittaikan*) which pervades Japanese society.

Like Kawai Hayao, Okonogi sees the obvious danger faced by a maternal moratorium society surrounded by an alert, competitive, and potentially hostile international community. In such a society, who will be mature enough to negotiate with foreigners who have not been gentled in the same way? Who will take responsibility for things if everyone regards himself as a "guest" living at the expense of the country? To meet this challenge, Kawai calls for the strengthening of paternal principles. Okonogi, however, believes that because the moratorium has its roots in child-rearing, it is something very human and therefore of great value. The democracy and pacifism of postwar Japan are predicated upon it. From this he concludes that state and society alike should be remolded to fit the needs of moratorium man. At the same time, he warns that the Establishment (bureaucrats, industrial and labor leaders, and politicians of all stripes) are ready to launch an "anti-moratorium" movement, for example, by rearming the country and instituting a military draft. This path must be avoided at all costs, he insists. The weaknesses of moratorium man must be overcome from within, not by hostile movements from without. Ominously, he warns that if international conditions (that is, the occupation of Japan) could initiate the moratorium, new developments on the international horizon could possibly bring it to an end.

Lacking the professional credentials to analyze these theories in any greater detail, I will simply say that I feel that there is probably something to the theories of amae, the maternal society, moratorium man, and the Ajase complex. I am not sure, however, whether this something has yet been expressed in a way that will pass muster as psychology.[10] Call it femininity or what you will, a number of writers have pointed out the delicacy, softness, and passivity that so often characterize the Japanese. One thinks, for example, of Kamishima Jirō's emphasis on the "soft rule" tradition in government, of Motoori Norinaga's delineation of the intuitive nature of the Japanese people, of Robert Bellah's analysis of the feminine aspect of the emperor, and the novelist Endō Shūsaku's feminine portrayal of Christ in his novel *A Life of Jesus*.

Deferring therefore to those who are better able to judge these matters, I would like to return to the problem of the relationship between the national identity which emerges in this psychological version of Japan theory and the international scene. It is here that we catch a glimpse of the defensive use of the theory. For example, Okonogi Keigo cites the words of a middle-aged Japanese woman who was taken as a hostage in the hijacking of a Japanese airliner in Dacca in 1977. "I just felt sorry for those kids [i.e., the terrorist hijackers]," she said. "Aren't they really pitiful, running around trying to escape but having no place to go? I wondered if it would be wrong just to forgive them [*yurushite yaru*]."[11] "Okonogi then cites with approval an article by the archetypal Japan theorist Yamamoto Shichihei (Isaiah Ben-Dasan) who concludes that this woman's generous attitude represents the traditional Japanese way of overcoming confrontation. Quoting Kawai Hayao, Okonogi points out that while the Germans, for example, think first of abstract principles (i.e., "giving in to terrorist demands is *wrong*"), the Japanese approach emphasizes forgiveness and the importance of human life.

The scenario warms up a very old chestnut. In effect, it takes us back to the contrast drawn by Motoori Norinaga between the abstract, masculine principles of the Confucian classics and the intuitive, feminine spirit of the Japanese and their "*natural* goodness." On the other hand, its contemporary meaning emerges when we think about the international context of the hijack. Around 1977, Japan was being roundly criticized by other countries for giving in too easily to the demands of hijackers. Western countries which were trying to take more stringent measures against airborne piracy felt their efforts were being undercut by Japan's shilly-shally response to the problem. In the face of such criticism, Japan theory seemed to say, "We have compromised with the hijackers because compromise (and *yurushi*) is part of our national character."

The hijacking affair and the reaction of the theorists to it are good examples of the important role national image-making plays in international relations. Japan theory is increasingly playing a role in the media, explaining and justifying Japanese attitudes and behavior to westerners who, unfortunately, still believe that the Japanese are inscrutable unless their actions are explained in terms of some equally inscrutable psychology.

Not long ago a young American, to protest the slaughter of dolphins by Japanese fishermen, went to Japan and cut the nets which the fishermen had laid for the dolphins. The case drew widespread interest among the Japanese people when the American was apprehended by Japanese authorities and brought to court. An article in the *Japan Times* by a professor at Gakushūin University attacked what the author called "dolphinism."[12] Dolphinism, the professor declared, is just one more western "ism" designed to force a tendentious abstraction down other peoples' throats. Dolphinism, he said, can be compared with the crusades of the Middle Ages and other western acts of violence. In fact, western history has been marked by continual violence—largely due to the excitement over "isms" (such as dolphinism)—whereas the Japanese "have lived peacefully in a Far East island country beyond the conflicts of other races, enjoying the beauties of nature." To the Japanese, "the history of Europe appears to be a history of " 'ism'-dictated killing." What is significant in this reaction to the dolphin affair is the way in which the theorist justifies Japanese reactions to international events by generating sets of highly stereotyped, emotional images of Japan versus the west.[13]

Another example of the function of Japan theory in international affairs comes from the pages of *Newsweek* (4 February 1980). In 1979, problems in Iran and Afghanistan began to dominate the headlines. At that time, the American government was pressuring Japan and other allied nations to take concrete action against the Khomeini regime in Iran and against the Soviets for their invasion of Afghanistan. In particular, the United States wanted its allies to join in a program of economic reprisals. Caught between diplomatic obligations and self-interest, Japan, like France and Germany, initially seemed to waver. In a highly critical article, Japan's indecisive attitude was explained, or rather justified, by Nakane Chie of Tokyo University as follows: "The Japanese way of thinking depends on the situation rather than on principle. We Japanese have no principles. Some people think we hide our intentions, but we have no intentions to hide."[14] If Japan's indecisiveness was resented in America, one can easily imagine how Americans responded to this kind of statement. Here was a highly respected Japanese anthropologist saying that the Japanese were dragging their feet because they had "no principles." Furthermore, Nakane's catchy, media-oriented way of stating her case inadvertently represented the Japanese as totally inhuman. (At least, in America and other western countries, people without principles, or even intentions, hardly qualify as human beings). The same issue of *Newsweek* also discussed the reluctance of France and Germany to follow the American lead against Iran and the Soviet Union. These countries too were hesitant to offend oil-rich Iran and weapons-rich Russia. But *Newsweek* explained the German and French reactions in simple geopolitical terms. And no German or French professor appeared to justify the response of his country in terms of "national character."

Japan theory also seems to be on the defensive when it seeks to explain or justify the unending diplomatic ineptitude of the Japanese government. Often, as in the 1990–1991 confrontation with Iraq, diplomatic and political waffling is excused as merely a quirk in the national character. It has been said, for example, that the furor over whether to characterize Japan's relations with the United States as an "alliance" is simply a matter of distinguishing between *tatemae* and *honne*, one of the stock elements in all Japan theory.[15] The same conceptual dichotomy is said to explain the fuss over whether or not nuclear-armed American vessels entering Japanese ports are in violation of Japan's three nuclear principles.[16] Likewise, in 1982 when South Korea and the People's Republic of China protested the whitewashing of Japan's wartime atrocities in public school textbooks approved by the Department of Education, a member of the textbook screening committee justified the revision on the grounds that the "national character" encourages the use of "soft language." A few months earlier when operatives from Hitachi and Mitsubishi were arrested in California for industrial espionage against IBM, the Japanese media immediately launched a massive editorial campaign on behalf of the defendants. Pictures of the diminutive Japanese engineers being led away in handcuffs by husky FBI agents filled the newspapers. The FBI itself was vilified in articles which zeroed in on its domestic surveillance of protesters during the Vietnam War and other true, but irrelevant, details. A highly respected financial paper, influenced perhaps by a TV program in which Franklin D. Roosevelt virtually caused the Japanese to bomb Pearl Harbor, suggested that the FBI caused the Japanese industrial spies to break American law. Another newspaper suggested that IBM was such a greedy giant that it deserved to have its secrets stolen—shades of Hop 'o my Thumb or Jack and the Beanstalk here!

The crowning argument for the defense, however, came from Murata Kiyoaki, editor of the *Japan Times* (2 July 1982). The spy incident, Murata declares, was simply a case of innocent Japanese engineers falling into a trap set for them by the Americans. In a tour de force of legal reasoning, he tries to prove that IBM property was neither stolen nor lost.[17] The crux of his argument, however, is that the Japanese defendants should be exculpated because of the "uniqueness of their culture." Now, what all of this has to do with culture is rather difficult to see. Such appeals to "national character" and "culture" seem to be little more than defensive ploys aimed at avoiding responsibility for past and present wrongdoing while, simultaneously, keeping the official policy of "building up the country through technology" (*gijutsu rikkoku*) on line at any cost.

Even the Japanese "work ethic" has a defensive edge. Not only do the Japanese regard themselves as hardworking (*kinben*); allegations that other nations are not so kinben are often used to justify existing trade imbalances.[18] At home, however, the work ethic functions to make industriousness next to, not godliness but, patriotism. That is, if the theory describes the Japanese as hardworking, then, indirectly, it is criticizing the not-so-kinben for being "un-Japanese." Nevertheless, as anyone familiar with Japanese universities can readily testify, the "average Japanese" is not likely to toil very diligently in institutions designed for low productivity. On the contrary, given the right institutional setting, the Japanese can be as indolent as anybody else. Much of the work ethic actually has its origin not among the people but among their rulers and industrial bosses. It can be traced back to the preachments of daimyos, landlords, and Confucian moralists of the Tokugawa period, the Imperial Rescript on Education (1890), the Boshin Rescript (1908), the creation and ideological use of the Ninomiya Sontoku legend, and continues to be promoted today in the "spiritual education" programs sponsored by Japanese industry. Like the less successful sermons by American presidents on the same subject, the officially promoted kinben-ness of Japan might better be called a work *ideology* than a work ethic. It inspires the work of others and legitimates accumulations of capital already in place.

While the use of feminine and maternal images by some Japan theorists suggests that the theory itself is playing a merely defensive symbolic role, recent talk in Japan about the need for "internationalism," "internationalization," and "international men," implies the birth of a more aggressive posture vis-à-vis the rest of the world. Today "internationalization" (*kokusaika*) and "international exchange" (*kokusai kōryū*) are among the most lively buzzwords in the vocabulary of the country's business, educational, and political elites. Exactly what is meant by these words is rather obscure, a fact that seems to give their users a feeling of self-assurance or even creativity. Yamamoto Mitsuru, professor of international politics at Hosei University, points out that "internationalization" is merely nationalism in mufti.[19] While the traditional Japanese businessman used to "smile, smoke and remain silent" (the three *S*s) during his unavoidable encounters with foreigners—here one thinks of Prime Minister Suzuki's passivity at the economic summit held in Ottawa in 1981 and other premier non-performances—the "international" Japanese is expected to take on foreigners in a more aggressive way. He is the kind of person who can say no to American demands; he can, with self-assurance, refuse demands for aid from Korea, China, or other third world countries; and he can drive hard bargains even with the Russians. He may prefer dining with other Japanese (*tatemeshi*) to socializing with foreigners (*yokomeshi*), but he is able to function, and negotiate, in a natural way in either setting.

The kind of internationalization promoted by the government may be a bit more complicated. While government, like business, naturally has a vested interest in securing a steady supply of hard-nosed negotiators, it would also like to project a more conciliatory self-image. "Internationalization" is therefore made to imply a new spirit of responsibility (for example, at the United Nations) and cooperation (in negotiations over import and export policies). By creating the image of a country now firmly committed to "free" or "open" trade principles, the government seems to be trying to ward off reprisals by western countries for its (de facto) restrictive import policies and aggressive export campaign.

While one could have predicted that the defensive, ideological use of Japan theory would be rejected out of hand by western scholars, one might have expected them to show more patience with, and certainly more interest in, the theorists' description of Japan's allegedly harmonious and consensual society. This has not been the case. Even sociologists and anthropologists have tended to react in a visceral way to the claims of Japan's theorists. In general, western social scientists seem to approach Japan theory not just from the point of view of their own academic disciplines, but also from the vantage point of the eighteenth century ideology of their own culture, i.e., a worldview based on the "naturalness" of self-interest, political pluralism, and free trade (in ideas and things), and a deeply held belief in the ontological priority of individuals to groups. Ever since Aristotle pointed out the damage too much unity could do to the Greek polis, there has been a tradition of liberal social thought in the west which has been intuitively skeptical of "togetherness" in all its forms. Because this tradition sees society in individualistic, pluralistic terms, consensus, hierarchy, and the subordination of individuals to groups are regarded as contrary to the spirit of modernity and dangerous to the health of democratic institutions. Recent wars with nations (including Japan) which have advocated fascist or communist versions of "togetherness" have served only to reinforce these convictions. Stuart Hampshire, an Aristotelian liberal, holds that we

> should look in society not for consensus, but for ineliminable and acceptable conflicts, and for rationally controlled hostilities, as the normal condition of mankind; not only normal, but also the best condition of mankind from the moral point of view, both between states and within states . . . Harmony and inner consensus come with death, when human faces no longer express conflicts but are immobile, composed, and at rest.[20]

From this point of view, the consensus of the Japan theorists would appear to be nothing short of the death mask of an inscrutable—or "premodern"—oriental civilization.

I point out the ideological basis of the western rejection of Japan theory not in order to pretend that my own paradigm stems from other roots—obviously it does not—but rather to warn against a hasty or hysterical rejection of the whole theory, root and branch.[21] While Japan theory is largely intuitive, generally anecdotal, and often ideologically motivated, I would contend that the theorists are trying to tell us, and their fellow Japanese, something important about their country, its traditions and basic values. Many of their claims could be restated in testable (falsifiable) terms, and then verified or disconfirmed. Many of the points the theorists are making can be accepted as they are. "Togetherness," for example, is not necessarily a prelude to fascism. Nor is there anything wrong with the theorists' claim that there is more than one way to become "modern," and that the west does not have a monopoly on modernity, let alone postmodernity.

I would like to suggest that the blitz of books dealing with the essence of Japanese culture and society is, in reality, a groping for a new national self-identity in the face of increasing contact, competition and friction with western countries. Looked at historically, many of the values and self-images of prewar Japan continue to flourish in the Japan theories of the postwar period. One thinks, for example, of the high premium placed on consensus, unity, harmony, paternalism (or hierarchy), asceticism, loyalty, flexibility, efficiency, and so on. In the civil religion of prewar Japan these values were securely grafted into the emperor system and the Way of the Warrior (*bushidō*), and were therefore suffused with the religious and patriotic emotionalism of that period of history. With the defeat of Japan in 1945, this civil religion was radically secularized. If in Japan nothing succeeds like success, nothing fails like failure. Thus, when Japan lost the war, the emperor and the other Shinto deities were thought to have let the country down.

In prewar ideology, such as the National Morality Movement (*kokumin dōtoku undō*) led by Inoue Tetsujirō and others, much was made of the national characteristics which set the Japanese off from the rest of the world.[22] In the civil religious atmosphere of the emperor system, the national character of the people (*kokumin*) was always grounded in the mystery of the ineffable National Essence (*kokutai*)—just as the people were racially, or mythologically, derived from the sacred ancestors of the imperial household. In today's more secular atmosphere, kokumin has replaced kokutai as the focal point of Japan theory. The essence of Japaneseness is seldom explained in religious terms, or even in terms of the imperial family. When religion is introduced in the theory at all, it is to bring home the overall uniqueness of Japanese society. Religious customs are simply one example, among many, of the incomparable "spirit of Japan" (*Yamato damashii*). Nevertheless, it is significant that Isaiah Ben-Dasan could sum up the nature of Japaneseness as a kind of religion (*Nihonkyō*).[23]

Many of the functions of the civil religion of pre-1945 Japan—the generation of national purpose, symbolic self-defense, value-consensus, etc.—are now being assumed by the symbols, values, and imagery produced by the literature of Japan theory. To be sure there are also significant differences. Militarism, for example, is still largely taboo in the theory, the Way of the Warrior yielding to the way of the "international" salaryman. Authors are now free to explore the gentler side of the Japanese personality and to worry, publicly, about its darker aspects (e.g., violence in schools and in homes and the decline of self-discipline and loyalty). Nevertheless, conservative scholars and politicians talk quite openly nowadays about revising the constitution in order to turn the self defense force into a genuine, world-class military organization. A handful have even dared to suggest that the Japanese, in spite of their "nuclear allergy," must develop their own weapons of mass-destruction. Ishihara Shintarō, a popular but highly controversial LDP politician, has called for the creation of a Japanese "Star Wars" program—"air mines," as he calls it—and has suggested that Japan use its technological prowess to play off the United States against the USSR. It goes without saying, that if proposals of this sort become part of mainstream Japan theory, Japan watchers will have good reason to be concerned about the future trajectory of the theory.

At the present time, Japan theory can hardly be called a unified movement. It is produced by authors working under competitive conditions of a free publishing market, and usually not by propagandists in the employ of the state. The self-images we see emerging in contemporary Japan theory are not the finished products of a new ideology, but an ongoing search for a new national identity by a people whose economic enterprise has recouped what generals, gods, and a divine emperor previously lost. Although I have described Japan theory as a secularization of a civil religion, because secularization itself is not inevitably a one-way or irreversible process, it is conceivable that Japan theory, under new historical circumstances, will give birth to a new religious self-understanding, or perhaps even to a new civil religion.

Notes

Preface

1. For an informative, but controversial account of these and other paradoxes, see Karel van Wolferen, *The Enigma of Japanese Power.* New York: Vintage Books, 1989.

2. The only place where my paradigms come close to an Eliadean pattern or archetype is in the discussion of Pure Activity in chapters 3 and 6.

3. Belief in "axilological parity" does not mean, however, that the boundary between scholar and informant has been erased. While I would affirm the usefulness of the controversial distinction between emic and etic discourse proposed by Kenneth Pike, Marvin Harris and other anthropologists, I am reluctant to attribute to one or the other a greater proximity to reality. Whether the scholar or the informant is "telling it like it is," is a question that would have to be debated anew every time it was raised. I therefore use '*etic*' to refer to arguments or paradigms which enjoy salience in the academic community, reserving '*emic*' for discourse that seems especially realistic, or commonsensical, in the informant's own world.

4. *Violent Origins: Walter Burkert, René Girard, and Jonathan Z. Smith on Ritual Killing and Cultural Formation,* edited by Robert G. Hamerton-Kelly. Stanford: Stanford University Press, 1987, p. 207.

5. Thomas S. Kuhn, *The Structure of Scientific Revolutions.* Chicago: University of Chicago Press, 1974, 2nd ed., p. 94. My emphasis.

6. *The Collected Dialogues of Plato,* edited by Edith Hamilton and Huntington Cairns. Princeton: Princeton University Press, 1985. Translation by J. B. Skemp, pp. 1043–45. My emphasis.

7. *Local Knowledge.* New York: Basic Books, 1983, p. 151.

8. E. Evans-Pritchard, *Theories of Primitive Religion.* Oxford: Oxford University Press, 1965, pp. 20–47.

9. Peter Berger and Thomas Luckmann, *The Social Construction of Reality.* Garden City: Doubleday, 1966.

10. Peter Berger, *The Sacred Canopy: Elements of a Sociological Theory of Religion*. Garden City: Doubleday, 1969.

11. See for example Alvin Y. So, *Social Change and Development: Modernization, Dependency, and World-System Theories*. Newbury Park, London, New Delhi: Sage Publications (Sage Library of Social Research 178), 1990, pp. 66–75 and pp. 85–87.

12. *The Fable of the Bees, or Private Vices, Publick Benefits*. Indianapolis: Liberty Classics, 1988, Vol. I, p. 356.

13. *Democracy in America.*, translated by Henry Reeve; edited by Phillips Bradley. New York: Alfred A. Knopf, 1972, Vol II, pp. 27–28. My emphasis.

14. In contrast to Weber, who explained asceticism in terms of religious anxiety, Tocqueville explains it as the outcome of *self-interest*. While self-interest "produces no great acts of self-sacrifice . . . it suggests daily small acts of self-denial. By itself it cannot suffice to make a man virtuous; but it disciplines a number of persons in habits of regularity, temperance, moderation, foresight, self-command; and if it does not lead men straight to virtue by the will, it gradually draws them in that direction by their habits." Ibid., Vol. II, p. 123.

Chapter 1.

1. For a detailed but brief account of the history of religious affiliations in Japan see my *Toward Modernity: A Developmental Typology of Popular Religious Affiliations in Japan*. Ithaca: Cornell University East Asia Papers, No. 12, 1977.

2. Several considerations make me wary of relying too heavily on conventional exchange theory. Many Anglo-American contributors to exchange theory have universalized the values of modern competitive societies and the concept of human nature generated by those societies. This obviously makes it difficult to deal with the moral obligations that tie individuals to families and churches. Jack N. Mitchell, for example, remarks that Peter Homans' theory of exchange "steadfastly denies the existence of any normative element existent on bases other than individual self-interest" (*Social Exchange, Dramaturgy and Ethnomethodology: Toward a Paradigmatic Synthesis*. New York: Elsevier, 1978, p. 28). He also points out that Peter Blau, another exchange theorist, treats norms as "nothing more than the derivatives of the economic motives of individuals" (ibid., p. 69). Sociological versions of exchange theory tend to amalgamate, without unifying, a bewildering variety of heterogeneous positions such as cybernetics, game theory, rational-choice theory, economic marginalism, and biological and social evolutionism, not to mention the psychologies of operant

conditioning and possessive individualism. Other theorists deal with values of terms of "preference schedules," "reference signals," and "selector functions," expressions which seem to reduce the obligatory or normative aspect of value to a de facto self-centered tendency to choose one thing over another. (See Harry C. Bredemeier, "Exchange Theory," in Tom Bottomore and Robert Nisbet, eds., *A History of Sociological Analysis.* New York: Basic Books, 1978, pp. 418–456. Anthropological theories of exchange generally take their categories from primitive societies, making direct application to modern societies hazardous. Marcel Mauss, for example, basing his theory of exchange on "the great neolithic stage of civilization," considered obligation and interest nearly inseparable aspects of "total prestation" (*The Gift: Forms and Functions of Exchange in Archaic Societies,* translated by Ian Cunnison. London: Cohen and West, 1969, p. 69). In this chapter, I follow Alfred Schutz and separate obligations and interests as two distinguishable ideal-types.

3. For a more aggressive and reductionistic use of exchange theory, see Rodney Stark and William Sims Bainbridge, *A Theory of Religion.* New York: Peter Lang, 1987 and my review of the book in *Journal of Religion,* Vol. 69, No. 2, pp. 287–88.

4. Charles E. Lindblom, *Politics and Markets: The World's Political-Economic Systems.* New York: Basic Books, 1977, p. 33.

5. Ibid., pp. 33–34.

6. *Collected Papers,* Vol 2 (*Studies in Social Theory*), edited by Arvid Brodersen. The Hague: Martinus Nijhoff, 1964 and *The Phenomenology of the Social World.* Evanston: Northwestern University Press, 1967.

7. In English and other languages, there is an overlap between the expressions 'in order to' and 'because'. For example, I can say that I went to the store 'in order to' buy some bread, or 'because' I wanted some. This, however, does not obscure the obvious distinction Schutz was trying to make. The meaning of the words in this case lies not just in their use, but in our stipulation of their use. A 'because' motive is "always an explanation after the event" and therefore covers various kinds of obligated, conditioned, and caused behavior. (Schutz, *Phenomenology,* p. 93). In this chapter I shall set aside conditioned and caused behavior and focus on Schutz's 'because' motives as the intentionality lying behind obligatory behavior, and on his 'in order to' motives as that which informs purposeful or intentional conduct.

8. George Simmel, one of the fathers of exchange theory, pointed out that in a market or exchange society "any selfless motives appear not to be natural and autochthonous but secondary and, as it were, artificially implanted. As a result, only self-interested action is considered to be genuinely and simply 'logical'. All devotion and self-sacrifice seem to flow from the irrational forces of feeling and volition, so that men of pure intellect treat them ironically as a proof of lack of intelligence or denounce them as the disguise of a hidden

egoism." The direct application of *this* concept of exchange to Japan naturally invites misunderstanding. See Simmel's *The Philosophy of Money,* translated by Tom Bottomore and David Frisby. London: Routledge and Kegan Paul, 1978, pp. 438–39.

9. For a discussion of Japanese ancestor worship in terms of exchange theory, see Harumi Befu, "Gift-Giving in a Modernizing Japan, " *Monumenta Nipponica* (Vol. 23, Nos. 3–4, pp. 445–56). A similar analysis could be applied to the cult of the Shinto domestic deities, the *yashikigami.*

10. In Japanese: *Yo no hitobito ni kansha shite imasu.*

11. The erosion of the ritual privileges of these families was largely the outcome of the development of a competitive money economy and the decline of traditional patron-client relations in the countryside. For a more detailed account see my "Parish Guilds and Political Culture in Village Japan," *Journal of Asian Studies,* Vol. 36, No. 1 (November 1976), pp. 25–36 and "The *Miyaza* and the Fisherman: Ritual Status in Coastal Villages of Wakayama Prefecture," *Asian Folklore Studies* (1977) No. 36, No. 2, pp. 1–29.

12. *Ujiko-iri* (literally, "entering [the ranks of] the children of the clan") is as involuntary as infant baptism in the churches of the west and plays a similar role in creating ascriptive identities.

13. I prefer to use Robert Bellah's expression "civil religion" and not Daniel Holtom's "Shinto nationalism" for the simple reason that nearly all of Japan's religions contributed to the political ideology of the 1930s and 40s. See my "Fundamentalism in Japan: Religious and Political," in *Fundamentalisms Observed,* edited by Martin E. Marty and R. Scott Appleby. Chicago: University of Chicago Press, Vol. I, forthcoming.

14. Cited in Kazuko Tsurumi, *Social Change and the Individual: Japan Before and After Defeat in World War II.* Princeton: Princeton University Press, 1970, p. 59.

15. *Religion in Changing Japanese Society.* Tokyo: University of Tokyo Press, 1975, pp. 39–72.

16. Closely related to the obligatory nature of Shinto parish affiliations is the particularism of its values. Traditionally, only local residents could participate in the rites of the ujigami. Newcomers might have to wait for a whole generation (or even longer) before they were accepted as fullfledged "children of the clan."

17. For the distinction between "natural" and "specifically religious" religions see Joachim Wach, *Sociology of Religion.* Chicago: University of Chicago Press, 1944, pp. 54–205.

18. In 1974, there were on average eighteen suicides by elderly Japanese every day. This was two more per day than in 1971, when Japan already had

the world's second highest rate of elderly suicides. *The Japan Times* (December 5, 1976), p. 14.

19. This ritual may possibly be related to the use of magical cloth sashes (*iwata obi*) by pregnant women in Kansai. Both types of undergarment are believed to help the individual into his or her next life.

20. See Naganuma Iwane, "Pokkuri-dera o yogiru oi to shi," *Asahi Jānaru* (December 19, 1975), Vol. 17, No. 54, pp. 86–91.

21. For a general survey of these religions see H. Neill McFarland's *The Rush Hour of the Gods: A Study of New Religious Movements in Japan.* (New York: Harper Colophon Books, 1970). Recent studies of specific New Religions include H. Byron Earhart's *Gedatsu-Kai and Religion in Contemporary Japan: Returning to the Center* (Bloomington: Indiana University Press, 1989), Helen Hardacre's *Lay Buddhism in Contemporary Japan: Reiyūkai Kyōdan* (Princeton: Princeton University Press, 1984), and my *Dojo: Magic and Exorcism in Modern Japan* (Stanford: Stanford University Press), 1980.

22. *Religion in Japanese History.* New York: Columbia University Press, 1966, p. 333.

23. For the distinction between substantial and functional rationality, see Karl Mannheim's *Man and Society in an Age of Reconstruction* (New York: Harcourt, Brace and World, 1940), pp. 53–59 and, for its application to one New Religion, my *Dojo,* op. cit., pp. 291–302.

24. Peter L. Berger and Thomas Luckmann, "Secularization and Pluralism," *International Yearbook for the Sociology of Religion,* Vol. 2, No. 2, pp. 73–84.

25. See *Dojo,* op. cit., pp. 99–114.

26. "Kō shūdan no shakaiteki seikaku," *Tetsugaku kenkyū* (Kyoto University), October 1957, Vol. 39, No. 7, pp. 15–35.

27. One can compare this potential for rebellion with another "Free Church," the Methodists in 19th century England. In 1807, the Anglican Bishop of Gloucester "depicted the Establishment as a 'citadel' which was 'beset on every side' by Methodists 'who wish not well to the civil and religious polity of this nation.' These 'malignant and subtle adversaries,' through their 'private conferences, their local classes, their extensive connections, their general assemblies . . . cooperate from one part of the Kingdom to another . . . for the purpose of concerting measures to undermine our civil and religious Constitution.' " While most Methodists were actually quite deferential, the translocal connections of their chapels and the itinerancy of their clergy seem to have raised bugaboos of sedition in the minds of their ecclesiastical and social Betters. See Bernard Semmel, "Introduction: Elie Halévy," in Elie Halévy, *The Birth of Methodism in England* (Chicago: University of Chicago Press, 1971), p. 19.

28. See chapter 5 for a detailed discussion of the political conservatism of the family temples.

29. Sects can be regarded as groups which take shape in response to a founder and his message. Cultic orders, on the other hand, are organized around preexisting holy places by religious entrepreneurs of various sorts. See James H. Foard, *Ippen Shōnin and Popular Buddhism in Kamakura Japan* (unpublished Ph.D. dissertation, Stanford University, 1977).

30. At the level of vernacular religion, the Japanese often do not distinguish between magic (good luck) and salvation itself ("lucking out" once and for all).

31. The following chart is based largely on Hori Ichirō, *Folk Religion in Japan: Continuity and Change,* edited by Joseph M. Kitagawa and Alan L. Miller. (Chicago: University of Chicago Press, 1968, pp. 32–81.

32. See Sakurai Tokutarō, *Kō shūkan seiritsu katei no kenkyū.* Tokyo: Yoshikawa Kōbunkan, 1962, pp. 554–579.

33. Waida Manabu, "Symbolism of 'Descent' in Tibetan Sacred Kingship and some East Asian Parallels," *Numen,* Vol. XX, Fasc. 1 (April 1973), pp. 60–78. Such myths seem to indicate that "supernatural powers and superior culture usually came from the outside to the exclusive in-group society. . . . The idea of a super-natural power and a superior culture coming from outside was probably related to general feelings of inferiority among the ancient villagers, who were aware of community exclusiveness and isolation. At the same time, they may have been conscious of cultural and religious distinctions between their own group and the out-groups, and felt a certain longing for the outsiders' cultures." Hori, *Folk Religion,* p. 69.

34. Tsurumi Shunsuke, *Nichijōteki shisō no kanōsei* [The Possibility of Everyday Thought]. Tokyo: Chikuma Shobō, 1975, pp. 34–38.

35. Sonoda Minoru, "The Traditional Festival in Urban Society," *Japanese Journal of Religious Studies,* Vol. 2, Nos. 2 and 3 (June-September 1975), pp. 103–136.

36. In the west, for example, a relationship with a "church" which typically falls under our 'because' motives, is often reinforced by answers to 'in order to' prayers, while family obligations ('because' motives) tend to reinforce commitments to 'in order to' sectarian groups.

37. For more on Japan theory, see chapter 8.

38. Cited in Rodney Clark, *The Japanese Company* (New Haven and London: Yale University Press, 1979), p. 137.

39. We shall take a closer look at a Buddhist form of "spiritual education" in chapter 6.

40. See Abegglen's *The Japanese Factory: Aspects of its Social Organization*. Glencoe, Ill.: The Free Press, 1958.

41. Perhaps the most balanced account of the obligations and motivations at work in Japanese industry is Rodney Clark's *The Japanese Company*, op. cit. Summarizing his findings on Japan's famous but widely misunderstood tenured employment, he points out that the system "could be construed as the effect of a labour market consisting of essentially self-serving individuals and firms. But this sort of explanation does not invalidate the proposition that 'lifetime employment' is at the same time an ideal, and a very powerful one, entailing an obligation of mutual attachment between firm and employee. Sanctioned by what is seen as tradition, morally correct, and emblemative of Japanese culture, 'lifetime employment' is the goal towards which both firms and individuals have to direct their efforts—or their apologies," p. 175.

Chapter 2.

1. For the theory of conflict structuralism, see Margaret M. Poloma, *Contemporary Sociological Theory*. New York: Macmillan, 1979, pp. 65–104.

2. *Sources of Japanese Tradition*, edited by Ryusaku Tsunoda, et al. New York: Columbia University Press, 1958, Vol. I, p. 48.

3. Shōtoku Taishi, to whom the Seventeen Article Constitution is conventionally attributed, believed that right views "spontaneously" gained acceptance only when the social and political hierarchy was respected: "When the lord speaks, the vassal listens; when the superior acts, the inferior yields compliance." (art. III). Class or status was therefore an indispensable part of his Confucian concept of harmony.

4. See for example *Conflict in Modern Japanese History: The Neglected Tradition*, edited by Tetsuo Najita and J. Victor Koschmann. Princeton: Princeton University Press, 1982.

5. R. J. Zwi Werblowsky, *Beyond Tradition and Modernity: Changing Religions in a Changing World* (London: Athlone, 1975), pp. 106, 113.

6. Victor W. Turner, *The Ritual Process: Structure and Anti-Structure* (Chicago: Aldine Publishing Co., 1969), and "The Center Out There: Pilgrim's Goal," *History of Religions* Vol. 12, No. 3 (February 1973), pp. 191–230.

7. Bryan Wilson, *Contemporay Transformation of Religion* (Oxford: Clarendon Press, 1979), p. 97. In all fairness it should be pointed out that individual Methodists also played an important role in reforming English society.

8. It could be argued that, even when Japanese religion seemed to be most disruptive of the social order (e.g., in the uprisings of the Ikkō and Hokke sects and the later rebellion of Christians at Shimabara), what religion provided was

the translocal social structure and occasion for dissent—not a theory for revolt (see chapter 1, on confraternities).

9. Shinjō Tsunezō, *Shomin to tabi no rekishi* (Tokyo: NHK Books, 1981), p. 197.

10. The determination of this time period was based on the sexagenary cycle, as well as on Chinese notions of divination based on yin and yang and the five elements. It was also related to the custom of having special celebrations for one's sixty-first birthday and other Japanese traditions. Sakurai Tokutarō, *Nihon minkan shinkōron* (Tokyo: Kōbundō, 1970), pp. 239–40.

11. In spite of these differences, I shall occasionally cite parallels from the ee-ja-nai-ka movement in this paper.

12. Ise dances had taken place throughout the Tokugawa period, most notably in 1614, 1621, 1624, 1653, 1678, and 1714. Like okage-mairi itself, these dances were often sparked by the "descent" of shrines, amulets, or the goddess Amaterasu from heaven, or by the falling of money or rice from the sky. In 1830 dancing broke out in the intercalary third month on the Tōkaidō. See Nakajima Kazuyoshi, "Bunsei jūsan-nen no okage-odori ni tsuite: Tōkaidō Hirakata-shuku o chūshin ni," in *Chihōshi kenkyū,* No. 168 (1980), pp. 11–30. In late April, a *segyō-odori* (alms dance) took place in Kawachi and included *odori-komi* attacks (dance-ins) on the homes of rich farmers. See Yano Yoshiko, " 'Okage-mairi' to 'ee-ja-nai-ka,' " in *Ikki,* ed. Aoki Michio et al. (Tokyo: Tōkyō Daigaku Shuppankai, 1981), Vol. 4, *Seikatsu, bunka, shisō,* p. 330.

13. *Ukiyo no arisama,* in *Nihon shisō taikei,* ed. Shoji Kichinosuke et al. (Tokyo: Iwanami Shoten, 1970), Vol. 58, *Minshū undō no shisō,* p. 357; cited hereafter as UA. The comical high-jinks dance (*kappore*) which developed later on seems to have its origin here too. Okage-odori was also influenced by the dancing which took place at the Mitaue, or rice transplanting ceremony, held at the Sumiyoshi Shrine in Osaka.

14. Fujitani Toshio, "*Okage-mairi*" *to* "*ee-ja-nai-ka*" (Tokyo: Iwanami Shinsho, 1973), p. 24.

15. *UA*, p. 370.

16. In the pilgrimages of 1650 and 1705 the word *nuke-mairi* was generally used instead of okage-mairi. This is probably an indication of how widespread the custom of French-leave pilgrimage had become. Nuke-mairi was also called "*kakure-mairi,*" i.e., hidden, or covert pilgrimage.

17. *UA*, p. 335.

18. Ibid., p. 339.

19. Reluctant givers were threatened with physical revenge, e.g., their homes might be rammed by a large float during the next Shinto festival (Yano [n. 11 above], pp. 325–26).

20. Cited in *UA*, p. 365. My emphasis.

21. Cited in Fujitani, pp. 29–30.

22. Minowa Zairoku, "Okage sangū Bunsei shin'i-ki" (1830), in *Jingū sanpaiki taisei* (Gifu-shi: Seinō Insatsu K.K., 1937), p. 513.

23. Besides two chapters dealing with okage-mairi, the *UA* also deals with the coming of foreign ships to Japan, natural disasters, peasant rebellions, the unrest of the Tempō period (including Ōshiro's rebellion), popular customs and morals, inflation, and so on. The section on okage-mairi (called "Okage no jimoku") is divided into two sections, the first containing important historical information, the second, made up largely of riddles, poems, word plays, and Ise songs (*ondo*), aims to entertain rather than to instruct. His description of the Ise-odori (which clearly shows its affinities with the *yonaoshi odori* of the ee-ja-nai-ka) is the most detailed account we have of these dances. The work was printed in the *Kokushi sōsho* (1917–20) in which poor editing occasionally distorted the meaning of the text. The entire *UA* is now available in *Nihon shōmin seikatsu shiryō shūsei* (Tokyo: San'ichi Shobō, 1971), Vol. 11. In this article, I have made use of the annotated edition of the first part by Yasumaru Yoshio in Shōji Kichinosuke et al., eds., pp. 308–72.

24. *UA*, p. 309.

25. Ibid., p. 321.

26. Ibid., p. 308.

27. Ibid., p. 310.

28. Ibid., p. 328.

29. Until a person was dead and buried his name was written in red. After his funeral it was painted black. The trick was therefore a deliberate confusion of the living and the dead.

30. *UA*, pp. 356–57. *Tengu* are mythical creatures, half human and half bird, with red faces and long phallic noses. They are thought to fly down from mountain tops to attack and bedevil human beings.

31. Nishigaki Seiji, *Ee-ja-nai-ka: Minshū undō no keifu* (Tokyo: Shinjinbutsuōraisha, 1981), p. 238.

32. *UA*, pp. 340–41.

33. Ibid., p. 340.

34. Ibid., p. 328.

35. Ibid., p. 351.

36. Ibid., pp. 336–37.

37. Ibid., p. 358.

38. This incident seems to be an extension of the custom of *shibari-Jizō*. People would bind a statue of Jizō with a rope and say "grant our request, Jizō, and we'll let you go." Or, they would take a statue of Jizō with a child (Jizō being the protector of children) and knock the child's statue to the ground, telling Jizō that they would not pick it up until he had answered their prayers. See Nakura Tetsuzō, "Kinsei no shinkō to ikki," in Aoki, ed. (note 12 above), pp. 304–5.

39. Ivan Morris. *The Nobility of Failure: Tragic Heroes in the History of Japan* (New York: Meridian Books, 1976), p. 204.

40. In 1655, Sōgorō and his wife were crucified after he presented a petition to the shōgun on behalf of the peasants in Shimōsa (Ibaraki). Before their death, the parents were forced to view the decapitation of their own children. Although the tale is largely fictitious, the discovery of the name "Sōgorō" in a contemporary public document has added some credibility to it.

41. The ruse was identical with that employed by the Hidden Christians who worshiped the Blessed Virgin Mary under the guise of the Buddhist deity Kannon.

42. Yasumaru Yoshio, "Minshū undō no shisō," in Shōji et al., eds. (n. 13 above), pp. 394–95.

43. Shōji et al., eds., p. 250. My emphasis.

44. Yasumaru, p. 393.

45. Ibid., p. 398.

46. For the concept of the "logic of relative contrasts," see chapter 7, p. 247–249.

47. Yasumaru (note 42 above), p. 399.

48. Fujitani, p. 150.

49. Ibid., p. 162. Whether this was a threat directed against moneylenders or simply a case of eschatological blather cannot be known. The word *oharai*, which I have translated "will be wiped away," is really a double entendre meaning both "to exorcize" and "to pay back money."

50. *UA*, p. 351.

51. The parody of upper classes was seen in other okage-mairi as well as during the ee-ja-nai-ka when commoners masqueraded as famous warriors such as the legendary fisherman of Miho-no-Matsubara, as Takenouchi-no-Sukune the retainer of Empress Jingū, as the famous Soga brothers, Sukenari and Tokimune (d. 1193), and as the forty-seven rōnin.

52. Minowa, pp. 514–15.

53. This area, which included Nakayama, Katsuodera, Minō, and Ikeda, was the center of the uprising in Nose and was deeply influenced by the rebellion of Ōshio Heihachirō in Osaka. During the Nose Uprising, rebels hoisted signs reading "no more loans" and "benevolent government," ideas they hoped the emperor would enforce. *UA*, p. 370 (editor's note).

54. Ibid., p. 370.

55. Ibid., pp. 361–62. The dancing, religious ecstasy and "world renewing" which came together in the ee-ja-nai-ka movement formed a volatile mixture. The dance-ins and masquerading (trasvestism) providing a symbolic cover under which resentment and protest could be revealed, while being concealed from the authorities. One person recounted the following story: "We went to the houses of chaps we used to hate or to the homes of people who pretended they were big shots and danced right in shouting 'ain't it great, ain't it great'! We'd destroy the floor mats and doors, taking any good-looking furniture, and dance around" (*Itō Sajirō-ō dan*, cited in Fujitani, p. 118). Another man recalled how during the ee-ja-nai-ka "while we were dancing around from shrine to shrine, completely naked and without a penny, when we came to the house where amulets had fallen, we'd dance at the doorway and shout 'ain't it great, ain't it great!' And then we'd force our way in—with muddy feet, straw sandals or whatever—and dance around the house. Then the people in the house would panic and give us something to eat and drink" (*Awa ee-ja-nai-ka*, cited in Fujitani, pp. 112–13).

56. *UA*, p. 324.

57. Similarly, during the ee-ja-nai-ka, officials arrested those who claimed to see rice, beans, and salt falling from the sky as well as individuals dressing in the clothes of the opposite sex. In some places people were even forbidden to worship falling amulets. In Edo, official notices condemned merrymaking in large groups, collecting money, and going into other neighborhoods to create a disturbance. Above all, the government was keen to promote a discrete religious attitude (*kokoroechigai nai yō ni seyo*) among the common folk. See Fujitani Toshio, "Okage-mairi to 'ee-ja-nai-ka'," (Tokyo: Iwanami Shinsho, 1973), p. 120; Yano Yoshiko, " 'Okage-mairi' to 'ee-ja-nai-ka'," in *Ikki*, ed. Aoki Michio et al. (Tokyo: Tōkyō Daigaku Shuppankai, 1981), Vol. 4, *Seikatsu, bunka, shisō*, pp. 324–25.

58. *UA*, p. 324.

59. Fujitani, p. 75.

60. *UA*, p. 335.

61. Ibid., p. 360.

62. Of the 488 disciples of Motoori Norinaga, 166 were said to be merchants, 114 farmers, 67 Shinto priests, 27 physicians, 25 Buddhist priests,

and 58 from samurai or other backgrounds. Of the approximately 550 students of Hirata Atsutane, as many as 330 were believed to be merchants, cultivators, or Shinto priests. In both cases, sub-samurai students greatly outnumbered warriors.

63. Fujitani, p. 160.

64. The idea that the okage-mairi was an omen of disaster was also found, to a lesser degree, among the common people. After the persecution of the "Toyota Christians" and married Buddhist priests by Ōshio Heihachirō in 1829, people remarked that "because okage-mairi has started, Buddhism is declining and Shinto has become dominant. The Yang spirit is predominant and there will probably be fires" (*UA*, p. 343).

65. Fujitani, pp. 76–77.

66. *UA*, p. 365.

67. Ibid., p. 367.

68. Minowa Zairoku, "Okage sangū Bunsei shin'i-ki" (1830), in *Jingū sanpaiki taisei* (Gifu-shi: Seinō Insatsu K. K., 1937), p. 518.

69. Gift giving, both real and symbolic, is especially significant in Japan where, even today, it plays an important role in cementing social ties, obliging acquaintances, and disarming enemies (see Harumi Befu, "Gift-Giving in a Modernizing Japan," *Monumenta Nipponica* 23 [1968]: 445–56). The segyō of the rich and powerful must therefore have helped to contain the resentment of the poor which, long seething, was apt to come to full boil when fueled by large-scale social movements. During peasant rebellions the rich resorted to gift giving to sooth nasty tempers. Some were seen in full ceremonial garb serving refreshments to fuming peasants. Accompanied by their servants, they obsequiously called out, "Most noble rebels, please have some *sake* and rice balls, or some straw sandals for your honorable, aching feet. And if there is anything else you need, please feel free to take it" ("Ōshū Shinobu-gun Date-gun no Onbyakushō-shū no ikki no shidai," in Shōji et al., op. cit., p. 276).

70. Minowa, p. 518.

71. Ibid., p. 495.

72. Ibid., p. 533.

73. Ibid., p. 505.

74. Ibid., p. 532. For a similar tale, see *UA*, pp. 339–40.

75. Watarai Hironori, "Ise Daijingū Zokushin'iki" (1705), in *Jingū sanpaiki taisei, op. cit.*, p. 416.

76. *UA*. p. 340. Similar tales of immobilized lovers were told in the Itami region northwest of Osaka (*UA*, p. 344).

77. Since the fifth century, Ise had been patronized exclusively by the imperial family which regarded the goddess Amaterasu of the Inner Shrine as its clan deity. A rule against private offerings and prayers (*shihei no kin*) suggests that even at this early date the shrines were thought to have national significance. Even empresses and crown princes who wanted to present offerings had to secure permission from the emperor. Before the time of the Meiji emperor, the emperors themselves did not go to Ise to make offerings. To enure that the shihei no kin rule was strictly observed, messengers were sent in their place. With the decline of the ancient aristocracy and the rise of the manorial economy, the Ise faith changed greatly. Warrior families who donated estates (*mikuriya* or *misono*) to the shrines replaced the aristocracy as their patrons. These donations led to the breakdown of the ancient rule against private offerings. For example, when Minamoto Yoritomo dedicated an estate to the shrines in 1183, he did so in order to have prayers said "for the country *(ōyake) and for himself*" (my emphasis). Although the Kamakura shōguns, like the emperors, did not visit the shrines themselves, later military rulers often went on pilgrimage. Ashikaga Yoshimitsu (1358–1408), for example, went to Ise ten times and his son, Yoshimochi (1386–1428), is said to have made seventeen pilgrimages. The wives of the shōguns also went along. On these family pilgrimages, personal prayers were naturally made for the healing of the diseases of family members, for safe childbirth, and so on. As the shrines began to accumulate estates, knowledge of the Ise cult spread widely even among the common people. The first commoners to visit the shrines were probably the porters and foot soldiers who accompanied the shōguns on their pilgrimages. Knowledge of the shrines was also spread by pilgrims passing through Ise on their way to the Kumano shrines at the southern end of the Kii peninsula. Around the beginning of the fifteenth century, confraternities for the promotion of the worship of the Ise gods were formed among the aristocracy and powerful provincial families (*dogō*). During the peace and relative prosperity of the Tokugawa period, similar confraternities spread among the common people. The faith was also propagated by itinerant priests (see note 97 below). Thus Ise passed through four major historical stages, each dominated by different social strata: the ancient period (the court), the early Middle ages (the warrior class), the late Middle Ages (the common people), and the modern period (the oligarchs and nationalists). See Nishigaki Seiji, "Ise Shinkō," in *Nihon no shūkyōshi no nazo*, ed. Wakamori Tarō (Tokyo: Kōsei Shuppansha, 1976), 2:159–68.

78. For a more detailed examination of the patterns of syncretism, social conflict and enfranchisement in Japanese religion, see Winston Davis, "Parish Guilds and Political Culture in Village Japan," *Journal of Asian Studies* Vol. 36, No. 1 (November 1976): 25–36, and "The *Miyaza* and the Fisherman: Ritual Status in Coastal Villages of Wakayama Prefecture," *Asian Folklore Studies* Vol. 36, No. 32 (.977): 1–29.

79. *UA*, p. 337.

80. Ibid., pp. 333–34.

81. The Shinshū sect was not the only group to suffer such apostasy. In the late sixteenth century a large number of baptized Christians in Bungo (Kyūshū) defied the church and went to Ise (Fijitani [note 57 above], p. 25).

82. Fujitani, p. 77.

83. Watarai, p. 412.

84. Minowa, pp. 505, 533–34.

85. Fujitani, p. 184.

86. Horiguchi Yoshibei, "Keiō Ise okage kenbun shokoku fushigi no hikae," in Shōji et al., eds., op. cit., p. 379.

87. Fujitani, p. 168.

88. Minowa, p. 514.

89. Ibid., pp. 498–99.

90. Minowa, pp. 511–12.

91. Ibid., pp. 519–20.

92. Watarai, p. 407.

93. Minowa, pp. 520–21.

94. Ibid., p. 501.

95. Ibid., p. 499.

96. For the idea of religious and moral "action guides," see David Little and Sumner B. Twiss, *Comparative Religious Ethics* (San Francisco: Harper & Row, 1978).

97. The oshi became active in Japanese religious life around the end of the Kamakura period when they were patronized by aristocratic families and warrior clans. Although one thinks of these priests today primarily in connection with the history of the Ise shrines, oshi were found at a number of well-known shrines, temples, and sacred mountains, e.g., at the Kumano, Iwashimizu, Hachiman, Kamo, Hiyoshi, Matsuo, Mishima, and Hakusan shrines, at Zenkōji in Shinano, as well as at Mount Kōya, Mount Fuji, and Dewa Sanzan. Originally, the oshi were of a social rank close to that of the up-and-coming *myōshu* and *jitō* who gained control of the new, semi-independent "federated villages" (*gōson*) of the Kinki region during the Muromachi period. With the appearance of the new "territorial ideology" of these communities, the Ise confraternities which had developed along the lines of the warrior clans were reorganized on the basis of territorial networks consonant with the organization of the gōson themselves. Thanks to the activities of the oshi, the Ise shrines were able to

move from manorial support to a system of direct contributions made by pilgrims and believers. In the new economic world of the *ryōshu* system, this put Ise (together with Honganji) in a position of considerable strength. In 1429 there was a *coup d'église* at Ise in which the lower-ranking oshi (or *shin'-yakunin*) overthrew priests of higher rank (*jinnin*) who had been closely associated with the ruling classes. Soon thereafter the Outer and Inner Shrines were rebuilt (in 1434 and 1462, respectively, after a hiatus of a century), and Ise began to emerge as a popular pilgrimage center. Throughout the Muromachi period, the oshi, with the help of feudal authorities, organized farmers into congregations (*danna*) and, before long, farmers and merchants were seen making the pilgrimage to Ise. As the shrines became more popular, the number of priests increased. By the end of the sixteenth century there were 145 oshi attached to the Outer Shrine alone. By the early eighteenth century their number had risen to 504, while those serving the Inner Shrine stood at 241. Documents seem to suggest that by the end of the Tokugawa period their number had declined significantly. For example, at the Inner Shrine in 1867 there were only 196 priestly families registered. It is likely, however, that these figures reflect the acquisition and consolidation of danna by the more powerful oshi. Some of these priests served as many as ten thousand families or more. (Less successful, unregistered priests presumably went to work for the more prosperous ones.) So successful were some of the oshi that the daimyō in some parts of the country tried to limit their visitations and collections lest the people be too drained to pay their taxes. See Shinjō Tsunezō, *Shaji sanrei no shakai-keieishiteki kenkyū* (Tokyo: Hanawa Shobō, 1964), pp. 710–20.

98. Sakurai Tokutarō, *Nihon minkan shinkōron* (Tokyo: Kōbundō, 1970), p. 259.

99. While the terms "folktale" and "folklore" are generally used of an anonymous genre of literature, I use them here because the tales spun by the oshi were nearly identical to the style, content, and outlook of traditional Japanese folklore.

100. *UA*, pp. 361–62.

101. Horiguchi, op. cit., p. 376.

102. Michael Walzer, *The Revolution of the Saints: A Study in the Origins of Radical Politics* (New York: Atheneum, 1968), p. 1.

103. Yano, op. cit., p. 357.

104. Yasumaru Yoshio, "Minshū undō no shisō," in Shōji et al. eds., op. cit., p. 393.

105. Fujitani, op. cit., p. 137 ff.

106. E. H. Norman, *Origins of the Modern Japanese State: Selected Writings of E. H. Norman* (New York: Pantheon Books, 1975), pp. 349–54.

107. In some places women were expected to go to Ise before they were regarded as eligible for marriage. Sakurai, p. 238 ff.

108. Yano, op. cit., pp. 322, 335.

109. In some cases the hayari-gami credited with powers to cure such-and-such disease was believed to be the spirit of a person who, before his death, had suffered from the same disease. The cult often took the form of visits to this person's grave. Better-known hayari-gami, such as the Seven Gods of Luck, Hachiman, or Inari, played similar functions. For example, Tarō Inari, the god of smallpox and measles, was periodically driven out of villages to prevent epidemics.

110. Miyata Noboru, *Kinsei no hayari-gami,* Nihonjin no Kōdō to shisō, no. 17 (Tokyo: Hyōronsha, 1972). For a more concise statement, see the same author's "Minkan shinkō no naka no hayari-gami," *Rekishi kōron* Vol. 5, No. 7 (July 1979): 38–46.

111. Mircea Eliade, *Le Mythe de l'éternal retour: Archétypes et répétition* (Paris: Gallimard, 1969).

112. Sakurai Tokutarō, "Kesshū no genten: Minzokugaku kara tsuiseki shita shochiiki kyōdōtai kōsei no paradaimu," in *Shisō no bōken: Shakai to henka no atarashii paradaimu,* ed. Tsurumi Kazuko and Ichii Saburō (Tokyo: Chikuma Shobō, 1979), esp. pp. 219–30. I present this material here because of its importance for our understanding of the religious context of pilgrimage and because of the contrast it offers to the sacred-profane dichotomy elaborated by Durkheim and others.

113. Fujitani, pp. 27–28.

114. Yano, p. 339.

115. Fujitani, pp. 80–81.

116. Nishigaki Seiji, p. 242.

117. Ibid., p. 243.

118. Faith in Maitreya (Japanese: Miroku) Buddha was long associated with social unrest and rebellion in Southeast Asia and China. In Japan, peasants since the turbulent Muromachi period expected Miroku's boat to land off the coast of Kashima. This vessel was supposed to be filled with rice which, when planted by thirteen *miko* (shrine maids), would bring about the age of eternal plenty, or Miroku's "world." Later, in the New Religions such as Fuji-kō, Ōmoto, Sekai-Kyūsei-kyō, and Sekai Mahikari Bunmei Kyōdan (Sūkyō Mahikari), faith in Maitreya was absorbed by messianic claims and apocalyptic visions. Under these new conditions the spirit of protest long implicit in the figure of the Future Buddha was transformed into an ethos supportive of traditional, feudalistic morality and hierarchical arrangements.

119. Miyata Noboru, "Nōson no fukkō undō to minshū shūkyō no tenkai," *Nihon rekishi 13* (Kinsei 5) (Tokyo: Iwanami Shoten, 1980), pp. 210–45.

120. See, for example, Stephen Vlastos, "*Yonaoshi* in Aizu" in Najita and Koschmann, op. cit., pp. 164–176.

121. Albert Camus, *The Rebel* (New York: Vintage, 1956), p. 56.

122. In 1889 the customary rebuiding of the Ise shrines took place. In the following year, which was the sixty-first anniversary of the okage-mairi of 1830, a pilgrimage was due to take place. The shrines therefore organized *kagura* dances and other special events. Many pilgrims made the trip using modern forms of transportation. Those coming from the Tokyo area could take the train as far as Nagoya. Others arrived by steamship. Although the steamship company offered free towels to their passengers, the traditional segyō was nowhere to be seen. While the number of pilgrims visiting the shrines that year was larger than in ordinary years, the massive migrations to Ise were already a legend from the past.

123. Norman (n. 106 above), p. 355, n. 54.

124. While faith in Maitreya was a common ingredient in peasant uprisings in China and Southeast Asia, in Japan it was often subordinated to loyalty to the feudal authorities and reverence for the emperor. A good illustration of this is the Maitreyan eschatology of the Fuji sect and its offshoots, the Fujidō and Maruyama-kyō movements. In the Genroku period, the fifth patriarch of the Fuji sect Gatsugyō Sōjū submitted a petition to the court asking the emperor to initiate the World of Maitreya. This apparently was to be a drastic change or metamorphosis (*furikawari*) during which "divine punishment would shake up the whole world." In 1789, a follower of the sect, a retainer by the name of Nagai Tokuzaemon, secluded himself on Mount Fuji and sent his wife with a petition to Matsudaira Sadanobu imploring the government to establish the World of Maitreya. In 1847, two disciples of Kotani Sanshi (1765–1841, a founder of the Fujidō sect), petitioned the Ōmetsuke to send Maitreya to help the frightened masses, citing as evidence of his (inevitable?) coming the decline of human character and heaven's mercy. Like other patriarchs, Itō Jikigyō (1671–1733) preached obedience to the feudal authorities and the emperor. Only in the Maruyama-kyō sect did popular unrest show itself directly. Perhaps the last truly popular, antiestablishment yonaoshi uprising took place in 1885 when Nishigaya Heishirō, a farmer in Shizuoka, led an antiwar movement among the followers of this sect. The founder of the Maruyama movement, Itō Rokurobee (1829–94), preached against conscription and the Sino-Japanese War (1894–95). His teaching about the coming "sunrise age of the pines" (*hi no de ni matsu no yo*) may have been inspired by the old yonaoshi faith. After his death the movement quickly declined. Those who remained gradually succumbed to the spirit of ultranationalism and emperor worship. See Yasumaru Yoshi and Hirota Masaki, " 'Yonaoshi' no ronri no keifu: Maruyama-kyō o

chūshin ni, Parts 1, 2," *Nihonshi kenkyū*, No. 85 (July 1966), pp. 1–25; No. 86 (September 1966), pp. 46–65.

Chapter 3.

1. While originally used to protect individuals from tear-gas, and to conceal their identity, face towels, together with the omnipresent helmets and staves, became a costume of protest that continues to be used in public demonstrations.

2. The word for these cudgels in Japanese is *gebabō*, a compound of the German term *Gewalt* (force) and the Japanese word *bō* (stick).

3. The radicals are often referred to euphemistically in Japanese as "problem posers" *(mondai teikisha)*.

4. Although the population of Japan increased by 12 percent between 1970 (104,665,171) and 1980 (117,060,396), membership in the Kyodan was down by 7 percent. [*Nihon Kirisutokyōdan Nenkan*. Tokyo: Nihon Kirisutokyōdan Sōmukyoku, 1968–1983 (foldouts); *Population of Japan*. Tokyo: Statistics Bureau, Prime Minister's Office, Vol. I, 1982, p. 2]. Between 1970 and 1977 the membership of the church dropped from 205,051 to 187,685, down 8 percent. After that, it grew slightly, reaching 191,971 in 1982, up 2 percent. Those regarded by the church as "active resident communicants" have declined from 94 percent of the membership in 1948 to about 50 percent in 1982. A somewhat more rapid decrease in their numbers was noted during the Kyodan struggle. This was followed by a modest recovery. *(Kyodan News Letter.* Tokyo: United Church of Christ in Japan, No. 133 (March 20, 1979), pp. 2–3). Average church attendance held steady from 1948 to 1968. Then it fell from 55,711 per Sunday to a low of 44,449 in 1974, down 20 percent. By 1982, however, attendance had nearly returned to its 1968 level: 55,149. Church school enrollments and attendance, which had been declining since 1948, fell still more rapidly during the first years of the controversy. Recent years have shown some improvement. The number of baptisms, which had been falling gradually since 1948, decreased from a total of 4,558 in 1970 to 2,654 in 1979, a drop of 40 percent for adults and 54 percent for children. Some of the decline in infant baptism may be due to a general decline in the birthrate which began in 1973 *(Kōsei-hakushō*. Tokyo: Kōsei-shō, pp. 544–545.) But the 24 percent increase in infant baptisms seen between 1979 and 1982 took place in spite of a birthrate that continued to decline.

5. Prof. Kitamori is the author of the well-known book, *The Theology of the Pain of God* (London: SCM Press, 1966).

6. Dohi Akio, *Purotesutanto kyōkai no seiritsu to tenkai*. Tokyo: Nihon Kirisutokyōdan Shuppankyoku, 1975 pp. 321, 329, 319.

7. One could compare the pavilion to the Narita airport which also became a symbol of the radicals' struggle against state power and capitalism in the 1970s. Narita was metaphorically reified by students and pictured as the "Narita within" *(uchinaru Narita)*, an evil spirit to be exorcized through the ritual of revolutionary self-criticism. Christian radicals urged the churches to "take up the Narita airport from the viewpoint of the Gospel."

8. This document was drawn up as a result of a visit to Japan by Dr. Martin Niemöller, who explained to the Japanese leaders the significance of the Stuttgart Confession, a document drawn up by the German church only five months after the end of the war. The Japanese Confession was a response to stinging criticism by Korean and Filipino participants in various Asian youth conferences held by the church. Another stimulus was the Japanese peace movement which caused a number of Christians to reflect on the role their church had played during the war.

9. For the complete English text of this and other "Documents of the United Church of Christ in Japan," see *The Japan Christian Quarterly,* XLV: 3, (Summer 1979), pp. 172–176.

10. I am making the distinction between causes and enablements not merely in order to extol the free will of sociological "agents" or the "subjects" of history, but to give expression to the "methodological humility" with which historians and sociologists should approach complex movements and events. By an "enablement" I do not mean a weak or soft cause. Unlike causes, "enablements" imply environments in which the relationship between actors and their surroundings is complex and "open," i.e., where there is room for surprises and maneuvering. Perhaps more important than so-called free will is the *looseness of situations* and the multiplicity of factors and hidden relationships at work at each moment. For example, in the history of religions, the development of a new technology (such as hunting, agriculture, or mechanics) does not "cause" new religions to appear. On the contrary, by opening up new possibilities (such as the symbologies of blood, bones, seeds, and machines) technology "enables" new ideas and images to take shape which may, *or may not,* gain acceptance. While the words *cause, impact, influence,* are nearly unavoidable from the point of view of style, they have unfortunate connotations derived from tired speculation on the collision of billiard balls or on the concept of mechanical causation. While direct causation is obviously indispensable in natural science and in the study of relatively simple socio-historical events, I find it insufficient for the kind of analysis I am undertaking here. For the distinction between positive and passive enablements see chapter 4.

11. Donald F. Wheeler, "Japan's Postmodern Student Movement," in *Changes in the Japanese University: A Comparative Perspective,* William K. Cummings, Ikuo Amano, and Kazuyuki Kitamura (eds.). New York: Praeger Publishers, 1979, p. 209.

12. See note 7.

13. Wheeler, op. cit., p. 207.

14. A combination of the Japanese word *uchi* (internal) and the German word *Gewalt* (force), *uchigeba* is slang for the fighting that has taken place between the Chūkaku-ha, the Kakumaru-ha, the Kuro-heri and other radical sects. The annual number of clashes ranged from two hundred to three hundred until 1975 when the figures finally began to taper off. In 1980, the total number of *uchigeba*-related deaths stood at eighty. See Murata Kiyoaki, "Savage Infighting: 'Uchigeba' Among Radical Groups Goes on Relentlessly," *The Japan Times* (7 November 1980), p. 16.

15. These themes were reflected in student manifestoes, handouts and other publications. They were also seen in graffiti painted on the walls of occupied buildings. The following are samples taken from the walls of Kwansei Gakuin University in Nishinomiya: "Utopia will consist of the everlasting handsome and beautiful, like us." "I live for love and revolution." "Deny life." "Blues are our poetry." "To die, to die, to die in the barricades." "It is not an ethical sense that drives me to struggle. Only the sense that I live is floating between the high sky and wide ocean *[sic]*." "I only hope that someone will play a burial melody which will be in harmony with continual tones of machine guns and the cries of a new strife and victory."

16. Some of these churches let students use their facilities as infirmaries and places of sanctuary. Younger pastors, recent university graduates themselves, were easily persuaded by the students that the real function of Japanese higher education was to crank out "pliant stooges" for the capitalist regime. Some of these pastors brought food to students manning the barricades and even conducted worship services for them.

17. These religious traditions often set up a contrast between Pure and Mundane Activity, the latter being the plodding, rehearsed, calculating, compromising, or "responsible" Activity of everyday life. For a general analysis of Pure Activity in Japanese culture see chapter 6.

18. See Fujita Ken, "Gakusei undō no Nihonteki tokusei to daigaku kaikaku ni tsuite, " *Kaihō*, No. 15, (March 1969) esp. pp. 53–54.

19. Kazuko Tsurumi, "Student Movements in 1960 and 1969: Continuity and Change," in Shun'ichi Takayanagi and Kimitada Miwa, eds., *Postwar Trends in Japan: Studies in Commemoration of Rev. Aloysius Miller,* S. J. Tokyo: Tokyo University Press, 1975, pp. 216–219.

20. See. J. Victor Koschmann, "The Debate on Subjectivity in Postwar Japan: Foundations of Modernism as a Political Critique," *Pacific Affairs*, 54: 4, (Winter 1981–1982), pp. 609–631.

21. Dohi, op. cit., p. 282.

22. Ibid., p. 327.

23. Koschmann, op. cit., p. 629.

24. Tsurumi, op. cit., p. 218.

25. Former TUTS president Ōki Hideo attacked the "radicalized" leadership of the church for its dependence on foreign support which he likens to "the foreign aid that propped up the Saigon government long after it had lost popular support." *The Japan Christian Quarterly,* XLV; 3 (Summer 1979) p. 189.

26. Kitamori Kazoh, "Kyū-ten-san Kyōjukai: Watakushi no sōkatsu ni kaete," *Fukuin to sekai* (September 1971), pp. 69–74.

27. Robert J. Smith, *Kurusu: The Price of Progress in a Japanese Village, 1951–1975.* Stanford: Stanford University Press, 1978 p. 231.

28. Ibid., p. 238.

29. Ibid., p. 233.

30. Ibid., p. 246.

31. Ibid., p. 239.

32. *Jōmin no seijigaku.* Tokyo: Dentō to Gendaisha, 1972, pp. 5–8.

33. I am indebted to Prof. Nakane Chie for the concept of "scripts."

34. In Japanese, this is called *nemawashi* after the practice of "binding the roots" of plants before they are transplanted.

35. In this respect, folk democracy is closer to the "soft rule" of the emperors and aristocrats of ancient Japan than to the "hard rule" of the military dictators of medieval and modern times.

36. Tsurumi, op. cit., p. 217.

37. From the point of view of the history of religions, one might argue that the only shutaisei produced by the Japanese tradition was that of the shaman. I suspect that this is why western scholars so often feel that Nichiren and other religious leaders look like "real individuals" or "prophets."

38. Others sheepishly returned to the more comfortable life of the university or seminary. A number of students, emotionally burned out by the struggle, or unable to get letters of recommendation from their teachers, dropped out of sight, and, to this day, continue to do menial work here and there.

39. Peter L. Berger, *Invitation to Sociology.* Garden City, N. Y.: Doubleday Books, 1963, p. 23.

40. One senses a deep moralism running through the politics of both sides. Many vote Socialist simply because they oppose the "money politics" of the Liberal Democrats. While conservative pastors seldom preach on social issues, sermons by radicals can hardly be called political harangues.

41. By 1980, the Kyodan was able to support about 25 percent of its 245 Western missionaries with Japanese funds. Most of these missionaries seem to be young "missionary associates" working in Japan as language teachers. Nearly one-third of the support for the remaining missionaries also comes from Japan. Some assistance for theological education and religious broadcasting continues to come from abroad. [*Kyodan News Letter.* Tokyo: United Church of Christ in Japan, No. 151 (20 January 1981) p. 5.]

42. Ōki Hideo, "Reflections on the Kyodan Problem," *The Japan Christian Quarterly,* op. cit., p. 169. Ōki himself was one of the drafters of the Kyodan's "Fundamental Policy for Social Action," which states that "the social action of a church, as a fulfillment of the church's social responsibility, includes the whole realm of social practice and social welfare work"—hardly the words of a reactionary. Ibid., p. 174.

43. In retrospect, one wonders how new or radical the students' tactics were. Was their prophetic wrath not basically similar to the symbolic violence Japanese rebels traditionally had used to block unpopular decisions? Was their inarticulate effervescence so different from the irrational spontaneity of the anarchists of the past?

44. Public debate, as we know it, was introduced in Japan only in the late nineteenth century by Fukuzawa Yukichi. Before that, discussions of policy had taken place only in private between rulers and their advisors, or in the carefully orchestrated scenarios of folk democracy. Debate itself presupposes a kind of public space that simply did not exist in Japan until modern times, that of the agora, forum, or parliament.

45. Suzuki himself was by no means universally admired—a common complaint being that he handled such problems as the Confession of War Responsibility "like a dictator or a Methodist bishop!"

46. An almost identical bifurcation can be seen in politically active mainline denominations in North America and Europe. From a structural point of view, this allows religious institutions to speak out on public issues in spite of their own internal differences. But from a practical standpoint, it means that ecclesiastical pronouncements generally mean very little indeed, except, of course, to the ecclesiocrats who are pleased to make them.

47. *The Japan Christian Quarterly,* op. cit., p. 189.

48. Phillips, op. cit., pp. 32–33.

49. By *heterogeneous* I refer to the social, theological, and ideological differences between the individuals and families making up a church. Internal heterogeneity within "the body of Christ" is probably the single most important reason why "mainstream denominations" usually must keep silent on major social and economic issues, and why, when they do speak out, they usually do so with great caution.

Chapter 4.

1. *Sources of Japanese Tradition,* edited by Ryusaku Tsunoda et al. New York: Columbia University Press, 1958, Vol. I, pp. 51 and 50.

2. Max Weber, *The Protestant Ethic and the Spirit of Capitalism,* translated by Talcott Parsons. New York: Scribner, 1958, p. 26.

3. *Scholarship and Partisanship: Essays on Max Weber,* edited by Reinhard Bendix and Guenther Roth. Berkeley: University of California Press, 1980, p. 114.

4. Weber, op. cit., p. 41.

5. Max Weber, *The Religion of China: Confucianism and Taoism,* translated and edited by Hans H. Gerth. New York: Free Press, 1951, p. 248.

6. Herbert Marcuse, *Negations: Essays in Critical Theory,* translated by Jeremy J. Shapiro. Boston: Beacon Press, 1969, p. 226.

7. Weber, *The Protestant Ethic,* op. cit., p. 13.

8. Ibid., p. 91.

9. For the concept of "cost of information," which I believe is valuable for unpacking Weber's idea of credit-worthiness, see Richard A. Posner, *The Economics of Justice.* Cambridge, Mass.: Harvard University Press, 1981.

10. Joseph A. Schumpeter, *Capitalism, Socialism and Democracy.* New York: Harper and Row, 1962, p. 84.

11. Ibid., p. 143.

12. Winston Davis, *Dojo: Magic and Exocism in Modern Japan.* Stanford: Stanford University Press, 1980, p. 299.

13. Max Weber, *Ancient Judaism,* translated and edited by Hans H. Gerth and Don Martindale. New York: Free Press, 1952, p. 223. My emphasis.

14. Max Weber, *Economy and Society: An Outline of Interpretive Sociology,* edited by Guenther Roth and Claus Wittlich. New York: Bedminster Press, 1968, Vol. 2, pp. 636–37.

15. On the role of fate in sociology, see Peter L. Berger, *The Sacred Canopy.* Garden City, N.Y.: Doubleday, 1967, p. 86.

16. See Chapter 7 below, and my *Dojo:,* op. cit., pp. 291–302.

17. Keith Thomas, *Religion and the Decline of Magic.* New York: Scribner, 1971, pp. 656–68. For a comparison of the decline of magic in England and Japan, see chapter 7, pp. 248–249.

18. Ibid., p. 657.

19. Jacob Viner, *Religious Thought and Economic Society: Four Chapters of an Unfinished Work,* edited by Jacques Melitz and Donald Winch. Durham, N.C.: Duke University Press, 1978, p. 36. My emphasis.

20. By religion, in this case, I mean the use of sacred symbols, rewards, and punishments to restrict greed and the spread of impersonal market values. Western examples of religious restraints range from attacks on urbanization and commerce by the biblical prophets to the teachings of the medieval church on usury. By magic, I have in mind cases, such as the "pauper's curse," that serve to enforce the (marginal) distribution of wealth. By traditional law, morality, and philosophy I am thinking of the formal and informal teachings that make market values subordinate to social ones (e.g., the medieval dictum: *homo mercator vix aut numquam potest Deo placere*—the merchant can seldom, if ever, please God). By taboos, I mean the limitation of commerce to certain classes or castes, rules limiting the hours of trade or the space allotted to the market, etc. By the folk tradition, I have in mind the countless tales of poetic justice in which the greedy get their comeuppance and the generous their just reward. (Japanese folklore seems especially rich in ethical material of this sort). Most traditional societies probably shared Durkheim's view that economic activity is a centrifugal force, religion a countervailing, centripetal one. (See Emile Durkhiem, *The Elementary Forms of the Religious Life,* translated by Joseph Ward Swain. New York: Free Press, 1965, pp. 245–55). Thus, it is significant that almost no one has seriously argued that the teachings of any of the world religions in their early or classical forms led directly to the growth of capitalism. All theories seem to posit some kind of *mutation* in religion before it becomes a force behind economic development: Christianity must turn into Calvinism. Buddhism must assume its Mahayana form, and Confucianism must be Japanized. Thus, the defensive function of the social teachings and practices of traditional religion seems indisputable.

21. Karl Polanyi, *The Great Transformation.* Boston: Beacon Press, 1942, pp. 61–62.

22. *Sermons and Society: An Anglican Anthology,* edited by Paul A. Welsby. Middlesex: Penguin Books, 1970, p. 19. My emphasis.

23. R. H. Tawney, *Religion and the Rise of Capitalism.* Harmondsworth: Penguin Books, 1980, p. 188.

24. Ibid., p. 189.

25. See Liston Pope, *Millhands and Preachers: A Study of Gastonia.* New Haven, Conn.: Yale University Press, 1942, and also John R. Darle, Dean D. Knudsen, and Donald W. Shriver, Jr., *Spindles and Spires: A Re-Study of Religion and Social Change in Gastonia.* Atlanta: John Knox Press, 1976.

26. Roy Hofheinz, Jr. and Kent E. Calder, *The Eastasia Edge.* New York: Basic Books, 1982, viii.

27. Ibid., p. 43.

28. That Confucianism is not mere morality, but a form of "moralism" is of great importance when we consider its putative impact on development. I mean by moralism *morality based on the fallacy of composition.* Whether taught by Confucius or by Billy Graham, moralism reduces complex social problems to the simpler level of individual moral conduct, teaching that social conditions can be improved only by converting all (or most) of the individual members of society to a proper moral (or religious) life. In other words, moralism assumes that the problems of society are simply the quantitative aggregation of individual moral issues. It recognizes no *qualitative* change in moral issues as one moves from individuals to complex organizations. Because it believes social ills can be remedied only by the moral or spiritual cultivation of individuals, moralism tends to be indifferent to "structural evils" and often counsels patience in the face of institutional injustice and exploitation. Under the right circumstances, moralism—which is pervasive in *both* Protestant and Japanese sects—can easily become a "passive enablement" of development.

29. Hofheinz and Calder, op. cit., p. 121.

30. Michio Morishima, *Why Has Japan "Succeeded"?: Western Technology and the Japanese Ethos.* Cambridge: Cambridge University Press, 1982, p. 201. My emphasis.

31. Ibid., p. 199.

32. Ibid., p. 43. My emphasis.

33. Joseph J. Spengler, *Origins of Economic Thought and Justice.* Carbondale, Ill.: Southern Illinois University Press, 1980, p. 51.

34. Cited in ibid., p. 58.

35. Wing-Tsit Chan, *A Source Book in Chinese Philosophy.* Princeton: Princeton University Press, 1963, p. 94.

36. Louis Dumont, "A Modified View of Our Origins: The Christian Beginnings of Modern Individualism," *Religion* (1982), Vol. 12: 1–27.

37. *Analects* 4:15. My emphasis.

38. Max Weber, *The Religion of India: The Sociology of Hinduism and Buddhism,* translated and edited by Hans H. Gerth and Don Martindale. New York: Free Press, 1958, p. 275.

39. Weber, *The Religion of China,* op. cit., p. 100. My emphasis.

40. Ibid., p. 95.

41. Ibid., p. 97.

42. Ibid., p. 102.

43. Ibid., p. 149.

44. Weber, *The Religion of India,* op. cit., p. 38.

45. Weber, *The Religion of China,* op. cit., p. 163.

46. Ibid., p. 228.

47. Weber, *The Protestant Ethic. . .* op. cit., p. 91.

48. Weber, *The Religion of China,* op. cit., p. 187.

49. Ibid., p. 225.

50. Ibid., p. 244.

51. *Analects* 18:6.

52. Albert Craig, "Science and Confucianism in Tokugawa Japan," in *Changing Japanese Attitudes toward Modernization,* edited by Marius B. Jansen. Princeton: Princeton University Press, pp. 130–60.

53. See Charles E. Lindblom, *Politics and Markets: The World's Political-Economic System.* New York: Basic Books, 1977, p. 13. Nearly all proposals for the reform of the Japanese economy during the Tokugawa period called for intervention by the state.

54. Morishima, *Why Has Japan "Succeeded"?,* op. cit., p. 200.

55. Ibid., p. 120.

56. Ibid., p. 115.

57. Charles David Sheldon, *The Rise of the Merchant Class in Tokugawa Japan, 1600–1868.* New York: Russell & Russell, 1973, p. 140.

58. Thomas C. Smith, *The Agrarian Origins of Modern Japan.* New York: Atheneum, 1966, p. 148.

59. For more information on the *miyaza* see chapter 1 in general, and, for further bibliography, note 11 in the same chapter.

60. For the importance of an active "participant citizenry" in the modernization of society see Alex Inkeles and David Horton Smith, *Becoming Modern: Individual Change in Six Developing Countries.* Cambridge, Mass.: Harvard University Press, 1974.

61. Melford E. Spiro, *Buddhism and Society: A Great Tradition and Its Burmese Vicissitudes.* Berkeley: University of California Press, 1982 (2nd ed).

62. Viner, op. cit., p. 163 and p. 169.

63. See chapter 1.

64. As important as the spirit of toleration has been, it would be impossible to measure its total impact and folly to regard it as a major or necessary factor in development. As Weber himself noted, all of Asia "was, and remains, in principle, the land of the free competition of religions, 'tolerant' somewhat in the sense of late antiquity." *The Religion of India,* op. cit., p. 329.

65. Tenshō-Kōtai-Jingū-Kyō, *The Prophet of Tabuse.* Tabuse, Japan: Nakamoto, 1954, p. 55 and p. 20.

66. Ibid., p. 154.

67. Ibid., p. 108.

68. Ibid., p. 115.

69. Tenshō-Kōtai-Jingū-Kyō, *Divine Manifestation.* Tabuse, Japan: Nakamoto, 1970, p. 134.

70. Ibid., p. 136.

71. Ibid., p. 135.

72. *The Prophet of Tabuse,* op. cit., p. 153.

73. Religious founders like Taniguchi Masaharu of the House of Growth (Seichō no Ie), who stood in the forefront of ultranationalism during the war, did a sudden about-face in 1945, presenting themselves as messengers of world peace. The theological ambiguity of these groups and their indifference to common logic (the "morality of thought") gave them a flexibility that enabled them to go along with "development" of all sorts.

74. See my *Dojo,* op. cit., pp. 298–302.

75. Weber, *Economy and Society,* op. cit., Vol. 1, p. 424 and *The Religion of India,* op. cit., p. 336.

76. Davis, *Dojo,* op. cit., p. 84.

77. The Rule of the Three Obediences, which can be traced back to India, held that, as a child, a woman must obey her parents; after marriage, her husband; and, after her husband's death, her own children.

78. The social teachings of Japan's vernacular religions often combine egalitarian dreams with an absolute respect for authority. For example, Deguchi Nao (1836–1918), foundress of the Ōmoto sect, proclaimed that someday the "World shall be equal all over." But she also taught that "everyone should be obedient to (the person) whom he should obey." Oomoto, *Ofudesaki: The Holy Scriptures of Oomoto.* Kameoka, Japan: Oomoto, 1974, p. 8 and p. 70.

79. The Fuji sect was banned in 1849 when it called for government reforms. Under the influence of the samurai, Shibata Shōgyō (1809–90), a related

movement called the Practice Sect appeared giving greater emphasis to nationalism and loyalty to the emperor. Shibata and his followers regarded Mount Fuji as the palladium of the nation, and even the "brain of the planet." After the Meiji period, this sect became closely aligned with State Shinto. The Maruyama sect, a branch supported by middle- and lower-level peasants in Kanagawa, Shizuoka, and Nagano, became actively involved in protests against the Sino-Japanese war. This antiwar activity came to a halt after the death of its founder, Itō Rokurobei. After this, the sect's social outlook was overcome by the growing spirit of nationalism. The Fuji sect is, therefore, a good example of the way in which vernacular religious movements (even eschatological ones) were coopted by the imperial system. It also illustrates the close connection between some versions of the traditional "work ethic" and nationalism.

80. *Divine Manifestation,* op. cit., p. 143.

81. *The Prophet of Tabuse,* op. cit., p. 113.

82. *Divine Manifestation,* p. 142.

83. Ibid., p. 136.

84. By 'civil religion' I mean to imply, as I did in chapter 1, a "network of moods, values, thoughts, rituals, and symbols that establishes the meaning of nationhood within an overarching hierarchy of significance. While civil religions are the precipitates of traditional religious communities, they transcend specific religious communities and dogmas. The symbols and suasions of the civil religion must speak to 'all sorts and conditions of men.' 'Civil theology,' on the other hand, is the articulation of civil religion by the elite. One could say that civil religion—a reticulation of implicit sentiments—is 'thought in.' Civil theology is 'thought out.' " Winston Davis, "The Civil Theology of Inoue Tetsujirō," *Japanese Journal of Religious Studies,* (March 1976), Vol. 3, No. 1, p. 6, n. 3.

85. Byron K. Marshall, *Capitalism and Nationalism in Prewar Japan: The Ideology of the Business Elite, 1868–1941.* Stanford: Stanford University Press, 1967, p. 117.

86. *Global Economics and Religion,* edited by James Finn. New Brunswick, N.J.: Transaction Books, 1983, p. 55, p. 135, and p. 202.

87. Marshall, op. cit., p. 4.

88. The term "business ideology" is used by Byron K. Marshall, op. cit. For a discussion of the "superordinate goals" of Japanese business, see Richard Tanner Pascale and Anthony G. Athos, *The Art of Japanese Management.* New York: Simon and Schuster, 1981, pp. 177–206.

89. See Thomas P. Rohlen, *For Harmony and Strength: Japanese White-Collar Organization in Anthropological Perspective.* Berkeley: University of California Press, 1974, pp. 34–61.

90. Weber, *The Religion of China,* op. cit., p. 237 and p. 85.

91. Mikiso Hane, *Peasants, Rebels and Outcastes.* New York: Pantheon, 1982.

92. In contrast to the American problem of child abuse, in Japan it seems to be the children who usually are the "aggressors," bludgeoning parents to death in their sleep, attacking teachers, destroying school property, and so on.

93. Two books by Okonogi Keigo (discussed in chapter 8) are good examples of this trend: *Moratoriamu ningen no jidai* (The Age of Moratorium Man) (Tokyo: Chūōkōronsha, 1978) and *Moratoriamu ningen no shinri kōzō* (The Psychological Structures of Moratorium Man) (Tokyo: Chūōkōronsha, 1979).

94. See Satoshi Kamata, *Japan in the Passing Lane: An Insider's Account of Life in a Japanese Auto Factory,* translated and edited by Tatsuru Akimoto. New York: Pantheon, 1983 and Jon Woronoff, *Japan's Wasted Workers.* Totowa, N.J.: Allanheld, Osmun, 1983.

95. For example, Sūkyō Mahikari, one of Japan's New Religions, predicts that in the twenty-first century, humankind will once again be ruled by the Japanese emperors, just as it was when the world was young. When the "Civilization of the Kingdom of God" is finally revealed, the humble folk who have joined the Mahikari sect will become the emperor's ruling elite. Thus, to quote the scriptures of another eschatological sect, "the first shall be last, and the last shall be first." See Winston Davis, *Dojo,* op. cit., passim.

Chapter 5.

1. Byron K. Marshall, *Capitalism and Nationalism in Prewar Japan: The Ideology of the Business Elite, 1868–1941.* Stanford: Stanford University Press, 1967, p. 35.

2. *The Japan Times* (7 December 1981), p. 8.

3. *The East,* Vol. 11, No. 3, (April 1975), p. 28.

4. British historians and sociologists like E. P. Thompson (*The Making of the English Working Class* [New York: Vintage, 1966]); and Robert Moore (*Pitmen, Preachers and Politics: The Effects of Methodism in a Durham Mining Community* [Cambridge: Cambridge University Press, 1974]) have moved away from Weber's preoccupation with the Puritans and give more attention to the economic rôle of Dissent and Nonconformity in the Industrial Revolution itself.

5. Recent examples of the treatment of religion as a passive enablement of economic development include Bernard Groethuysen, *The Bourgeois: Catholicism versus Capitalism in Eighteenth Century France* (New York: Holt,

Rinehart & Winston, 1968); and Jean Delumeau, *Le Catholicisme entre Luther et Voltaire* (Paris: Presses Universitaire de France, 1971). My emphasis on passive enablements should not be construed as an absolute denial of the positive role sometimes played by "this-worldly asceticism" in economic development. Religion, in my view, may simultaneously contribute to development actively (e.g., through the this-worldly asceticism of its values) and passively (e.g., by retiring from its role as the institutional guardian of the community and social order). I emphasize passive enablements simply in order to encourage a sense of historical balance and perspective.

6. I have in mind here the discussion of embedded economies in chapter 4, symbolized by figure 3 (p. 122). To review: an embedded economy is one in which the ultimate economic goal is not the "profit maximization" of "acquisitive individuals," but the well-being of kith, kin, and, in many cases, the religious community.

7. *Miraculous Stories from the Japanese Buddhist Tradition: The Nihon Ryōiki of the Monk Kyōkai.* Cambridge: Harvard University Press, 1973, pp. 257–59.

8. *Sources of Indian Tradition*, edited by Wm. Theodore De Bary. New York: Columbia University Press, 1958, Vol. 1, p. 122.

9. See the "disembedding" scenario described in chapter 4 and summarized in figure 4, p. 123.

10. These concepts were elaborated by Confucian and Buddhist thinkers alike. While Confucians conceived of *on* in relation to concrete hierarchical relationships, Mahayana Buddhists linked them to concepts in their own philosophical repertoire, e.g., to karma, the ontological unity of self and others (*jita funi*), and the bodhisattva ideal. The concepts of *on* and *hō-on* were of vital importance to all Japanese religious founders from Kūkai to Nichiren. In the Tokugawa period, Confucian connotations began to permeate Buddhist thought about *on*. See Naitō Tatsu, "Bukkyō no hō-on setsu ni tsuite," in *Indogaku/Bukkyōgaku Kenkyū*, Vol. 4 (January 1955).

11. While the duties owed to the parents and the sovereign are always mentioned, some lists of the Four Duties include the individual's obligation to his master or friends and the monk's obligation to lay patrons. The *Heike Monogatari* even lists one's obligation to heaven and earth.

12. Because virtue was conceived as a response to benefits already received, the morality of *on* was completely antithetical to the western idea of rights. From the point of view of traditional Buddhist morality, talk about rights outside of the context of complementary moral exchanges was regarded as the epitome of selfishness. The ethic of benefits and their return was therefore easily coopted by the ideology of the Meiji bureaucrats, which focused on duty to the emperor, the family, and the "family-state."

13. Robert Bellah, *Tokugawa Religion: The Values of Pre-Industrial Japan* (Boston: Beacon, 1957), p. 5. Since Bellah's book was written before Japan's postwar economic nationalism was in full view, his perception of the centrality of the country's political values was especially prescient.

14. Republication of the writings of these thinkers in the Meiji period made their conservative work ethic a vital force in the period of industrialization itself.

15. See Kashiwahara Yūsen, "Bakumatsu ni okeru 'Myōkōnin-den' henshū no imi," *Indogaku/Bukkyōgaku Kenkyū* 6 (1958): 277–80.

16. Nakamura Hajime, *Nihon shūkyō no kindaisei* (Tōkyō: Shunjūsha, 1964), p. 193.

17. Ibid., p. 194.

18. The self-interest of the priestly editor is pathetically obvious in such tales.

19. Ikeda Eishun, *Meiji no shin Bukkyō undō* (Tōkyō: Yoshikawa Kobunkan, 1976), p. 32 ff.

20. See Martin Collcutt, "Buddhism: The Threat of Eradication," in *Japan in Transition: From Tokugawa to Meiji*, ed. Marius B. Jansen and Gilbert Rozman (Princeton, N.J.: Princeton University Press, 1986), p. 162, table 6.1; and Mikiso Hane, *Modern Japan: A Historical Survey* (Boulder, Colo., and London: Westview Press, 1986), p. 108.

21. The Three Teachings included 1. precepts (*kai*), 2. concentration (*jo*), and 3. wisdom (*e*). Emphasis was laid on such important platitudes as "doing good and not evil," "calming the heart," "clearing away worldly thoughts and excessive desires," and "seeking for the truth in all things."

22. For the concept of "plausibility structures," see Peter Berger, *The Sacred Canopy: Elements of a Sociology of Religion* (New York: Doubleday, 1967), passim. Plausibility structures include theodicy (symbolic systems that provide consolation in the face of excessive misfortune) and legitimation (symbolic systems that justify an excess of power or wealth).

23. The anti-Christian prejudice of Meiji Buddhists seems to have been rooted not only in their fear of religious rivalry but also in the nativism of the late Tokugawa period. Thus haja-kenshō probably had its origin in the feelings expressed by the earlier political slogan, "honor the emperor, expel the barbarians" (*sonnō-jōi*).

24. Talcott Parsons, "Religion in a Modern Pluralistic Society," *Review of Religious Research* 7 (Spring 1966): 125–45.

25. The only members of the Meiji Six Society (*Meirokusha*, an archetypal Enlightenment group) not to hold public office were Fukuzawa Yukichi and Mitsukuri Shūhei.

26. A helpful account of his life in English is "The Life of Manshi Kiyozawa," in *December Fan: The Buddhist Essays of Manshi Kiyozawa*, trans. Nobuo Haneda (Kyōto: Higashi Honganji, 1984), pp. 77–90.

27. See Kashiwahara Yūsen, *Nihon kinsei, kindai Bukkyōshi no Kenkyū* (Kyōto: Heirakuji Shoten, 1969), pp. 400–424.

28. Haneda, trans., p. 24.

29. Nakamura Hajime et al., eds., *Ajia Bukkyōshi (Nihonhen VII: Kindai Bukkyō)* Tōkyō: Kōsei Shuppansha, 1972), pp. 278–79.

30. See chapter 6, pp. 212–221.

31. Haneda, trans., p. 3.

32. Ibid., p. 18.

33. See J. Victor Koschmann, "The Debate on Subjectivity in Postwar Japan: Foundations of Modernism as a Political Critique," *Pacific Affairs* 54 (Winter 1981–82): 609–31.

34. Akamatsu Tesshin, "Kindai Nihon shisōshi ni okeru Seishinshugi no risō: Kiyozawa Manshi no shinkō to sono kansei," in *Bukkyōshigaku ronshū*, ed. Chiba Hakeshi, Kanreki Kinen Kai (Kyōto: Nagata Bunshōdō, 1977), pp. 225–26.

35. Fukushima Hirokata, "Teikokushugi seiritsuki no Bukkyō: 'Seishinshugi' to 'Shin Bukkyō' to" in Chiba Hakeshi, Kanreki Kinen Kai, ed., p. 486.

36. The most obvious examples of this are Ittōen (discussed in the next chapter) and Itō Shōshin's Muga-Ai (Selfless Love Community).

37. In 1899 this group was reorganized as the Fellowship of Reformed (literally, "Pure") Buddhists (Bukkyō Seito Dōshikai) under the leadership of Sakaino Kōyō, Watanabe Kaigyoku, Tanaka Jiroku, and Takashima Beihō. In 1903, it was reorganized once again as the New Fellowship of Reformed Buddhists.

38. Yoshida Kyūichi, *Nihon no kindai shakai to Bukkyō* (Tōkyō: Heibonsha, 1970), pp. 165–66.

39. Nakamura et al., eds. (n. 29 above), p. 272, citing *Shin Bukkyō*, vol. 6, no. 10.

40. Tetsugakkan (later, Tōyō University) was founded by Inoue Enryō in 1887. In 1902, Kumamoto Aritaka, inspector of schools from the Ministry of Education, found that the students of Nakajima Tokuzo had been using as their textbook *Elements of Ethics* (New York: Charles Scribner's Sons, 1892) written by the British philosopher John Henry Muirhead. The ministry concluded from this that Nakajima's students were insufficiently prepared for their graduation

examinations and that the school's ethical instruction did not correspond to the national essence. The attack on Tetsugakkan by the ministry created an uproar throughout the Japanese academic world. Many New Buddhists graduated from this school.

41. Yoshida, p. 189. Among the ideals of the Hōtoku Society was that the rich and the poor should mutually "give way" (*suijō*) to one another.

42. Ibid., pp. 196–97.

43. In 1910, Miyashita Takichi and other radical socialists schemed to assassinate the emperor. Using this as an excuse to attack left-wing activists, the police arrested large numbers of socialists and communists before the plot could be carried out. In the following year, twelve were executed, including Kōtoku Shūsui, who was completely innocent; others were sentenced to life in prison. The incident was the prelude to the repression of the political left.

44. Yoshida (n. 38 above), p. 205.

45. His attack on rice taxes was inspired by the Zen teaching "he who does not work shall go hungry" (*fukō donshoku*).

46. Quoted in Kashiwahara, *Nihon Kinsei, Kindai Bukkyōshi no kenkyū* (n. 27 above), p. 435.

47. Kashiwahara Yūsen, "Kindai Bukkyō ni okeru shakai dōtokukan no seiritsu," in *Bukkyō to seiji, keizai,* ed. Nihon Bukkyōgakkai (Kyōto: Heirakuji Shoten, 1972), pp. 297–300.

48. Yoshida, p. 220.

49. Ibid., pp. 56–57.

50. Kashiwahara, "Kindai Bukkyō ni okeru shakai dōtokukan no seiritsu," p. 304.

51. Yoshida (n. 38 above), p. 149.

52. "Kōjō fukyō zettai hantai," cited in Yoshimuro Keijō, *Nihon Bukkyōshi* (Kyōto: Hōzōkan, 1969), p. 418.

53. Yoshida, p. 83.

54. Shimaji called for the spread of systematic charitable work and the adoption of techniques developed by the Vincent de Paul movement in the Roman Catholic Church.

55. Max Weber, *The Religion of China: Confucianism and Taoism* (New York: Free Press, 1951), p. 248.

56. See Jacob Viner, *Religious Thought and Economic Society* (Durham, N.C.: Duke University Press, 1978), pp. 165–76.

57. Carol Gluck, *Japan's Modern Myths: Ideology in the Late Meiji Period* (Princeton, N.J.: Princeton University Press, 1985), pp. 50–57.

58. For Max Weber on Buddhism, see *The Religion of India: The Sociology of Hinduism and Buddhism* (New York: Free Press, 1958), pp. 204–90. "Moody" is something Buddhism has never been except in its aristocratic, literary manifestations. Buddhism regards moods as emotional obstacles to enlightenment.

59. See chapter 6.

60. This does not mean that on occasion strategically situated religions will not stand at the forefront of innovation.

61. See for example, Smith's *The Theory of Moral Sentiments* (edited by D. D. Raphael and A. L. Macfie. Indianapolis: Liberty Classics, 1976), pp. 85–86.

62. Richard Helmstadter, "The Nonconformist Conscience," in *The Conscience of the Victorian State*, ed. Peter Marsh (Syracuse, N.Y.: Harvester Press, 1979), pp. 135–72.

63. See Byron K. Marshall, op. cit., (note 1 of this chapter).

64. Cited in ibid., p. 58. Soeda's words sound remarkably like the Seventeen Article Constitution of the early seventh century.

65. Although the Pure Land sects and the New Religions appealed to the lower classes and outcastes, Japanese religions generally did not develop the class-consciousness that beset the churches and the sects of Great Britain. When they did, the effect was muted.

66. See K. S. Inglis, *Churches and the Working Classes in Victorian England* (London: Routledge and Kegan Paul, 1963); J. F. C. Harrison, *The Common People of Great Britain* (Bloomington: Indiana University Press, 1985), pp. 211–347; Hugh McLeod, "The Dechristianization of the Working Class in Western Europe (1850–1900)," *Social Compass* 27 (1980): 191–214.

67. See Ronald Dore, *Taking Japan Seriously: A Confucian Perspective on leading Economic Issues* (Stanford, Calif.: Stanford University Press, 1987), passim.

Chapter 6.

1. The *dramatis personae* of Ittōen include: 1. *dōnin,* i.e., members, faithful and lax; 2. *tōbans,* the leaders of the community; 3. the stalwart, i.e., the orthodox and orthoprax *dōnin;* 4. retreatants, people who are not *dōnin,* but are

making a private retreat in the community; and 4. participants, those taking part in one of the monthly training sessions held for outsiders.

2. Nishida Tenkō, *Jiyū no seikatsu: Ittōen seikatsu gojūnen no kaiko* (A spontaneous life: reflections after fifty years of the Ittōen life) (Kyoto: Ittōen Shuppanbu, 1959), pp. 4–5 (hereafter cited as *JS*).

3. The four cardinal virtues extolled by Ninomiya were: 1. diligence (*kinben*), 2. thrift (*setsuyaku*), 3. learning the limits of one's talents and living accordingly (*bundo*); and 4. giving away (*suijō*)— a transpersonal and transgenerational form of asceticism the object of which is the well-being of one's family, friends, village, and nation. Of these, *suijō* was the most difficult for Tenkō san to achieve. In fact, until he "threw himself away," he was unable to put it into practice at all (see his *Sange no seikatsu* (The life of repentance) (Tokyo: Shunjūsha, 1971), pp. 77–78 [hereafter cited as *SS*]). It is significant that Tenkō san's image of Ninomiya was essentially the ideological version of his life promoted by the Meiji regime (see Naramoto Tatsuya, *Ninomiya Sontoku* [Tokyo: Iwanami Shoten, 1971], pp. 145–52.

4. *SS*, p. 83.

5. Ibid., p. 85.

6. Ibid., pp. 86–87. The obvious religious symbolism of these experiences will be discussed below; italics added.

7. *SS*, p. 88.

8. Ibid., p. 89. This is a reference to Christ's words in John 16:33.

9. Literally, "inactive activity" or the "activity of being idle." In Chinese Taoism, this is *wu-wei* (nonactivity) (see below).

10. *SS*, p. 89.

11. *Takuhatsu,* a word used for the begging of monks (according to strict rules) in Buddhism since the Sung period, continues to be practiced today in Japan where one occasionally sees a group of monks going out on a mendicant expedition (*shūdan takuhatsu*).

12. *Roku* (six) refers to the six paths to enlightenment in the Zen sect: alms giving, keeping the Buddhist precepts, perservance, practice, equanimity, and attaining wisdom. *Man* (ten thousand) refers to Tenkō san's hope that in ten years' time he would be able to clean ten thousand toilets throughout Japan as a means to world peace and self-negation. (He hoped to visit five homes each day which would amount to one thousand toilets cleaned per year if he went out two hundred days out of the year). Ittōen's mass toilet-cleaning expedition became the most famous, or infamous, feature of the community.

13. Official translation from the pamphlet "Guide to Kōsenrin (Ittōen Village)" (no publication data).

14. Japanese: *Sange no seikatsu.* A partial translation of this book is Ittōen Tenko-san, *A New Road to Ancient Truth,* trans. Makoto Ohashi in collaboration with Marie Beuzeville Byles (London: George Allen & Unwin, 1969).

15. *Junshaku:* another Buddhist term.

16. Mizutsu Hikō, *Nihon no yūtopia (Japan's utopias) (Tokyo:* Taihei Shuppansha, 1973), p. 67.

17. According to one youth who has now left the village, the Ittōen school system discourages independence and initiative, aiming, rather, at the creation of a docile communitarian personality.

18. The word *tōban* is often used for offices which rotate (Japanese: *rinbansei*). Shinto priests in the countryside were often called "toban" (or *tōya* or *kannushi*). During the war the word sometimes had more authoritarian connotations.

19. The Chinese characters for this word could be roughly translated as "Alpha" and "Omega."

20. Of even more importance to Ittōen was the way the bodhisattvas in this sutra provide Vimalikīrti (Yuima) with all his needs—with boundless food and shelter. Because of the bountifulness of this heavenly gift, in Vimalikīrti's world there is no "competition" (*sōdatsu*) (*SS,* p. 15).

21. A reference to Shinran Shōnin (1173–1262).

22. Official Ittōen translation.

23. Mizutsu, p. 66. Tenkō san believed that knowledge, as well as power and money, leads to *ikizumari* (SS, p. 91).

24. Harakawa Yoshio, *Tōsō naki keizai seikatsu: Ittōen no keizai o kataru* (Economic life without conflict: a discussion of Ittōen's economics) (Kyoto: Ittōen Shuppanbu, 1966), p. 4.

25. The opposite interpretation could also be given to this act. That is, one might also show *respect* for the emperor by dropping the character from his name. As is often the case in Japan, protest is rendered safe by wrapping itself in obscure symbolic gestures.

26. Mizutsu, p. 79.

27. Part of the moral legitimation of leadership in Japan is the idea that the founder of an institution suffered in order to bring it into existence. The sacred ancestors of the family, industrial entrepreneurs and emperors alike, are thought to have suffered in order to bestow upon the people the "blessings" they now enjoy.

28. *JS,* p. 79.

29. Nishida Tenkō, *Selflessness: Selected Sayings of Tenko Nishida*, bilingual ed. (Kyoto: Ittōen, 1958), p. 11.

30. *SS*, p. 82.

31. *Selflessness*, pp. 14–15.

32. See Mizutsu, p. 64. The idea of *sange*, while translated as "repentance," did not mean remorse over sin. Rather, Tenkō san maintained, "true repentance is, above all, the Absolute Death of self-attachment" (*Selflessness*, p. 8).

33. Mizutsu, p. 85, chart 1.

34. On their return from gyōgan participants like to compare their experiences. "How many did you clean?" "Only two." (Incidentally, my own record was six, including two urinals.)

35. *Sābisu* (Japanese for the English word "service") in a Japanese store can mean anything from a free and not-too-valuable gift to a three-for-the-price-of-two kind of sale.

36. *JS*, p. 45.

37. *Selflessness*, pp. 4–5.

38. Peter L. Berger, *The Sacred Canopy: Elements of a Sociological Theory of Religion* (New York: Doubleday & Co., 1967). The attitude is nicely summed up in Job's words, "though he slay me, yet will I trust him" (ibid., p. 74).

39. The traditional religious disciplines (*shugyō*) of Japan have almost always involved some kind of physical endurance and pain.

40. *SS*, p. 76.

41. *Selflessness*, pp. 16–17.

42. *JS*, p. 50.

43. Nishida Tenko, *Hōki no ato* [Traces of a broom] (Tokyo: Shunjūsha, 1970), p. 105.

44. Victor W. Turner, *The Ritual Process: Structure and Anti-Structure* (Chicago: Aldine Publishing Co., 1969), pp. 95–96.

45. Ibid., p. 95.

46. Ibid., p. 125.

47. Ibid., p. 128.

48. Ibid., p. 103.

49. Ibid., p. 96

50. Ibid., p. 129.

51. Ibid., pp. 106–7.

52. *SS*, p. 46.

53. *JS*, p. 40.

54. Harakawa (note 24 of this chapter).

55. *JS*, p. 40.

56. Ibid., p. 51.

57. Émile Durkheim, *The Elementary Forms of the Religious Life* (New York: Free Press, 1965), p. 470.

58. As Turner points out, "property rights are linked with structural distinctions" (op. cit., p. 111). The Ittōen ideal of overcoming conflict (*arasoi*) and struggle (*ubaiai*) naturally comes into conflict with the ideals of management which, after all, must deal with the "outside world." Turner also shows that "the concept of 'conflict' has come to be connected with the concept of 'social structure,' since the differentiation of parts becomes opposition between parts, and scarce status becomes the object of struggles between persons and groups who lay claim to it" (ibid., p. 126).

59. *JS*, p. 25.

60. Ibid., p. 36.

61. Ibid., p. 32.

62. Ibid., p. 29.

63. I was once told by a stalwart that if I had the spirit of *zazen* (meditation) I would not need an electric fan, even in Kyoto's insufferable summer heat. I later noticed, however, that I was not the only one in the village who needed more of the "spirit of *zazen*" that summer! Electric fans and other conveniences are beginning to proliferate throughout the community.

64. Plath's "Afterword: The Unintentional Utopia," in *Sensei and His People: The Building of a Japanese Commune*, edited by Yoshie Sugihara and David W. Plath (Berkeley: University of California Press, 1969) p. 187.

65. Here I shall be satisfied with a simplistic definition of "reality" as "the way the community looks to critical outsiders and alienated *dōnin*."

66. See Suzuki Gorō, *Kono sannin: Tenkō, Hyakuzō, Torusutoi no shisō to seikatsu* [These three men: the life and thought of Tenkō, Hyakuzō, and Tolstoy] (Tokyo: Shunjūsha, 1972), pp. 141–47.

67. Clifford Geertz, *The Interpretation of Cultures* (New York: Basic Books, 1973), pp. 126–41.

68. *Fukuden* (Buddhist: "gratitude and charity") becomes "purified wealth." *Takuhatsu* (Buddhist: "begging") becomes "purified labor." *Gyōgan* (Buddhist: "vowing to attain the Buddhist perfections") becomes "toilet cleaning." *Kuyō* (Buddhist: "mass for the dead") becomes "contribution to the Village." Even the fee paid by firms for the food, lodging, and training of their employees is a "religious offering" (*osonae*).

69. *Tanomaretara nan de mo sasete morau,* Harakawa, op. cit., p. 10.

70. See the quotation from the *Ichi-Jijitsu,* p. 000.

71. I prefer to call this a ritual even though Takeshi san and the dōnin refer to it as an "experience" (*taiken*). Many of the young people who are skeptical—even cynical—about it, think of it as "theater." I prefer the word *ritual* for two reasons. In the first place, the time, place, action, and implied meaning of the events seem to be fixed. The words—even the "discussion" held by the Friends of Light to decide whether to invite the dōnin to return to their homes—are stereotyped. One can easily imagine the day when they will be written down and recited as part of an unvarying liturgy.

72. This function of the rotō rituals was explicitly recognized by Tenkō san himself (see *JS,* p. 37).

73. *Mondai wa jibun ga kono azukatte oru mono ó ippen hanarete shimau to iu koto no taiken* (taped interview).

74. Turner op. cit., p. 104.

75. *SS,* p. 16.

76. *SS,* p. 40.

77. *JS,* p. 66.

78. Harakawa Yoshio, op. cit., p. 16.

79. De Bary et al., eds., *Sources of Japanese Tradition* (New York: Columbia University Press, 1967), 2:16.

80. Alfred Bloom, *Shinran's Gospel of Pure Grace* (Tucson: University of Arizona Press, 1965), p. 44.

81. Yanagita Izumi, "Meiji Nihon no yūtopia shisō" [Utopian ideas in Meiji Japan], *Sekai* (January 1964), p. 241.

82. Cited in Holmes Welch, *Taoism: The Parting of the Way* (Boston: Beacon Press, 1966), p. 33.

83. Arthur Waley, *The Way and Its Power: A Study of the "Tao Te Ching" and Its Place in Chinese Thought* (New York: Grove Press, 1958), p. 201.

84. Max Kaltenmark, *Lao Tzu and Taoism* (Stanford, Calif.: Stanford University Press, 1969), p. 55.

85. Waley, op. cit., p. 193.

86. Ibid., p. 143.

87. Waley, cited in Welch, p. 80.

88. Official translation from the pamphlet "Guide to Kōsenrin (Ittōen Village)" (no publication data).

89. Waley, p. 178.

90. Ibid., p. 169.

91. Kaltenmark, p. 38. Magical liquids were also related to immortality in popular Taoism. Especially in Taoist alchemy, mercury and liquefied gold were thought "to strengthen our bodies and thereafter enable us not to grow old nor to die" (*Sources of Chinese Tradition,* edited by Wm. Theodore De Bary, et al. (New York: Columbia University Press, 1970) Vol. 1, p. 261.

92. *SS,* p. 90.

93. Waley, p. 199.

94. Ibid., p. 243.

95. A. C. Graham, *The Book of Lieh-tzu* (New York: Paragon Book Gallery, 1960) p. 5.

96. Taoism, too, had its own version of muga: "The perfect man has no self; the spiritual man has no achievement; the true sage has no name" (*Sources of Chinese Tradition,* Vol. 1, p. 66) Tenkō san's own version of the concept has more in common with the Zen tradition.

97. Ruth Benedict, *The Chrysanthemum and the Sword: Patterns of Japanese Culture* (Cleveland: Meridian Books, 1967), p. 251. My own analysis does not presuppose an acceptance of Benedict's shame-culture hypothesis. Nevertheless, it is important to recognize that *satori* and Pure Activity alike are both grounded in the culture of Japan.

98. Daisetz T. Suzuki, *Zen and Japanese Culture* (Princeton, N.J.: Princeton University Press, for the Bollingen Foundation, 1970), p. 361.

99. Nakamura Hajime, *Ways of Thinking of Eastern Peoples: India, China, Tibet, Japan* (Honolulu: East-West Center, 1966) p. 350.

100. Ibid., p. 352.

101. Suzuki, p. 375.

102. Ibid., p. 27.

103. Ibid., p. 376.

104. Masunaga Reihō, *The Sōtō Approach to Zen* (Tokyo: Layman Buddhist Society Press, 1958), p. 102. My thanks to Professor Delmer M. Brown for drawing my attention to this passage.

105. Benedict, p. 248.

106. *Sources of Japanese Tradition,* 2:199–200; modified and my emphasis.

107. Kenneth B. Pyle, *The New Generation in Meiji Japan: The Problem of Cultural Identity 1885–1895* (Stanford, Calif.: Stanford University Press, 1969), p. 175.

108. Donald Keene, *Landscapes and Portraits: Appreciations of Japanese Culture* (Palo Alto, Calif.: Kodansha International, 1971), p. 303.

109. Ibid., p. 304; my emphasis.

110. *SS,* p. 90.

111. Ibid., p. 91.

112. I am indebted to the late Victor Turner for these insights (personal conversation).

113. Victor Turner, "The Waters of Life: Some Reflections on Zionist Water Symbolism," in *Religions in Antiquity: Essays in Memory of Erwin Ramsdell Goodenough,* ed. Jacob Neusner (Leiden: E. J. Brill, 1968), pp. 517–18.

114. For a speculative, Freudian analysis of the community's "collective unconscious," see my "Ittōen: The Myths and Rituals of Liminality," *History of Religions* (August 1975) Vol. 15, No. 1, pp. 2–13.

115. Yanagita Izumi, p. 240.

116. Ibid., p. 242.

117. The number of labor disputes during the two years before the publication of *The Life of Repentance* totaled 3,457, over four times the total recorded during 1917–18 (John K. Fairbank, Edwin O. Reischauer, and Albert M. Craig, *East Asia: The Modern Transformation* [Boston: Houghton Mifflin Co., 1965], p.527). For a general description of the economic growth during this period, see ibid., pp. 493–500.

118. Plath, p. 95.

119. Anthony F. C. Wallace, "Revitalization Movements," *American Anthropologist* 58 (1956): 264–81.

120. Nigel Harris, *Beliefs in Society: The Problem of Ideology* (Harmondsworth, Middlesex: Penguin Books, 1971), p. 83.

121. *SS,* p. 33. Ittōen is not alone among the New Religions to stress this traditional Japanese virtue. One of the Seven Commandments of Kurozumi-kyō is "be grateful every day" (Harry Thomsen *The New Religions of Japan.* (Rutland, Vt.: Tuttle, 1963, p. 65). The first of Seichō no Ie's Articles of Faith is about the same: "Be grateful to all beings in the universe." This sect stresses

the words *arigatō gozaimasu* (thank you). "It is used, apparently in almost any circumstance, as a greeting or a countersign; but it also has essentially the force of a magical incantation (though no teacher of Seichō no Ie would consent to this terminology)" (H. Neill McFarland, *The Rush Hour of the Gods: A Study of New Religious Movements in Japan* [New York: Harper Colophon, 1970], p. 163).

122. Plath, p. 180.

123. "Let the producers be many and the consumers be few. Let there be activity in the production and economy in the expenditure. Then the wealth will always be sufficient" (James Legge, trans., *The Four Books: Confucian Analects, the Great Learning, the Doctrine of the Mean, and the Works of Mencius* [Shanghai: Chinese Book Co., 1933], "The Great Learning," sec. 19, p. 343).

124. *Life against Death: The Psychoanalytical Meaning of History* (Middletown, Conn.: Wesleyan University Press, 1959), p. 303, after Shumpeter.

125. Doi Takeo, "*Amae:* A Key Concept for Understanding Japanese Personality Structure," in *Japanese Culture: Its Development and Characteristics,* ed. Robert J. Smith and Richard K. Beardsley (Chicago: Aldine Press, 1962), pp. 132–39. See also the same author's more recent work, *Amae no kōzō* [The structure of intimate dependency relations] (Tokyo: Kōbundō, 1972).

126. Tenkō, *What Is Itto-en?: Its Theory and Practice* (Kyoto: Itto-En Publishing House, 1959), p. 39.

127. For example, a pamphlet put out by the Moralogy group in Chiba Prefecture and distributed recently by Japanese banks carried an article on the causes of environmental pollution. Its lead story was headed by the motto: "Instead of throwing away your garbage, throw yourself away!" Within the context of the Japanese moral community, the idea is perfectly comprehensible.

128. Cited in Adam Ulam, "Socialism and Utopia," in *Utopias and Utopian Thought,* ed. Frank E. Manuel (Boston: Beacon Press, 1967), p. 126.

129. Kagawa Toyohiko, *Brotherhood Economics* (New York: Harper & Bros., 1936), p. 115.

Chapter 7.

1. See Larry Shiner, "The Meanings of Secularization," in *Secularization and the Protestant Prospect,* ed. James Childress and David Harned. Philadelphia: Westminster Press, 1970, pp. 30–42.

2. "The Progressive Course of the Human Mind," in *Sociology and Religion: A Book of Readings,* ed. Norman Birnbaum and Gertrud Lenzer. Englewood Cliffs, N.J.: Prentice-Hall, 1969, p. 28.

3. G. van der Leeuw, *Religion in Essence and Manifestation.* New York: Harper Torchbook, 1963, Vol. II, p. 600.

4. Rudolf Otto, *The Idea of the Holy.* New York: Oxford University Press, 1958; Mircea Eliade, *The Sacred and the Profane.* New York: Harcourt Brace, 1959, p. 23, writes: "To whatever degree he may have desacralized the world, the man who has made his choice in favor of a profane life never succeeds in completely doing away with religious behavior."

5. Otto, op. cit., p. 15, 176. Otto, of course, did not argue that all men actualize this potential; see p. 149.

6. Robert Nisbet, *The Sociological Tradition.* New York: Basic Books, 1966, p. 261.

7. Talcott Parsons, "Christianity and Modern Industrial Society," in *Sociological Theory, Values, and Sociocultural Change: Essays in Honor of Pitirim A. Sorokin,* ed. Edward Tiryakian. New York: Free Press, 1967, pp. 33–70; "Religion in a Modern Pluralistic Society," *Review of Religious Research* 7 (1966), pp. 125–46.

8. Robert Bellah, *Beyond Belief: Essays on Religion in a Post-Traditional World.* New York: Harper and Row, 1970, p. 21.

9. For a critique of the functionalist's tendency to assume that cultural and social change are always synchronic see Clifford Geertz, *The Interpretation of Cultures.* New York: Basic Books, 1973, pp. 142–69.

10. Reinhard Bendix, *Embattled Reason: Essays on Social Knowledge.* New York: Oxford University Press, 1970, pp. 250–314.

11. Jospeh M. Kitagawa, "Some Reflections of a Historian of Religions," unpublished manuscript, p. 10.

12. Shiner, op. cit., p. 41.

13. *Gallup Opinion Index Reports, No. 130: Religion in America.* Princeton: Gallup International, 1976, pp. 1–17.

14. Ibid., p. 2.

15. *Shūkyō Benran* (Nihon Shūkyō Renmei). Tokyo, 1948, pp. 350–61; Suzuki Norihisa, "Nihonjin no shūkyō ishiki kenkyū ni tsuite," *Shūkyō Kenkyū,* 38 (1965), pp. 119–30.

16. *Nihonjin no Kokuminsei,* ed. Hayashi Chikio et al. Tokyo: Tōkei Sūri Kenkyūjo, 1982, No. 4, p. 457.

17. One reason for the low scores on religious commitment in all of these surveys is that the word religion (*shūkyō*) seems to imply 1. doctrines and 2. specific public commitments to them—neither of which is part of the genius of

Japanese religion. Many people usually forget to include their Shintō affiliations when asked to name their *shūkyō*. Notice that in this survey's principle question regarding belief, the words *shinkō* (faith) and *shinshin* (religious attitude) were used and not *shūkyō*.

18. Fernando Basabe, *Religious Attitudes of Japanese Men: A Sociological Survey.* Tokyo and Rutland: Tuttle, 1968.

19. *Nihonjin no Kokuminsei,* 1970, No. 2, p. 50.

20. Basabe, op. cit., p. 121.

21. See Winston Davis, *Toward Modernity: A Developmental Typology of Popular Religious Affiliations in Japan,* Ithaca: Cornell East Asia Papers, No. 12 (1977); Morioka Kiyomi, *Religion in Changing Japanese Society.* Tokyo, 1975, pp. 39–72, 155–67.

22. Thomas Smith, "Ōkura Nagatsune and the Technologists," in *Personality in Japanese History,* ed. Albert Craig and Donald Shively. Berkeley: University of California Press 1970, p. 140ff. During this period there were others, however, like Ninomiya Sontoku, who tried to *combine* traditional religious pi ety with a this-worldly work ethic.

23. See Winston Davis, "Parish Guilds and Political Culture in Village Japan," *Journal of Asian Studies,* Vol. 36 (1976), pp. 25–36.

24. Yanagita Kunio, *Nihon no matsuri.* Tokyo: Kōbundō, 1942, p. 49.

25. Chiba Masaji, *Matsuri no hōshakaigaku.* Tokyo: Kōbundō, 1970, pp. 70–71; Edward Norbeck, "Pollution and Taboo in Contemporary Japan," *SW Jour. Anthr.* 8 (1952), pp. 269–85.

26. Yanagita Kunio, *Japanese Manners and Customs in the Meiji Era.* Tokyo: Ōbunsha, 1957, *passim.*

27. The saying is the epigraph of Hakuin's sermon, "The Plain Looking Courtesan's Ballad of Bravado," *The Embossed Tea Kettle.* London, 1963: Allen, p. 157. See Yanagita, *Japanese Manners,* p. 257.

28. *Ibid.,* 261.

29. For the role of *hare* and *ke* in pilgrimage, see chapter 2, pp. 76–78.

30. Yanagita, *Nihon no matsuri,* pp. 53, 48.

31. "Ujigami to ujiko," *Teihon Yanagita Kunio shū.* Tokyo: Chikuma Shobō, p. 430.

32. *Nihon no matsuri,* pp. 229–43.

33. In one village which I visited in Shiga prefecture cattle used to be taken to the shrine once a year to drink sacred rice wine and be blessed. After the

introduction of vaccinations this custom disappeared, though amulets for the protection of cattle are still sold.

34. God-carts or palanquins used to transport symbols of kami during processions.

35. Winston Davis, "The *Miyaza* and the Fishermen: Ritual Status in Coastal Villages of Wakayama Prefecture," *Asian Folklore Studies* 36 (1977), pp. 1–29.

36. One thinks of the automated mausoleums in which a push of a button produces a recorded recitation of Buddhist sutras; and of the fact that it is often the undertaker who finds a Buddhist priest to perform the funeral, just as the manager of a wedding hotel often contacts a Shintō priest for a wedding.

37. Discontinued after the war, this festival was revived as part of a commercial and industrial festival (*shōkō matsuri*), which is why it is celebrated one month late. (The word *matsuri* is often used in a purely commercial context).

38. D. C. Holtom, *The National Faith of Japan*. New York: Dutton, 1938, pp. 23–24.

39. Yoshito Hakeda, trans., *The Awakening of Faith Attributed to Asvaghosha*. New York: Columbia University Press, 1967, p. 37.

40. Cited in Nakamura Hajime, *Ways of Thinking of Eastern Peoples*. Honolulu: East-West Center, 1964, p. 352.

41. Edmund Leach, "A Definition of Religion and its Uses," *J. Royal Anth. Inst.* 90 (1960), p. 202.

42. Itō Mikiharu, "Nihon bunka no kōzōteki rikai o mezashite," *Kikan jinruigaku* 4 (1973), 3–30. See Durkheim's distinction in *The Elementary Forms of the Religious Life*. New York, 1965, p. 53.

43. See chapter 1, pp. 26–27.

44. For an example of "existential drift" of this sort, see my discussion of Robert Jay Lifton's "Protean Man" in chapter 8, p. 261.

45. *Nihonjin no Kokuminsei*, No. 2, p. 47.

46. Whether these occasions should be called instances of faith or mere custom has become a legal as well as an academic conundrum. In 1965, for example, some of the citizens of Tsu, a city in Mie prefecture, sued town officials for hiring four Shinto priests to conduct a ground-breaking ceremony at the city's expense. The litigation that ensued went from court to court until the supreme court ruled that the ceremony was merely a "custom" which did not violate the constitutional separation of state and religion.

47. New York, 1971, p. 656f. See also Christoper Hill, *Society and Puritanism in Pre-Revolutionary England*. New York: Schocken, 1967, pp. 124–44;

Robert Merton, *Social Theory and Social Structure*. New York: Free Press 1968, pp. 628–60; E. P. Thompson, "Time, Work-Discipline, and Industrial Capitalism," *Past and Present* 38 (1967), pp. 56–97.

48. Sugiyama Meiko, "Religious Behavior of the Japanese," *Seminar on Theory, Methods and Applications of Multidimensional Scaling and Related Techniques* (August 20–24, 1974, University of Calif. at San Diego), p. 159. My thanks to Hayashi Chikio for drawing this research to my attention.

49. Tsurumi Shunsuke, *Nichijōteki shisō no kanōsei*. Tokyo: Chikuma Shobō, 1967, pp. 34–55.

50. Again, I must make clear that I am not arguing that *all* religion hinders social change, but only—in a rather ironic, Machiavellian way—that, in some cases, a lack of religious (and even moral) commitments gives a country's developers a freer hand.

Chapter 8.

1. Yasuda Saburō, "Nihon shakairon no tenbō" (Perspectives on the theory of Japanese society), *Gendaishakaigaku*, 13, 7 (1): pp. 3–14.

2. See for example *Nihonjinron* (Japan theory). NRI Refarensu No. 2. Kamakura: Nomura Sōgō Kenkyūjo, 1978.

3. For a more detailed study of the development of Japan theory from a somewhat different perspective, see my essay, "Fundamentalism, Nationalism and Science: a Study of Political Fundamentalism in Japan," in *Fundamentalism Observed*. Chicago: University of Chicago Press, Vol. II, forthcoming.

4. *The Napoleon of Notting Hill*. New York and London: John Lane, 1904, p. 134.

5. Ross Mouer and Yoshio Sugimoto, "Some Questions Concerning Commonly Accepted Stereotypes of Japanese Society." Canberra: Australia-Japan Economic Relations Research Project. The Australian National University, Research Paper No. 64, 1979, p. 12.

6. Kawai Hayao, *Bosei shakai Nihon no byōri* (The pathology of Japan as a 'maternal society'). Tokyo: Chūō Kōronsha, 1976.

7. The difficulty with Kawai's Jungian perspective—and his valiant effort to prove the "feminine" or "maternal" nature of Japanese society—is that it is completely ahistorical. Gender roles, especially in modern societies, are anything but absolute or static. It is therefore extremely risky to stereotype these roles and assign them as labels for entire societies.

8. Robert Jay Lifton, *Boundaries*. New York: Touchstone, 1976.

9. Okonogi Keigo, *Moratoriamu ningen no jidai* (The age of moratorium man). Tokyo: Chūō Kōronsha, 1978, p. 252.

10. I find it odd that these writers have turned to an *Indian* legend to uncover the quintessence of the Japanese psyche. It is also rather curious that those parts of the Ajase story that deal with the tensions between the *father* and his son are passed over in silence. Before the birth of the prince, a fortune-teller announced that Ajase would cause his father to come to grief. Hearing this, the father, King Bimbisara, tried to kill the boy. When he grew up, Ajase revenged himself by putting his father under house arrest until the old man died. Furusawa and Okonogi have seen fit to repress this part of the legend, perhaps because it could very well be cited by those who subscribe to the universality of the Oedipus complex itself.

11. Okonogi, op. cit., pp. 206–8; see also p. 303ff. Okonogi's comparison of Japanese and western families is a good example of the way in which Japan theory uses negative stereotypes of other nations to generate positive self-images. Morality in the west, Okonogi declares (following Freud), is grounded in absolute commands, taboos, and the fear of punishment, e.g., castration (p. 210). He pictures the western family as living in a home where parents erotically kiss and embrace in the presence of their children and where mothers (unable to control their lust) sleep with their husbands and not with their children (the custom in Japan). Such egocentrism and lust lead, he says, to the spread of pornography, child abuse, and a rising divorce rate (p. 221 ff). In Japan, children would find such a sexualization of parental roles extremely disturbing. The mother who is seen as a woman by her children would be regarded as their betrayer.

12. Koyama Ken'ichi, "Dolphinism: Ragtag Remnant of 'Imperial Isms,' " *The Japan Times* (20 April 1980), p. 12.

13. The peacefulness of Japan (in contrast to the violence of the rest of the world) is one of the more potent self-images created by Japan theory. It harks back to prewar literature of a similar nature, e.g., to propaganda contrasting the unbroken imperial lineage of Japan with the turbulent dynastic history of China. In the postwar period, the peaceful image of Japan has been artificially sustained by official revisions of the nation's textbooks which minimize Japan's military aggression against its Asian neighbors. Right-wing organizations have even prevented the renovated Hiroshima Peace Memorial Museum from including displays that would remind the visitor of Japan's role in the beginning of the Pacific War.

14. Most Japanese have just the opposite opinion of themselves. For example, Kobayashi Koji, the president of Nippon Electric Company, declared at the beginning of the trade war between the United States and Japan: "While the Americans, by and large, take a pragmatic way of thinking and think in terms of power relations, the Japanese tend to emphasize morality and principles" (*The Japan Times*, 13 September 1971, p. 11).

15. *Tatemae* refers to a principle averred to in public, or to ideological window dressing used to smooth over one's real intentions or opinions (*honne*).

16. Murata Kiyoaki, "The Japanese Duality: *Tatemae* and *Honne* May Help Understanding of Nuclear Furor" (*The Japan Times*, 5 June 1981), p. 14.

17. This line of thought is odd indeed. After all, the FBI entered the case only *after* IBM reported that vital information had been stolen. The Japanese defendants volunteered to the undercover agents that they had *already* obtained secret IBM materials and wanted more. The agents, in turn, repeatedly informed them that obtaining this information would be illegal. The Japanese nevertheless pushed ahead and knowingly purchased the materials.

18. Japan theory deals with the problem of trade imbalances almost exclusively in terms of *cultural* tension—and therefore does nothing to help solve, or conceptualize, the problem. Some have alleged that the real cause of trade friction is the west's own racism, especially its fear of the "yellow peril." See Ouchi Tsutomu, "Bōeki masatsu o umu kion kōzō wa nani ka?" (What is the real nature of trade friction?), *Ekonomisuto* (4 and 11 May 1982, Vol. 60, No. 19, p. 12), and more recently, Morita Akio and Ishihara Shintarō, *No to ieru Nippon: Shin Nichibei kankei no kādo* (A Japan That Can Say No: The "Card" of the New Relationship between Japan and the United States) (Tokyo: Kōbunsha, 1989). Others have suggested that the best way to relieve these tensions is to export Japanese culture so that foreign countries will "understand" Japan and accept her trade practices in the spirit of yurushi. But clearly, no *Bildungsblitz* is going to have this effect. Economic and diplomatic dilemmas are not going to go away simply by shrouding them in the cultural mists of Noh drama and the tea ceremony.

19. Yamamoto Mitsuru, "Nihon ga kokusai shakai de ikiru jōken" (Prerequisites for Japan's survival in international society). *Economisuto* (20 January 1981), pp. 10–17.

20. *Innocence and Experience*. Cambridge: Harvard University Press, 1989, p. 189.

21. This, I fear, is the shortcoming of Peter N. Dale's, *The Myth of Japanese Uniqueness* (New York: St. Martin's Press, 1986).

22. See Winston Davis, "The Civil Theology of Inoue Tetsujirō," *Japanese Journal of Religious Studies*, 1976, Vol. 3, No. 1, pp. 5–40.

23. Isaiah Ben-Dasan (Yamamoto Shichihei), *Nihonkyō ni tsuite* (On the Faith of Japan). Tokyo: Bungei Shunjū, 1975.

Index